Perilous Prospects

Perilous Prospects

The Peace Process and the Arab-Israeli Military Balance

Anthony H. Cordesman

Routledge
Taylor & Francis Group
New York London

First published 1996 by Westview Press

Published 2019 by Routledge
52 Vanderbilt Avenue, New York, NY 10017
2 Park Square, Milton Park, Abingdon, Oxon OX14 4RN

First issued in hardback 2019

Routledge is an imprint of the Taylor & Francis Group, an informa business

Library of Congress Cataloging-in-Publication Data
Cordesman, Anthony H.
    Perilous prospects : the peace process and the Arab-Israeli
military balance / Anthony H. Cordesman.
        p.   cm.
    Includes bibliographical references.
    ISBN 0-8133-2939-6.—ISBN 0-8133-3074-2 (pbk.)
    1. Israel—Defenses.   2. Arab countries—Defenses.   3. Israel-Arab
conflicts.   4. Israel. Treaties, etc. Munaẓẓamat al-Taḥīr al-
Filasṭīnīyah, 1993 Sept. 13.   I. Title.
UA853.I8C67   1996
355′.03305694—dc20   96-7426
                                                                             CIP

ISBN 13: 978-0-367-31720-1 (hbk)
ISBN 13: 978-0-8133-3074-7 (pbk)

To Judith, Dick, Arnaud, Bill, Ahmed,
David, and my other colleagues at
the Center for Strategic and International Studies

Contents

Tables and Illustrations

Figures

Maps

Acknowledgments

The author would like to thank Kimberly Goddes, Melissa Lynn Owens, Kiyalan Balmanglidi, and Ara Jabagchourian for researching portions of this book—especially Kimberly Goddes for her patience in editing various drafts. He would also like to thank Jed Snyder for helping to start the project, and Frederick W. Axelgard for comments on the role it might play.

Several analysts played a role in commenting on the manuscript, and in correcting some of its many errors. The author would especially like to thank Dr. Abdullah Toukan, General Ahmed Fakhr, Dore Gold, Michael Eisenstadt, Tom Neuman, and Robert Satloff. He would also like to thank the many analysts and officials in the Egyptian, Israeli, Jordanian, and US governments, and Palestinian Authority, who cannot be acknowledged by name.

Anthony H. Cordesman

1

INTRODUCTION

The security and stability of Egypt, Israel, Jordan, Lebanon, the Palestinians, and Syria are shaped by many factors. These include the economic and demographic trends in the region, domestic politics, internal security, and the peace process. Nevertheless, the Arab-Israeli military balance still shapes much of the security situation in the Middle East.

The peace process has not put an end to military threats or the regional arms race. Israel's peace agreements with Egypt and Jordan have led to only limited cuts in military forces, and Israel is still negotiating with Syria and Lebanon. Even the best outcome of the peace process will still be "peace with violence," and it may often be difficult to tell the difference between the "Cold War" that preceded the Oslo Agreements and the "Cold Peace" that has followed. There will be many incidents of violence between Israelis and Palestinians before the final stages of a peace settlement are agreed upon and fully implemented and "peace" may sometimes escalate to low-intensity warfare.

Even if all the current peace negotiations are successful, it is likely to be a decade or more before Israel and its neighbors achieve a major reduction in their war fighting potential. Fundamental changes in the military balance—and the risks it poses for further war—will require fundamental shifts in the present security polices of the nations in the region, major reductions in future military spending, and a process of confidence building measures and arms control to reduce the potential destructiveness of any future conflict. Peace may even increase some aspects of the regional arms race, at least in the short run, as nations attempt to adapt their force postures to the new demands of peace. This may be particularly true of Israel, which may have to make significant military investments to compensate for the loss of the Golan and territory in the West Bank.

It is also dangerous to assume that there is anything inevitable about the success of the peace process. While it is an axiom that "all wars must end," history is equally consistent in warning that "all peaces fail." Israeli political support for the peace process is uncertain and Israeli public opinion is becoming increasingly polarized. Yitzak Rabin was assassinated by an Israeli extremist in an effort to end

Israel's support for peace, and a far less supportive or even hostile government may come to power.

Palestinian support for the peace process is still heavily dependent on the leadership of one man—Yasser Arafat—and might also collapse. There are many "final settlement" issues that have not been fully addressed, much less resolved. There is political instability in Egypt, Jordan, and Syria. New incidents of terrorism or repression can undermine public support and pro-peace leaders. Forging an exception to history is anything but easy.

The peace process may freeze into an uneasy status quo, or it may fail altogether. If the peace process does fail, the political and military risks of war are almost certain to increase. The present conventional arms race and the search for weapons of mass destruction are almost certain to accelerate. The risk of a sustained low conflict between Israel and the Palestinians will grow. A failing peace is likely to discredit and undermine moderate secular Arab regimes, encourage both Israel and Arab extremists, lead to violent exchanges of terrorism and counterterrorism, and possibly drag outside Arab and Islamic states into any future conflict.

Even if a full peace is followed by arms control, it will still be a long time before such arm control efforts bring added security. During this process, arms reductions may increase military risks, even as they decrease political risks. Any asymmetries that unilateral force cuts or arms control create in the military balance may lead to more extreme forms of escalation. Lower levels of arms may lead to less technology-oriented conflicts that last longer and involve more close combat—fighting which inevitably produces higher casualties and more risk of involving civilian targets than brief intense wars directed at destroying key weapons and military facilities. Some confidence building measures or moves toward "parity" may encourage risk taking or reduce deterrence in a political crisis. Reductions in conventional military power may encourage irregular warfare or the use of weapons of mass destruction. A rise in the military power of the Gulf states at a time when Israel and its neighbors are disarming may encourage interventions by radical states like Iran or Iraq.

The threat of the proliferation of weapons of mass destruction, very long range delivery systems, and more lethal conventional weapons may radically change the balance of power and deterrence in the region. It already is linking nations like Iran and Iraq into existential conflicts with Israel and presenting major new problems for arms control.

Finally, the trends in the military balance will have a major domestic impact on Egypt, Israel, Jordan, Lebanon, the Palestinians, and Syria—regardless of the outcome of the peace negotiations. At least in the near term, Israel and its neighbors will continue to spend some 20% to 30% of their central government expenditures, as much as 10% of their GDP, and as much as 10% of their annual hard currency imports on military forces—a critical drain on their capability for development at a time when their total population will increase by over 50% during the coming decade.[1]

The "Conventional Balance"

The Arab-Israeli balance is still shaped largely by the conventional balance between Israel and its immediate neighbors—Egypt, Jordan, Lebanon, and Syria—the so-called ring states. At the same time, a wide range of different factors are reshaping the way in which the Arab-Israeli balance must be measured and the contingencies that must be examined in determining that balance.

Some of the factors that are changing the military balance are positive. They aid in the deterrence of war, and reduce the incentive to maintain large military forces and acquire more arms and weapons of mass destruction. These factors include the progress in the peace process, the impact of the end of the Cold War, the impact of the Gulf War, and the relative weakness of threats to Israel from outside the "ring states" like Iran, Iraq, and Libya.

Other factors, however, are negative or potentially negative, and increase the probability and/or possible intensity of a conflict. These factors include the impact of the rise of Islamic extremism, the political and economic instability in the Arab states surrounding Israel, the deep divisions within the Palestinian movement and the instability of the peace process, and the proliferation of weapons of mass destruction. These negative factors also affect the kind of contingencies that must be examined in evaluating the balance. There is still a threat of the kind of major conventional war that occurred in 1948, 1956, 1967, and 1973. At the same time, the peace process brings new threats of low level conflict, and proliferation inside and outside the Arab-Israeli "ring states" creates the risk of far more threatening types of war.

This mix of trends makes the Arab-Israeli balance difficult to characterize and predict. There are other problems that affect any attempt at analysis. Ever since 1948, the Arab-Israeli balance has been determined primarily by uncertainty and "intangibles," not force numbers.

The primary source of such uncertainty has been the rapidly evolving changes which have taken place in the strategic and political conditions affecting the use of force. Disarray and disunity prevented Arab forces from being effective in 1948. A sudden British and French intervention over the Suez Crisis shaped the outcome in 1956. Israeli surprise and tactical innovation, coupled with Egyptian unpreparedness, led to a massive Israeli victory in 1967. The Canal War of 1970 was an unexpected battle of attrition shaped largely by major Soviet deliveries of new air defense weapons. Arab surprise shaped the initial outcome of the 1973 war, only to see the course of the fighting reversed by a daring Israeli thrust across the Suez Canal. A fundamental Israeli misreading of the situation in Lebanon, and a rogue effort to transform a limited action against the PLO into an attack on Syria, turned an initial Israeli victory into a war of occupation and a strategic defeat in 1982. In each case, the course of the fighting and its final outcome were shaped as much by the specific scenario as by force quality or force quantity.

At the same time, once combat began, its outcome was shaped largely by "intangibles" like leadership, training, manpower quality, tactics, innovativeness, flexibility, effective use of combined arms and jointness, command and control capability, and battle management skills. The outcome of Arab-Israeli conflicts has never been determined by easily quantifiable force ratios or pre-conflict orders of battle.

Uncertainty and "intangibles" are certain to be equally dominant in the future. The peace process, proliferation, and the end of the Cold War make future scenarios even more unpredictable, and make sweeping comparisons of the total size of Arab and Israeli forces even less relevant. At the same time, the changes now taking place in tactics, training, and technology emphasize the value of force quality relative to force quantity. As the Gulf War has demonstrated, the "revolution in military affairs" is changing the nature of warfare and large inventories of older or mediocre equipment are more likely to be targets than assets.

Counting Total Forces

These factors raise serious doubts about the value of any assessment of the Arab-Israeli balance that simply counts the total size of Israel's forces relative to those of the largest potential threat. While such comparisons are often used as strategic shorthand, or for political purposes, they bear little relation to reality.

Table 1.1 and Figure 1.1, for example, reflect such a classic view of the balance. They show an Israeli estimate of the total conventional forces the Arab states can deploy against Israel. The total Arab forces include the total forces of Egypt, Jordan, Lebanon, the PLO, and Syria, the entire Libyan Navy and selected forces from the Saudi Army (three brigades), Iraq (five divisions, 100 combat aircraft, 100 helicopters, 10 surface-to-surface missile [SSM] launchers), Kuwait (one combat aircraft squadron), the Algerian Army (two brigades and two combat aircraft squadrons), Morocco (one brigade and one combat aircraft squadron), Libya (six brigades, two combat aircraft squadrons, one attack helicopter squadron, and 20 SSM launchers and minor elements of land forces from Iran).

It is difficult to know how serious Israeli analysts and planners are in advancing such comparisons of Israel's total forces with the total forces that all Arab states could conceivably deploy against Israel. While Iraq did play a significant role in the October War, and such "worst case" force comparisons may be useful in supporting Israeli defense budgets and aid requests, they include large numbers of undeployable and unsustainable Arab forces, and imply a degree of Arab unity that never existed during the period before Egypt, Jordan, and the PLO signed peace agreements with Israel. Further, many of the Arab states involved are now far more concerned with other Arab enemies.

The trends in Table 1.1 and Figure 1.1 also illustrate the problems inherent in relying on gross measurements of force strength. They reflect a valid build-up in Middle Eastern land forces since 1984, and the fact that armored forces and ar-

TABLE 1.1 The Arab-Israeli Balance: The Israeli View of the Trends in the Total Threat

Category/Weapon	1984 Arabs	1984 Israel	1984 Ratio	1994 Arabs	1994 Israel	1994 Ratio
A. Land Forces						
Divisions						
Armor	10	11	0.9	16	12	1.3
Mechanized	10	–	–	14	–	–
Infantry	3	–	–	3	4	0.8
Total	23	11	2.1	33	16	2.1
Independent Brigades	51	20	2.5	44	13	3.4
Tanks	8,065	3,650	2.2	10,400	3,850	2.7
Other Armored Vehicles	8,470	8,000	1.1	13,250	8,100	1.6
Artillery & Mortars	6,050	1,000	6.0	6,100	1,300	4.7
B. Air Forces and Air Defense						
Interceptors						
High Quality	130	40	3.3	215	75	2.9
Others	620	–	–	478	–	–
Total	750	40	18.8	693	75	9.5
Strike/FGA						
High Quality	496	445	1.1	72	204	0.4
Others	354	185	1.9	467	463	1.1
Total	850	530	1.6	539	667	1.2
Total Combat Aircraft	1,635	670	2.4	1,236	742	1.8
Helicopters						
Attack	161	55	2.9	280	115	2.4
Other	324	133	2.4	362	138	2.6
Total	485	188	2.6	642	253	2.5
Military Airfields	48	11	4.4	65	11	5.9
C. Naval Forces						
Major Missile Surface	8	0	–	14	0	–
Major Non-Missile Surface	8	0	–	2	0	–
Submarines	18	3	6.0	17	3	5.7
Missile Patrol Boats Landing Craft	67	24	2.8	67	19	3.5

Source: Adapted by the author from Shlomo Gazit, Zeev Eytan, *The Middle East Military Balance, 1984–1994,* JCSS/Westview, Tel Aviv/Boulder, 1995, pp. 494–499.

FIGURE 1.1   Israeli Estimate of Israel's Forces Versus Total Arab Potential Threat (All Forces of Egypt, Jordan, Lebanon, PLO, Syria, and Selected Forces of Algeria, Kuwait, Iran, Iraq, Libya, Morocco, and Saudi Arabia)

Land Weapons - Total Main Battle Tanks

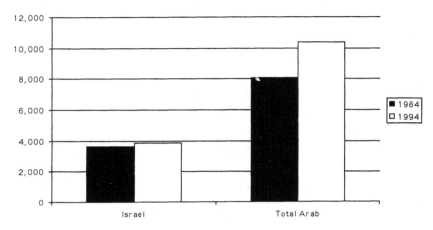

Air Forces - Total Combat Aircraft

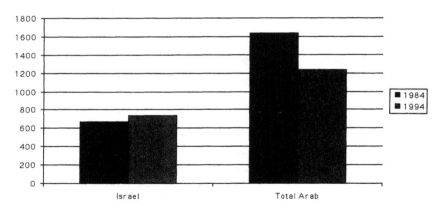

tillery have increased in size. However, much of the military build-up in Arab land forces between 1984 and 1994 is the result of the rising tensions in the Gulf region and the impact of the Iran-Iraq War and Gulf War. It has nothing to do with the real threat to Israel. Further, the increase in the total inventory of Arab land weapons is the product of the retention of many older and low quality systems that have only limited capability.

Table 1.1 and Figure 1.1 indicate that Arab aircraft numbers have decreased relative to Israel. This trend is valid to the extent it reflects Israel's continuing emphasis on the excellence of its air force, and reductions in the size of Arab forces in response to factors like attrition and the rising cost of aircraft. At the same time, it is important to note that Arab combat aircraft counted in these totals have improved strikingly in relative quality—and that the counts of fixed wing aircraft in Figure 1.1 do not reflect the fact that both sides now have significantly larger numbers of attack helicopters. Further, it overstates the strength of both Israel and Arab air forces by counting a number of aircraft in storage or training units.

In short, comparisons of the total size of Arab and Israeli forces are valid only as a warning that other Arab states and Iran may play a more significant role in the military balance in the future than they do today, and that much depends on the success of the peace process and the politics of the individual Arab states. Iraq, for example, did play a major role in the fighting on the Golan in October 1973, and broadened its theater of war to launch missile strikes on Israel in 1990. Peripheral radical states like Iran, Iraq, and Libya are now extremely weak and moderate Arab states have little incentive to engage in military confrontation with Israel. Iran, Iraq, and Libya may become stronger if a sudden rise takes place in real oil prices or if they can break out of their current level of containment. A major breakdown in the peace process could lead some moderate Arab states to make at least limited military commitments.

The trends in the Arab-Israeli balance can only be understood by counting forces in a way that accurately reflects the level of resources available to each country, that distinguishes between different Arab states in counting force numbers, that examines force quality as well as force quantity, that looks at the impact of changes in military technology, and that ties such analysis to the kinds of contingencies and scenarios most likely to affect the future.

2

MILITARY EXPENDITURES
AND ARMS SALES

Comparisons of military expenditures and arms sales can provide important insights into the broad trends in military effort but they must be kept in careful perspective. Countries differ sharply in the size of their economy, and in the relative military effort they make at any given time. All international statistics present problems in reliability and comparability, and the data available on the detailed annual military expenditures and arms imports of the key Arab-Israeli countries have important weaknesses and inconsistencies that limit their value.

Differences in Economic Size and Level of Military Effort

The economies of Israel, Egypt, Jordan, Lebanon, and Syria differ sharply in size, structure, and relative wealth. Israel is the only highly industrialized state in the region, with industrial production worth 30% of the GDP and growing at an annual rate of 8%. Although Israel has a population of only 5,433,000, the CIA estimates that Israel had a GDP worth $70.1 billion in 1994, measured in terms of purchasing power parity, and a per capita GDP of $13,880. Its exports consist largely of industrial goods and light manufactures and were worth $16.2 billion. Its imports were worth $22.5 billion.[1]

In contrast, Egypt had a population of 62,360,000 in 1994, and a GDP worth $151.5 billion. More than half of its work force was employed by the state sector. Its industrial production was a relatively low percentage of the economy, and growing at only 2.7% per year. Egypt's exports were only worth $3.1 billion, while its imports cost $11.2 billion. Put differently, Egypt has more than 10 times Israel's population, a little over twice its GDP, but only 8% of its GDP per capita. As a result, Egypt faces much more severe limits in allocating money to military expenditures and manufactures than Israel.[2]

Jordan and Lebanon have much smaller economies than Israel and Egypt. Jordan had a population of 4,101,000, and a GDP worth $17 billion in 1994. Its per capita GDP was $4,280. Jordan's exports were worth $1.4, while its imports cost

$3.5 billion. Jordan is, however, one of the few countries in the region to make significant economic reforms and has improved its economic performance since its recession following the Gulf War. It has improved its debt service and debt to export ratios to some of the best in the region, and has passed new investment, financial market corporate tax, and foreign exchange laws.

Lebanon had a population of 3,696,000, and a GDP worth $15.8 billion. Its per capita GDP was $4,360. Lebanon's exports were worth $925 million, while its imports cost $4.1 billion. Syria's economy was roughly the size of that of Israel, although its population was nearly three times larger. Syria had a population of 15,452,000, and a GDP worth $74.4 billion. Its per capita GDP was $5,000. Syria's exports were worth $3.6, while its imports cost $4 billion.[3]

In total, Egypt, Jordan, Lebanon, and Syria had a total GDP worth $258.7 billion, or about 3.7 times larger than that of Israel. This comparison, however, has never had much impact on the military balance because the Arab states have never approached Israel's efficiency in mobilizing its economy to fund military forces.

Both Israel and its Arab neighbors have made significant reductions in the percent of their total economies devoted to military spending. Figure 2.1 shows the recent trends in military spending as a percentage of GDP. It reflects a major drop since the crisis years following Israel's 1982 invasion of Syria. Israel, in particular, has cut its level of military effort by over 50%. As a result, Egypt, Israel, Jordan, Lebanon, and Syria all have the potential to make major increases in military spending if they choose to do so. Unlike the period between roughly 1948 and 1984, Arab-Israeli military spending is no longer near the maximum level each country can allocate.

Problems in Dollar Comparisons of Military Expenditures and Arms Sales

There are three major sources of comparable data of the military expenditures and arms sales of Egypt, Israel, Jordan, Lebanon, and Syria: ACDA, SIPRI, and the IISS. The SIPRI data use relatively crude estimating methods and are little more than sophisticated guess work. The IISS data only report on military expenditures. They vary in definition from year to year and country to country in ways which make trend and inter-country comparisons impossible.[4] Only ACDA has access to US intelligence data, and can draw on the major analytic effort that goes on within the US intelligence community.

The ACDA data are taken from material provided by the US intelligence community, and are the best data available, but they still have severe problems. These data are presented in Table 2.1. The data in italics represent data missing in the original ACDA source data that have had to be estimated by the author, and these gaps alone illustrate how difficult it is to make meaningful comparisons. There are, however, other problems in the ACDA data:

FIGURE 2.1   Trends in Arab-Israeli Military Spending: 1983–1993 (In Constant 1993 Dollars)

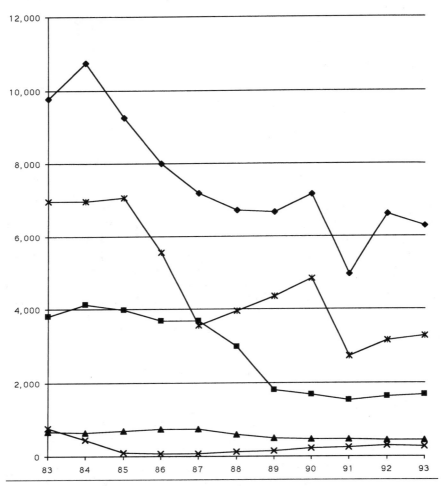

Source: Adapted by Anthony H. Cordesman from Arms Control and Disarmament Agency, "World Military Expenditures and Arms Transfers, 1983–1993," Washington, GPO, 1995, Table I.

- A review of past ACDA documents shows these problems cannot be explained by past military expenditures to pay for later arms deliveries.
- The ACDA data in Table 2.1 do not track with national reporting on military expenditures in budget documents, and the data on military expenditures for Egypt, Jordan, Lebanon, and Syria are exceptionally rough estimates.[5]

TABLE 2.1   Arab-Israeli Military Expenditures and Arms Purchases in Constant 1993 Dollars

	1983	1984	1985	1986	1987	1988	1989	1990	1991	1992	1993	TOTAL
A. Total Military Expenditures												
Israel	9,779	10,740	9,256	8,006	7,195	6,724	6,687	7,155	4,967	6,634	6,290	83,433
Egypt	3,801	4,131	3,976	3,690	3,690	2,979	1,787	1,680	1,526	1,612	1,670	30,542
Jordan	660	633	680	728	730	600	500	465	462	441	438	6,337
Lebanon	760	444	*100*	*75*	*75*	*120*	*150*	233	246	288	274	2,765
Syria	6,965	6,959	7,078	5,540	3,564	3,950	4,342	4,836	2,730	3,150	3,270	52,384
Total Arab	12,186	12,167	11,834	10,033	8,059	7,649	6,779	7,214	3,967	5,494	2,652	88,034
B. Arms Deliveries												
Israel	683	1,022	1,315	576	2,482	1,315	1,258	630	554	795	850	11,480
Egypt	1,993	2,453	2,104	1,409	2,110	837	858	630	712	897	1,100	15,103
Jordan	1,566	313	822	736	683	538	366	110	53	21	20	5,228
Lebanon	370	286	26	12	12	12	6	0	5	0	10	739
Syria	4,983	2,999	1,973	1,409	2,482	1,554	1,258	1,041	685	538	120	19,042
Total Arab	8,912	6,051	4,925	3,566	5,287	2,941	2,488	1,781	1,455	1,456	1,250	40,112

Note: Definitions of military expenditures and arms transfers are not comparable between countries shown. Different military and paramilitary force elements are counted, different levels of construction and support costs are included, expenditures on weapons of mass destruction and major long range missile programs are generally excluded. Foreign borrowing and some foreign exchange costs often are not included. The very different cost of manpower in a largely reserve Israeli force, and Arab force with extremely low conscript and regular salaries is not made comparable. The arms import data also disguise the large role of Israel's military industry in supplying Israel's military forces, while the Arab states are far more dependent on arms imports.

Source: Adapted by Anthony H. Cordesman, CSIS, from US Arms Control and Disarmament Agency, *World Military Expenditures and Arms Transfers, 1993–1994*, Washington, GPO, 1995. Italics show areas where the author has provided estimates for Jordan, Lebanon, and Syria because of gaps in the ACDA data.

- The ACDA data on military expenditures are not comparable in definition from country to country. They generally exclude expenditures on weapons of mass destruction, and exclude many imports of long range missiles.
- The data are not comparable in terms of the amount of military imports included or in terms of the extent to which they include new foreign debt and/or past interest payments on military foreign debt—data excluded from the budget reporting of all of the Arab states listed.
- The data are not comparable in terms of the amount of non-military goods and services used by the military, and include very different levels of military infrastructure expenditures.
- There also is no way to adjust for the very different costs each country pays for manpower. Israel, for example, pays for high quality regular manpower, but is primarily a reserve force. Arab states pay almost nothing for conscripts and very low salaries for other ranks and many junior officers.

The detailed arms import data in Table 2.1—which are summarized in Figure 2.4—present additional problems. They exclude many expenditures on weapons of mass destruction, and exclude many imports of long range missiles. They are not comparable in terms of the kind of contractor services and advisory efforts, military construction, and civil/dual use equipment included. Annual changes in the dollar value of imports rarely correlate to major weapons deliveries or the level of US FMS aid, and there is no way of relating dollar values to the value of the weapons technologies being purchased. There is a an uncertain correlation to actual expenditures in foreign currencies, and to data on military foreign assistance and borrowing. There is little correlation between the ACDA arms import estimates and the flow of FMS aid. ACDA's estimates to Egypt's total annual arms imports from some countries are sometimes lower than the value of the arms delivered through US FMS aid.

Comparing data on the dollar value of arms imports also presents problems because there often is only a limited correlation between the dollar figure and the number of weapons transferred or the importance of technology transferred. Such comparisons can be particularly misleading in examining the Arab-Israeli balance because Israel has a major military industry and often imports components which are not included in the figures for arms imports. Egypt is the only Arab "ring state" with significant military industrial output, but the sophistication of its output does not approach that of Israel.

Further, the data do not reflect the very different prices given nations pay for weapons or the fact that some countries get weapons that are provided as surplus equipment or pay far less for given types of weapons than other countries. Throughout the Cold War, for example, the Arab states buying from the Soviet bloc paid far less per weapon than states buying from the West. Since the end of the Cold War, states buying from Russia, the PRC, and Central Europe have had to pay more than in the past, but have still paid far less per weapon than nations buying similar types of weapons from Western countries. These price differences are so striking in the case of arms transfers to the Middle East that there is sometimes an inverse correlation between the ratio of arms transfers to given states measured in dollars and the relative number of weapons transferred.[6]

What Can Be Learned from Comparisons of Military Expenditures

In spite of the problems, the military expenditure data in Figures 2.2 and 2.3 and the first part of Table 2.1 provide some important insights into the defense effort in each country:

- The data are almost certainly accurate in reflecting a broad decline in real total military spending since the end of 1982. They are equally accurate in reflecting a massive drop in the percent of GDP that Israel and Syria spend on military forces. The level of total GDP allocated to military spending in both countries is less than half of what it was in the early 1980s—shortly after the 1982 war.
- Israeli military spending has dropped from $10 billion annually, in constant 1993 dollars, in the early 1980s to around $6 billion in 1993. Israeli reporting, which uses somewhat different definitions and conversion factors, indicates that the Israeli military budget was $8.25 billion in current dollars in 1995 and $8.28 billion in 1996. This cut for 1996 came after a major debate within the Israeli cabinet, a debate that illustrated some of the problems Israel faces in making peace. The Israeli military had requested an additional $492.6 million to cover current and planned withdrawals from Gaza and the West Bank. However, the military budget was cut by $123 million and parallel reductions were made in the security agencies.[7]
- Syrian military spending has dropped from around $7 billion annually in the early 1980s to around $6 billion in 1993—with a limited rise at the time of the Gulf War. It too has continued to drop since 1993.
- Jordanian military spending, which has always been low by the standards of its neighbors, has declined since 1987.
- Egyptian domestic military spending dropped from around $4 billion annually during the early 1980s to below $2 billion in 1989, and has remained close to this level.
- Lebanese military spending has shown a slight recovery since the Syrian intervention in Lebanon's civil war, but continues to be so low that Lebanon has little hope of developing serious military capabilities.

These trends are reinforced by some important shifts in Arab-Israeli military spending that have taken place since the end of the Cold War, and as a result of the Gulf War.

Syria, for example, was able to seek parity in equipment numbers with Israel during the mid-1980s because of a combination of aid from the Gulf and free or cheap arms from the Soviet Union and the Warsaw Pact. Although Syria did re-

FIGURE 2.2   Trends in Percentage of GDP Spent on Military Forces: 1983–1993

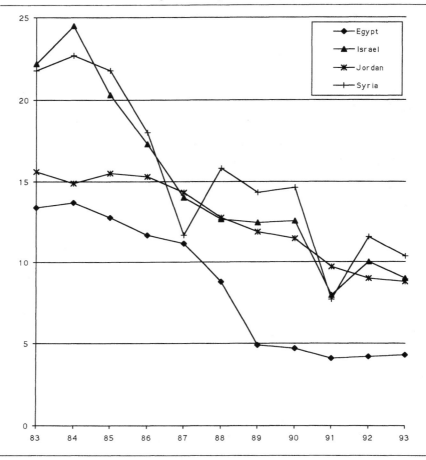

Source: Adapted by Anthony H. Cordesman from Arms Control and Disarmament Agency, "World Military Expenditures and Arms Transfers, 1983–1993," Washington, GPO, 1995, Table I.

ceive a onetime allotment of aid close to $1 billion at the time of the Gulf War, this money only allowed it to continue modernizing its armor and self-propelled artillery and was not sufficient to allow it to fund the other major force improvements it needed.

Syria has received little or no Gulf aid since 1991. It ceased to obtain free or nearly free arms from the Soviet Union and the Warsaw Pact in the mid- to late 1980s, and had to buy on credit. Syria also found that it could not meet its arms

FIGURE 2.3   Trends in Arab-Israeli Arms Import Deliveries: 1983–1993 (In Constant 1993 Dollars)

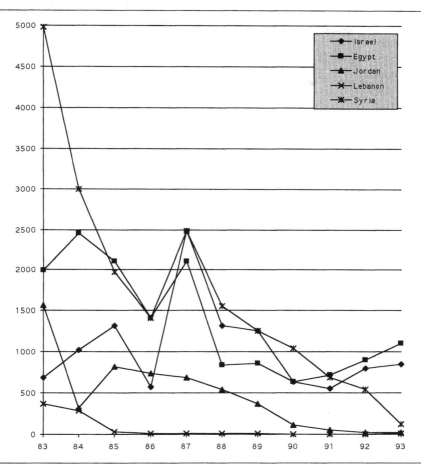

Source: Adapted by Anthony H. Cordesman from Arms Control and Disarmament Agency, "World Military Expenditures and Arms Transfers, 1983–1993," Washington, GPO, 1995, Table II.

debt to Russia. This effectively halted Russian credit to Syria, along with Syrian ability to buy arms for cash without dealing with its debt problem. Further, Syria's external civil debt rose from $786 million in 1975 and $10.8 billion in 1985, to $20.0 billion in 1993 and $20.4 billion in 1994.[8] As a result, the real drop in Syrian military spending is at least twice as great as the figures in Figures 2.2 and 2.3 and the first part of Table 2.1 indicate.

Jordan too used outside aid to buy arms to supplement its military spending, although it never received anything approaching the level of Gulf and Soviet bloc aid provided to Syria. Jordan, however, saw this aid decline sharply in the late 1980s and virtually halt after it supported Iraq during the Gulf War. Most Jordanians and Palestinians working in the Gulf were forced to return to Jordan, which lost much of the income it obtained from expatriates, while its trade with Iraq declined sharply as a result of UN sanctions.

Jordan's economy entered a crisis from which it is only beginning to recover. External debt—which had been $348 million in 1975 and $4.0 billion in 1985— rose to $6.9 billion in 1993 and $7.4 billion in 1994.[9] Further, Jordan had to cut its domestic civil and military spending sharply in 1990, and still operates under sharp government spending constraints. For example, it cut military spending again in 1994—to a total of only about $400 million in current dollars. As a result, net Jordanian military expenditures—including foreign aid to buy military equipment—have dropped far more than the data in Figures 2.2 and 2.3 and the first part of Table 2.1 indicate.[10]

Egypt's economy has shown only limited real growth in recent years, and its population growth has been so rapid that it has experienced little growth in per capita income. Egypt, however, has received in excess of $1 billion annually in Foreign Military Funds (FMF) and over $800 million in Economic Support Funding (ESF). It recently has received a total of $1.3 billion in FMF and $815 million in ESF, for an annual total of $2.1 billion. Only a small portion of this aid seems to be counted in Figures 2.2 and 2.3 and the first part of Table 2.1, and virtually all of Egypt's capital spending is now provided through US aid in addition to the figures shown.[11]

Israel may have tightened its military spending, but its economy is one of the most robust in the Middle East. A combination of the peace process and improved economic relations with other countries, Russian immigration, and some $10 billion in US loan guarantees is rapidly making Israel a fully developed country. According to some estimates, Israel's gross domestic product grew nearly 40% from the beginning of 1990 to the end of 1995. The Israeli Finance Ministry estimates that Israel's economy grew by 7% in 1995. Israel's per capita income, which ranged under $10,000 during the 1980s, has grown to nearly $16,000 in current dollars—a level similar to that of developed European nations like Britain and Italy. Foreign investment has tripled since 1990, reaching a total of $1.72 billion by the end of 1994, and foreign investors have invested $967 million in the stock market alone in 1995. Exports rose by 60% during 1993–1995, and reached $19 billion in 1995.[12]

Israel also continues to receive massive amounts of US aid, and this includes both direct FMF and ESF. Israel has long received $1.8 billion in annual FMS grant aid and $1.2 billion in Economic Support Fund grants. As a result, it has received $3 billion a year during most of the period shown in Table 2.1, only part of which is counted in the totals shown for Israeli military spending. Israel's actual defense effort is considerably larger than current reporting indicates, although there is no way to determine its exact size.

As a result, the current trends in military expenditures favor Israel and Egypt—proven partners in the peace process—far more than most reporting on such expenditures indicates. This difference affects every aspect of military capability, but it has a particularly important impact on the modernization and recapitalization of Egyptian, Israeli, Jordanian, Lebanese, and Syrian forces.[13] It is also important to understand that these differences have a powerful cumulative effect. The gap between Israel and Egypt and the other Arab states grows with time as Israel and Egypt continue to modernize and maintain their readiness, and Jordan, Lebanon, and Syria lack the funds to compete in modernization and maintain their existing force structure. This is particularly true in the case of Syria, which chooses to maintain very large force numbers even at the cost of letting them become progressively more hollow.

Further, these trends are reinforced by the relative efficiency of each nation in using its military budget. Israel compensates for high manpower costs by heavy reliance on conscription and reserves, and through efficient manpower management. It has a large and efficient manufacturing base, a modern infrastructure, and the ability to import the latest military technology from the US with minimal constraints on technology transfer. Unlike all of its Arab neighbors, it has the domestic resources to develop or modify the technology and complex systems needed to create the advanced command, control, communications, computer, intelligence (C^4I), and battle management systems necessary to take advantage of the "revolution in military affairs."

Like Israel, Egypt has the advantage of being able to manage its defense acquisition efforts with the knowledge it can count on a substantial flow of US aid and something approaching Israel's level of access to advanced US military technology. Egypt also has the advantage of a substantial industrial base and low cost manpower. Egypt, however, has high bureaucratic military forces with many fiefdoms and rivalries. It is only beginning to acquire modern management systems. Manpower and training management is poor, and the potential advantages of low cost manpower are more than offset by a failure to fully modernize training programs, make proper use of trained manpower, develop strong and respected NCO and technical cadres, and properly encourage the career development of junior and mid-level officers.

Egypt attempts to support far too large an active force structure for its financial resources, and still maintains a large number of units with low grade Soviet-supplied equipment—which places a further burden on its inadequate logistic and maintenance system. If Israel's military industries are often of only moderate efficiency, Egypt's are generally of low efficiency and lack effective management and capital. Egypt's military facilities and infrastructure have often been allowed to decay—because funds are allocated to new acquisitions instead—and Egypt lacks a "maintenance ethic" that ensures its equipment has proper readiness.

Jordan uses its resources more efficiently than Egypt, but it has very few resources indeed. Even though it has adopted successively smaller modernization plans over a period of more than a decade, it has been unable to fund any of these plans. This has constantly disrupted Jordan's efforts to create an efficient acquisition plan and its effort to develop its military maintenance and modernization facilities. It has also meant that Jordan has had only very limited access to advanced technology, and while it has relatively high quality manpower, the divisions between Trans-Jordanian and Palestinian limit its ability to exploit its manpower skills on the basis of merit or to create a large pool of reserves. Jordan is also faced with a steadily growing problem in dealing with diseconomies of scale and aging and obsolete equipment. Its force structure is too small in many areas to allow the efficient use of resources, and it is forced either to retire equipment from service or to spend more and more to service and modify aging equipment to get less and less in terms of relative effectiveness.

Lebanon has made minimal progress in improving the inadequate management of its heavily politicized, and often corrupt, military forces. It has never had anything approaching an effective acquisition and maintenance capability, its officer corps is traditionally recruited from the "failed sons" of Lebanese families, and it has recently turned its manpower system into a military disaster by reducing conscription to a single year of service.

Syria has many effective small combat formations, particularly in its land forces, but a highly inefficient central structure, and does a very poor job of using its military expenditures. It has been far less successful than Egypt in modernizing its overall manpower management and training system, in developing strong and respected NCO and technical cadres, and in developing effective training and career systems for its junior and mid-level officers. It does an exceptionally poor job of funding the training of senior officers.

Inter-service and inter-branch rivalries present major problems in using money efficiently, and corruption and the political use of funds are common throughout the Syrian armed forces. Its acquisition policy strongly favors the purchase of large numbers of modern weapons at the expense of effective sustainability, maintenance, infrastructure, and support. Large amounts of low grade equipment are retained in the force structure that cannot be deployed effectively in virtually all foreseeable scenarios, and which consume financial and manpower resources.

If Egypt sometimes lacks a "maintenance ethic," Syria sometimes lacks a basic consciousness of basic maintenance requirements—particularly for equipment in storage or units with older equipment. Syria has only limited domestic major military repair, overhaul, and modernization capability and its military management system is organized around dependence on imports, rather than the manufacture of spares, support equipment, etc. Most of the manufacturing resources Syria does have either produce aging Soviet light weapons and ammunition for older

Soviet systems, or are devoted to Syria's effort to acquire weapons of mass destruction and the means to deliver them.

Comparisons of Arms Sales and Imports

As might be expected, many of the trends in total military expenditures are reflected in the data on trends in arms sales. While such data again can only be used to measure the broad vector in national efforts, they still provide some useful insights into the balance. The data in the bottom half of Table 2.1 and Figure 2.4 show arms import deliveries in constant dollars during 1983–1993, and reveal several interesting patterns:

- Syria has seen a steady and massive drop in arms imports over the period from 1983 to 1993. Its deliveries in the early 1990s were so low that they only equaled a small fraction of the deliveries necessary to sustain or modernize Syria's massive force structure. Although any such judgments are speculative, deliveries seem to be less than 15% of the volume required to maintain and "recapitalize" Syria's forces.
- Jordan exhibited the same trend as Syria, with a crippling loss in the volume of its arms imports.
- Lebanon's arms imports were so low that Lebanon's already largely ineffective military forces became even more hollow.
- Israeli arms exports were erratic, but reflect relatively high levels of deliveries.
- Egypt had substantially higher levels of arms deliveries than Israel.

Table 2.1 and Figure 2.4, however, tell only part of the story. They need to be supplemented by data on the source of Egyptian, Israeli, Jordanian, Lebanese, and Syrian arms imports, and data on US military assistance. Table 2.2 is based upon slightly more current data from the work of Richard F. Grimmett of the Congressional Research Service. Like the ACDA data, they are taken from unclassified estimates made by the US intelligence community.[14]

These data are shown in Table 2.2—and summarized in Figure 2.3. The data cover two four-year periods before and after the Gulf War. These periods roughly correspond to periods before and after the break-up of the Soviet Union and the Warsaw Pact. They also illustrate the very different relationships between new arms sales agreements and new arms deliveries.

The data in Table 2.2 are particularly striking in the case of Syria. They indicate that Syria signed orders for $5.6 billion worth of arms during 1987–1990. In contrast, Syria only signed orders for $900 million during 1991–1994—16% of the level it had signed during the earlier period. Similarly, Syria only received 27% of the deliveries during 1991–1994 as it did during 1987–1990. Syrian new arms agreements fell far behind those of Egypt and Israel. Further, Table 2.2 shows that

TABLE 2.2 Arms Sales Agreements and Deliveries Affecting the Arab-Israeli Balance
(Millions of Current US Dollars)

Recipient Country	US	Russia	PRC	Major West European	All Other European	All Others	Total
New Arms Transfer Agreements							
1987–1990							
Israel	2,300	0	0	0	0	0	2,300
Egypt	5,900	500	0	0	100	0	6,500
Jordan	100	200	100	100	200	100	800
Lebanon	0	0	0	0	0	0	0
Syria	0	5,300	0	0	100	200	5,600
1991–1994							
Israel	3,000	0	100	1,200	0	0	4,300
Egypt	4,000	300	0	200	100	200	4,800
Jordan	100	0	0	0	0	0	100
Lebanon	0	0	0	0	0	0	0
Syria	0	500	0	0	200	200	900
1987–1994							
Israel	5,300	0	100	1,200	0	0	6,600
Egypt	9,900	800	0	200	200	200	11,300
Jordan	200	200	100	100	200	1000	900
Lebanon	0	0	0	0	0	0	0
Syria	0	5,800	0	0	300	400	6,500
Arms Transfer Deliveries							
1987–1990							
Israel	2,400	0	0	0	0	0	2,400
Egypt	2,300	500	100	400	200	200	3,700
Jordan	200	400	100	400	100	100	1,300
Lebanon	0	0	0	0	0	0	0
Syria	0	5,000	0	0	200	0	5,200
1991–1994							
Israel	2,800	0	100	400	0	0	3,300
Egypt	4,400	100	0	0	100	200	4,800
Jordan	100	0	0	0	0	0	100
Lebanon	0	0	0	0	0	0	0
Syria	0	1,000	0	0	100	300	1,400
1987–1994							
Israel	5,200	0	100	400	0	0	5,700
Egypt	6,700	600	100	400	300	400	8,500
Jordan	300	400	100	400	100	100	1,400
Lebanon	0	0	0	0	0	0	0
Syria	0	6,000	0	0	300	300	6,600

Source: Adapted by Anthony H. Cordesman, CSIS, from Richard F. Grimmett, "Conventional Arms Transfers to Developing Nations, 1987–1994," CRS 85-862F, Congressional Research Service, August 4, 1995, pp. 56–57 and 67–69. All data are rounded to nearest $100 million. Major West European states include Britain, France, Germany, and Italy.

FIGURE 2.4   New Arab-Israeli Arms Agreements and Deliveries: 1987–1994 (Current Millions of Dollars)

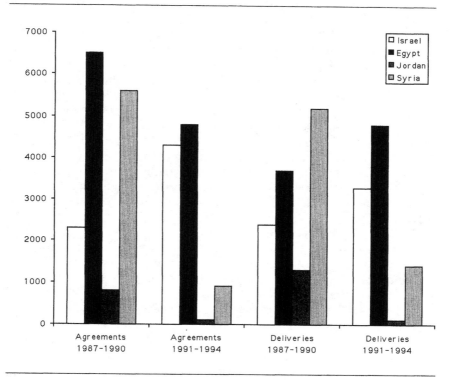

Source: Adapted by Anthony H. Cordesman from Arms Control and Disarmament Agency, "World Military Expenditures and Arms Transfers, 1983–1993," Washington, GPO, 1995, Table I.

Syria only received limited deliveries of arms from Russia, and no major deliveries from the West.

This drop in Syrian imports reflects a combination of the impact of the end of the Cold War, Syria's continuing problems in meeting its past arms debt to Russia, Russia's insistence on cash payments for arms, reductions in outside aid to Syria, and Syria's inability to control its balance of payments deficit. Syria was able to modernize many of its tanks and some of its aircraft—largely because of aid Syria received during the Gulf War—but it had accumulated a debt to Russia for past arms deliveries totaling between $13 billion and $16 billion. When Syria sought another $2 billion deal with Russia in 1992, the deal collapsed because of Russia's insistence on cash payments. The deal would have included 24 more MiG-24 fighters, 12 Su-27 fighter-bombers, 300 T-72 and T-74 tanks, and an unspecified number of SA-16 and SA-10 missiles.[15]

Syria has been able to buy some arms since that time, but outside aid has dropped from an average of $800 million per year during 1973–1993 to only $40 million a year since 1993. Syria has not been able to obtain major new sources of aid since the Gulf War. In fact, wartime promises of aid for a major new steel mill and phosphate fertilizer plant have been kept in the tender stage ever since the war because of a lack of Gulf aid. Syria is gradually reforming its fiscal institutions to improve its borrowing capability, but it has had to reschedule its past civil debts to limit its arrears on payments due on past loans to $400 million, and its current account balance has dropped from a surplus of $1.7 billion in 1990 and $700 million in 1991, to a surplus of $55 million in 1992, and a deficit of $607 million in 1993, $930 million in 1994, and $875 million in 1994.[16] In spite of the growth in Syria's GDP resulting from liberalization and privatization, it has been in a poor position to generate anything like the resources it needs to maintain and modernize its force structure. Both the decline in new arms agreements and deliveries and the lack of access to high technology systems will steadily weaken Syrian forces in the future.

Similarly, Table 2.2 and Figure 2.4 reflect a massive cut in Jordanian new arms agreements after 1990. This cut resulted from the near total cut-off of foreign aid to Jordan following Jordan's tilt toward Iraq during the Gulf War. This aid had to-taled up to $1.2 billion a year, although it declined in the period before the Gulf War.[17]

While Jordan had nothing approaching the level of arms debt, it did have a debt to the US of $275 million. It also had to devote most of its economic resources to dealing with the loss of aid, and the massive influx of Jordanian and Palestinian workers forced to leave the Gulf as a result of Jordan's support of Iraq. This helped drive Jordan's civil debt up to $8 billion in 1992. While a rescheduling of this debt and an improving economy brought the debt down to $6 billion in 1995, the rescheduling came at the cost of an IMF imposed austerity program that sharply limited Jordan's flexibility in using its domestic resources to buy arms.[18] As a result, Jordan only signed about 13% of the arms agreements during 1991–1994 that it signed during 1987–1990, and only received 8% of the deliveries. Jordan had better access to Western arms and technologies, but lacked anything approaching the funds it needs to recapitalize and modernize its forces.

The Impact of US Military Assistance

All of the previous data on Israeli arms imports have the defect that they sharply understate the true nature of Israeli military imports. While it is sometimes difficult to determine why the estimates of Israeli arms deliveries are so sharply understated, the reason seems to be that the arms import data generated by the US intelligence community only reflect the value of fully assembled weapons at the price the US charged, and do not reflect anything like the total value of FMS grants.

As has been discussed earlier, Israel has regularly received $1.8 billion in annual FMS grant aid. This is reflected in the data shown in Table 2.3, which shows that Israel got a total of $17.5 billion in FMF grant aid during 1985–1994. Put differently, Israel got $7.2 billion worth of FMF aid during 1991–1994, although Table 2.2 indicates Israel signed only $4.3 billion worth of new agreements during this period and received only $3.3 billion worth of deliveries.

Further, Israel also received $1.2 billion annually in ESF grants, which allowed it to shift its own funds away from domestic spending to areas like its arms industries. The US has provided Israel with $10 billion in loan guarantees since FY1993, at a rate of $2 billion per year. While these loan guarantees have been subject to penalties for Israel's funding of new settlements on the Occupied Territories, these penalties have been reduced to help Israel pay for the cost of the peace process and have been changed to exclude the value of any "private" construction. As a result, their net impact has dropped from $437 million in penalties in FY1993 to $60 million in FY1995. Further, the government of Israel has been allowed to use the entire $4 billion due during FY1996 and FY1997 to finance its national budget deficit.

The US has also invested several hundred million dollars in development of the Arrow, which allowed Israel to procure more arms, and the appropriations bill of November 5, 1990, provided Israel with grant military equipment valued at $700 million.[19]

Table 2.3 shows the annual levels of new FMS agreements and deliveries, and commercial military imports Israel received during 1985–1994. Any comparison between these data on annual US aid with the annual data in Table 2.1 reinforces the point that current estimates of Israeli arms imports do not provide a valid picture of the size of Israel's military effort. Further, Israel has been able to tailor many of its imports to support its military industries and has often received large amounts of US technology at little or no cost.

Israel has sometimes wasted this money. Particularly during the 1980s, it used US aid to subsidize inefficient military industries and projects which were more grandiose than practical. In other cases, however, Israel was able to increase the efficiency of its arms imports by combining US technology and domestic production into systems tailored specifically to Israel's strategic and tactical needs. If Israel's politically and export-driven decisions regarding its military industries were usually wasteful and inefficient, its "IDF-driven" decisions usually produced equipment that did a far more cost-effective job of meeting Israel's special military needs than simply importing equipment tailored to the global needs of US forces.

Table 2.3 also shows that Egypt received massive amounts of US military assistance. Nevertheless, the data in the previous tables and charts do not understate the value of Egyptian arms imports by anything approaching the extent to which they understate Israel's arms imports because almost all of this US aid was provided in the form of fully manufactured military goods and FMS services that are

TABLE 2.3   The Comparative Size of US Military Assistance and Commercial Arms Sales to the Arab-Israeli "Ring States": 1985–1994

	1985	1986	1987	1988	1989	1990	1991	1992	1993	1994
Israel										
Foreign Military Financing Program	1,400	1,722.6	1,800	1,800	1,800	1,800	1,800	1,800	1,800	1,800
Payment Waived	1,400	1,722.6	1,800	1,800	1,800	1,800	1,800	1,800	1,800	1,800
FMS Agreements	84.7	168.3	100.2	1,358.2	333.2	381.9	370.1	99.4	167.7	2,447.2
Commercial Sales	613.0	401.1	1,024.8	474.8	997.2	387.3	169.1	27.8	21.6	0.9
FMS Construction Agreements	–	–	–	–	–	–	–	–	–	0.2
FMS Deliveries	475.3	164.2	1,229.6	754.1	230.3	151.2	245.9	721.4	796.1	934.6
MAP Program	–	–	–	–	–	74.0	43.0	47.0	491.0	4.0
MAP Deliveries	–	–	–	–	–	–	114.7	0.6	44.7	–
IMET Program/ Deliveries	1.8	1.7	1.9	1.7	1.9	2.1	1.1	0.6	0.5	0.8
Egypt										
Foreign Military Financing Program Payment Waived	1,175.0	1,244.1	1,300.0	1,300.0	1,300.0	1,300.0	1,300.0	1,300.0	1,300.0	1,300.0
FMS Agreements	325.3	486.4	342.5	1,393.8	2,274.9	988.0	1,860.4	724.4	456.8	473.6
Commercial Sales	95.3	58.1	55.4	73.1	252.5	206.0	75.6	31.0	15.8	1.0
FMS Construction Agreements	16.3	19.6	112.4	121.4	65.3	48.1	233.9	107.5	14.0	0.9
FMS Deliveries	579.8	602.6	955.1	473.0	297.5	368.3	480.6	1,026.4	1,187.2	932.3
MAP Program	–	–	–	–	–	–	–	–	–	13.5
MAP Deliveries	–	–	–	–	–	–	–	–	–	–

IMET Program/Deliveries	1.4	1.6	1.7	1.5	1.5	1.5	1.8	1.5	1.7	0.8
Jordan										
Foreign Military Financing Program	90.0	81.3	–	–	10.0	67.8	20.0	20.0	9.0	9.0
Payment Waived	–	–	–	–	10.0	67.8	20.0	20.0	9.0	9.0
DoD Guaranty	90.0	81.3	–	–	–	–	–	–	–	–
FMS Agreements	108.8	24.2	34.1	30.1	10.1	27.8	0.6	7.1	16.9	53.4
Commercial Sales	613.0	401.1	1,024.8	474.8	997.2	387.3	169.1	27.9	21.6	0.9
FMS Deliveries	124.9	61.0	49.7	55.4	59.5	42.1	22.9	19.6	25.2	32.7
MAP Deliveries	7.0	1.2	1.1	0.8	–	–	–	–	0.1	–
IMET Program/Deliveries	0.7	0.5	0.5	0.4	0.4	0.1	–	–	0.6	0.3
Lebanon										
FMS Agreements										
Commercial Sales	3.9	6.8	3.9	2.9	1.5	3.5	2.3	7.4	1.7	0.1
FMS Deliveries	43.1	11.6	12.1	11.9	3.9	2.0	0.3	1.3	4.9	3.6
IMET Program/Deliveries	–	–	–	–	–	0.1	–	–	0.6	0.3
Syria										
FMS Agreements										
Commercial Sales	0.1	–	–	–	–	–	–	–	–	–
FMS Deliveries	–	–	–	–	–	–	–	–	–	–

Source: Adapted from US Defense Security Assistance Agency (DSAA), "Foreign Military Sales, Foreign Military Construction Sales and Military Assistance Facts as of September 30, 1994," Department of Defense, Washington, 1995.

counted in the estimates in Tables 2.1 and 2.2. As a result, Tables 2.1 and 2.2 are almost certainly correct in showing that Egypt's arms imports have been significant relative to those of Israel, and that Egypt received far more arms than Jordan, Lebanon, and Syria.

Table 2.2, for example, indicates that Egypt signed about five times more new arms agreements during 1991–1994 than Syria, and 48 times more than Jordan. Such figures are hardly surprising, given the fact that Table 2.3 shows Egypt received $1.3 billion a year in FMF Grant Aid, or $5.2 million in aid over the four year period, plus substantial value from the delivery of excess defense articles and commercial sales.[20]

Table 2.3 does not reflect significant US aid to Jordan or Lebanon, or any meaningful aid to Syria, but US and Jordanian relations have improved in recent years—particularly since Jordan's peace agreement with Israel. This has resulted in both the forgiveness of Jordan's $275 million FMF debt to the US and an increase in US aid.[21] The Clinton Administration requested $18.8 million worth of US aid to Jordan in FY1994 ($9 million in ESF, $9 million in FMF, and $0.8 million in IMET). It requested $15.5 million worth of US aid to Jordan in FY1994 ($7.2 million in ESF, $7.3 million in FMF, and $1.0 million in IMET), and requested $38.4 million worth of US aid to Jordan in FY1994 ($7.2 million in ESF, $30.0 million in FMF, and $1.2 million in IMET).[22]

On September 27, 1995, King Hussein met with US Secretary of Defense William Perry to discuss a larger aid program involving the transfer of up to 72 used USAF F-16 fighters, upgrades to Jordan's tanks, conversion of its IHawk surface-to-air missiles to the Pip 3 version, upgrades to its air defense C^{4}I/BM system, conversion of its M-113A1 armored personnel carriers to the M-113A3 version, upgrades of its anti-tank guided missiles, the provision of rocket assisted artillery rounds, supply of 18 UH-1H scout helicopters, and the supply of spare parts.[23]

The F-16 fighters would be excess equipment worth up to $1.5 billion, and the provision of more M-60A3s or the M-1s with 120 mm guns could cost $200 to $400 million. Another aid package could provide $300 million worth of upgrades to Jordan's fixed IHawks and obsolete aid defense system. The US has also discussed a mission to upgrade Jordan's military training effort.

Even if the Congress accepts such plans—and Congress has resisted the Clinton Administration's efforts to raise military aid to Jordan to $100 million a year—they would only alleviate Jordan's problems and not solve them. Jordan has not made any major deliveries of land weapons since 1980, except for captured Iranian equipment transferred by Iraq. Its last purchase of a new combat aircraft consisted of the moderate performance Mirage F-1s it bought from France in 1979.[24]

Since 1993, the US has provided Lebanon with 32 UH-1 helicopters, more than 800 M-113 APCs, spare parts for Lebanon's M-48 tanks, 80 other military vehicles, and other equipment worth more than $58 million. This aid, however, is only sufficient to make the Lebanese forces more effective for internal security purposes. The US will not help Lebanon build up serious modern military forces as long as it remains under Syrian occupation and permits Iran and Syria to supply and fund the Hizbollah in attacks on Israel.[25]

More broadly, US aid is certain to play an important role in the future of the peace process. There is a broad consensus among those who are actively involved in the peace process that US economic and military aid to Israel, Egypt, Jordan, and the Palestinians will play a critical role in ensuring the stability of the Camp David accords, the Oslo accords, and the Israeli-Jordanian peace agreement. Something close to current US levels of aid to Egypt and Israel will probably be needed for half a decade or more simply to underpin the current peace agreements. Military aid to Jordan will be needed to provide both security and internal stability, and economic aid to the Palestinians will be needed to reduce the risk of internal upheavals and create a stable Palestinian Authority.

Israeli officers and officials are divided over whether Israel will need a major increase in US aid to adjust to a withdrawal from the Golan. Politicized Israelis, and those who base their assessments on worst case threats, feel that withdrawal from the Golan will result in an increase in the risk to Israel that requires significant additional aid. Some indicate that they intend to use withdrawal as an excuse for asking for a massive new aid package worth up to $5 billion.

Those Israeli officers and officials who have analyzed the military situation in detail generally seem to have more modest demands. They feel the current mix of grant aid and loan guarantees will be largely sufficient if Israel is not forced to suddenly withdraw before it can restructure its forces. Most do, however, feel added technical aid will be needed and that either a direct US role in ensuring the peace accords or some increase in US military aid will be needed to compensate for full withdrawal.

Much, however, will depend on the force limitation agreements, confidence building and warning measures, verification regime, and international peace keeping force that will almost certainly be part of any Israeli-Syrian peace agreement. There also is little prospect that the US will provide significant aid to Syria, even if Syria agrees to a comprehensive peace agreement with Israel. This could, however, present problems. Syrian implementation of a strong force limitation agreement could be expensive and require some additional equipment like improved air defenses as compensation. This may mean Syria will need aid from a third party to implement the military aspects of a peace agreement.

3

QUANTITATIVE COMPARISONS: COMPARING MILITARY FORCES BY COUNTRY

While economics can provide important insights into the trends in the balance, it is military forces, not economics, that determine current war fighting capabilities. Table 3.1 provides a more realistic picture of the military forces that must be considered in assessing the trends in the balance than does Table 1.1. The data do not have a pro-Israel bias, and are based on a combination of information provided by US experts and information taken from the International Institute of Strategic Studies (IISS).

Table 3.1 compares the forces of Israel with the individual forces of Egypt, Jordan, Lebanon, and Syria—the Arab "ring states." Such a country-by-country breakdown avoids the assumption that the balance should be measured in terms of the total forces of a combination of Arab states relative to Israel. The charts that follow provide both an overview of the totals in Table 3.1 and the details of each nation's holdings of some of the key weapons that shape the balance.

There are several broad conclusions that can be drawn from this kind of data. Table 3.1 shows that:

- Syria remains a major regional military power in spite of its recent problems in financing arms imports. Syria's military build-up after the October War—which was given further impetus by its defeat in 1982—has still left it with near quantitative parity in many areas of land force strength, and numerical superiority in a few areas like armored infantry fighting vehicles, anti-tank weapons launchers, and artillery. Syria also has rough parity in total combat aircraft and attack helicopters.
- The sheer mass of Syrian forces cannot be ignored, and could be particularly important in a surprise attack or a defensive land battle. At the same time, there are many qualitative differences between Israeli and Syrian forces which almost universally favor Israel. Syria is also unquestionably wasting re-

sources in preserving low capability forces that would be better spent on new equipment or making its better units more effective.

- Egypt remains a major Middle Eastern power. Egypt has near numerical parity with Israel in terms of total force strength. It has fewer tanks than Israel or Syria, but it is well equipped with other armored fighting vehicles and anti-tank guided weapons. Egypt also has large numbers of modern US weapons, although it does not match Syrian artillery in mass or Israeli artillery in mobility.

- Jordan is now a small military power relative to Egypt, Israel, and Syria. It has adopted a new five year plan, which went into effect on January 1, 1995. This plan calls for Jordan to make major cuts in its headquarters, training, and support functions, and to consolidate its land forces from four divisions to three. It consolidates logistics centers and depots under a single directorate, combines the air and army staff colleges, and places weapons acquisition under a single directorate. The new five year plan also restructures the Jordanian military staff system from one based on British models to one using the G-1 to G-5 organization of the US Joint Chiefs of Staff—a measure designed to make Jordanian-US cooperation more effective in operations like peace keeping.

- Jordan still has considerable armored and artillery strength, but it only has a small air force and negligible naval capability. It has been able to improve the mobile and manportable SHORAD coverage of its ground forces, but it lacks modern fighters and mobile medium range surface-to-air missiles and can only provide its land forces with very limited air defense coverage.

- Lebanon's regular military forces are too small to be a meaningful player in the Arab-Israeli balance. Lebanon has only negligible military strength by the standards of Egypt, Israel, Jordan, and Syria. It has some 100 M-48A1/A5s, 200 T-54s/T-55s, and 620 other armored fighting vehicles, but its armored and mechanized forces have very limited training and war fighting capability. Similarly, Lebanon has little ability to mass, manage, and sustain its artillery assets. It has only three combat aircraft and four armed helicopters in its air force, and these include obsolete Hunter fighters and obsolescent SA-342 helicopters with AS-11/AS-12 missiles. The 3,000-odd men in the Iranian and Syrian-backed Hizbollah and the 2,500-odd men in the Israeli-backed South Lebanon Army are far more active in the Arab-Israeli conflict than Lebanon's regular forces, and are likely to remain so.

Understanding the Details Behind Quantitative Comparisons of Total Forces

The kind of force totals shown in Table 3.1 require considerable additional explanation if their implications are to be fully understood and kept in the proper per-

TABLE 3.1   The Arab-Israeli Balance:
Forces by Country in the Arab-Israeli "Ring States"

Category/Weapon	Israel	Syria	Jordan	Egypt	Lebanon
Defense Budget (In 1995 $Current Billions)	$6.9	$2.62	$0.448	$2.96	$0.343
Mobilization Base					
Men Ages 13–17	266,000	869,600	256,400	3,264,000	197,000
Men Ages 18–22	262,600	702,400	232,600	2,739,000	198,200
Arms Imports— 1991–1994 ($M)					
New Orders	4,300	900	100	4,800	–
Deliveries	3,300	1,400	100	4,800	–
Manpower					
Total Active	185,000	330,000	110,000	440,000	55,000
(Conscript)	138,500	–	–	–	–
Total Reserve	430,000	400,000	35,000	245,000	–
Total	615,000	808,000	145,000	685,000	55,000
Paramilitary	6,050	8,000	10,000	374,000	13,000
Land Forces					
Active Manpower	125,000	220,000	95,000	310,000	53,000
Reserve Manpower	365,000	100,000	30,000	150,000	–
Total Manpower	490,000	320,000	125,000	460,000	53,000
Main Battle Tanks	4,700	4,600	1,141	3,450	350
AIFVs	350	2,300	50	280	50
APCs/Recce/Scouts/ Half-Tracks	10,650	2,500	1,150	4,590	850
ATGW Launchers	1,005	5,050	640	2,340	20
SP Artillery	1,150	470	390	200	0
Towed Artillery	500	1,630	160	1,100	150
MRLs	100+	480	—	340	30
Mortars	6,500	4,500+	750	3,700	280
SSM Launchers	20	46+	0	0	0
AA Guns	1010+	1,985	360	1,677	220
Lt. SAM Launchers	945	?	900+	2,200	–
Air Forces					
Active Manpower	32,000	100,000	8,000	110,000	800
Reserve Manpower	55,000	92,000	–	90,000	–

TABLE 3.1   *(Continued)*

Category/Weapon	Israel	Syria	Jordan	Egypt	Lebanon
Aircraft					
Total Fighter/FGA/					
Recce	453	440	75	487	3
Fighter	56	280	30	340	0
FGA/Fighter	325	0	0	0	0
FGA	50	154	45	121	3
Recce	22	6	0	20	0
Airborne Early					
Warning (AEW)	4	0	0	5	0
Electronic Warfare					
(EW)	28	10	0	10	0
Maritime					
Reconnaissance (MR)	3	0	0	2	0
Tanker	5	0	0	0	0
Transport	40	29	9	32	0
Combat Training	60	91	14	70	2
Helicopters					
Attack/Armed	117	140	24	99	4
Other	160	110	24	113	14
Total	277	250	48	212	18
SAM Forces					
Batteries	20	99	14	38+	0
Heavy Launchers	–	698	80	738	0
Naval Forces					
Active Manpower	6,600	6,000	600	20,000	500
Reserve Manpower	10,000	8,000	–	14,000	0
Total Manpower	16,600	14,000	600	34,000	500
Submarines	3	3	0	3	0
Destroyers/Corvettes					
Missile	3	0	0	4	0
Other	–	2	0	1	0
Missile Patrol	20	18	0	26	0
Coastal/Inshore Patrol	35	11	7	18	9
Mine	–	7	0	8	0
Amphibious Ships	1	3	0	3	0
Landing Craft	4	5	3	16	2

Source: Adapted by Anthony H. Cordesman from data provided by US experts and the IISS, *Military Balance, 1995–1996*

spective. First, there are many ways to count the balance, and each tends to provide a different picture of relative capability. Second, there are many possible sources of such data, and the estimates of the force strengths and equipment holdings used throughout this book differ significantly according to the source. The primary source of these estimates is a series of interviews and comments by US experts and the IISS, *Military Balance, 1995–1996.*[1] Third, quantitative comparisons tend to be most meaningful when they are organized to portray important aspects of force capability and put in analytic content.

Total Force Strength and Differences in National Force Structure

There also are some important measures of force numbers that cannot be compared in direct quantitative terms. Table 3.1—and the rest of the tables and charts in this analysis—do not attempt to compare numbers of major combat units because each nation involved defines its combat units so differently. Numerical comparisons of formations that have such different individual manpower and equipment strengths are virtually meaningless. Some divisions may be twice the size as others. Furthermore, some countries have "brigades" and "regiments" that are as large as other countries' divisions or as small as other countries' large battalions.

The only thing that Israel, Syria, Jordan, and Egypt have in common in organizing their major combat units is that they all structure the organization of their land forces with a common emphasis on armored and mechanized land units, supported by some element of elite airborne and special forces units.

Israel organizes its forces into 3 different corps, plus territorial border defenses. It has a total of 11 armored divisions (3 active, 8 reserve), 3 regional mechanized infantry divisions (with 10 reserve regional brigades), an airborne division, 2 additional division headquarters for internal security operations, 4 active independent mechanized infantry brigades (1 airborne), and 1 reserve air mobile/mechanized infantry division with 3 brigades manned by paratroop trained reservists.

Jordan organizes its forces into two armored and two mechanized divisions, one special forces brigade, and one independent royal guard brigade. These are all full-time active forces and have relatively high readiness by regional standards. Jordan is, however, consolidating its land forces into three divisions. These three divisions will have a total of the same number of combat elements, but will convert four tank battalions to units better suited for border surveillance and will have sharply reduced support and headquarters strength. They will be relatively heavily mechanized if Jordan can obtain suitable aid, but Jordan's financial problems may force it to regroup its army into one armored division, one mechanized division, and a light strategic reserve division that could be used as a frontier force.

Jordan is also reorganizing its land force deployments to improve coverage of the Iraqi and Syrian borders and provide a lighter border force to cover its border with Israel, which will emphasize border security over defense against Israel. This new border force will be highly mobile, will have improved surveillance technology, and may be supported by an electrified border fence and systems of thermal TV cameras. Talks are under way between Israel and Jordan on cooperative border surveillance.[2]

Egypt organizes its forces into two armies and four major military districts. Its combat strength emphasizes heavy forces, and Egypt has four armored and eight mechanized infantry divisions, one Republican Guard armored brigade, two independent armored brigades, two air-mobile brigades, four independent mechanized brigades, one paratroop brigade, and seven commando groups. Like Syria, a substantial part of this order of battle is composed of relatively low grade and poorly equipped units, many of which would require substantial fill-in with reservists—almost all of which would require several months of training to be effective.

Syria organizes its ground forces into 2 corps. It has 6 armored divisions, each with 3 armored brigades, 1 mechanized brigade, and 1 artillery regiment. It has 3 mechanized divisions, each with 2 armored brigades, 2 mechanized brigades, and 1 artillery regiment. It has 1 Republican Guard division, with 3 armored brigades, 1 mechanized brigade, and 1 artillery regiment, and a special forces division, with 3 special forces regiments. Its active smaller formations seem to include 1 border guard brigade, 3 infantry brigades, 1 anti-tank brigade, 1 tank regiment, 7 special forces regiments, and 1 artillery brigade. According to some reports, it has 1 reserve armored division and 30 reserve regiments, including infantry and artillery formations.

Lebanon has a "paper strength" of 11 infantry brigades, 1 Presidential Guard Brigade, 1 commando/ranger regiment, three special forces regiments, 2 artillery regiments, and 1 air assault regiment. In fact, its formations differ widely in actual manning, equipment, and readiness, and some of its brigades are close to being nothing more than reinforced battalions.

The Importance of Reserve Forces and Strategic Warning

The manpower data in Table 3.1 and Figures 3.1 and 3.2 reflect another important aspect of the balance. The data in Table 3.1 provide a rough measure of the comparative size of each nation's current military establishment. Figure 3.2 provides a rough picture of the trends in total active military manning since the 1973 war.

However, Israel organizes its forces and military manpower in very different ways from those of its Arab neighbors, and comparisons of either total active manpower or total active and reserve manpower have only limited meaning in measuring military effectiveness. Israel has only about 172,000 active men and women in its peacetime force structure, and this total includes some 138,500 conscripts. Israeli conscripts serve a total of 36 months (21 months women, 48 months officers), and a significant number are still in training or gathering com-

FIGURE 3.1   Total Arab-Israeli Active Military Manpower: 1973–1995

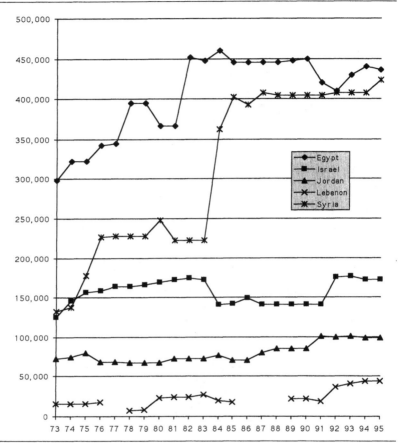

Source: Adapted from the IISS, *Military Balance,* various years. Some data adjusted or estimated by the author.

bat experience at any given time. Israel's military effectiveness depends heavily on the ability to call up the key elements of a reserve manpower pool of about 430,000 men. In fact, 8 of Israel's 11 armored "divisions" are reserve forces, as are 1 air mobile mechanized division, 4 out of 7 artillery brigades, and the 10 regional infantry brigades it uses to guard its borders.

Syria, Jordan, and Egypt also have reserve forces. Syria has 400,000 reserves, including 300,000 in the army, 92,000 in the air force, and 8,000 in the navy. Jordan has 35,000 men (30,000 in the army), and Egypt has 254,000. These reserves provide a pool of hundreds of thousands of men, but the war fighting capability of

FIGURE 3.2   Arab-Israeli Army Manpower: 1973–1995

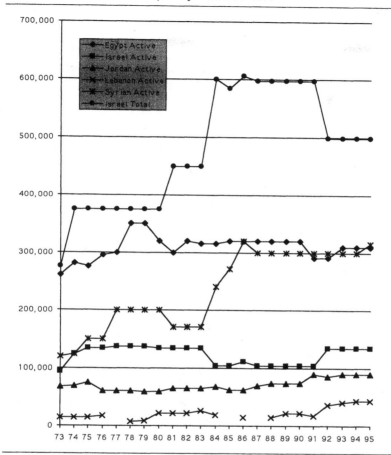

Source: Adapted from the IISS, *Military Balance*, various years. Some data adjusted or estimated by the author.

most Arab reserves is limited. They receive little call-up training and most are not
integrated into an effective unit structure or mix of active and reserve force elements. Syria has never made effective use of most of its reserves, and Egypt and
Jordan have steadily cut back on reserve activity—in part for financial reasons.

On paper, Syria has one low grade reserve armored unit with about half the effective strength of its active divisions, plus 30 infantry and one artillery reserve
regiment. All of these Syrian reserve units are poorly equipped and trained. Those
Syrian reserves that do train usually do not receive meaningful training above the
company to battalion level, and many train using obsolete equipment that is dif-

ferent from the equipment in the active units to which they are assigned. The Syrian call-up system is relatively effective, but the Syrian army is not organized to make use of it. Virtually all of the Syrian reserves called up in the 1982 war had to be sent home because the Syrian army lacked the capability to absorb and support them.

Egypt has a 254,000 man reserve (150,000 army, 20,000 air force, 70,000 air defenses, 14,000 navy). The Egyptian reserve system has been allowed to collapse into decay since the 1973 war. Reserves still have nominal assignments to fill in badly undermanned regular units, but they have little training for their mission. Like Syria, those Egyptian reserves that do train usually do not receive meaningful training above the company to battalion level, and many train using obsolete equipment that is different from the equipment in the active units to which they are assigned.

Jordan cannot significantly increase its combat unit numbers with reserves. It has had to cut back on reserve training to the point where its reserves now have little effectiveness, and has recently frozen its intake of conscripts for its active forces to reduce the cost of its forces. This freeze effectively ensures that Jordan's active and reserve forces will not grow with its population, and Jordan may have to make additional cuts in both its active and reserve strength. Lebanon has no meaningful reserve system.

Where Israel's reserves are the key to its effectiveness, the cost of maintaining Syrian and Egyptian reserve forces may actually reduce the total military effectiveness of each country by wasting resources on low grade forces that would be better spent on more effective units.

Figure 3.2 illustrates the resulting impact of Israel's reserves on the balance by showing how both the active and mobilized strengths of Israel's land forces compare with the active manpower in Arab armies. The Israel total that includes reserves shows just how much Israel can increase its pool of highly trained manpower in an emergency, and it is that total that should really be compared to the Arab armies. As a result, Israel has far more real world manpower strength than its total active military manpower would indicate.

At the same time, Israel's use of reserves makes it dependent on timely mobilization for its war fighting capability, and Israel requires 36–48 hours of strategic warning and reaction time to fully prepare its defenses in the Golan—its most vulnerable front. Only about one-third of Israel's total manpower consists of full time actives, and much of this manpower consists of conscripts. Some of Israel's best troops consist of its younger reserves.[3]

High Quality Weapons Versus Total Weapons

There are many different ways to count weapons, and many different estimates of weapons numbers. Table 3.1 has provided a "snapshot" of the current balance, based on the estimate of US experts. Several of the following charts provide a graphic portrayal of the same data, highlighting key aspects of weapons numbers. Other charts show the trend in equipment numbers from 1973 to the present, based largely on data provided by the International Institute of Strategic Studies (IISS).

Another set of charts provide a more selective picture of force strengths, based on counts of the highest performance weapons. As the Gulf War and past Arab-Israeli conflicts have shown, high quality weapons tend to dominate modern conflicts. Accordingly, these charts provide a very different picture of the force strength on each side, and provide a rough measure of how force quantity is affected by force quality.

At the same time, any counts of high performance or modern weapons are inherently controversial. One man's definition of "high performance" is almost inevitably different from another's. For example, Figure 3.5 provides an estimate of high quality tanks. The data exclude all older generation Soviet tanks, but include all M-60s and Chieftains. Many experts would argue that the M-1 and Merkava II and III are the only truly advanced tanks that should be counted in the balance, while others would argue that the Chieftain and M-60A1 are not equal to the M-60A3 and T-72.

The count of true armored fighting vehicles in Figure 3.7 is even more controversial. Many experts would argue that Figure 3.7 should include more types of armored reconnaissance vehicles, particularly those armored vehicles which have heavy weaponry. This count is highly selective, and only includes the vehicles US experts classify as high performance, based on recent combat experience.

The count of high performance aircraft in Figure 3.12 differs sharply from many estimates, which define all supersonic aircraft as "high performance." The author feels that such distinctions are obsolete and never reflected the realities of air combat. Supersonic speed is largely a measure of intercept or escape speed for most combat aircraft, which are forced to fly at subsonic speeds the moment they engage in air-to-air combat and lose energy of maneuver. Only a few modern aircraft are effective if they fly attack missions at supersonic speeds. In contrast, modern avionics plays a critical role in determining situational awareness, night and poor weather mission capability, and the ability to fly look-down, shoot-down missions, carry out beyond-visual-range intercepts, and use precision guided weapons effectively. As a result, Figure 3.12 is based on modern mission capability and not aircraft speed.

Unfortunately, there is no meaningful way to score or "weight" different weapons systems using either static or dynamic analysis that provides a convincing picture of present force-wide effectiveness or future combat capability. The author has been involved in various efforts to "score" weapons by type since the development of the revised firepower scores in the 1960s and the development of the weapons effectiveness indicators (WEI). None of these attempts to date resolve the problem of accurately comparing direct and indirect fire weapons, dealing with weapons upgrades and modifications, trading off one aspect of weapons effectiveness against another, assessing the value of modern fire control systems, or aggregating very different mixes of combined arms in units with very different tables of equipment. They may simplify the problem of developing databases for war games, or aggregating weapons data into simply scores for entire combat units, but they do so at the cost of both transparency and credibility.

Main Battle Tanks

Figure 3.4 shows the trends in tank strength and Figure 3.5 shows high quality armored weapons—perhaps the most important measure of land force strength. It also provides a broad index of the most important measure of maneuver and direct fire warfare capability. It should be noted that the total shown for high quality tanks in Arab forces is about 75% higher than the total for Israel, but that no Arab state individually equals the total for Israel.

A comparison of Figure 3.5 with the data in Figure 3.3 shows how different the tank strength of each nation is when one looks only at high quality tank forces. Israel's total tank strength includes about 2,200 Merkavas and M-60s. This total includes at least 930 Merkava I/II/IIIs, 750 M-60A3s, and 500 M-60A1s. This is a total of 2,000 high quality tanks out of a total strength of 4,700, or 48%. Israel's percentage of high quality tanks would drop to 37% if one only included its Merkavas and M-60A3s, but Israel continues to build Merkavas and is getting deliveries of additional M-60A3s.[4]

Syria has given its tank forces high priority and has a total of about 4,600 main battle tanks, and this total includes some 1,550 relatively capable T-72 and T-72M tanks. The remaining tanks, however, include 2,100 relatively low quality T-54s and T-55s and 1,000 obsolescent T-62M/Ks. About 1,200 of these T-54, T-55, and T-62 tanks are also emplaced in revetments or in storage, and are not part of Syria's operational or maneuver forces. Syria has, therefore, emphasized numbers over quality and war fighting capability. Further, many of the tanks Syria has in storage, or assigned to its reserve units, have never been properly prepared for storage, and are stored in the open. A number of experts believe they would now require extensive rebuilding to become operational.

Jordan's tank strength includes 1,141 tanks, but most of its 270 M-47 and M-48 tanks are now in storage. This total also includes 293 obsolete Tariq (Centurion) tanks that have been upgraded, but are strikingly inferior to all of Israel's tanks, and would have severe difficulties in successfully engaging Syria's T-62s and T-72s. Jordan's only tanks that can compete effectively against the T-72 and T-80 are its 218 M-60A1/A3s and 360 Khalids (Chieftains).

These problems help explain Jordan's reorganization from four to three divisions. One of its restructured divisions is supposed to acquire 300 tanks with 120 mm guns—preferably a variant of the M-1. Jordan is seeking the M-1 with the 120 mm gun in order to be able to defeat Syria's T-72s and possible acquisition of the

FIGURE 3.3   Arab-Israeli Armored Forces

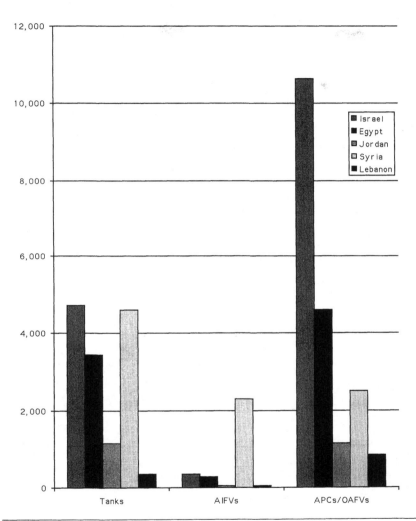

Source: Prepared by Anthony H. Cordesman, based upon discussions with US experts.

T-80—although it may have to settle for surplus US M-60A3s. A second division will use about two-thirds of Jordan's upgraded Chieftains—or Khalids. A third division will use Jordan's upgraded M-60A1/A3s. Jordan's remaining M-47/M-48s and upgraded Centurions (Tariqs) will be dropped from service and sold.

FIGURE 3.4   Arab-Israeli Main Battle Tanks: 1973–1995

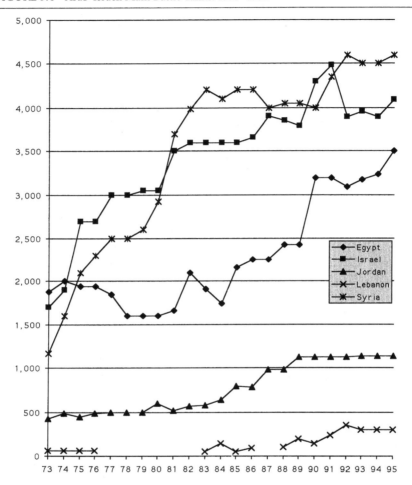

Source: Adapted from the IISS, *Military Balance,* various years. Some data adjusted or estimated by the author. Data differ significantly from estimates by US experts.

Jordan's upgraded M-60A1s and M-60A3s are still effective against tanks like the T-72, but the Khalids are worn and have a number of power train problems. Jordan has not been able to finance the upgrading of most of its Khalids, although it still hopes to upgrade their armor. As a result, only about 20% of Jordan's tanks are really modern. Like Syria, many of the tanks Jordan has placed in storage are stored in the open.

Egypt has a large number of modern tanks. These include 700 M-60A1, 847 M-60A3, and 230 M-1A1 tanks, or 52% of Egypt's total of 3,450 tanks. Egypt is

FIGURE 3.5   Israel Versus Egypt, Syria, Jordan, and Lebanon: High Quality Tanks (High Quality Tanks include T-72s, Chieftains, M-60s, M-1s, Merkavas)

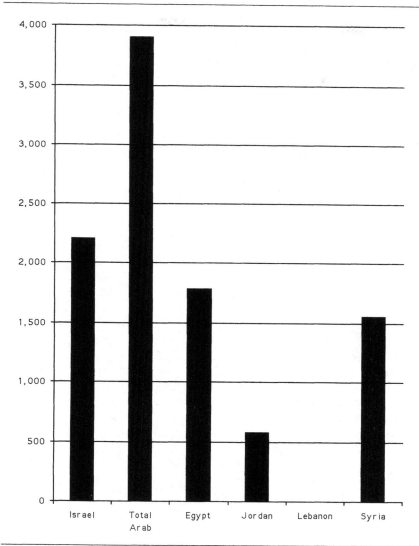

Source: Prepared by Anthony H. Cordesman, based upon discussions with US experts.

also continuing to get deliveries of M-1A1s and surplus US M-60s. It will coproduce a total of 524 M-1A1s by the end of 1997, and is considering follow-on production of the M-1A1 or M-1A2 and using its tank production plant to upgrade its M-60s and M-113s with new turrets.[5]

Egypt still, however, has 750 worn obsolete T-54 and T-55 tanks in its active force structure; 600 worn, obsolescent T-62s; and 260+ Ramses conversions of the T-54 and T-55—a conversion of very uncertain value in combat against first line tanks. These lower quality tanks might be of value against a low grade enemy like Libya or the Sudan, but they have very doubtful value against an opponent like Israel. They may well represent a waste of Egyptian resources in which Egypt invests in useless mass at the cost of force equality. Like Syria and Jordan, many of the tanks Egypt has in storage, or assigned to its reserve units, have never been properly prepared for storage and are stored in the open.

Other Armored Fighting Vehicles

The data on armored fighting vehicles (AFVs) shown in Figures 3.6 and 3.7 reflect significantly greater differences in each nation's forces than the data on tanks. Egypt, Israel, Jordan, and Syria have all emphasized the main battle tank, and Lebanon has sought to increase its holdings of each weapon. The story is very different in the case of AFVs. Each country has taken a different path toward mechanizing its infantry, support, and artillery, and acquiring specialized reconnaissance and infantry fighting vehicles.

Israel has nearly 11,000 APCs and half-tracks, but this number needs to be kept in context. Most of these armored vehicles are armored personnel carriers (APCs). These include low grade systems like the BRDM-2 and BTR-50 as well as better performing systems like the M-113A1/A2, Nagmashots, Achzarits, Fuchs, and Ramta conversion of the M-113. Israel also still uses 3,000 obsolete M-2 and M-3 half-tracks.

Some of Israel's more modern APCs have been up-armored, are relatively well armed, and can support tanks from positions only slightly to the rear in direct tank engagements. This makes it difficult to distinguish their war fighting capability from systems that were originally designed as armored fighting vehicles like the BMP and Scorpion, and some almost certainly can outperform the BMP in armored maneuver warfare.

Nevertheless, most US experts feel that Israel should not be counted as having significant holdings of AFVs intended to have the armor, firepower, and mobility to directly support tanks in maneuver combat or engage well-armed and well-placed infantry with modern anti-tank weapons. They only classify 350 of Israel's other armored fighting vehicles as designed for this role, although Israel is now deploying more armored vehicles modified to provide direct support of tanks and is giving the procurement of an advanced APC/AFV a higher priority.[6]

Syria has purchased large numbers of other armored vehicles, although these are of very mixed quality. Syria has 700 obsolescent BRDMs which it uses as armored reconnaissance vehicles. These vehicles performed relatively poorly in Afghanistan. They have limited visibility and poor angles of fire for rough and mountainous terrain of the kind on the Golan and in the Galilee, are highly vul-

FIGURE 3.6 Arab-Israeli Other Armored Fighting Vehicles (OAFVs): 1973–1995

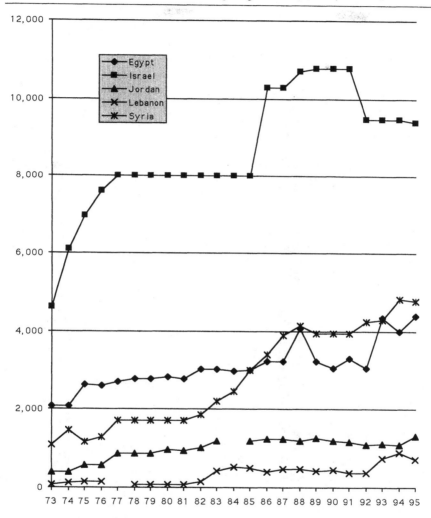

Note: Includes APCs, scout cars, half-tracks, mechanized infantry fighting vehicles, reconnaissance vehicles, and other armored vehicles other than tanks.

Source: Adapted from the IISS, *Military Balance,* various years. Some data adjusted or estimated by the author.

FIGURE 3.7   Israel Versus Egypt, Syria, Jordan, and Lebanon: True AFVs (AFVs include
BMP-1, BMP-2, Ramta, M-2/3, Scorpion)

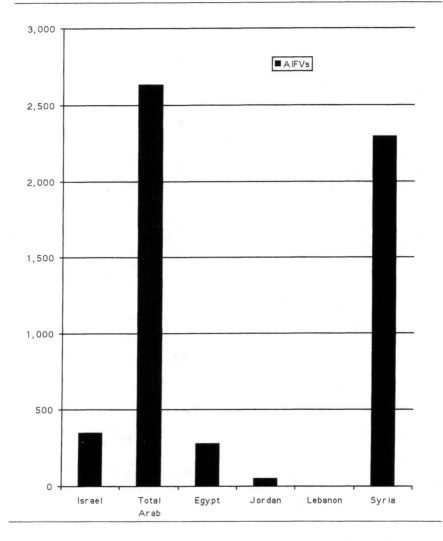

nerable even to light anti-tank weapons, and are difficult to exit rapidly once the
vehicle is hit. Syria also has 1,500 obsolescent and relatively low quality BTR-40s,
BTR-50s, BTR-60s, and BTR-152s, which are Korean War vintage designs it uses
as APCs.

Syria's most capable armored fighting vehicles consist of 2,250 BMP-1s and 50
BMP-2s that it uses as armored infantry fighting vehicles (AIFVs). The BMP is a

Soviet designed weapon intended to support tanks in combat. It is an effective system in some respects, but has light armor and has proven to have severe ergonomic problems in the design of its fire ports and in the operation of its main gun and anti-tank guided weapons system.

The BMP-1 and BMP-2 performed relatively poorly in the Iran-Iraq War, the Gulf War, and the fighting in Afghanistan. Russian armored vehicles have been extensively modified as a result of these conflicts, and the BMP-3 seems to have corrected many of the crippling ergonomic problems that limited the effectiveness of the BMP-1 and BMP-2. The BMP-3 has a much more effective 100 mm gun, and its use of a gun-launched variant of the AT-10 "Bastion" (9M117) missile may give it the first effective anti-tank guided missile capability ever deployed on a BMP. Syria, however, has no immediate ability to buy the BMP-3 or upgrade its existing BMPs, and even the BMP-3 is relatively heavy for its power train and has demonstrated serious reliability problems.[7]

Like Israel, Jordan has comparatively large numbers of APCs, many of which carry heavy weapons, but relatively few other armored vehicles that are classified as armored fighting vehicles dedicated to the direct forward support of tanks. Its holdings include 19 Scorpion light tanks, 150 obsolete Ferret armored reconnaissance vehicles, and 35 relatively modern BMP-2 armored infantry fighting vehicles. The rest of Jordan's holdings consist of 1,100 variants of the M-113 APC. Some of these M-113s have minor improvements in armor, some have been equipped with cannon/machine guns and mortars, and 70 have TOW anti-tank weapons.

Jordan is now much better equipped for armored personnel movement and dismounted support of tanks than the direct support of tanks with armored fighting vehicles. It is actively seeking US aid to convert its M-113A1s to M-113A3s to improve their survivability and firepower in combined maneuver operations, and to upgrade the armor of its M-113s. It also, however, plans to cut its total operational strength of M-113s by about 15% to free resources to maintain its remaining forces.

Egypt has comparatively large numbers of armored fighting vehicles, but much of its strength is worn and/or obsolete. Egypt has some 3,000 operational APCs, including 1,685 M-113s, 44 M-577s, roughly 1,000 BTR-50/OT-62s, over 600 Walids, and over 150 Fahds. Egypt's armored reconnaissance vehicles include 300 obsolescent BRDM-2s and 112 light armored Commando Scouts that are not suited for missions in areas with large amounts of heavy armor. Its holdings of armored infantry fighting vehicles include 250 BMR-600Ps and 220 worn BMP-1s. Egypt did, however, order 599 YPR-765 armored infantry fighting vehicles from the Netherlands in 1994, as well as 12 M-577 command vehicles. Deliveries of the YPR-765s began in October 1994, and the Netherlands is providing technical and training assistance.[8]

It should be noted that some Israeli and Jordanian officers do not feel that their respective lack of an advanced armored fighting vehicle is likely to be significant in combat on the West Bank, on the Golan, or in Lebanon. They feel that advanced armored fighting vehicles may be useful in supporting tanks and direct fire in the relatively open terrain in the Sinai, but that moving through rough terrain requires infantry to dismount from armored vehicles, or allows AFVs with softer armor and less speed to be positioned where their anti-tank weapons and mortars can be used "hull down" or in less vulnerable positions.

They feel that both tanks and AFVs fighting in the Golan, and much of the West Bank and Lebanon, will have to advance along the same relatively predictable routes for terrain reasons, will have to compete for maneuver room in major engagements, and that armed helicopters, close air support, and rapidly responding, precision fire artillery will provide more effective support for tanks in hunting down and suppressing enemy tanks and anti-tank weapons than AIFVs. US experts also question the value of Syria's emphasis on massing direct fire armored weapons in the vicinity of the Golan Heights and the Galilee because of the geographic factors that limit cross country movement and "channel" armored vehicles.

Israeli officers with extensive experience with unattended airborne vehicles (UAVs) also stress the new degree of situational awareness that modern sensors can give combined arms forces in locating and suppressing both tanks and AFVs. In contrast, Egyptian officers who served in the Gulf War are more impressed with the advantages of weapons like the M-2 Bradley and the impact of a mix of M-1A1 tanks and the M-2 in armored maneuver combat. In short, Egypt, Israel, Jordan, and Syria not only have different views of their desired relative mix of tanks and AFVs, but differ over the role of AFVs in combined arms.

Anti-Tank Weapons

There is no way to develop exact counts of Israel's, Egypt's, Jordan's, Lebanon's, and Syria's holdings of anti-tank guided weapons, but all of the countries involved have acquired relatively large numbers of modern crew-served, vehicle mounted, and manportable anti-tank guided weapons. These systems play a major role in shaping the balance of armored warfare capabilities.

Israel has at least 200 modern crew-served TOW anti-tank guided missile launchers (some mounted on Ramta M-113s), 1,000 aging manportable Dragon anti-tank guided missile launchers, 25 Mapats, and some captured AT-3 Saggers. It also has large numbers of B-300 82 mm rocket launchers, Carl Gustav 84 mm rocket launchers, and 250 M-40A1 107 mm rocket launchers.

Syria relies largely on 3,700 low quality Soviet-bloc AT-3 Sagger anti-tank guided weapons with second generation guidance systems. It does, however, have 200 modern manportable Milan and 150 modern AT-4 Spigot anti-tank guided weapons with third generation guidance systems.

Jordan has emphasized anti-tank weapons as a way of offsetting its weakness in armor. It has 200 TOW launchers (90 mounted in APCs) and 310 Dragons. It also has some 2,500 LAW-80 94 mm rocket launchers, 2,300 112 mm APILAS rocket launchers, and 330 M-40A1 106 mm rocket launchers. Jordan is seeking to upgrade its TOW missiles to the TOW-2A and find a replacement or upgrade package for its Dragons.

Egypt has a mix of low quality Soviet-bloc and British anti-tank guided weapons with second generation guidance systems, and modern manportable Milan and crew-served TOW weapons with third generation guidance systems. Its holdings include 1,400 AT-3 Sagger launchers (some on BRDM-2s), 200 Swingfire launchers, 220 Milan launchers, and 520 TOW launchers, including improved TOWs and TOW-2As (52 mounted on M-901 armored vehicles). The AT-3s and Swingfires are obsolescent and are another case where Egypt has tended to maintain force numbers at the expense of force quality. Egypt is, however, seeking more TOW-2As as one of its highest procurement priorities.[9]

Lebanon has 20 TOW launchers and ENTAC and Milan anti-tank guided weapons. It has very large inventories of RPG-7 and M-65 anti-tank rocket launchers and recoilless weapons like the M-40A1 106 mm recoilless rifle.

Egypt, Israel, Jordan, and Syria all recognize the advantages of modern anti-tank guided weapons which combine high lethality, long range, and ease of operation. They also mix the use of AFVs that can fire anti-tank guided weapons at long ranges with an emphasis on defensive tactics that use anti-tank weapons in fortifications and pre-surveyed locations.

Israel and Syria have made anti-tank guided weapons a key part of their fortifications on the Golan, and Jordan relies heavily on such weapons for the defense of the slopes on the Eastern Bank of the Jordan. Israel, however, does a far better job of supporting its anti-tank guided weapons crews with C4I/BM systems than Syria and of training its crews for integrated combined arms operations.

Artillery Forces

Figures 3.8, 3.9, and 3.10 provide a broad picture of the relative artillery strength of Israel, Egypt, Jordan, Lebanon, and Syria, and a rough measure of their indirect fire capability. These charts illustrate the fact that Israel has emphasized artillery maneuver warfare since the 1973 war, while its Arab neighbors have tended to place more emphasis on massing artillery and sheer fire. One important aspect of this table that may have considerable impact in future wars is that maximum artillery ranges now extend from 27 to 40 kilometers.[10] This is a significant increase in range since 1973, and a near doubling of range since 1967. It means both sides can fire at military and civilian targets much deeper in their opponent's territory.

Egypt and Syria have massive total artillery forces. At the same time, the data in Figure 3.10 reflect the fact that Israel has built up a considerable force of modern self-propelled artillery weapons, including some 1,150 weapons out of a total of 1,650 self-propelled, toward, and multiple rocket launcher weapons—or 72%. Israel's best artillery weapons include 530 M-109A1/A 155 mm, 200 M-107 175 mm, and 220 M-110 203 mm weapons. Israel has an additional advantage in tech-

FIGURE 3.8   Arab-Israeli Artillery Forces

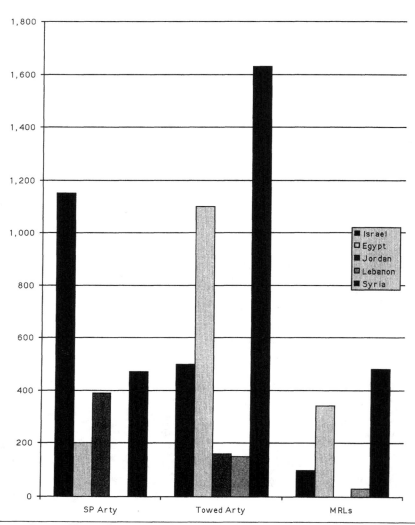

Source: Prepared by Anthony H. Cordesman, based upon discussions with US experts.

nology because it has much better counter-battery, long range targeting, and battle management and fire control systems and capabilities than Egypt, Jordan, and Syria, and conducts much more realistic combined arms exercises than its Arab neighbors.

FIGURE 3.9   Arab-Israeli Total Artillery Strength (Towed and Self-Propelled Tube Artillery of 100 mm + and Multiple Rocket Launchers): 1986–1995

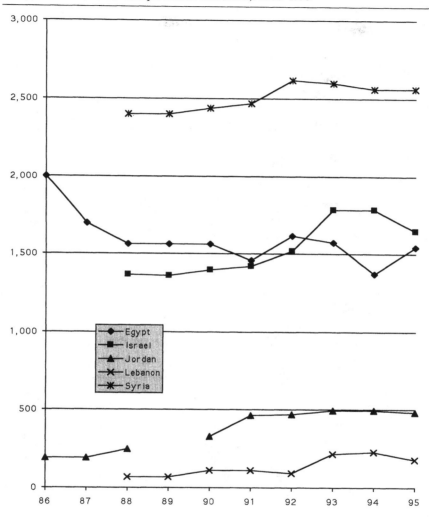

Source: Adapted from the IISS, *Military Balance,* various years. Some data adjusted or estimated by the author.

Syria has improved its artillery to add more maneuver capability, and now has 400 122 mm S21 self-propelled artillery weapons, and 50 152 mm S23 self-propelled artillery weapons. It does, however, remain reliant on some 1,630 older Soviet-bloc supplied towed artillery weapons. These towed weapons include 100

FIGURE 3.10   Israel Versus Egypt, Syria, Jordan, and Lebanon: High Performance
Artillery

Modern Self-Propelled Artillery

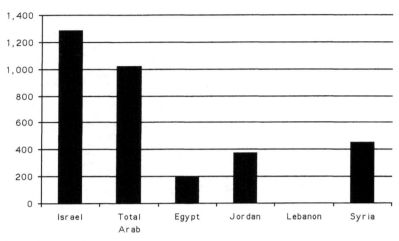

Multiple Rocket Launchers

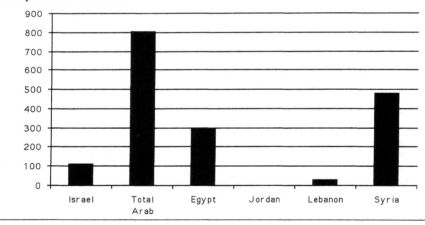

M-1931 and M-1937, 100 M-1938, and 500 D-30 122 mm weapons. They also include 800 M-46 130 mm weapons, 20 D-20 and 50 M-1937 152 mm weapons,
and 20 S23 180 mm siege guns. A substantial number of Syria's towed weapons
are in storage or low grade reserve units. Syria has significant inventories of
chemical rounds for its artillery.

FIGURE 3.11   Arab-Israeli Combat Aircraft: 1973–1995

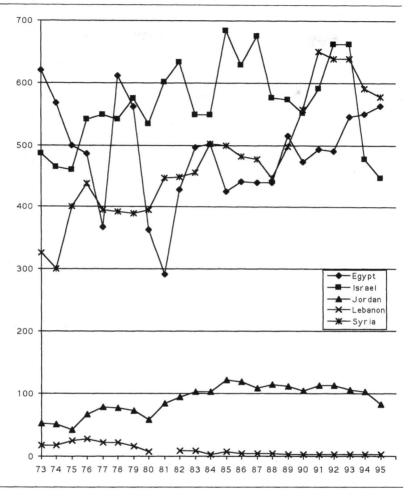

Source: Adapted from the IISS, *Military Balance*, various years. Some data adjusted or estimated by the author.

Syria does have counterbattery radars and some long range target acquisition capabilities, but it is much less sophisticated in organizing and training its artillery forces for maneuver warfare than Israel, and is significantly less sophisticated than Egypt and Jordan. Syria still divides much of its artillery command structure and training in ways that do not involve combined arms capability, and fails to conduct realistic training above the battalion and regiment level. Syria places more emphasis on bringing sustained, high rates of fire against pre-surveyed or relative static targets than it does on rapidly locating targets, rapidly bringing precision fire to bear, and then rapidly shifting fires to meet combined arms needs.

Jordan has low total artillery holdings by the standards of its Arab neighbors, but it has joined Israel in emphasizing self-propelled artillery and the role of artillery in combined arms. Jordan has 550 major artillery weapons, 390 of which are self-propelled. Its holdings include 30 obsolescent M-52 105 mm weapons, 20 M-44 and 220 relatively modern M-109A1/A2 weapons, and 100 M-100 203 mm weapons. A number of Jordan's towed artillery weapons seem to be in storage. Jordan has AN TPQ-36 and AN TPQ-37 counterbattery radars, and has shown good capability to use them. (Jordan has deployed a company with TPQ-37s in its peace-keeping forces in Bosnia.) Jordan also has a French artillery fire control and battle management system. It is seeking rocket assisted projectile rounds for its 155 mm weapons to compensate for the range advantage of Iraqi and Syrian artillery, and is at least experimenting with UAVs for artillery targeting.

Egypt has 200 modern self-propelled M-109A2 artillery weapons, and its best artillery units—which are equipped with these weapons—reflect a new emphasis on improved training, combined arms doctrine, more sophisticated target acquisition, and more rapid shifts of fire. Egypt does not have Israel's capability to use these weapons to acquire targets at long ranges, rapidly shift and mass fires, and maneuver its artillery, but it does have modern counterbattery radars like the AN/TPQ-37 and uses modern artillery fire management vehicles like the Rasit.

Egypt, however, is still largely dependent on 1,100 towed Soviet-bloc weapons. Its towed artillery assets include 36 M-31 and M-37 122 mm weapons, 359 M-1938 122 mm weapons, 156 D-30M 122 mm weapons, 420 M-46 130 mm weapons, and an unknown number of larger weapons or mixed size. Many of these weapons are heavy, obsolete Soviet-supplied weapons with awkward ergonomics and limited fire support technology, although Egypt does have the ability to manufacture artillery barrels and refurbish such weapons. The artillery units using these towed weapons continue to use relatively obsolete tactics, lack more fire control support, and lack mobility and effective combined arms training. They have substantially less effectiveness than Egypt's units with self-propelled weapons. Egypt has the capacity to manufacture chemical rounds, but there is no evidence it has large numbers in inventory or that its forces train to use such rounds.

Multiple Rocket Launchers

The data in Figures 3.8, 3.9, and 3.10 show that Israel, Egypt, Jordan, Lebanon, and Syria have large inventories of multiple rocket launchers (MRLs).

Israel has the smallest numbers, with less than 150 multiple rocket launchers. This total is somewhat misleading, however, because it does not reflect the qualitative advantages provided by Israeli holdings of highly accurate long range systems with advanced conventional warheads. Israel is also acquiring the Multiple

Launch Rocket System (MLRS) from the US—a system with far greater accuracy and warhead lethality than any deployed in the forces of the Arab "ring states." It has ordered 42 MLRS launchers and 1,500 tactical rockets at a cost of $103.5 million in US FMF aid.[11]

At the same time, the data in these charts are representative of the fundamental asymmetry between Israel's artillery forces and those of Egypt and Syria. Israel emphasizes maneuver and precision; Syria—and to a lesser degree Egypt—emphasize volume of fire and surge capability over precision and mobility.

Syria has at least 480 multiple rocket launchers. These include 200 Type 63 107 mm Chinese weapons and 280 BM-21 Soviet bloc weapons. The Type 63s are towed weapons, and the BM-21s are mounted on trucks. Multiple rocket launchers have historically been most effective in terms of their shock effect on relatively static troops, and have only had high lethality against exposed infantry forces or large, static area targets. Syria's holdings can provide a considerable amount of surge fire to harass and suppress enemy activity or attack area targets, but it has not modernized its C⁴I/BM capabilities to improve the accuracy and rapid reaction capabilities of its MRL forces or to support them effectively with real-time beyond-visual-range targeting. Syria has significant inventories of chemical weapons for its MRLs.

Jordan has no multiple rocket launchers.

Egypt has at least 340 multiple rocket launchers. These include 96 BM-11 122 mm weapons and 200 BM-21, as Saqr 10, 18, and 36 barrel 122 mm weapons. Egypt manufactures modern 122 mm rockets with enhanced stability and possibly enhanced lethality warheads. Egypt has the capability to manufacture chemical warheads for its MRLs, but there is no evidence that such rounds are currently deployed.

Mortars

Both Israel and the Arab "ring states" use extensive numbers of mortars, which add a significant firepower capability. Mortars are important in urban warfare, static infantry combat, and in rough terrain. They allow rapid reaction direct fire at targets in visual range and the use of suppressive fire without complex command and control problems. This eliminates many of the organizational and tactical problems that countries like Syria face in coordinating the use of longer range systems, and mortars have produced as many casualties as long range artillery in a number of clashes between Israeli and Arab forces.

Israel has some 6,500 mortars, including some 1,600 81 mm mortars, 900 120 mm mortars, and 240 160 mm mortars. A number of these weapons are mounted in APCs.

Syria has over 4,500 mortars, but it is not clear how many are actively deployed. Syria's holdings include 82 mm mortars, 350 M-1943 120 mm mortars, 100 M-160 160 mm mortars, and 8 M-240 240 mm mortars.

Jordan has a total of 750 mortars, including 450 81 mm mortars, about 150 of which are mounted on APCs. Jordan also has 50 M-30 107 mm mortars, and 300 Brandt 120 mm mortars.

Egypt has well over 3,000 mortars. These include some 1,800 M-43 120 mm mortars; a large number of 82 mm mortars (at least 50 mounted on armored vehicles); a number of 107 mm mortars (at least 50 mounted on armored vehicles); and a number of 160 mm mortars (at least 60 mounted on M-160 armored vehicles).

FIGURE 3.12   Israel Versus Egypt, Syria, and Jordan: Air Forces

High Quality Combat Aircraft: Phantom 2000, Mirage F-1, F-15, F-16, Su-20/22, Su-24, MiG 25/25R, MiG-29, E-2C

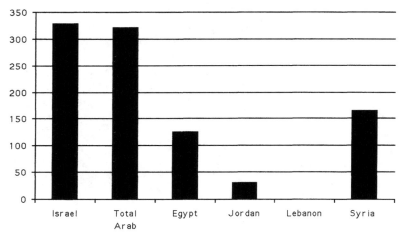

Attack and Armed Helicopters: Hughes 500MD, AH-1, AH-64, Mi-25, Mi-24, SA-342

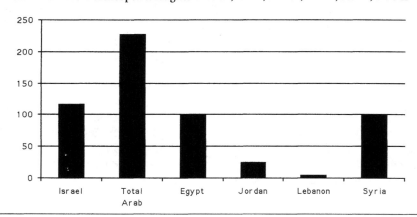

Combat Aircraft

Most of the previous charts have been relatively self explanatory, but Figures 3.11 and 3.12 illustrate just how difficult it is to count Egyptian, Israeli, Jordanian, and Syrian combat aircraft in meaningful terms. Estimates of the total inventory of combat aircraft differ sharply according to source, and estimates of the number of aircraft that are actually operational in combat units are even more controversial. The difference is critical because many of the combat aircraft in each country are in storage or are assigned to training units. Also, many of the older aircraft in Egypt and Syria are assigned to very low grade units with token or no combat capability against an air force with surviving air defense capabilities.

Figure 3.11 is based on IISS data, and is more valuable for the warning it provides about the constant variations in unclassified estimates of combat aircraft numbers than as a portrayal of the trends in the forces of each side. It should also be noted that US experts believe that counts that lump fighter, fighter ground attack (FGA), dual role, reconnaissance, and special purpose aircraft into one total for combat aircraft are relatively meaningless, and that only counts of operational aircraft have value in assessing the balance. They also question the value of the kind of breakdown of combat aircraft strength into fighter, fighter ground attack, and dual role aircraft shown in Table 3.1. Many believe that unclassified estimates of such missions ignore real-world training and mission allocations.

At the same time, Figure 3.11 is accurate in showing that Egypt, Israel, Jordan, and Syria have made no major increases in combat aircraft numbers in recent years. This reflects a growing emphasis on aircraft quality over aircraft quantity, and the combined impact of losses through attrition and the need to limit aircraft numbers in order to pay for aircraft that have grown far more costly in constant dollars, as well as more capable and sophisticated.

Figure 3.12 shows the strength of high quality fixed-wing combat aircraft and the strength of attack helicopters. It also provides a rough measure of air warfare capability. As has been discussed earlier, it emphasizes total mission capabilities and the sophistication of avionics over speed. The aircraft included in Figure 3.12 have significant mission capabilities that were not widely available in 1973 or 1982. Many of the fixed wing aircraft shown now have significant beyond-visual-range air combat capability. Many also have the ability to use advanced precision air-to-surface weapons at ranges outside the coverage of many short range air defenses, and aircraft like the F-15 and Su-24 are capable of very long range strikes—with or without refueling.

It is important to note that Israel has the only air force which heavily emphasizes dual-capability squadrons with both air combat and attack capabilities—although Egypt and Jordan have such units and Egypt has steadily improved the dual capability of its F-16 units. Israel also has significant airborne early warning (AEW), airborne command and control, airborne intelligence and electronic warfare (EW), and advanced reconnaissance capabilities. As was the case for Coalition aircraft during the Gulf War, these special purpose aircraft help Israel to manage its combat aircraft as an integrated force, rather than as a series of individual squadrons, to manage sophisticated beyond-visual-range combat, to maintain force cohesion in large scale air-to-air combat, to conduct near real time targeting and rapid reaction missions, and to allocate interdiction and act missions effectively in complex joint operations. The only Arab air force to support its combat aircraft with modern command, control, communications, intelligence and battle management (C⁴I/BM), and reconnaissance capabilities is Egypt.

Israel's combat aircraft are far more modern and more capable than those of its Arab neighbors, with the exception of Syria's MiG-29s and Su-24s, and Egypt's F-16Cs. Israel has received a total of 80 F-15s and 300 F-16s, although some have been lost to attrition. Israel also has 50 Phantom 2000s, 14 RF-4Es, 2 F-15DRs, 4 E-2C AWACS-like aircraft, and up to 28 electronic warfare and signals intelligence aircraft. This gives Israel about 478 highly sophisticated active combat aircraft. In addition, Israel retains up to 20 Kfir C2/C7s, 6 Kfir RC-2s, and 50 A-4Ns. Israel has up to 120 Kfir C2/C7s and 130 A-4Ns in storage.

Israel has also integrated its combat aircraft into the kind of "system of systems" that is essential to take advantage of modern air power. It has developed and modified a large number of guided offensive weapons. These include a large rocket boosted glide bomb called "Popeye" which the US used as the AGM-142 or "Have Nap" on B-52s flown in Desert Storm. It is a TV-guided missile which uses a Mark 84 bomb as a warhead, and has a large 895 kilogram warhead, inertial guidance with TV or imaging IR homing, a digital data link, and a maximum range of about 80 kilometers. It can be launched by the Kfir, F-15, and F-16.[12] Israel also has an air-launched version of the Gabriel anti-ship missile with a range of 35 kilometers, sea skimming capabilities, and a 150 kilogram semi-armor piercing warhead. A medium-range laser guided air-to-surface missile called the Nimrod is in development. It has a range of 25 kilometers and a 15 kilogram warhead suited for anti-armor or small point target killing.[13]

Israel has continued to make improvements in its ability to use aircraft to support ground forces. It is steadily improving its air-to-ground munitions lethality and range—with an emphasis on high volumes of accurate delivery of dumb but more lethal munitions in low vulnerability attack profiles. It has taken full advantage of its access to US air-to-air and air-to-ground avionics and weapons. It has steadily improved the tactics and avionics it uses to deliver precision guided weapons and is buying advanced all-weather navigation and targeting systems like LANTIRN.

Israel is one of the few Middle Eastern air forces capable of providing a full range of defensive countermeasures for its aircraft, and has heavily modified these countermeasures to suit local combat conditions or introduced designs of its own. It regularly deploys onboard chaff and flare dispensers and radar homing and warning receivers. It has both its own and US active countermeasure systems and ECM pods.[14] Pilots receive excellent training in using these systems and they normally have high standards of maintenance and operational readiness.

The IAF has steadily improved its reconnaissance, electronic warfare, and C⁴I/battle management capabilities as a result of the lessons of the 1982 war and the Gulf War. The IAF now has 14 RF-4Es, 6 Kfir RC-12s, and 2 F-15s dedicated to the reconnaissance role. Its has four updated and Israeli modified E-2C airborne early-warning aircraft. The E-2Cs are fitted with AN/APS-125/138 surveillance radars and AN/ALR-73 passive detection systems.[15]

The IAF's electronic intelligence and ECM squadrons include a number of specially modified aircraft and RPVs, including 6 E-707s, 6 RC-12Ds, 3 IAI-200s, 15 Do-28s, and 6 King Air 2000s.

The E-707s seem to use Elta electronic support measure (ESM) and communications support (CSM) equipment for electronic intelligence, communications intelligence, and command analysis. According to some reports, they can cover a band-width of 70 megahertz to 40 gigahertz over a 360° area and sense transmitters up to 450 kilometers away from the aircraft. They provide a continuously updated electronic display at communications intelligence and ELINT consoles and have a secure air-ground data link. Some may have special naval electronic support measure or ELINT systems. The IAI 200 and RC-12D are configured for tactical signals intelligence missions. The IAI-200s carry ELINT and signals intelligence equipment. The RU-21As are fitted for airborne direction-finding against hostile communications nets. The RC-12Ds are fitted with the US Guardrail V target location and identification system.[16]

The E-2Cs play a critical role in large scale air combat. They provide a much better capability to allocate for Israeli fighters and vector them toward possible targets than can be done by regional control centers on the ground. They perform electronic intelligence missions, help reduce the IFF problem, and manage overall IAF fighter deployments according to the needs of the battle. Israel also, however, uses the long range radars on its F-15s so that an F-15 in the rear can help direct forward deployed Israeli fighters into combat without having to risk direct engagement. The E-2Cs do not have the same range or capability to detect aircraft flying over land as the E-3A AWACS, and may still use the AN/APS-124 radar, rather than the AN/APS-138 used by the US Navy. They still, however, provide Israel with very good low altitude radar coverage, filling in the gaps left by land based radars and greatly extending the range of detection and IAF battle management capability. They allow Israeli fighters to take advantage of their excellent low altitude combat training. The IAF is one of the few forces in the Middle East capable of training and controlling its fighter forces for low altitude combat.

Israel has designed a new variant of its B-707s called the Falcon, which combines Israeli-designed early warning and command and control equipment with improved radars, IFF equipment, ELINT equipment, electronic warfare systems, and a variety of display systems. If this system is successful, it will be the first

AWACS-type aircraft to eliminate the radar dome above the aircraft. It uses an Elta EL/M-2075 phased array radar of about 800 transmit/receive modules in six antenna arrays molded to conform with the aircraft fuselage. This allows 360° operation without interference from the wings, engines, or tail. It is claimed to be able to detect a 5 square meter target at ranges of up to 350 kilometers, ships at up to 500 kilometers, and cruise missiles at up to 230 kilometers. It also allows all of the arrays to be concentrated in one area, provides tracking within 4 seconds versus 20–40 seconds for a rotating dome radar, and is supposed to be more sensitive to slow moving and hovering helicopters.[17]

Israel also has 24 "Wild Weasel" F-4Es which are specially equipped to carry the US AGM-78B Standard anti-radiation missile. These aircraft were used extensively in the Beka'a Valley operations in 1982, and reflect the fact that one of the key lessons that Israel drew from the 1973 fighting was the need for effective anti-radar missiles as a key air defense suppression weapon. The Wild Weasel F-4Es can carry four AGM-78Bs each. They have special J79-17B engines, AN/APQ-120(V)4 radars, and TISEO long range optical visual identification systems. There are special displays and provision for the launch of AGM-65 missiles. The aircraft do not have emitter location equipment separate from the missile, and Israel put its own improved Purple Heart seeker on the AGM-78Bs as a result of the lessons it learned in 1982. Some experts indicate that Israel has a number of other aircraft which can deliver anti-radiation missile (ARM) systems and is phasing out the F-4Es.[18]

Israel continues to expand its use of unmanned airborne vehicles (UAVs) or remotely piloted vehicles (RPVs). It currently operates hundreds of the Mastiff, Scout, Teledyne Ryan 124R, MQM-74C Chukar I, Chukar II, Samson, Pioneer, Searcher, and Delilah (decoy) UAVs. These systems perform a wide range of targeting and intelligence functions and use photo, IR, ELINT, and possibly small radar sensors. Israel is the world's first major user of RPVs, and its Mastiffs and Scouts had logged some 10,000 flight hours and over 1,000 sorties by the mid-1980s, including the several hundred sorties they flew in 1982. It is believed to have some RPVs modified for attack purposes, including some designed to home in on radar emitters.

Israel has deployed third and fourth generation UAVs. These include the Pioneer. The Pioneer has a payload of 45 kilograms versus 38 for the Scout, and an endurance of eight to nine hours versus four to six hours for Israel's older RPVs. Its speed is increased from 60 to 70 nautical miles per hour, and its airframe is made from composite materials rather than metal to reduce its radar signature. Like previous Israeli RPVs, the Pioneer is very silent and normally is hard to see. It has a ceiling of 15,000 feet and a video transmission range of up to 200 kilometers.

The equipment on the Pioneer includes a TV camera, a thermal imager, electronic warfare equipment, and a laser range finder or designator. It will be deployed in field units with four Pioneers each, and can be launched with a pneumatic catapult and rocket booster or on any 250 meter long stretch of road. It can land on a 70 meter road using a catch net. The Pioneer has a greatly improved down link and display system and can be turned over to remote forward deployed control stations. The normal range of the down link is 30 to 40 kilometers.[19] It gives Israel an even greater advantage in tactical reconnaissance and surveillance capability than it had in 1982, and allows the IDF to carry out such missions without exposing personnel.[20]

Israel has more advanced systems in deployment and development. In 1992, it began to deploy the Searcher, a 318 kilogram system that builds on the lessons learned from the Scout and Pioneer. Systems in development include a twin engine system with about twice the range-payload of the Pioneer. This system is called the Impact, and can operate at ranges from 150 to 300 kilometers beyond Israel's front lines. It is designed to have a much lower radar cross section than previous RPVs, has a 150 pound payload, an endurance of 12 hours, a maximum speed of 120 knots, a loiter speed of 60 knots, and a multi-mission stabilized TV/FIR sensor payload. It can be deployed as a containerized unit of the back of a pickup truck. It has a long loiter system called the Heron with a demonstrated world endurance record of 51 hours and 21 minutes, and has claimed to have UAVs with the ability to fly at altitudes as high as 30,000 feet.[21]

Several Israeli UAVs have been developed for air defense suppression. The Delilah is a modular system that can either be used with an active payload to simulate the presence of an attack aircraft—and draw enemy fighters, surface-to-air missiles, and anti-aircraft fire away from real attack aircraft—or with a passive payload to saturate an area with chaff to blind enemy air defense radars. It uses both active elements in the A, C, and L radar bands to simulate aircraft and a passive Luneberg lens reflector to expand its apparent size to enemy radars. It weighs only 180 kilograms, and can be carried by an attack fighter like the F-4. It can fly at speeds of Mach 0.4 to 0.8, has a range of up to 400 kilometers, and can simulate fighter maneuvers in the target area with a positioning accuracy of better than 91 meters.

Israel has also developed a remotely piloted vehicle or drone called the Harpee or STAR-1. This would be able to loiter for extended periods over the battlefield and then home in immediately on any radar that started to operate in the area, even if it only emitted for very short periods of time.[22] The Harpee is similar in concept to the US Seek Spinner and Tactic Rainbow missiles. While the details are classified, the system evidently can loiter for several hours waiting for a threat radar to emit and then home in on it and kill it. This would allow it to replace the much more costly, aging, and vulnerable F-4E wild Weasels. It seems to have been tested in simulated missions where it did home in and hit military radars. Such a system would give Israel a greatly improved capability to destroy Arab air defense systems without exposing high cost aircraft, and would confront an Arab force with the fact that it could never predict when its air defense systems would be attacked.[23]

All of these various airborne or flying assets are linked to battle management and fusion centers and to field mobile C^4I/BM systems that can directly support the land forces. It is important to note that the IDF's integration of land and air intelligence, sensor, and battle management systems gives it a further advantage in the air-land battle. They are backed by a range of active and passive electronic warfare systems. Israel has succeeded in improving its edge over Syria in every aspect of electronic warfare. Israel has also greatly increased the sophistication of its ground-based forward electronic warfare and targeting efforts, although the details remain classified.

Israel has eight tanker aircraft, which provide a significant refueling and long range strike capability—although some are only equipped for probe and drogue recovery and cannot refuel the F-15 and F-16. Israel is continuing to modernize its aircraft with improved avionics, electronic warfare suites, and precision weapons. It also continues to either purchase US fighters or receive deliveries of surplus equipment—including the F-16 and at least 20 new F-15I long range strike-attack fighters. This should allow Israel to eliminate its remaining low-to-moderate performance Kfir C2/C7s, A-4Ns, and F-4Es by the year 2000.[24]

The Syrian air force has long emphasized numbers over quality, tactics, and training. It currently has about 40,000 men and 500 operational combat fixed wing aircraft, with well over 100 more that are not operational, derelict, or in storage. While such estimates are highly uncertain, the IISS estimates that Syria has 10 fighter-ground attack squadrons, equipped with 44 obsolete MiG-23BNs, 20 aging S-20s, and 70 moderate capability Su-22s. Syria also has 18 fighter-air defense squadrons equipped with 150 MiG-21 and 80 MiG-23 fighters that have low grade avionics and radars and limited air-to-air combat capability.

Syria's front line strength does, however, include 20 modern Su-24 long range strike-attack aircraft, 30 MiG-25s which are effective at high altitude, and 20 modern MiG-29 fighters that are capable of beyond-visual-range combat and effective look-down, shoot-down capability. Syria's only reconnaissance aircraft are six MiG-25Rs with low quality sensor packages. Syria's only electronic warfare aircraft include 10 Mi-8J/K helicopters.

Syria's MiG-29s and Su-24s illustrate the path it must take to modernize its air force and make it competitive with Israel. Its MiG-29 aircraft are designed for forward area air superiority and escort missions, including deep penetration air-to-air combat. Their flight performance and flying qualities are excellent, and are roughly equivalent to that of the best Western fighters.[25] They have relatively modern avionics and weapons, and an advanced coherent pulse-Doppler radar with look-down, shoot-down capabilities that can detect a fighter-sized, two square meter target at a range of 130 kilometers (70 nautical miles) and track it at 70 kilometers (38 nautical miles).

The MiG-29 also has a track-while-scan range of 80 kilometers (44 nautical miles) against a 5 square meter target and is designed to operate with the radar off or in the passive mode, using ground-controlled intercept.[26] It has an infrared search and track system collimated with a laser range finder, a helmet-mounted sight, internal electronic countermeasure systems, SPO-15 radar warning receiver, modern inertial navigation, and the modern Odds Rod IFF. The range of the infrared search and track system is 15 kilometers (8.2 nautical miles) against an F-16-sized target. The maximum slant range of the laser is 14 kilometers (7.7 nautical miles) and its normal operating range is 8 kilometers (4.4 nautical miles).

The MiG-29 can carry up to six air-to-air missiles, a 30 mm gun, a wide mix of bombs, and 57 mm, 84 mm, and 240 mm air-to-ground rockets. A typical air combat load would include 250 rounds of 30 mm gun ammunition, 335 gallons of external fuel, 4 AA-8 Aphid infrared guided missiles, and 2 AA-10 Alamo radar-guided medium range air-to-air missiles. Iran may have acquired AA-8, AA-10, and AA-11 Archer air-to-air missiles from Russia.

The MiG-29 does, however, have a number of ergonomic problems. The cockpit frames and high cockpit sills limit visibility. The cockpit display is fussy and uses outdated dials and indicators similar to those of the F-4. There is only a medium angle heads-up display and only partial hands-on system control. The CRT display is dated and the cockpit is cramped. The helmet mounted sight allows the pilot to slave the radar, IRST, and heads up display (HUD) together for intercepts and covert attacks using off-boresight cueing, but the weapons computer and software supporting all combat operations are several generations behind those in fighters like the F-15C.[27] This makes it doubtful that even a well-trained MiG-29 pilot has the air-to-air combat capability of a well-trained pilot flying an F-16C/D, F-15C, F/A-18D, or Mirage 2000 in long range missile or beyond-visual-range combat, or in any form of combat when only the other side has the support of an AWACS-type aircraft.

The Su-24 is a twin seat, swing wing strike-attack aircraft that is roughly equivalent in terms of weight to the F-111, although it has nearly twice the thrust loading and about one-third more wing loading. The Su-24 can carry payloads of up to 25,000 pounds and operate on missions with a 1,300 kilometer radius when carrying 6,600 pounds of fuel. With a more typical 8,818 pound (4,000 kilogram) combat load, it has a mission radius of about 790 kilometers in the LO-LO-LO profile and 1,600 kilometers in the LO-HI-LO profile. With extended range fuel tanks and airborne refueling by an aircraft like the F-14, the Su-24 can reach virtually any target in Iraq and the southern Gulf.[28]

Although it is not clear what variant of the SU-24 has gone to Syria, it seems likely to be the Su-24D, which includes a sophisticated radar warning receiver, an improved electronic warfare suite, an improved terrain avoidance radar, a bean, satellite communications, an aerial refueling probe, and the ability to deliver electro-optical, laser, and radar-guided bombs and missiles.[29]

The Su-24D is an excellent platform for delivering air-to-surface missiles and biological, chemical, and nuclear weapons. The air-to-ground missiles it can carry include up to three AS-7 Kerry radio command guided missiles (5 kilometers range), one AS-9 Kyle anti-radiation missile with passive radar guidance and an active radar fuse (90 kilometers range), three AS-10 Karen passive laser-guided missiles with an active laser fuse (10 kilometers range), three AS-11 Kilter anti-radiation missiles with passive radar guidance and an active radar fuse (50 kilometers range), three AS-12 Kegler anti-radiation missiles with passive radar guidance and an active radar fuse (35 kilometers range), three AS-13 Kingposts, and three AS-14 Kedge semi-active laser-guided missiles with an active laser fuse (12 kilometers range). It can also carry demolition bombs, retarded bombs, cluster bombs, fuel air bombs, and chemical bombs. Some experts believe that Russia has supplied Iran with AS-10, AS-11, AS-12, and possibly AS-14/AS-16 air-to-surface missiles.

It will not be enough, however, for Syria to buy advanced fighters, attack aircraft, and reconnaissance aircraft. Even if one ignores "intangibles" like leadership and training, Syria lags far behind the West and its most advanced neighbors in the ability to command an air force in large-scale battle. If Iran is to compete effectively with Saudi and US forces in air combat, it will also need an Airborne Warning aircraft, advanced beyond-visual-range missiles and combat capabilities, advanced stand-off air attack ordnance, a new C^{4}I/BM system, and much more advanced electronic warfare capabilities.

The practical problems are whether Syria can obtain such aircraft from Russia, whether Iran can afford them in sufficient numbers, whether Syria can manage the complex conversion from US to Russian aircraft efficiently, and whether Syria fully understands and can accomplish the need to convert from an air force organized to fight at the squadron or small flight level, to one that can conduct coherent force-wide operations and fight modern joint warfare.

Equally important, the problems Syria faces go far beyond modernizing its air order of battle and require fundamental changes in its ability to conduct force-on-force warfare. Where Israel has integrated its air force into a "system of systems," the Syrian air force still consists of "pieces of pieces." Where Israel stresses joint operations, Syria cannot even conduct effective battle management of its air forces in large scale individual air operations.

It is far from clear that Syria can accomplish all these tasks in the near to midterm. Syria is also unlikely to obtain any assistance from the US and Europe as a substitute for Russia. Further, Chinese capabilities are unlikely to evolve to the point where China can be an adequate supplier of advanced aircraft, munitions, and technology before 2010.

Jordan now has only a very limited strength of combat aircraft, including 78 operational fixed-wing fighters. These aircraft are organized into fighter ground attack squadrons with F-5Es and F-5Fs, and two air defense squadrons with less than 30 operational Mirage F-1CJs and F-EJs. Jordan has no modern attack fighters and no air defense fighters with advanced radars and beyond-visual-range air combat capability. It has no dedicated reconnaissance and electronic warfare aircraft.

Jordan has had a long history of being unable to finance its aircraft modernization plans. In 1989, it had to cancel a $860 million order for 8 Tornado attack aircraft it had placed in September, 1988. In September, 1991, Jordan had to cancel a $1 billion order it placed with France in April, 1988 because it lost Saudi funding as a result of the Gulf War. This deal would have given it 12 Mirage 2000s with an option to buy 8 more and would have upgraded 15 of its Mirage F-1Js. Jordan denies reports that it has signed a $21 million contract with Singapore Aerospace to upgrade up to 40 of its F-5s with look-down shoot-down Doppler radars and advanced avionics, and has financed this order by selling Singapore Aerospace 7 other F-5E/Fs.[30]

Even though the US is increasing aid, Jordan is still negotiating with the US over whether it can obtain surplus F-16s or will have to seek further upgrades of its F-5Es from the US. It has sought 60 to 72 ex-USAF Block 10 F-16A/Bs as aid in the form of US excess defense articles. This would allow Jordan to remove all of its Mirage F-1s and F-5Es from combat units, and to standardize on the F-16—although it would keep one squadron of F-5Es for training purposes. Jordan feels that it could support such an F-16 force more cheaply than its present combination of F-1s and F-5Es and has even held informal talks with Israel about cooperative efforts at major overhaul and maintenance. It is unclear, however, whether Jordan will get this level of aid from the US.[31]

Egypt has about 600 combat aircraft, including armed helicopters. It is one of the few Arab air forces organized and equipped with modern air control, reconnaissance, and electronic warfare assets. It has seven squadrons of fighter ground attack aircraft with 40 Alphajets, 25 F-4Es, 40 Chinese J-6s, and 16 Mirage 5E2s. These forces have significant problems because the J-6s have limited payload, endurance, and avionics, and are very low performance aircraft. The Alphajets are light daytime attack aircraft which are only effective in line of sight visual close support missions. The Mirage 5E2s have limited range-payload and mediocre avionics, and Egypt's F-4Es are worn and aging aircraft that have not been modernized to improve their attack and electronic warfare capabilities.

Egypt also has 16 air defense squadrons. Five of these squadrons are equipped with modern aircraft including 80 F-16Cs, 30 F-16As, and 16 Mirage 2000Cs. The remainder are low quality forces largely limited to visual intercepts. They include 60 obsolete low performance Chinese J-7s, 100 obsolete low performance MiG-21s, and 54 aging and marginal performance Mirage 5D/Es. The J-7s, MiG-21s, and Mirage 5D/Es are supersonic, but lack the radars, avionics, and missiles to be highly effective.

Egypt's reconnaissance aircraft are largely obsolete photo reconnaissance aircraft, including 6 Mirage 5SDRs and 14 MiG-21Rs. Egypt does, however, have 5 modern E-2C airborne early warning and control aircraft and a number of electronic warfare aircraft—including 2 CH-130s, 4 Beech 1900s, and 4 Commando 2 ECM helicopters.

Egypt is, however, giving priority to the modernization of its air force. It hopes to acquire a total of 190 F-16 fighters by 1998, as part of the Peace Vector program, and almost 80% of the US military aid it has received under the second and current US-Egyptian military modernization programs has gone to the Egyptian air force. Egypt would also like to acquire a total of 40 Mirage 2000 fighters and 48 L-29 advanced trainers which have dual capability in the close support role. It also is seeking to phase out its F-4Es, which present severe maintenance and spare parts problems. It is doubtful that Egypt can afford this level of modernization, but it is clear that Egypt recognizes the seriousness of its modernization problems.[32]

More generally, Egyptian officers also recognize that the Egyptian air force is effectively organized into three different forces: an obsolete and ineffective force using its older Soviet-bloc aircraft; a somewhat more capable force using its newest Soviet-bloc aircraft, Mirage 5s, and Alphajets; and a relatively modern force using its F-16s and Mirage 2000s. Some officers recognize that the retention of the older Soviet-bloc aircraft does little more than waste financial and skilled manpower resources on militarily ineffective units, but others see force size as a matter of Egyptian prestige.

Egypt has made progressively better use of its E-2Cs for large scale air defense operations. Egyptian pilot training and maintenance have also improved as a result of cooperation with the US, and Egypt has many pilots equal to those of the USAF in individual training. Nevertheless, Egypt does not approach Israeli standards of maintenance, squadron, and force-on-force training, and the ability to support its best combat aircraft with the special purpose aircraft, electronic warfare, and C⁴I/BM technology necessary to integrate them into a "system of systems" and provide effective large-scale joint warfare capabilities.

Syria, Jordan, and Egypt also lack the facilities, equipment, trained ground crews, and doctrine to generate anything approaching Israel's surge and sustained sortie rates—although Egypt's F-16 forces are significantly more capable than any Syrian air units. This is a critical technical and organizational defect. Both past Arab-Israeli conflicts and the Gulf War have shown that combat air strength is as much a function of the ability to generate and effectively allocate sorties as are aircraft numbers. Historically, Israel has been able to sustain up to three times as many combat sorties per operational aircraft as Egypt, and four to five times as many as Syria.

Attack and Armed Helicopters

Figure 3.12 also shows the number of attack and armed helicopters in each force. Attack and armed helicopters may play an important role in changing the nature of the next Arab-Israeli conflict. They provide a considerable increase in maneuver and long range strike capability which has been lacking in past Arab-Israeli conflicts. They also allow operations deep into the battlefield which are not limited by terrain or defensive barriers, and they can be combined with troop-carrying helicopters to seize key points or bypass ground troops.

It should be noted, however, that attack and armed helicopters differ as much in combat capability as fixed wing aircraft. Only a relatively small number of the armed helicopters on each side have the avionics, armor, maneuverability, anti-armor missiles, night and poor weather sights, and ergonomics to allow rapid acquisition of targets, high lethality strikes, and rapid evasion of air defenses. With the exception of the AH-64 and AH-1s, the combat helicopters in Egyptian, Israeli, Jordanian, Lebanese, and Syrian forces have only limited anti-armor capability and are highly vulnerable to short range air defenses. Many use semi-obsolete missile guidance systems that require exceptional training to be effective and which force the exposure of the aircraft for relatively long periods during the attack phase. Some are large slow-flying helicopters, while others have ergonomic problems in attacking from nap of the earth and pop-up profiles unless the pilot has exceptional proficiency and training.

Israel now has 117 attack and armed helicopters, including 42 AH-64s, 35 Hughes 500MDs, and 40 AH-1Fs. The AH-64s give Israel a major new long range strike and maneuver weapon.[33] Its AH-1Fs are also relatively effective attack aircraft. Unlike its Arab neighbors, Israel has also done an effective job of integrating its attack helicopters into joint operations and its C⁴I/BM system, ensuring they have the training and suppression systems to deal with the steady improvement in threat short range air defenses, and ensuring that its ground forces have suitable training to recognize and kill threat attack helicopters. While Israel has taken full advantage of its sometimes painful lessons from the 1982 war, Syrian doctrine, training, and C⁴I/BM capabilities have remained static in many ways.

Israel also has excellent heliborne mobility by regional standards, with 42 heavy lift CH-53Ds; 30 medium lift UH-1Ds, 10 UH-60s, and 54 Bell 212s; and 39 light Bell 206s. Israeli helicopter readiness standards are very high, and Israel has made procurement of more Blackhawk UH-60s a high priority.[34]

In contrast, the Arab states have larger total numbers of attack and armed helicopters, but only Egypt is getting helicopters that equal the AH-64 in effectiveness, and Syria has no fully modern attack helicopters. Syria has 50 Mi-25s and 50 SA-342Ls. These forces do not have advanced sensors, targeting, and night combat systems, but Syria has trained these forces relatively well.

Jordan has 24 relatively high performance AH-1S attack helicopters armed with TOW. This force has had high readiness, but has lacked effective scout helicopters. This explains why Jordan had obtained agreement from the US to provide 18 UH-1H helicopters to use as scouts. Jordan has little heliborne mobility for its ground forces—it only has 9 AS-332M Super Pumas. Jordanian helicopter pilot and ground crew training standards have been high, but its funding problems have created some problems in sustaining operations and advanced training.

Egypt has a number of armed Mi-8s and Mi-25s, but its true attack helicopter assets include four squadrons of 75 SA-342Ks. About 30 of these SA-342Ks are armed with HOT anti-tank guided weapons, but the avionics and guidance systems for these missiles present moderate ergonomic problems. The rest of Egypt's 342Ks are armed with 20 mm guns. The forces equipped with SA-342Ks have moderate training and readiness standards. Egypt is also in the process of converting to a force of 24 AH-64s armed with Hellfire. This force will give Egypt significant attack helicopter capabilities once it becomes fully operational.

Major Surface-to-Air Missile Defenses

There is no easy way to count surface-to-air missile defenses. There are significant differences in the data, and the systems involved have little comparability. Table 3.2 does however, provide an overview of each nation's air defense forces, showing its strength by weapons type. This table illustrates the fact that surface-to-air missile defenses are a vital part of Egyptian, Israeli, Jordanian, and Syrian air defenses.

At the same time, effective surface-to-air missile defenses require integration into a system of overlapping defenses supported by a highly sophisticated and fully integrated C⁴I/BM system. They require modern sensors and electronic warfare support, sophisticated central and regional command and control centers, and the capability to simultaneously manage air-to-air combat, surface-to-air missile combat by different types of missiles, and different types of anti-aircraft guns. In practice, fighting an effective air war also requires a nation to have the capability to rapidly suppress at least part of its opponent's air defense system and achieve enough air superiority to allow effective attack operations.

Once again, Israel is the only state that has the resources, technology, organizational skills, war planning capability, and leadership to provide such a comprehensive approach to air defense and air warfare. Jordan has the technical understanding, but lacks the equipment and resources. Egypt again combines some modern capabilities with large obsolete forces and a lack of military coherence. Syria relies on an imitation of Soviet systems, the most modern of which date back to the early 1980s, which are poorly executed in detail and lack effective systems integration, electronic warfare capability, and truly modern C⁴I/BM capabilities.

Israel has long emphasized airpower over land-based surface-to-air missile forces. It now, however, has 17 batteries of MIM-23 Improved Hawk surface-to-air missiles, 3 batteries of upgraded Patriot missiles with improved anti-tactical ballistic missile capabilities, and 8 short range Chaparral missiles. Israel integrates these systems and its air defense aircraft into an effective air defense battle management (BM) and command, control, communications, computers, and intelligence (C⁴I) system. This system may lack the full sophistication of US systems, but it is believed to have main control centers in the Negev and near Tel Aviv and to make use of the Hughes technology developed for the USAF, including many elements of the USAF 407L tactical command and control system and Hughes 4118 digital computers. It has a mix of different radars, including at least two AN/TPS-43 three dimensional radars. This system is tailored to Israel's local threats and has sufficient technology to meet these threats in combat. Israel also has the ability to coordinate its air defenses from the air, has superior electronic warfare and systems integration capability, and has a clear strategy for suppressing enemy land-based air defenses and the ability to execute it.

Syria has a large separate Air Defense Command with nearly 60,000 personnel. Its forces are organized into 22 regional brigades and a countrywide total of 95 air defense batteries. These forces, however, include large numbers of worn obsolete

TABLE 3.2   Arab-Israeli Land-Based Air Defense Systems

Country	Major SAM	Light SAM	AA Guns
Egypt	738 launchers 360 SA-2 210 SA-3 60 SA-6 72 I Hawk 30 Crotale	2,000 SA-7 Ayn as Saqr 20 SA-9 *26 M-54 Chaparral SP* 18 Amoun Skyguard/ RIM-7F 36 quad SAM Ayn as Saqr	475 ZPU-2/4 14.5 mm 550 ZU-23-2 23 mm 117 ZSU-23-4 SP 23 mm 45 Sinai SP 23 mm 150 M-1939 37 mm 300 S-60 57 mm *40 ZSU-57-2 SP 57 mm* 36 Twin 35 mm 23 mm guns
Israel	3 Patriot Bty. 17 I Hawk Bty.	Stinger 900 Redeye 45 Chaparral 8 Chaparral Bty. (IAF)	850 20 mm, Vulcan, TCM-20, M-167 20 M-163 Vulcan/ Chaparral 100 ZU-23 23 mm 60 ZSU-23-4 SP M-39 37 mm L-70 40 mm
Jordan	2/14/80 I Hawk	SA-7B2 50 SA-8 50 SA-13 300 SA-14 240 SA-16 250 Redeye	360 guns 100 M-163 SP 20 mm 44 ZSU-23-4 SP 216 M-42 SP 40 mm
Lebanon	None	SA-7 SA-14	20 mm ZU-23 23 mm 10 M-42A1 40 mm
Syria	22 Ad Brigades 95 SAM Bty. 11/60/450 SA-2/3 11/27/200 SA-6 1/248 SA-5	20 SA-13 SA-9 SA-7 60 SA-8	1,985 Guns 600 ZU-23-2 400 ZSU-23-4 SP 300 M-1938 37 mm 675 S-60 57 mm 10 ZSU-5-2 SP KS-19 100 mm

Adapted by Anthony H. Cordesman from the IISS, *Military Balance, 1995–1996*

Soviet-bloc systems which have only had limited upgrading. These assets include 11 SA-2 and SA-3 brigades with 60 batteries and some 450 launchers. They include 11 brigades with 27 batteries that are armed with 200 SA-6 launchers and some air defense guns. In addition, there are two regiments which have two battalions with two batteries each, and which are armed with 48 SA-5 and 60 SA-8 surface-to-air missile launchers. The SA-5 is an obsolescent long range system whose primary value is to force large, fixed-wing aircraft like Israel's E-2Cs to stand off outside their range. The SA-8 is a light mobile short range system that is more effective.

Syria needs a new type of missile system to develop the range of air defense capabilities it needs. Its SA-2s, SA-3s, SA-6s, and SA-5s are vulnerable to active and passive countermeasures. If Syria is to create the land-based elements of an air defense system capable of dealing with the retaliatory capabilities of the Israeli air force, it needs a modern, heavy surface-to-air missile system that is part of an integrated air defense system. Such a system will not be easy for Syria to obtain. No European or Asian power can currently sell Iran either an advanced ground-based air defense system or an advanced heavy surface-to-air missile system. The US and Russia are the only current suppliers of such systems, and the only surface-to-air missiles that can meet Syria's needs are the Patriot, SA-10, SA-12a, and SA-12b.

Syria has no hope of getting the Patriot system from the US, making Russia the only potential source of the required land-based air defense technology. This explains why Syria has sought to buy the SA-10 heavy surface-to-air missile/anti-tactical ballistic missile systems and a next generation warning, command, and control system from Russia. The SA-10 (also named the Fakel 5300PMU or Grumble) has a range of 90 kilometers or 50 nautical miles. It has a highly sophisticated warning radar, tracking radar, terminal guidance system, and warhead, and has good electronic warfare capabilities. The SA-10 is a far more advanced and capable system than the SA-2, SA-3, SA-5, or SA-6.[35]

Much depends on Russian willingness to make such sales in the face of Syria's debt and credits problems. Russia has the capability to quickly provide Syria with the SA-10 or SA-12 quickly and in large numbers, as well as support it with a greatly improved early warning sensor system and an advanced command and control system for both its fighters and land-based air defenses. Such an advanced land-based Russian air defense system would, however, give Syria far more capability to defend against retaliatory or preemptive raids. It would allow Syria to allocate more fighter/attack aircraft to attack missions and use its interceptors to provide air cover for such attack missions. It would also greatly complicate Israel's problem in using offensive air power against Syria, require substantially more Israeli forces to conduct a successful air campaign, and increase Israel's air losses.

Such a Russian system would, however, still have important limits. Russia has not fully completed integration of the SA-10 and SA-12 into its own air defenses. It also has significant limitations on its air defense computer technology and relies heavily on redundant sensors and different, overlapping surface-to-air missiles to compensate for a lack of overall system efficiency. A combination of advanced Russian missiles and an advanced sensor and battle management system would still be vulnerable to active and passive attack by the US.

It would also take Syria at least three to five years to deploy and integrate such a system fully, once Russia agreed to the sale. Its effectiveness would also depend on Russia's ability both to provide suitable technical training and to adapt a Russian system to the specific topographical and operating conditions of Syria. A Russian system cannot simply be transferred to Syria as an equipment package. It would take a major effort in terms of software, radar deployment, and technology—and considerable adaptation of Russian tactics and siting concepts—to make such a system fully combat effective. As a result, full-scale modernization of the Syrian land-based air defense system is unlikely to occur before 2005 under the most optimistic conditions, and will probably lag well beyond 2010.[36]

Jordan has modernized some aspects of its ground-based air defense C⁴I/BM system with US aid, but has lacked the funds to compete with Israel in systems integration, sensor and sensor integration capability, digital data links, and electronic warfare capabilities. It now has two incompatible air defense systems: Its air force and Improved Hawk forces use a US system supplied by Westinghouse, and its land forces use a Russian system. Jordan has 14 batteries of Improved Hawk launchers, organized into two brigades with a total of 80 launchers.

Jordan's Improved Hawk forces, however, have important limitations. They are not mobile, they have blind spots in their low altitude coverage, and Israel can easily target them. The Improved Hawks are also vulnerable to Israeli and Syrian electronic countermeasures and have not been upgraded in recent years. Jordan is seeking to upgrade its US-supplied Improved Hawks to the Pip (product improvement program) 3 version, to upgrade its Westinghouse supplied system, and to replace its Russian supplied system with a US supplied system for its land forces.

As a result of the Canal War of 1970, Egypt has developed one of the largest dedicated air defense forces in the Middle East. It has a separate Air Defense Command with nearly 80,000 personnel. Its forces are organized into five divisions with regional brigades and a countrywide total of 100 air defense battalions. These forces include large numbers of worn obsolete Soviet-bloc systems which have had only limited upgrading. These assets include 40 SA-2 battalions with 360 launchers, 40 SA-3 battalions with 144 launchers, and 14 SA-6 battalions with 60 launchers. These Egyptian forces have low readiness and operational sustainability and only limited capability to resist modern jamming and other air defense suppression techniques. They are vulnerable to modern anti-radiation missiles.

Egypt does have substantial holdings of more modern and more effective Western supplied systems. They include 24 batteries of Improved Hawks with 144 launchers. Egypt also is developing an integrated command and control system, with US assistance, as part of Program 776.[37] This system is not highly advanced by US standards, but it will allow Egypt to integrate airborne and land-based air defenses into a common air defense system, create a single C⁴I/BM network, and allow Egypt to manage a defense against air attacks that bring a moderate number of sorties together at the same time and near the same area.

Short Range Air Defenses

Egypt, Israel, and Syria have large numbers of anti-aircraft guns and light surface-to-air missiles. These systems are not highly sophisticated, but can provide considerable defense against attack helicopters and low altitude coverage against attacking fighters of a kind that is not reliant on radar. They also can force most attack aircraft to use very high speed attack profiles that lack accuracy or to use long range precision guided missiles to attack at stand-off ranges. Many of the attack aircraft in Arab forces lack the range to conduct such attacks. Even Israel, however, faces problems in trying to suppress such defenses, and faces low altitude survivability problems in attacking targets with sophisticated short range air defenses (SHORADS).

Israel has large numbers of Stinger and 900 obsolescent Redeye manportable surface-to-air missiles, and 45 Chaparral crew-served missiles. It also has some 850 20 mm anti-aircraft (AA) guns—including TCM-20s and M-167 Vulcans. It has 35 M-163 Vulcan/M-48 Chaparral gun-missile systems, 100 ZU-23 23 and 60 ZSU-23-4 23 mm AA guns, and some M-39 37 mm and L-70 40 mm AA guns. These assets give Israel comparatively low total forces and air defense mobility relative to its neighbors, but Israel relies primarily upon its air force for such defense.

Jordan has attempted to use purchases of large numbers of short range air defense systems to compensate for its lack of modern air defense aircraft and survivable surface-to-air missile defenses. Its lower quality manportable surface-to-air missile launchers include large numbers of SA-7Bs and 250 Redeyes. Its more effective manportable weapons include 300 SA–14s and 240 SA-16s. Its vehicle mounted surface-to-air missile forces include 50 SA-8s and 50 SA-13s. Its 360 AA guns include 100 20 mm M-163 Vulcans, 44 23 mm ZSU-23-4s, and 216 40 mm M-42 self-propelled weapons. These assets give the Jordanian army considerable air defense mobility, which partially compensates for its static Improved Hawk defenses.

The Egyptian ground forces have large numbers of AA weapons. The army's surface-to-air missile assets include some 2,000 obsolete SA-7s and slightly better performing Egyptian made variants of the SA-7 called the Ayn-as-Saqr. The army also has 12 batteries of short range Chaparrals with 50 M-54 self-propelled Chaparral fire units, 14 batteries of short range Crotales with 36 launchers, and at least 20 SA-9 fire units.

The Egyptian Army's holdings of air defense guns include 475 14.5 mm ZPU-2/4, 550 23 mm ZU-23-2/4, 150 37 mm M-1939, and 300 57 mm S-60 towed unguided guns. They also include 117 ZSU-23-4 and 45 Sinai radar guided self-propelled guns. The SA-9s, Chaparrals, ZSU-23-4s, and Sinais provide the

Egyptian army with maneuverable air defenses that can accompany Egyptian armored forces.

In addition, Egypt's Air Defense Command has some 2,000 Soviet-bloc supplied unguided towed AA guns ranging from 20 mm to 100 mm, and a number of light air defense systems. These include 18 Amoun (Skyguard/RIM-7F Sparrow) systems with 36 twin guns and 36 quad launchers, a number of ZSU-23-4s, and Sinai-23 systems which are composed of Dassault 6SD-20S radars, 23 mm guns, and short range Ayn-as-Saqr missiles. These weapons provide low altitude defense of military installations and critical facilities, and can often be surprisingly effective in degrading attack sorties or destroying attack aircraft that attempt to fly through a "curtain" of massed anti-aircraft fire.

The Size and Role of Naval Forces

The size of Egypt's, Israel's, Jordan's, Lebanon's, and Syria's navies is summarized in Figure 3.13. All lack strong "blue water" navies of the kind that can play a decisive role in controlling the flow of supplies to an enemy power or dominating lines of communication. Egypt and Israel do, however, have considerable anti-ship capability in local waters, Egypt has considerable strength relative to other Red Sea powers, and Israel and Egypt have some "blue water" capability in the eastern Mediterranean.

Israel's naval forces have 6,600 men, which rise to 11,000 men upon mobilization. Its forces are based at Haifa, Ashdod, and Eilat. At this point in time, Israel has little or no capability in the Red Sea—reflecting its peace with Egypt and Jordan. Jordan has no real navy, although it is acquiring three improved Vosper-Thorneycroft patrol boats.

Israel does, however, have three operational Gal-class submarines in the Mediterranean which are armed with Mark 37 torpedoes and Harpoon anti-ship missiles. It is also taking delivery on two modern Dolphin-class submarines, with an option for a third. Israeli navy plans call for Israel to maintain all five submarines after the delivery of the Dolphins, but it is uncertain that Israel has the funds to do this.

Israel has Sa'ar 5-class 3 missile corvettes. These are new 1,127 ton ships, each of which has two quad launchers for Harpoon missiles with a range of up to 130 kilometers, eight Gabriel anti-ship missiles with radar and optical homing and ranges of up to 36 kilometers, two 32 cell launchers for Barak air defense missiles, one 76 mm gun, a Dauphin SA-366G helicopter, and six torpedo launchers.[38] The ships give Israel its first true "blue water capability," and are much more advanced than any ships in service with Israel's Arab neighbors.

Israel has 20 additional missile craft—including 3 Sa'ar 4.5-class ships with 8 Harpoons and 6 Gabriels each; 2 Sa'ar 4.5-class ships with 4 Harpoons and 4 Gabriels; 8 Sa'ar 4-class ships with 2–4 Harpoons and 4–6 Gabriels, and 6 Sa'ar 2-class ships with 2–4 Harpoons and 5 Gabriels. The Sa'ar 4.5s and 4s have been ex-

FIGURE 3.13   Arab-Israeli Large Naval Ships by Category in 1995

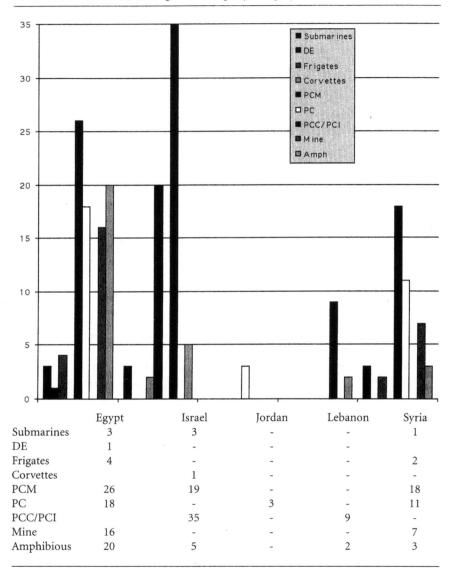

	Egypt	Israel	Jordan	Lebanon	Syria
Submarines	3	3	-	-	1
DE	1	-	-	-	
Frigates	4	-	-	-	2
Corvettes		1	-	-	-
PCM	26	19	-	-	18
PC	18	-	3	-	11
PCC/PCI		35	-	9	-
Mine	16	-	-	-	7
Amphibious	20	5	-	2	3

Source: Adapted by Anthony H. Cordesman from material provided by US experts and the IISS, *Military Balance,* 1995–1996.

tensively modernized. All Sa'ar 3s have been retired, and the Sa'ar 2s are being withdrawn from service.[39]

Israel also has 12 Dvora-class fast attack craft, 22 Dabur-class coastal patrol boats, 3 LCTs and 1 LCP, and 1 Bat Sheva-class transport. Its 4 E-2Cs provide maritime surveillance as well as airborne early warning, and it has 25 Bell 212 helicopters for coastal surveillance tasks. It has 2 Sea Panther helicopters for its Sa'ar 5s, and Sea Scan UAVs for maritime surveillance and targeting.[40]

Israel is the only navy in the Middle East with advanced electronic warfare design and modification capabilities, and the ability to manufacture and design its own sensors and anti-ship missiles. It is currently upgrading its Sa'ar 4 missile boats, integrating the new Sa'ar 5 into its force structure, and constructing the Dolphin submarines to replace its existing submarines.[41] These developments should allow Israel to maintain a decisive edge over Syria in the Mediterranean and more limited advantage in tactics, training, and technology over the Egyptian navy—although the Egyptian navy is now receiving significant modernization.

Syria has a small 6,000 man navy based in Latikia, Tartus, and Minet el-Baida. It has 18 surface ships and 3 non-operational Romeo-class submarines moored at Tartus. Its only significant surface ships include: 2 obsolete 2 Petya III class frigates, and 4 Osa I, 10 Osa II, and 5 Komar missile patrol boats. These ships date back to the 1970s, and many have only limited operational capability while others are on the edge of being laid up. Syria did, however, modernize some of its Osas in the mid-1980s and modernized its Komars in 1990.[42]

Syria also has 11 light patrol boats and 10 obsolescent mine warfare craft—only 7 of which are operational and at least 1 of which has had its minesweeping gear removed. Syria has 3 medium landing ships (LSMs). The Syrian navy's readiness, training, and funding levels are low, and it has little war fighting capability.[43]

Jordan's naval forces consist of a 600 man force with 7 coastal patrol boats (4 Faysal-class and 3 Al Hussein-class), and 3 Rotork craft capable of carrying 30 troops each. All are based at Aqaba.[44]

Lebanon has seven small coast patrol craft and two French landing craft. Its navy has no war fighting capability.[45]

Egypt has a 20,000 man navy, including a 2,000 man coast guard. These forces are based at Port Said, Mersa Matruh, Safaqa, Port Tewfiq, and Hurghada. They include four Romeo-class submarines that are now aging designs, but which have been modernized to fire Harpoon missiles and use modern torpedoes. All four will be in service by 1996.

Egypt's major surface ships include one obsolete British Z-class destroyer which dates back to 1955 and one Black Swan-class frigate dating back to the 1940s, both of which are actually training ships. Egypt also has 2 low quality Jianghu 1-class Chinese frigates, each equipped with four HY-2 anti-ship missiles with a maximum range of 80 kilometers and four 57 mm guns. Egypt does, however, have two FF-1051 Knox-class frigates, each equipped with eight Harpoons, a 127 mm gun, four torpedo tubes, and relatively modern radars and fire control.

Egypt is seeking to modernize its major combat vessels by acquiring two modern FFG-7 Oliver Hazard Perry–class guided missile frigates from the US, by equipping a limited number of its F-16s to carry Harpoon anti-ship missiles, and by acquiring ten anti-submarine warfare helicopters. The FFG-7s would be delivered as part of a package of five surplus ships the Clinton Administration is seeking to transfer or lease to allied Middle Eastern countries, including Turkey, Bahrain, Oman, and the UAE, but there has been congressional objection to providing the ships as grant aid because they cost $60 million each to procure.[46]

Egypt has 26 missile patrol craft, 12 of which are relatively modern ships armed with the Otomat anti-ship missile. These include 2 Descubierta-class 1,479 ton ships, each of which has 8 Harpoons, a 76 mm gun, Albatros air defense missiles, and 6 torpedo tubes; 6 Ramadan-class ships, each with 4 Otomat I anti-ship missiles and 76 mm guns; 6 October-class with 2 Otomat I missiles and 30 mm guns; 6 Osa I-class with 4 SS-N-2A Styx missiles; 6 Hegu-class vessels with SY-1 missiles; and 2 Komar-class vessels with SS-N-2A missiles. Egypt has 18 other patrol ships, some armed with 122 mm multiple rocket launchers.

Egypt has 8 operational but obsolete mine vessels, although it is taking delivery on 3 modern Swiftsure coastal mine hunters. It has 3 major amphibious vessels and 11 LCUs. The Egyptian navy is improving, but has received very low funding priority, and many of its holdings are worn and obsolete and have little or no operational effectiveness. Unless it receives FFG-7 frigates from the US, its major surface ships will all be obsolete by the year 2000.

The Egyptian navy has already had to phase out four obsolete frigates (two Russian and two Chinese), and 80% of its ships are antiquated. Even if it can carry out all of its modernization plans, it could only be a limited threat to Israel. Egypt does not have the training or electronic warfare capabilities to challenge Israel's best Sa'ar-class vessels except in Egyptian water, where Egyptian ships might have air cover and protection from its submarines. At the same time, Egypt can play an important role in dealing with the much less sophisticated naval and air forces of potentially hostile Red Sea countries.

The Inevitable Limits of Quantitative Comparisons

Even with these qualifications regarding the composition and employment of the weapons held by each country, quantitative force comparisons retain many of the defects of the data in Table 1.1. As the previous discussion has shown, even the most detailed breakout of weapons strengths inevitably includes equipment with a wide range of different capabilities.

The previous tables and charts count total inventories and not total operational forces. Much of the equipment counted in these totals is deployed in low grade active and reserve units with only limited readiness and limited combat capability. A substantial amount of the total equipment in Israeli and Arab inventories is in storage or has only limited operational readiness. Unfortunately, there is no way to make accurate estimates of deployable forces, to relate these estimates to mobilization times and readiness rates, or to estimate which portion of a given national force can be deployed in a given contingency or on a given front. While it is possible to make intelligent guesses, estimates of the balance always have this defect.

These tables and charts focus on weapons numbers at a time when the integration of weapons with other technologies into war fighting systems is increasingly more critical in shaping actual war fighting capability. The Arab-Israeli balance has never been determined by force numbers alone. Since the Suez War of 1956, the outcome of conflicts between Israel and various Arab states has been determined primarily by Israel's "edge" in integrating superior tactics, training, and technology.

The key missing dimensions in all quantitative comparisons is the synergy between numbers, technology, tactics, and training—an area where Israel often has a significant advantage. Similarly, there is no way to quantify or reflect very different capabilities in modern command, control, communications, computers, intelligence and battle management (C⁴I/BM), electronic warfare (EW), and reconnaissance (recce) capabilities. These differences are equally critical to joint operations, combined arms, and the other synergies of modern warfare, and Israel again enjoys a significant advantage.

4

THE IMPACT OF QUALITATIVE FACTORS AND THE "REVOLUTION IN MILITARY AFFAIRS"

Table 4.1 provides a very different picture of the relative capabilities of Arab-Israeli forces from the previous tables. It provides a qualitative ranking of their war fighting capabilities in the critical areas shaping the balance judged by Western standards, and specifically by the standards of the forces the US had built up at the time the UN Coalition began the liberation of Kuwait.

It should be clear that the judgments made in Table 4.1 are highly subjective and are anything but easy to make and validate. Further, such comparisons inevitably raise the question of whether peak US military capabilities are the proper standard of reference for judging Arab-Israeli forces. Many Arab forces that have severe limitations by Western standards have moderate to good capability if they are judged by their ability to fight other Arab states, and some might argue that this is the proper standard of comparison.

The Israeli Organizational and "Cultural" Edge

The fact remains, however, that Israel has dominated Arab forces in every war it has fought. The Suez War of 1956, the June War of 1967, the Canal War of 1970, the October War of 1973, and the Lebanon conflict of 1982 all show that the Arab-Israeli balance cannot be judged by force numbers or by the standards of military effectiveness set by the Arab states—although Egypt achieved relatively high technical proficiency during the Canal War, and Egypt and Syria demonstrated considerable innovation and military competence during their initial surprise attacks in 1973. It is Israel's ability to match Western military quality and to add significant capabilities of its own, which are tailored to fighting its Arab neighbors, that have determined the outcome of every Arab-Israeli conflict.

Israel continues to emphasize leadership and demanding exercise training, to promote on the basis of competence, to maintain a relatively young and aggressive officer corps, and to insist on forward leadership. It uses training that develops battlefield initiative and it allows flexibility in executing orders. In contrast, Arab forces often require highly detailed written orders and systems of accountability in order to ensure that orders are obeyed, and commanders are taught not to deviate from orders when presented with new battlefield opportunities or unanticipated problems.

Israeli military forces are far closer to Western forces in tactics, training, and technology than they are to the forces of Third World countries, and the standard of comparison used in judging the trends in the Arab-Israeli military balance must be based on the force with the highest qualitative standards and which is most likely to dominate the outcome of combat. In fact, Israel's Advanced Training and Simulations, Ltd. now has a partnership with Siemens Nederlands called Simagine Simulation Systems for the export of gunnery, training simulators for tanks, the Dragon and TOW anti-tank guided weapons, field artillery observers, and light air defense systems like the Stinger and Vulcan.[1] The outcome of the Gulf War reinforces this conclusion. While capabilities for guerrilla, revolutionary, low intensity, and some aspects of urban warfare are less subject to changes in training, tactics, and technology, the Gulf War has demonstrated that the military balance is changing strikingly for those nations that can begin to exploit the potential of the revolution in military affairs.

Israel has done a much better job of using its resources and of taking advantage of the advances in tactics, training, and technology which make up the "revolution in military affairs" (RMA) than its Arab neighbors. As a result, Table 4.1 reflects the fact that Israel has many of the same strengths that Western forces enjoyed at the time of the Gulf War. These are strengths which—as the Gulf War showed—are fundamentally changing the importance of joint and combined operations, the tempo and precision of air power, beyond-visual-range combat, rates of armored maneuver and ranges of armored engagement, the use of precision-directed long range artillery, sustainability in armored maneuver and air operations, and the ability to conduct "24 hour" warfare.

Israel has also done a better job of developing the ability to manage the sheer complexity of modern military forces. This complexity is reflected in Table 4.1 and may be hard for the lay reader to understand. Yet each of the variables listed in Table 4.1 is directly relevant to the performance of forces in modern war fighting that involves mid- to high intensity combat. There are also many other important variables which are not listed in this table.

The variables in Table 4.1 also interact to determine how one nation's mix of forces compare to another. War fighting capability is heavily dependent on the integration of complex qualitative factors into a "system of systems" that emphasizes tactics, training, and all aspects of technology rather than reliance force strengths and weapons performance.

Israel also links superior land maneuver warfare to one of the most effective air forces in the world. The Israeli Air Force (IAF) destroyed many of its opponent's aircraft on the ground in the 1967 war and then scored 72 air-to-air kills over the

TABLE 4.1   The War Fighting Capabilities of the Individual "Ring States"
Judged by Western Standards: Part One

Capability & Quality	US	Israel	Syria	Jordan	Egypt	Lebanon
Active Manpower						
• Officer quality	E	E	P-VG	M-E	P-E	N
• NCO quality	E	E	P-M	M-E	P-E	N
• Enlisted quality	E	VG-E	VP-M	M-G	P-M	N
Reserve Manpower						
• Officer quality	VG	E	P	M	P	N
• NCO quality	VG	E	P	P	P	N
• Enlisted quality	VG	VG-E	VP	P	VP	N
Combined Operations	E	E	VP	P	P	N
Land Forces						
• Combined arms	E	E	P-M	M	P-M	N
• Advanced maneuver	E	E	P-M	M	P-M	N
• Armored warfare	E	E	P-M	M	P-M	N
• Infantry warfare	VG	G	P-VG	G	P-G	N-M
• Advanced artillery	E	VG	P	P	P-G	N
• Heliborne	E	VG	P-M	P	P-M	N
• Advanced night	VG	VG	P	P	P	N
• Unconventional	VG	E	M-E	M	M-E	N
• C⁴I/BM	E	VG	P	P	P-M	N
• Sustainability	VG	VG	P	M	P-M	N
• Standardization	E	VG	M	P	VP-M	N
• Interoperability	E	VG	P	M	P-M	N
Naval Forces						
• Combined operations	E	M	VP	N	VP	N
• Anti-Ship missile	E	G	P-M	N	P-M	N
• ASW	E	P	VP	N	VP	N
• Offensive mine	M	P	M	N	P	N
• Defensive mine	P	P	P	N	P	N
• Amphibious	VG	M	P	N	P	N
• C4I/BM	E	M	P	N	P	N
Sustainability	VG	P-M	P	N	P	N
Standardization	E	G	G	N	P	G
Interoperability	VG	P	P	N	P	G

The War Fighting Capabilities of the Individual "Ring States"
Judged by Western Standards: Part Two

Air Forces						
• Combined operations	E	VG	P	P	P-M	N
• Day air defense	E	E	P-G	P-G	P-VG	N

TABLE 4.1 *(Continued)*

Capability & Quality	US	Israel	Syria	Jordan	Egypt	Lebanon
• AWX/BVR air defense	E	E	VP	N	VP-M	N
• Day attack	E	E	P	P	P-M	N
• Close support	E	VG	P	M	P-M	N
• Advanced anti-armor	VG	VG	VP	VP	VP-P	N
• Night/AWX attack	E	VG	VP	P	P-M	N
• Reconnaissance	E	E	P	P	P-M	N
• Electronic warfare	E	G	P	N	P	N
• Attack helicopter	E	M	P	P	P	VP
• C⁴I/BM	VG-E	E	VP	P-M	P-M	N
• Sustainability	VG	E	VP	P	P-M	N
• Standardization	E	E	M	P	VP-M	N
• Interoperability	VG	VG	P	P	VP-M	N
Strategic Mobility						
• Air	VG	M	VP	VP	P-M	N
• Sea	G	P	N	N	N	N
• Prepositioning	M	–	–	–	–	–
Counterproliferation						
• Missile defense	P-M	P-M	N	N	N	N
• Bio. offensive	N	N	P	N	P	N
• Bio. defensive	VP-N	P	P	N	P	N
• Chem. offensive	VP	P	M	N	P	N
• Chem. defense	M-G	P-M	P-M	N	P	N
• Nuclear offensive	E	E	N	N	N	N
• Nuclear defensive	M-VP	N	N	N	N	N
• Conventional retaliation	VG	E	P	VP	P	N

E = Excellent, VG = Very Good, G = Good, M = Moderate, P = Poor, VP = Very Poor, N = Negligible

Note: *Interoperability* refers to the Israeli ability to interoperate broadly with other Gulf and Western forces and Arab country ability to operate flexibly with other Arab forces. *Standardization* refers to whether equipment pool in a given service in a given country is standardized enough to permit effective cross-service and resupply. *C⁴I/BM* refers to overall command, control, communications, intelligence, and battle management capabilities.

rest. It destroyed 113 Egyptian and Syrian aircraft in air-to-air combat during the war of attrition, and killed 452 Egyptian, Syrian, Iraqi, and Jordanian aircraft during the October War in 1973. It killed at least 23 Syrian aircraft between 1973 and 1982, and killed 71 fixed wing aircraft during the fighting in 1982. It shot down three Syrian fighters between 1982 and 1992. While it has lost 247 aircraft in combat since the beginning of the 1948 war, only 18 have been lost in air-to-air combat. In contrast, Arab forces have lost at least 1,428 fixed wing and rotary wing aircraft in combat, and 817 have been lost in air-to-air combat.[2]

Two Arab air forces—Egypt and Saudi Arabia—have high training standards, modern combat aircraft, and advanced battle management systems like the E-3A and E-2C. Israel is the only Middle Eastern air force, however, that combines all of the elements of modern air power into an efficient and integrated whole. Israel has advanced combat, electronic warfare, intelligence and targeting, and battle management aircraft. These are supported by a host of advanced and special purpose weapons systems, Combat electronics, unmanned airborne vehicles, night and all-weather combat systems, and command and control facilities.

Israeli pilot and air crew selection and training standards are the highest in the Middle East and some of the highest in the world. Nearly 90% of those selected as possible pilots do not make the grade as fighter pilots. Israel has a ruthless selection process to keep its pilots at a high standard. It promotes on the basis of performance rather than seniority. High quality pilots and air crews now serve in a reserve capacity after leaving active service, giving Israel a significant ability to expand its combat air strength in wartime—particularly with attack aircraft. El Al, the national airline, can be mobilized immediately for transport and resupply missions and to provide added technical personnel, as can skilled workers in Israel's defense industries.

The Israeli air force has about 2.5 pilots per combat aircraft versus less than 1 in most Arab air forces. It is equipped with first line aircraft like the F-15 and F-16, continues to emphasize training, and has one of the most advanced combat training systems in the world, as well as the advantage of US training centers. The IAF's excellence in pilots is supported by excellence in the human dimension at all levels. Some Arab air forces have good training standards for a limited to moderate number of their pilots, but the IAF has the most demanding pilot training and performance standards of any air force in the Middle East. In fact, initial selection for pilot training is so demanding that the IAF has attrition levels approaching 90%. The IAF has equally demanding standards for maintenance, logistics, command and control, intelligence and targeting, and all of the other functions necessary to maintain effective air operations.

In addition, Israel has developed a reserve system that requires exceptional performance from its air force reservists. There are no reserve squadrons in the IAF, and all squadrons can operate without mobilization. However, about one-third of the air crew in each squadron are reservists. Reserve air crews train 55–60 days a year and fly operational missions with the squadron to which they are assigned. In the event of a call-up, the reserve air crews and operations support personnel report first, and then support personnel for sustained operations. About 60% of the IAF reserves are in air and ground defense units.

In contrast, other Middle Eastern forces are weakened by their failure to enforce rigorous selection procedures for assignments other than combat pilot, and by their failure to create a highly professional class of non-commissioned officers that are paid, trained, and given the status necessary to maintain fully effective combat operations. In most cases, these problems are compounded by poor overall manpower policies and promotion for political and personal loyalty. Other Middle Eastern air forces also tend to be weakened by a failure to see command and control, intelligence and targeting, high intensity combat operations, and sustainability as being equal in importance to weapons numbers and quality. While Egypt, Iraq, and Saudi Arabia have moved toward the idea of force-wide excellence in supporting an overall concept of operations, they still have a long way to go before approaching Israel's level of capability.

While the Israeli air defense system is scarcely leak proof—a fact demonstrated when a defecting Syrian pilot flew undetected deep into Israeli air space—a fully alert Israeli air defense is capable of coordinating its sensors, fighters, and land-based defenses with a level of effectiveness that no other Middle Eastern air force can approach.[3] Israel has a better overall mix of systems, better trained personnel, and a far better ability to integrate all its assets with its own technology and software than any other Middle Eastern air force.

Israel's advantages in strategic and long range offensive operations are even greater. The IAF is the only air force in the Middle East that is seriously organized for strategic attacks on its neighbors. Other Middle Eastern air forces may have long range strike aircraft, effective munitions, and even a limited refueling capacity. They are, however, essentially amateurs in using their assets to inflict strategic damage on an enemy nation or conduct effective long range strategic strikes.

Israel has the ability to strike deep into the Arab world, and has greatly improved its long range strike capability since its attacks on Osirak in 1981 and on Tunisia in 1985.[4] It has greatly improved refueling capability, targeting capability, stand-off precision munitions, and electronic warfare capability. Israel could probably surgically strike a limited number of key targets in virtually any Arab country within 1,500 nautical miles of Israel and could sustain operations against Western Iraq. It would, however, probably be forced to use nuclear weapons to achieve significant strategic impact on more than a few Iraqi facilities, or if it has to simultaneously engage Syrian and Iraqi forces.

At the same time, Israel is not "10 feet tall." The active manpower Israel does maintain is very expensive and accounts for nearly half of the defense budget. A once lean IDF now has some 600 colonels performing headquarters and staff functions. Israel cannot afford the state of the art in many aspects of C⁴I/BM and training, and Israeli officers often confuse the development of tactics and technology tailored to their local theater with the state of the art outside their theater of operations.

Morale and retention have been affected by the Intifada, the peace process, and competition from the private sector, and the IDF's reliance on reserves and conscripts presents some inevitable manpower problems. For example, during the 1960s, some nine out of ten young Israelis who were offered promotion to platoon commander of paratroops in the regular army would accept. This figure has slowly dropped to one in ten in 1995. Reserve call-ups are shorter and less demanding, and some of the IDF's best regular officers now leave early for civilian careers.

There is a growing "generational" debate over the quality of the IDF within Israel. This debate focuses on the fact that today's IDF lacks the combat experience that Israeli forces had in the past, and charges that the IDF is becoming bureaucratized and has eased its standards. At least some retired Israeli commanders are increasingly critical of what they see as a shift away from a "war fighting" to a "garrison" mentality and to an overreliance on technology. Other critics feel that the morale of the IDF still suffers from the impact of the Intifada. They charge that the peace process is leading to a relaxation of standards, that there is a tendency to shift to more defensive tactics, that conscript and reserve training is no longer as demanding as in the past, and that the government is taking peace dividends at the expense of overall readiness and capability.

There is no doubt that there have been major struggles for resources within the IDF between services and branches of a given service, debates over strategy and tactics, and arguments over organization and command. These debates have been interwoven with the broader debates in Israeli society. These debates have taken place over trading territory for peace or preserving control of the Occupied Territory, the Intifada and relations with the Palestinians, civil versus military spending, economic reform, and Israel's relations with the US and its dependence on US aid.

The IDF has also has been divided by a number of more technical military issues:

- The extent to which Israel's land forces should be capable of decisive sudden offensive action against Syria—or any combination of Syria, Lebanon, and Jordan—as distinguished from being capable of defending Israeli territory by halting any invasion.
- The specific contingencies Israel should plan for, and the level of capability of Syria, or Syria in combination with other Arab states, to carry out a surprise attack on Israel across the Golan or through Lebanon and/or Jordan.
- The level of readiness Israel needs within its land and air forces to deal with a surprise or limited warning attack.
- The ability of the Israeli Air Force and advanced conventional technology to inflict a decisive series of strikes on the Syrian military and Syrian economy within a few days using conventional weapons and without a major land offensive, or to inflict similar damage on any other neighbor.
- The level and type of force that should be used to control Palestinian activity within Gaza and the West Bank, and ultimately what level of compromise or relations with the Palestinian Authority will preserve Israeli security.
- The amount of territory that might be traded for peace, and the conditions under which such a trade might take place.

- The level of forces and other resources that Israel should commit to the defense of south Lebanon.
- The extent to which Israel needs a "blue water" navy that is capable of securing its lines of communication and long range strike capability, as distinguished from securing its coasts and immediate waters.
- The level of anti-tactical ballistic missile defense that can be provided.
- The level of defense Israel can provide its soldiers and population against biological, chemical, and nuclear weapons.
- The extent to which Israel should reveal or publicize its nuclear and missile capabilities.
- The extent to which the Israeli defense industry should be encouraged both to reduce dependence on the US and to create a technology base for advanced exports overseas.
- The level of resources that should go to defense versus absorbing the Russian Jews and economic development.

Israel has been involved in the same debate over downsizing and converting to the "revolution in military affairs" that has affected US and European forces and that challenges the effectiveness of current Western military plans and capabilities. These debates take place at every professional level within the IDF. Perhaps the most serious public critique of Israeli capabilities, however, is still the one written by Colonel Emanuel Wald. In a report originally written for Israel's then chief of staff Moshe Levi, Wald argued that the IDF had evolved into a slow moving and feuding bureaucracy that lost the 1982 war because of its inability to effectively manage combined arms and combined operations and make effective decisions at the command level.[5]

Further, Wald argued that the IDF had lost its professionalism at the command and combat unit level, had fragmented along branch and service lines, and had promoted according to bureaucratic performance. It no longer realistically trained and selected its officers for combat, could not effectively coordinate or manage operations at the corps level, could not sustain a high tempo of continuous operations, wasted resources on a large and unproductive staff and support structure, inflated its number of high ranking officers, could not effectively maneuver to engage all of its forces with the enemy, had limited night combat capability, had uncertain ability to use its intelligence collection in effective battle management, and lacked the ability to set meaningful politico-military objectives for battle and pursue them to a meaningful conclusion.

The IDF has, however, responded to many of these criticisms. It has steadily improved its use of technology, and has acted aggressively to take advantage of the lessons of the 1982 war and the Gulf War. It has eliminated many career officer and civilian positions from the IDF—particularly in headquarters, support, and "bureaucratic" functions. It has reduced or phased out IDF functions, including the Training Branch, Women's Corps, Education Corps, and Gadna Youth Corps.

These changes were instituted as part of broader reforms that began when Lt. General Ehud Barak was appointed as chief of staff of the IDF on April 1, 1992. Barak immediately summoned 3,000 officers from Lt. Colonel to Major General to a meeting where he issued a message that the IDF had become too fat and over-manned, lacked sufficient rigor and training, needed to tighten discipline, had to focus on arming and training for the high technology battlefield of the 1990s, and had to plan to live within tighter resources. Barak then proceeded to slash head-quarters and rear area support functions by 10–20%, cut paperwork, abolish some 30 out of 32 IDF publications, and remove officers who failed in command exercises or who failed to react quickly to terrorism. He also cut reserve service and training to provide added funds for high technology modernization. Barak's changes came very close to many of those recommended by Wald.[6]

In spite of some decline in interest in the military, 86% of eligible young Israelis still served in the military in 1995, and service was still three years for men and 22 months for women. Elite combat units still get adequate numbers of volunteers in spite of arduous service conditions, and the number of Israelis who do not report for service has increased by only 1.5% over the last four years—including Israeli Arabs and those Orthodox Jews who refuse all military service.[7]

As a result, many Israeli officers feel that much of the criticism of today's IDF ignores recent reforms and ignores the fact that the IDF is now a high technology force with different needs. They feel that modern combined arms and joint war-fare training must emphasize different skills and technical competence over phys-ical effort. They feel that Israel's technical edge necessarily requires a far more so-phisticated support and administrative structure than past IDF forces, and that the kind of emphasis on aggressive armored warfare that was decisive during 1967–1973 must be modified to deal with different Arab forces, equipment, and tactics. They also feel that some reductions in military spending are justified given the high level of US aid, the limitations of the Syrian threat, and the success of the peace process.

There is no way to resolve this debate short of war. It is probably true that the IDF no longer acts as if it were constantly on the brink of an existential challenge to Israel's existence requiring total national mobilization in a matter of hours. At the same time, this no longer seems to be the force posture the IDF needs, given current Israeli military technology. Maintaining this kind of knife's edge readiness also does not seem to be a realistic use of Israel's national resources.

The more relevant question may be whether future Israeli governments sup-port the peace process with the mix of resources and arms control measures nec-essary to ensure that the IDF has the capability to maintain its present level of de-terrence and war fighting capability relative to the Arab threat. The real issue is not whether the IDF of 1995 is the IDF of 1975, but whether the IDF of 2000 or 2010 will meet Israel's future needs.

There is also nothing magical about the IAF's superiority, and it has perfor-mance problems and limitations of its own. As was demonstrated during the

Canal War in 1970 and on many other occasions, individual Arab pilots are certainly as good as their Israeli counterparts. The IAF is vulnerable to a saturation attack, particularly if this was achieved at a time of strategic surprise, when the IAF either was not fully ready or failed to react properly. Carefully planned raids, with or without weapons of mass destruction, might well reach an urban target like Haifa or Tel Aviv.

The IAF has had some scandals and problems with incidents involving senior commanders.[8] It has experienced financial pressures, in part because of the massive costs of the now canceled Lavi program and in part because of recent cutbacks in new programs. These resource compromises have led to reductions in procurement and supply, the mothballing of some units, cuts in training levels and flight hours, a loss of operational tempo, and early grounding for a number of qualified pilots.

Like many nations in the West, Israel has also been unable to strike an efficient balance among defense industry, modernization, and operational readiness. Israel does not have the kind of satellite and long range targeting and intelligence assets available to the US, although its UAVs are a partial substitute. Any large scale battle with Syria or Syria and some combination of other Arab allies would force Israel to engage with a wide range of tactics, weapons, and C[4]I/BM systems and techniques that are experimental and subject to failure or problems.

The Arab Organizational and "Cultural" Problem

The comparison of the judgments made in Table 4.1 with the relative force strength data in Tables 1.1 and 3.1 also shows that the individual Arab states have far more strength in numbers than they have as yet translated into real-world war fighting capability. While the Arab states—particularly Egypt—have steadily improved their forces over time, they still suffer from a lack of effective organization, realistic large scale combat training, an overemphasis on mass relative to quality, an emphasis on attrition over maneuver, an emphasis on weapons numbers over C[4]I/BM systems and capabilities, and a lack of proper emphasis on standardization and sustainability.

Part of this Arab failure to develop force quality that can compete with Israel is the result of a lack of resources and/or access to first-line Western technology. Jordan, for example, has lacked the resources to modernize and equip its forces with high technology weapons and systems. Syria's opposition to the peace process and its ties to the former Soviet Union have meant it has been denied Western weapons and technology for political reasons. There is no question that Jordan and Syria would have far more effective forces if they had the same level of aid and access to advanced technology the US provided to Egypt and Israel.

Most of their problems, however, are the result of national and/or cultural failures to come to grips with the demanding realities of making modern military forces effective. In general, the Arab states have lacked the educational base and emphasis on management and technical skills to transform their large holdings of equipment into effective forces. They have tended to emphasize equipment purchases over tactics, training, manpower management, and sustainability. Procurement and promotion have been politicized and subject to corruption and nepotism.

Such generalizations are dangerous because they can disguise the fact that Arab forces differ sharply in quality and that individual Arab units can be as effective as Israeli or US forces. These problems do not mean that Arab forces are incapable of strategic innovation or military effectiveness. The Egyptian-Syrian surprise attack on Israel in October, 1973 was one of the major feats of arms of the twentieth century and involved considerable strategic and tactical innovation. Each Arab "ring state" has some high quality forces. Syria has several effective armored divisions and some elite special forces units. Jordanian forces have a high degree of military professionalism within their technical limits. Egypt has developed some high quality units equipped with modern American arms, and has gained experience in US concepts of warfare through its experience during the Gulf War and its participation in the biannual "Bright Star" exercises.

At the same time, each Arab "ring state" has a number of military problems. In broad terms, Syria has emphasized sheer force size and the acquisition of lead technology weapons systems with a high "glitter factor" over a balanced and effective approach to force modernization. Jordanian forces lack the technology and resources to fully modernize and develop effective combined operations and joint warfare capabilities. Egypt has paid too little attention to manpower quality and management, systems integration, C^{4}I/battle management, and sustainability, and far too much attention to the "glitter factor" of the latest technology and sheer mass. For example, Egyptian forces would be significantly more effective if Egypt did not try to support a large bloc of low grade forces equipped with obsolete Soviet-bloc equipment supplied before 1974, and concentrated its resources on making its Western supplied forces as effective as possible.

It is also impossible to ignore the fact that far too many Arab governments, ministries of defense, and military leaders fail to place a realistic emphasis on "intangibles." While Arab forces have steadily improved in quality over time, they still fail to emphasize aggressive leadership and the need for innovation and change. Ministries of defense are highly bureaucratic and rigid, and there is extensive inter-service and intra-service rivalry and over-compartmentation of procurement, manpower, and other functions. The layering of new functions and responsibilities over older bureaucratic structures is confused with effective reorganization. Senior commanders and officials serve too long, lack effective professional training, and are often chosen for political skills or loyalty rather than professional competence.

Arab forces fail to train effective combat leaders at every level. They have failed to create a strong and respected corps of NCOs and technicians, and the gap between officer and NCO is still too great—particularly in units where the experience and technical competence of other ranks are critical to the effective use of new technologies. Junior and mid-ranking officers do not receive sufficient training, and they are not forced to become aggressive and competent leaders and administrators. Junior officers are not given sufficient opportunities to innovate and lead, and both junior and mid-level officers are still promoted as much for time in service and political ties to senior commanders as for professionalism.

The leadership problem is compounded by a failure to force officers to assume personal responsibility for technical tasks and to work with their troops in areas involving manual labor and administrative detail. Improvements in training at the squad to battalion level are not matched by realistic and demanding training at the regimental or wing level and above. Both field and command post exercises are generally undemanding, limited in effort, and without penalty for anything other than the most mediocre performance. There is little realistic adversary training that forces officers to accept the prospect of defeat and innovate in the face of superior forces. Far too often, Arab officers become progressively less competitive with their Israeli counterparts and other officers in the world's most effective military forces as they rise in rank.

There is little acceptance of the need for "make or break" exercises to ruthlessly identify those field grade officers who can or cannot command and to force inferior field grade officers out of the military. There is little acceptance of the need to make a major investment in realistic, large unit training and to force effective joint and combined arms performance on the training process. There is insufficient effort to demand that officers exhibit superior situational awareness and the ability and will to lead from the front at every level. There is far too great a tendency to blame foreign support and equipment and accept conspiracy theories as a substitute for competence.

These problems are often compounded by an obsessive focus on force numbers, equipment numbers, and an effort to procure the latest and most advanced weapons system. Once again, Arab forces are improving with time and differ according to country and service. Nevertheless, there is still far too little acceptance of the fact that training and sustainability are often more important aspects of war fighting capability than numbers. There is a basic confusion between the technical advantages of buying the latest new weapon and the war fighting advantages of integrating weapons into a "system of systems" that ensures overall force-on-force effectiveness. There is insufficient attention to the need to support weapons systems and combat units with service support, sustainability and maintenance, associated technologies for targeting and intelligence, and effective C^4I/BM systems. There is insufficient understanding of the need to integrate firepower, maneuver capability, and sustainability as three pillars of high intensity, "24 hour a day" combat operations.

The Qualitative Weaknesses in Arab and Third World Military Forces

The importance of the qualitative judgments made in Table 4.1 is further illustrated by the qualitative lessons of past Arab-Israeli conflicts and the Gulf War.

The Arab-Israeli conflicts of 1967, 1973, and 1982, and the Gulf War revealed a fundamental disparity between the limited number of nations who can use new methods of warfare and the vast majority of nations who cannot. This is an important strategic reality that no nation can ignore. It raises serious questions about the value of many of the force structures and weapons systems in the Arab states surrounding Israel and about the ability of such states to engage "First World" states like Israel in mid- to high intensity, high technology conflict.

At the risk of oversimplifying trends that are country and contingency dependent, the Gulf War revealed major weaknesses in the forces of Iraq and the Arab members of the UN Coalition, weaknesses that are also present in the forces of Iran. The following weaknesses in Arab forces seem equally likely to play an important role in shaping the war fighting outcome of the Arab-Israeli military balance:

- *Authoritarianism and overcentralization of the effective command structure:* The high command of many countries is dependent on compartmented and overcentralized C⁴I/BM systems that do not support high tempo warfare, combined arms, or combined operations and lack tactical and technical sophistication. Many forces or force elements report through a separate chain of command. C⁴I/BM systems often are structured to separate the activity of regular forces from elite, regime security, and ideological forces. Systems often ensure that major sectors and corps commanders report to the political leadership, and separations occur within the branches of a given service. Intelligence is compartmented and poorly disseminated. Air force command systems are small, unit oriented, and unsuited for large scale force management. Coordination of land-based and air defense and strike systems is poorly integrated, vulnerable, and/or limited in volume handling capability. Combined operations and combined arms coordination are poor, and command interference at the political level is common.
- *Lack of strategic assessment capability:* Many Third World nations lack sufficient understanding of Western war fighting capabilities to understand the impact of the revolution in military affairs, the role of high technology systems, and the impact of the new tempo of war. Other countries have important gaps in their assessment capabilities reflecting national traditions or prejudices.
- *Major weaknesses in battle management, command, control, communications, intelligence, targeting, and battle damage assessment:* No Third World country has meaningful access to space-based systems or advanced theater reconnaissance and intelligence systems. Most lack sophisticated reconnaissance, intelligence, and targeting assets. Beyond-visual-range imagery and targeting are restricted largely to vulnerable and easily detectable reconnaissance aircraft or low performance RPVs. Many rely on photo data for imagery and have cumbersome download and analysis cycles in interpreting intelligence. Many

have exploitable vulnerabilities to information warfare. Most are limited in the sophistication of their electronic warfare, SIGINT, and COMINT systems. Their communications security is little better than commercial communications security. They have severe communications interconnectivity, volume handling, and dissemination problems. Additionally, they cannot provide the software and connectivity necessary to fully exploit even commercial or ordinary military systems. They lack the C4I/BM capability to manage complex deep strikes, complex large-scale armor and artillery operations, effective electronic intelligence, and rapid cycles of reaction in decision-making.

- *Lack of cohesive force quality:* Most countries' forces have major land combat units and squadrons with very different levels of proficiency. Political, historical, and equipment supply factors often mean that most units have much lower levels of real-world combat effectiveness than the best units. Further, imbalances in combat support, service support, and logistic support create significant additional imbalances in sustainability and operational effectiveness. Many states add to these problems, as well as lack of force cohesion, by creating politicized or ideological divisions within their forces.
- *Shallow offensive battlefields:* Most states face severe limits in extending the depth of the battlefield because they lack the survivable platforms and sensors, communications, and data processing to do so. These problems are particularly severe in wars of maneuver, in wars involving the extensive use of strike aircraft, and in battles where a growing strain is placed on force cohesion.
- *Manpower quality:* Many states rely on the mass use of poorly trained conscripts. They fail to provide adequate status, pay, training, and career management for NCOs and technicians. Many forces fail to provide professional career development for officers and joint and combined arms training. Promotion often occurs for political reasons or out of nepotism and favoritism.
- *Slow tempo of operations:* Most Third World military forces have not fought a high intensity air or armored battle. They are at best capable of medium tempo operations, and their pace of operations is often dependent on the survival of some critical mix of facilities or capabilities.
- *Lack of sustainability, recovery, and repair:* These initial problems in the tempo of operations are often exacerbated by a failure to provide for sustained air operations and high sortie rates, long range sustained maneuver, and battlefield/combat unit recovery and repair. Most Third World forces are heavily dependent on resupply to deal with combat attrition whereas Western forces and Israeli forces can use field recovery, maintenance, and repair.
- *Inability to prevent air superiority:* Many states have far greater air defense capability on paper than they do in practice. Most have not fought in any kind of meaningful air action in the last decade, and many have never fought any significant air action in their history. C4I/battle management problems are

critical in this near real-time environment. Most countries lack sophisticated air combat and land-based air defense simulation and training systems, and do not conduct effective aggressor and large scale operations training. Efforts to transfer technology, organization, and training methods from other nations on a patchwork basis often leave critical gaps in national capability, even where other capabilities are effective.

- *Problems in air-to-air combat:* Air combat training levels are low and unrealistic. Pilot and other crew training standards are insufficient, or initial training is not followed up with sustained training. There is little effective aggressor training. AWACS and ABCCC capabilities are lacking. EW capabilities are modified commercial grade capabilities. Most aircraft lack effective air battle management systems and have limited beyond-visual-range and look-down shoot-down capability. Most Soviet/Communist supplied air forces depend heavily on obsolete ground-controlled vectoring for intercepts. Key radar and control centers are static and vulnerable to corridor blasting.

- *Problems in land-based air defense:* Most Third World states must borrow or adapt air defense battle management capabilities from supplier states and have limited independent capability for systems integration—particularly at the software level. They lack the mix of heavy surface-to-air missile systems to cover broad areas or must rely on obsolete systems which can be killed, countered by EW, and/or bypassed. Most Third World short range air defense systems do not protect against attacks with stand-off precision weapons or using stealth.

- *Lack of effective survivable long range strike systems:* Many Third World nations have the capability to launch long range air and missile strikes but also have severe operational problems. Refueling capabilities do not exist or are in such small numbers as to be highly vulnerable. Long range targeting and battle damage assessment capabilities are lacking. Training is limited and unrealistic in terms of penetrating effective air defenses. Platforms are export systems without the full range of supplier avionics or missile warheads. Assets are not survivable or lose much of their effective strike capability once dispersed.

- *Combined (joint) operations, combined arms, and the AirLand Battle:* Many states fail to emphasize the key advances in the integration of war fighting capabilities from the last decade. When they do emphasize combined arms and joint operations, they usually leave serious gaps in some aspects of national war fighting capability.

- *Rough/special terrain warfare:* Although many Third World forces have armed helicopters, large numbers of tracked vehicles, and can create effective rough terrain defenses if given time, they have severe problems in conducting such operations in high tempo operations. Many tend to be road-bound for critical support and combined arms functions and lack training for long range, high intensity engagements in rough terrain. Many are not properly trained to exploit the potential advantages of their own region. They are either garrison forces or forces which rely on relatively static operations in predetermined field positions. These problems are often compounded by a lack of combat engineering and barrier crossing equipment.

- *Night and all-weather warfare:* Most Third World forces lack adequate equipment for night and poor weather warfare, and particularly for long range direct and indirect fire engagement and cohesive, sustainable, large scale maneuver.

- *Failure to defend in the proper depth—the shallow defensive battlefield:* Many Third World states have doctrines and defense concepts that attempt to hold long forward lines, with too few forces and too few forces in support and reserve. They rely on only one major belt of barrier and mine defenses. Many keep artillery and immediate support units too close to the forward line—enhancing vulnerability to air operations and armored penetration. They are vulnerable to Western forces who rely on swift deep armored penetrations, modern combat engineering, and air power.

- *Misuse and maldeployment of reserves:* Iraq is scarcely unique in relying on the uses of reserves to support forward deployed forces in ways that assume the forces in reserve have adequate air cover and sufficient time to react and either support the forward deployed units or halt a breakthrough. The problems in relying on slow moving, vulnerable forces in reserve—combined with growing threats posed by improving Israeli and Western "look deep/strike deep" capabilities—provide added capability to disrupt the enemy concept of battle.

- *Infantry operations:* Many Third World units maintain low quality infantry units which they use for defensive purposes. Many of these forces lack training and the capability to maintain cohesion in the event of disruptive air attacks or outflanking maneuvers. Many differ sharply in actual manning and equipment levels between individual units. Exploiting the character of individual units, as distinguished from relying on generalized order of battle/table of organization and equipment (OB/TO&E) analysis, allows the West to exploit these weaknesses effectively.

- *Armored operations:* Most countries have sharply different levels of armored warfare proficiency within their armored and mechanized forces. Few units have advanced training and simulation facilities. Most land forces have severe interoperability and standardization problems within their force structure—particularly in the case of other armored fighting vehicles where they often deploy a very wide range of types. Many are very tank heavy, without the mix of other capabilities necessary to deploy infantry, supporting artillery, and anti-tank capabilities at the same speed and maneuver proficiency as tank units. Most forces have poor training in conducting rapid, large scale armored and combined operations at night and in poor weather. Effective battle management declines sharply at the force-wide level—as distinguished from the major combat unit level—and sometimes even in coordinating brigade or division-sized operations.

- *Artillery operations:* Many Third World states have large numbers of artillery weapons but serious problems in training and tactics. They lack long range targeting capability and the ability to rapidly shift and effectively allocate fire. Many rely on towed weapons with limited mobility or lack off-road support vehicles. Combined arms capabilities are limited. Many units are only effective in using mass fire against enemies that maneuver more slowly than they do.
- *Combat training:* Third World military training generally has serious problems and gaps, which vary by countries. Units or force elements differ sharply in training quality. Training problems are complicated by conversion and expansion, conscript turnover, and a lack of advanced technical support for realistic armored, artillery, air-to-air, surface-to-air, and offensive air training. Mass sometimes compensates, but major weaknesses remain.
- *Inability to use weapons of mass destruction effectively:* Any state can use weapons of mass destruction to threaten or intimidate another, or to attack population centers and fixed area targets. At the same time, this is not the same as having an effective capability and doctrine to obtain maximum use of such weapons or to manage attacks in ways that result in effective tactical outcomes and conflict termination. Many states are acquiring long range missiles and weapons of mass destruction with very limited exercise and test and evaluation capabilities. This does not deny them the ability to target large populated areas, economic centers, and fixed military targets, potentially inflicting massive damage. At the same time, it does present problems in more sophisticated military operations. Many will have to improvise deployments, doctrine, and war fighting capabilities. In many cases, weaknesses and vulnerabilities will persist and they will only be able to exploit a limited amount of the potential lethality of such systems.

The Qualitative Advantages of Israeli Forces

It is difficult to go beyond such a generic list of weaknesses without making highly subjective judgments about the capabilities of Israeli, Syrian, Egyptian, and Jordanian forces. At the same time, a great deal is known about the doctrine, training, and/or exercise performance of Israeli and individual Arab forces. Further, some of the weaknesses in Syrian, Egyptian, and Jordanian forces are the product of limits in deployed weapons and technology and not "intangibles." Past Arab-Israeli conflicts have also shown that some of these factors are likely to be equally relevant in future Arab-Israeli conflicts—*if* Israeli forces have the time to deploy and fully organize and prepare, and *if* they do not face major challenges in terms of threats from weapons of mass destruction or guerrilla, urban, and revolutionary warfare—areas where many of the qualitative advantages of Israeli forces do not apply.

The impact of these advantages and weaknesses affecting the current trends in the Arab-Israeli balance include:

- *Decoupling of political and military responsibility:* No war is ever free of command controversy or friction between political and military leadership. However, the Coalition forces fought the Gulf War with effective delegation of responsibility for military decisions to military commanders. Israel is likely to enjoy the same advantage in mid- to high intensity wars. Syrian military forces are highly politicized and organized more to suit the regime's internal security needs than to conduct modern joint operations. Jordan's small forces are under tight political control, but are selected for their professionalism. Egypt's military forces are involved in politics, but operational units are under professional, rather than political, command. Egypt still, however, has a severe problem in reporting objectively—particularly in reporting bad news—through its chain of command. Egyptian intelligence is often politicized.
- *Unity of command:* The level of unity of command and "fusion" achieved during the Gulf War was scarcely perfect, but it was far more effective than that possible in most Arab states. Israel has steadily improved its unity of command and ability to conduct joint operations since 1973. Syrian command is still compartmented by command, service, and branch. Jordan has a limited combined operations capability, but lacks the technology and resources to develop a high degree of effectiveness. Egyptian command is also heavily compartmented by command, service, and branch.
- *Combined operations, combined arms, and the "AirLand Battle":* While US doctrine had always placed a pro forma emphasis on combined operations, many US operations in Vietnam did not properly integrate combined arms. Common inter-service training in combined operations was limited, and air operations were not properly integrated into land operations. In the years that followed, the US reorganized to place far more emphasis on combined arms and combined operations. It greatly strengthened combined operations training and career rotations into joint commands. At the same time, it developed tactics that closely integrated air and land operations into what the US came to call the "AirLand Battle." These tactics were critical to the success of the ground battle. Israel cannot afford the level of technology and sophisticated training systems used by the US, but has adopted lower cost and equally effective methods to its theater of operations. Syria has not made similar advances. Jordan's military doctrine recognizes the need for such advances, but Jordan lacks the resources and technology to move beyond defensive operations. Some Egyptian units equipped with US weapons and

technology have performed adequately during preplanned exercises, but overall Egyptian capabilities are poor.

- *Emphasis on maneuver:* The US had emphasized firepower and attrition until the end of the Vietnam War. In the years that followed, it converted its force structure to place an equal emphasis on maneuver and deception. This emphasis was supported by Britain and France and was adopted by Saudi Arabia. Israel has long emphasized wars of maneuver, although it faces obvious limits in using such techniques in offensive land warfare against entrenched Syrian forces on the Golan. Syria still emphasizes preplanned set piece maneuvers. These might prove adequate on the Golan if the Syrians achieve strategic surprise, but Syrian forces lack true maneuver capability and flexibility. Jordanian land forces recognize the importance of maneuver doctrine, but Jordan lacks the resources to adequately equip and train for modern maneuver warfare. Egypt's best units have moderate maneuver capability but even these units still need to improve their combined operations and sustainability. The bulk of Egyptian forces are relatively static and defensive in capability.
- *Emphasis on deception and strategic/tactical innovation:* No country has a monopoly on the use of deception and strategic/tactical innovation. The Coalition, however, demonstrated capabilities that were far superior to those of Iraq. Egypt and Syria made brilliant use of deception and innovation against Israel in the opening battles of the October War, but this operation took long preplanning and lacked operational flexibility once the initial battle plan was executed. Israel now has the technology and tactical sophistication to conduct "soft strike" air and land-based weapons attacks that are likely to achieve a high degree of "surprise" and has a distinct advantage in crisis-driven innovation. Syria retains the ability to use deception in preplanned operations, and has some elite units which showed considerable tactical flexibility in 1982, but lacks overall flexibility and speed of reaction. Jordan has considerable skill, but faces severe technical limits on its range of action. Egypt also retains the ability to use deception and innovation in preplanned operations, but only a relatively few elite units seem to exhibit tactical innovation and flexibility under pressure. In some ways, Egypt seems to have become more rigid since 1973—perhaps because of the problems inherent in trying to operate forces with such diverse equipment and training levels and such limited interoperability.
- *"24 hour war"—superior night, all-weather, and beyond-visual-range warfare:* "Visibility" is always relative in combat. There is no such thing as a perfect night vision or all-weather combat system or way of acquiring perfect information at long ranges. US and British air and land forces, however, have far better training and technology for such combat than they ever had in the past, and were the first forces designed to wage warfare continuously at night and in poor weather. Equally important, they were far more capable of taking advantage of the margin of extra range and tactical information provided by

superior technology. Israel cannot afford all of the systems and high technology training aids available to the US, but does have a distinct advantage in technology and training over its neighbors. Syria is still largely a daytime, visual-range, military force. Jordan has many similar limitations, although Jordanian land forces have night warfare training superior to Syria's. Egyptian capabilities are erratic. A few elite land units have some night warfare capability, and some US supplied air units have good all-weather and beyond-visual-range aircraft and training. Overall Egyptian proficiency is poor.

- *Near real-time integration of C⁴I/BM/T/BDA:* The Coalition took advantage of major US C⁴I/BM/T/BDA organization, technology, and software to integrate various aspects of command, control, communications, computers, and intelligence (C⁴I); battle management (BM), targeting (T), and battle damage assessment (BDA) to achieve a near real-time integration and decision-making-execution cycle. Israel has many of these same capabilities while its neighbors lack a similar combination of organization, technology, and training. Syrian ground forces use techniques at least a decade old, Syrian air units still rely primarily on obsolete ground controlled intercept techniques and grindingly slow cycles of air attack planning. Syrian surface-to-air missile C⁴I/BM/T/BDA systems are a decade out of date. Jordan has lacked the resources to adequately modernize its C⁴I/BM/T/BDA systems, although it has sometimes adapted low cost solutions to obtain partial capability. Egypt has modernized some aspects of its C⁴I/BM/T/BDA systems, but its integration of these capabilities is uncertain and its improvements in C⁴I/BM/T/BDA systems only affect the US equipped portion of its forces. Egypt has poor force-wide C⁴I/BM/T/BDA capabilities.
- *A new tempo of operations:* The Coalition exploited a superiority in every aspect of targeting, intelligence gathering and dissemination, integration of combined arms, multiservice forces, and night and all-weather warfare to achieve both a new tempo of operations and one far superior to that of Iraq. Israel has long emphasized tempo of operations while Syria remains a relatively low tempo force, Jordan lacks the air and artillery capabilities to support high tempo armored operations, and Egyptian forces have very mixed quality. Syria can only briefly sustain high tempo land operations under conditions where it has previously planned and trained for the specific operation involved and its battle plans are not disrupted by preemption or massive enemy air superiority. Jordan has had the training and doctrine for high intensity land operations, but now lacks the resources to keep most of its land forces at this level of proficiency. It can only briefly surge air operations. Egyptian capabilities to sustain high tempo operations are very erratic and the bulk of Egyptian forces lack detailed doctrine, training, support capabilities, and supply capabilities for such operations.
- *A new tempo of sustainability:* Coalition forces had maintainability, reliability, reparability, and the speed and overall mobility of logistic, service support,

and combat support force activity that broadly matched their maneuver and firepower capabilities. The benefits of these new capabilities were reflected in such critical areas as the extraordinarily high operational availability and sortie rates of US aircraft and the ability to support the movement of heliborne and armored forces during the long thrust into Iraq from the West. Israel has long demonstrated it has the ability to sustain high intensity air and land operations. Syria lacks the doctrine, training, specialized equipment and support vehicles, and stocks and supply system to give sustainability the emphasis needed in modern warfare. Jordan lacks the resources to fund adequate levels of sustainability for its land and air units. Egypt has placed a proper conceptual emphasis on sustainability, but lacks the detailed doctrine, training, specialized equipment and support vehicles, and stocks and supply system to give most of its forces the sustainability needed in modern warfare

- *Beyond-visual-range air combat, air defense suppression, air base attacks, and airborne C⁴I/BM:* The Coalition had a decisive advantage in air combat training, beyond-visual-range air combat capability, anti-radiation missiles, electronic warfare, air base and shelter and kill capability, stealth and unmanned long-range strike systems, IFF and air control capability, and airborne C⁴I/BM systems like the E-3 and ABCCC. These advantages allowed the Coalition to win early and decisive air supremacy. Israel has a mix of aircraft, E-2Cs, RPVs, electronic warfare systems, and command and control assets which give it many of the same advantages in its particular theater of operations against the forces of its Arab neighbors. Virtually every aspect of Syrian operations in these forms of combat is a decade behind the state of the art. Jordan lacks the equipment to implement such combat effectively. Egypt can use its E-2Cs effectively in air defense missions, but only with its US supplied air and surface-to-air missile units. Its F-16s are capable of good beyond-visual-range (BVR) combat capability, but are limited by their rules of engagement and a concern for fratricide and cannot compete with Israel in overall battle management capability, air defense suppression, and air field suppression/attack capabilities.

- *Focused and effective interdiction bombing:* While the Coalition strategic bombing effort during the Gulf War had limitations, many aspects of the Coalition's use of offensive air power were highly successful. The interdiction effort was successful in many respects. The Coalition organized effectively to use its deep strike capabilities to carry out a rapid and effective pattern of focus strategic bombing where planning was sufficiently well coupled to intelligence and meaningful strategic objectives so that such strikes achieved the major military objectives that the planner set. At the same time, targeting, force allocation, and precision kill capabilities had advanced to the point where interdiction bombing and strikes were far more lethal and strategically useful than in previous conflicts. Israel has given the development of focus attack and interdiction capabilities high priority since the 1973 war. It has advanced conventional bombing or "soft strike" capabilities and has the technology, tactics, and training to conduct similar operations in its theater of operations. Syria has yet to demonstrate anything approaching modern doctrine, tactics, and training for using its strike and attack aircraft, although it has some effective attack helicopter units. Jordan has developed a more sophisticated doctrine, but lacks virtually every technical capability needed for advanced attack and interdiction missions. Egypt has improved the capability of its Western equipped fighter-ground attack and F-16 units, but has poor overall doctrine and training for force-wide air attack and interdiction missions. It also seems to lack advanced targeting and striking planning techniques, and has a force mix filled with many low capability Soviet-bloc and European aircraft and weapons.

- *Expansion of the battle field: "deep strike":* As part of its effort to offset the Warsaw Pact's superiority, US tactics and technology emphasized using AirLand battle capabilities to extend the battlefield far beyond the immediate forward "edge" of the battle area (FEBA). The Coalition exploited the resulting mix of targeting capability, improved air strike capabilities, and land force capabilities in ways that played an important role in the attrition of Iraqi ground forces during the air phase of the war, and which helped the Coalition break through Iraqi defenses and exploit the breakthrough. This achievement is particularly striking in view of the fact that the US was not yet ready to employ some "deep strike" targeting technologies and precision strike systems designed to fight the Warsaw Pact that were still in development. Israel has long emphasized long range conventional air strikes or "soft-strike" capabilities and should be able to penetrate Syrian and Jordanian air defenses early in the air war. Syria has done little to refine its capabilities beyond developing the ability to fire missiles at area targets. It has not exploited its acquisition of Su–24 strike aircraft by providing effective training and doctrine. Jordan lacks modern strike aircraft and weapons. Egypt has some capability to use rockets against targets of moderate depth, and modern dual-capable aircraft, but has concentrated its modern aircraft in air defense units and does not seem to have developed an effective doctrine—and suitable targeting and battle management capabilities—for "deep strike" missions.

- *Technological superiority in many critical areas of weaponry:* The Coalition scarcely had a monopoly on effective weapons, but it had a critical "edge" in key weapons like tanks, other armored fighting vehicles, artillery systems, long range strike systems, attack aircraft, air defense aircraft, surface-to-air missiles, space, attack helicopters, naval systems, sensors, battle management, and a host of other areas. As has been discussed in Chapter 1, this superiority went far beyond the technical "edge" revealed by "weapon on weapon" comparisons. Coalition forces exploited technology in "systems" that integrated weapons into other aspects of force capability and into the overall force structures of the US, Britain, France, and the Saudi air force to a far greater degree than Iraq and most military forces in Third World states. Israel has a similar overall mix of technological superiority, while Syria and Jordan lack anything approaching a broad base of high technology systems, and Egyptian forces are split between forces with modern US equipment and forces with obsolete and/or worn Soviet-bloc and European supplied equipment.

- *Integration of precision guided weapons into tactics and force structures:* The Coalition exploited a decisive US technical "edge" in the ability to use precision guided weapons against Iraq. US forces had far more realistic training in using such weapons, and the US had the ability to link their employment to far superior reconnaissance and targeting capability. Israel has capabilities similar to those of the US. With the exception of a few units that use anti-tank guided missiles, Syrian capabilities to use precision guided weapons and related targeting and battle management systems are very poor. Jordanian capabilities are severely limited by a lack of equipment and sophisticated training aids. Egypt has a few well trained units, but most elements of all four Egyptian services are not trained effectively to use such weapons—particularly in complex, combined, and joint operations.

- *Realistic combat training and use of technology and simulation:* During the Gulf War, the US and Britain used training methods based on realistic combined arms and AirLand training, large scale training, and adversary training. These efforts were far superior to previous methods and were coupled to a far more realistic and demanding system for ensuring the readiness of the forces involved. Equally important, they emphasized the need for the kinds of additional training that allowed US forces to adapt to the special desert warfare conditions of Desert Storm. Israel has fully adopted this emphasis on realistic training and has adapted US techniques and systems for simulation using lower cost technology plus innovations of its own. Syrian units differ sharply in training quality, and even the most highly trained Syrian units use obsolete training methods with inadequate technical support. Jordan trains relatively well, but lacks the resources and organization for realistic aggressor training and simulation. Egypt has some units with high training levels, and some Egyptian units perform well in joint exercises with the US. Most Egyptian forces in all four Egyptian military services, however, have low levels of training with poor technical aid and support, and a lack of realistic aggressor training.

- *Emphasis on forward leadership and delegation:* During the Gulf War, virtually all of the successful Coalition forces were aggressively led from the front. In contrast, Iraqi forces were often led from the rear and the officers in forward units were sharply constrained in terms of delegation of authority, overall information on the battlefield situation, and the ability to take independent action. The performance of the forces in the Arab "ring states" is constrained by the same problems. Jordanian commanders, as well as the best Egyptian and Syrian commanders, lead from the front. Israel, however, has made this a force-wide doctrine and long demonstrated its excellence in this area of operations. Delegation of command authority is a problem in the Jordanian army and in all of the Egyptian and Syrian services. The lack of emphasis on command initiative is compounded by a lack of realistic force-wide exercise training.

- *Heavy reliance on NCOs and enlisted personnel:* There was nothing new about the heavy reliance that Western forces placed on the technical skills, leadership quality, and initiative of non-commissioned officers (NCOs) and experienced enlisted personnel. This is a reliance which is common to virtually every Western military force, and which has given them a major advantage over Soviet and those Third World forces which do not give the same authority and expertise to NCOs and career enlisted personnel. However, better educated, trained, and experienced NCOs and enlisted personnel were critical to the British, French, and US ability to exploit technology and sustain high tempo operations. Syria has done a poor job of developing well trained and professional NCOs and technicians, and has generally done a poor job of training junior officers and forcing them to work closely with enlisted men in training and technical tasks. Egyptian manpower management and training policies have been erratic. There are some good Egyptian units, but in broad terms, Egyptian NCO, technician, and junior officer cadres are poorly paid and their training and technical level is significantly lower relative to Israel than it was during 1971–1974. Jordan is the only Arab state which has consistently emphasized the development of a cadre of high quality NCOs and technical personnel, and Jordan has lacked the funds and equipment to approach Israel's recent levels of training and proficiency.
- *High degree of overall readiness:* Military readiness is a difficult term to define since it involves so many aspects of force capability. Western forces entered the Gulf War, however, with two great advantages. The first was far more realistic standards for measuring readiness and ensuring proper reporting. The second was adequate funding over a sustained period of time. Israel emphasizes overall readiness while its neighbors tend to emphasize force size or major weapons procurement. Syria has not attempted to develop high overall standards of readiness since the mid-1980s. Jordan used to emphasize readiness over force size, but can no longer afford high overall force readiness. Egypt maintains higher readiness standards for its best US equipped units, but has low force-wide readiness.

The Limits of Israel's Qualitative "Edge"

At the same time, the importance of Israel's qualitative advantages should not be exaggerated. This is not simply a matter of the potential problems in the IDF discussed earlier. There also are inherent limits in the IDF's present structure. It may prove less decisive in dealing with unconventional warfare, politically dominated low intensity and guerrilla conflicts, urban warfare, and other specialized types of conflict. There is also little reason to assume that an Arab-Israeli conflict is likely to be a repetition of the Gulf War. The terrain is different and generally less open; urban and mountain warfare are very real possibilities. Israel has far less strategic depth and room for maneuver than the UN Coalition. The Arab states are more aware of many of their own weaknesses and are unlikely to attack under the conditions where they are most vulnerable.

Most important, Israel has special vulnerabilities and weaknesses of its own. The limits to Israeli military capabilities may be summarized as follows:

- *Sudden or surprise attack:* Israel is dependent on strategic warning, timely decision-making, and effective mobilization and redeployment for much of its military effectiveness. Egypt and Syria achieved a level of strategic and military surprise during their initial attacks in October, 1973 that confronted Israel with its most serious threat of defeat to date and remains one of the most significant achievements in modern warfare. Some key lessons that Arab states are likely to draw from both the October War and Desert Storm are the potential advantage of sudden and decisive action and the potential value of exploiting the problems Israel faces in mobilizing and deploying its forces. Any attack that succeeds in its initial objectives before Israel can mobilize gives an Arab attacker significant advantages.[9]

- *Saturation:* There is no way to determine the point at which mass, or force quantity, overcomes superior effectiveness, or force quality—historically, efforts to emphasize mass have been far less successful than military experts predicted at the time. Even the best force, however, reaches the point where it cannot maintain its "edge" in C^{4}I/battle management, air combat, or maneuver warfare in the face of superior numbers or multiple threats. Further, saturation may produce a sudden catalytic collapse of effectiveness, rather than a gradual degeneration from which the Israeli Defense Forces could recover.

- *Taking casualties:* War fighting is not measured simply in terms of whether a given side can win a battle or conflict, but of how well it can absorb the damage inflicted upon it. Israel is highly sensitive to casualties and losses. This sensitivity may limit its operational flexibility in taking risks and in sustaining some kinds of combat if casualties become serious relative to the apparent value of the immediate objective.

- *Inflicting casualties:* Israel's dependence on world opinion and outside support means it must increasingly plan to fight at least low and mid-intensity conflicts in ways that limit enemy casualties and collateral damage to its opponents and show that Israel is actively attempting to fight a "humanitarian" style of combat.

- *Low intensity combat:* Israel has had more recent practical experience in low intensity conflict than the US, but it cannot exploit most of its technical advantage in such combat—because low intensity wars are largely fought against people, not things. Low intensity wars are also highly political. The battle for domestic Israeli, Palestinian civilian, and Western public opinion is as much a condition of victory as killing the enemy. The outcome of such a battle will be highly dependent on the specific political conditions under which it is fought, rather than Israeli capabilities.

- *Hostage taking and terrorism:* Like low intensity warfare, hostage-taking and terrorism present the problem that the IDF cannot exploit their conventional strengths and must fight a low level battle primarily on the basis of infantry combat. HUMINT is more important than conventional military intelligence, and much of the fight against terrorism may take place in urban or heavily populated areas.

- *Urban and built-up area warfare:* Israeli military forces have never come fully to grips with the problem of urban warfare. They did not perform particularly well in urban warfare in Egypt and Lebanon, and have far fewer technical advantages in fighting in populated areas. Western forces are not trained or equipped to deal with sustained urban warfare in populated areas in regional combat—particularly when the fighting may affect large civilian populations on friendly soil.

- *Extended conflict and occupation warfare:* Not all wars can be quickly terminated, and many forms of warfare—particularly those involving peacekeeping and peace enforcement—require prolonged military occupations. Israel faces severe economic problems in fighting any war or major confrontation that forces mobilization for more than a few weeks and has nothing to gain from prolonged military occupation of enemy territory. It also faces major risks in any conflict where it would have to attempt to attack into Egypt or Syria. Both nations have defensive capabilities that are much better than their offensive capabilities, and Syria demonstrated the risks Israel faces in an extended campaign during the 1982 fighting in Lebanon.

- *Weapons of mass destruction:* The UN Coalition emerged from Desert Storm claiming a victory over Iraq in destroying its weapons of mass destruction that, in fact, it never achieved. It had firmly identified only 2 of 21 major Iraqi nuclear facilities before the war, struck only 8 by the time the war ended, did not properly characterize the functions of more than half the facilities it struck, and never completed effective BDA. Coalition strikes on Iraqi chemical facilities left 150,000 chemical munitions intact—most of which suffered far more from design defects than Coalition attacks. Iraq's biological warfare capabilities seemed to have been evacuated and remain largely intact. The Coalition "Scud Hunt" failed and never produced a confirmed kill. It is far from clear that Israel has any better ability to target and destroy Syrian and Egyptian chemical and biological warfare facilities and capabilities, and it has only limited ability to defend effectively against Syrian missiles or less conventional delivery means.

- *Dependence on foreign assistance and technology transfer:* Israeli dependence on US military and economic assistance and technology transfer constitutes a strength in many ways. US military assistance and technology transfers have played a key role in giving Israel its present "edge" and in allowing Israel to simultaneously develop its economy and maintain strong military forces. Israel's ties to the US also provide an intangible security guarantee that no Arab state can ignore. While the US has no formal commitment to Israel's security, the 1973 war showed that the US will resupply Israel in an emergency, and the process of American diplomacy has focused on Israel's security virtually since the existence of Israel as a state. It is doubtful that the US would ever allow Israel's naval and air lines of communication to be threatened or allow any combination of Arab navies to dominate Israeli waters. It is also doubtful that the US would stand by if Israel faced an existential threat as the result of either conventional defeat or attacks with weapons of mass destruction. At the same time, dependence is dependence. Aid levels can vary and the need to pay close attention to US views and public opinion does impose significant constraints on Israel's possible tactics and levels of escalation.
- *The inability to win an ultimate grand strategic victory:* Israel faces the problem that no military victory can—in itself—bring it security. Israel can—and has—used military force to defeat Arab forces and occupy Arab territory. It has the nuclear capability to threaten and destroy the existence of given regimes. As all of the Arab-Israeli wars have shown, however, each military victory breeds new threats and new problems. As Israel's 1982 invasion of Lebanon has shown, victory and occupation cannot force lasting new political structures on even a weak and divided Arab state. The Intifada has shown that Israel cannot ignore the political costs of even decisive military victory in the territory it already occupies. No amount of military superiority can compensate for one central strategic reality that affects all the trends in the Arab-Israeli balance: Only a mix of peace supported by a stable balance of deterrence—Sun Tsu's "perfect victory" of winning without fighting and not Clausewitz's strategy of destroying enemy forces—can bring Israel lasting security.

5

POSSIBLE WAR FIGHTING OUTCOMES: A DYNAMIC NET ASSESSMENT

An understanding of the quantitative and qualitative factors that shape the military balance can provide considerable insight into the factors that must be considered in moving from peace to arms control, or the possible war fighting consequences if peace fails. At the same time, no assessment of total national military strength—regardless of the mix of quantitative strength and qualitative factors used in the assessment—can accurately measure the military balance, describe its impact on the peace process, or predict the nature and outcome of future wars.

Aggression, deterrence, and defense are not products of how leaders and nations calculate total national force strengths. They are products of different calculations about the outcome of war fighting in given contingencies. An analysis of contingency capabilities, however, presents serious analytic problems of its own. Crisis and war fighting behavior has rarely been predictable.

While foreign policy analysts sometimes talk about the end of the Cold War as having created new sources of conflict, the reality is very different. Roughly 20 to 30 low intensity civil wars and international conflicts have gone on every day since the end of World War II. The end of the Cold War did not create a "new world disorder." All it did was remove the West's central focus on the East-West conflict and expose an underlying reality that was already there.

Such conflicts also are not just endemic to the Middle East. Some 900 conflicts took place between 1945 and 1988, ranging from low level civil wars to major combat.[1] A total of 105 states intervened a total of 131 times in other states and territories. At least 639 military interventions were serious enough to involve clashes between armed forces. A total of 269 conflicts escalated to the point where they had some international and military significance.

While the Middle East is often thought of as a key source of conflict, these clashes and conflicts were spread throughout the world. There were 8 in the Caribbean, 15 in Central America, 14 in South America, 12 in Europe, 13 in West Africa, 18 in Central Africa, 11 in the Horn of Africa, 20 in East Africa, 14 in Southern Africa, 15 in North Africa, 14 in the Persian Gulf, 27 in the Arab-Israeli confrontation states and the Levant, 13 in southern Arabia, four in Southwest Asia, 17 in East Asia, 20 in South Asia, 26 in Southeast Asia, and three in Oceania.[2] It is impossible to accurately estimate the total deaths that these wars caused— from direct casualties, famine, and disease—but we are talking at least 10 million lives.

It is equally important to note that most of these wars and crises occurred with only limited warning and took on a form that at least one of the nations involved never intended or predicted. They involved very different kinds of forces and levels of intensity, and the opponents often had very different types of forces and technology. The pattern of the conflicts within given nations and subregions has also varied sharply over time, and low level conflicts have sometimes suddenly escalated into major struggles.

Ironically, two of the most publicized wars—Vietnam and Afghanistan—were decisively lost by high technology regular modern forces fighting against relatively primitive forces organized more for guerrilla combat than regular war. Vietnam and Afghanistan were also lost by sides that spent most of each war reporting that they had won every battle. We need to remember this when we talk about the role of new technologies in combat and the "revolution in military affairs."

Further, the outcome of such wars has had little to do with prewar force ratios and there has been little correlation between the use of modern technology and the number of casualties in a conflict. The outcome of war has been determined more by skill than size. While there have been some exceptions, conflicts involving prolonged infantry combat and guerrilla warfare have tended to be far more bloody than direct conflicts between states which both employ high technology forces. Similarly, "static" wars of attrition between ground forces that have been fought under tactical conditions that prevented decisive battles have tended to be far more bloody than quick and decisive wars of maneuver.

Sun Tsu warned nearly 2,500 years ago, "there never has been a protracted war from which a country has benefited," and this fact is reflected in part by Arab-Israeli conflicts. The 1948 war was a prolonged infantry conflict, and was the most costly of all the Arab-Israel conflicts. The 1982 war involved high levels of military technology, but most Israeli and Syrian losses took place after Israel had achieved its initial objectives in a war of maneuver and the conflict had bogged down in a prolonged slow moving effort to occupy parts of Lebanon. In contrast, high technology conflicts like the Gulf War and October War have tended to be quick and decisive and to produce far fewer casualties. Table 5.1 shows the size of these casualties and illustrates the lack of any predictable outcome from given wars and prewar force ratios.

This pattern too could easily change in future Arab-Israeli conflicts. There have been two major restraints on the use of high technology in most conflicts since the end of World War II which may not apply in the future. The first is that states have made only very limited use of weapons of mass destruction. The second is that most high technology conflicts have not involved major attacks on non-mili-

TABLE 5.1 Losses in the Arab-Israeli Wars: 1948–1982—Part One

A. 1948–1973 Wars

	1948		1956		1967	
	Arab	Israel	Arab[a]	Israel	Arab	Israel[b]
Killed	4,800	4,500	1,000	189–210	4,296	750–983
Wounded	25,000	15,000	4,000	899	6,121	4,517
Total	40,000	21,000	5,000	1,088–1,109	10,417	5,267–5,500

Equipment Losses

Main Battle Tanks[c]	–	–	30	40	965–1,000	200–394
Aircraft	–	– 215–390	15–20	444–500	40
Combat Vessels	–	–	2	0 ?	0

B. Land, Air, and Naval Losses: 1973 War

	Israel	Total Arab	Egypt	Syria	Jordan	Iraq	Other Arab
Casualties							
Killed	2,838	8,528	5,000	3,100–3,500	28	218–260	100
Wounded	8,800	19,549	12,000	6,000	49	600	300
Prisoners/Missing	508	8,551	8,031	370–500 500	–	20	?
Equipment Losses							
Main Battle Tanks[d]	400–840	2,554	1,100	1,200	54	100–200	?
Other Armor	400	850+	450	400	–	?	?
Artillery Weapons	?	550+	300	250	–	?	?
SAM Batteries	–	47	44	3	–	–	?
Aircraft	102–103	392	223	118	–	21	30
Helicopters	6	55	42	13	–	?	?
Naval Vessels	1	15	10	5	–	–	–

Losses in the Arab-Israeli Wars: 1948–1982—Part Two

C. Losses in the 1982 War

	Israel	Total Arab	Syria	PLO
Killed	368	3,000	1,000	2,000
Wounded	2,383	6,000	3,000	3,000
Total	2,751	11,000	4,000	7,000
Prisoners of War	7	–	250	–
Tanks, OAFVs, and Trucks	–	–	–	2,600[e]
Tanks	150	–	350–400	–
OAFVs	175	–	350–400	–

TABLE 5.1   *(Continued)*

	Israel	Total Arab	Syria	PLO
Artillery Weapons	–	–	–	1,700[e]
Aircraft	2	92	92	0
Helicopters	3	–	?	0
Munitions (Tons)	–	–	–	6,000[e]

[a]Includes only Egyptian casualties in fighting with Israel. Equipment losses include total Egyptian losses, including those to France and the United Kingdom.

[b]Prisoner of war and missing data are too unreliable to be included.

[c]Lower end of range often reflects losses that could not be returned to combat by the end of war. Higher end shows "kills" that put tank temporarily out of combat.

[d]Lower end of range often reflects losses that could not be returned to combat by the end of war. Higher end shows "kills" that put tank temporarily out of combat.

[e]Totals are equipment and munitions captured by Israel. No total is available for combat losses.

Sources: Estimates for 1948–1973 losses differ widely from source to source, which is the reason for not comparing all data in the same section of the table. The figures shown are adapted from Trevor Dupuy, *Elusive Victory,* New York, Harper and Row, 1978; Chaim Herzog, *The Arab-Israel Wars,* New York, Random House, 1982; and from various editions of the *Born in Battle Series,* Tel Aviv, Eshel Drammit. The estimates for 1982 are drawn from Anthony H. Cordesman, *The Lessons of Modern War, Volume I,* Boulder, Westview, 1990, pp. 152–153; data provided by the IDF spokesman and Embassy of Lebanon; and Yezid Sayigh, "Israel's Military Performance in Lebanon, June, 1982," *Journal of Palestine Studies,* Vol. 13, No. 1 (Fall 1983).

tary targets in population centers or national populations. As Iraq's use of gas warfare has demonstrated, however, nations are capable of using this technology with far less discrimination.

In short, such discussions can illustrate potential war fighting capability, but cannot predict the point at which current tensions will explode into a future conflict. No amount of static analysis, modeling, or war gaming can reliably estimate the outcome of conflicts between forces that have not fought a major conflict since 1973 or 1982. Their composition, training, C^{4}I/BM systems, weapons and technology, and objectives have changed so much in character since that time that many aspects of Arab and Israeli war fighting capabilities are uncertain.

No one can predict whether the dominant weapon will be the tank or the rifle, the chemical weapon or the car bomb. No one can predict timing, duration, or intensity of existing wars or new ones. War simply is not predictable in terms of its timing, duration, intensity, and cost. This is a truth that far too many political leaders and military planners ignore. History is proof of Santayana's warning that those who forget the past will be condemned to repeat it.

These analytic problems are compounded by the fact that it is not possible to translate many of the negative trends in the balance into a particular contingency based on clear military incentives to fight a given type of conflict. The fact that the overall trends in the Arab-Israeli balance and the success of the peace process currently favor deterrence has an ironic side effect. If war does occur, it may be the result of miscalculation or a serious failure in crisis management. This can lead to highly unpredictable patterns of conflict and escalation.

At the same time, neither the current state of the military balance nor the peace process provides any assurance that more predictable forms of war will not occur. It is possible to make rough subjective estimates of the potential outcome of a range of conflicts that illustrate the current and near term risks in the balance, as well as possible considerations for force planning. While such estimates are scarcely a means of predicting the future, they do highlight the importance of key trends in the balance and illustrate how the character of a future war could differ from a past conflict. They also help illustrate the fact that wars involving Israeli and Palestinian forces, or Israel and different combinations of the Arab ring states, have very different probabilities and are likely to have very different outcomes.

6

CASE ONE: THE PEACE PROCESS FAILS AND A NEW "INTIFADA" TAKES PLACE

Despite the progress in the peace process, it is still possible that the peace negotiations will fail, and that Israelis and the Palestinians will become locked in a new political and military struggle for power. Alternatively, it is possible that the peace process can proceed in a way in which Israel continues to deal with Arafat and/or the Palestinian Authority or some other Palestinian entity that supports the peace process, but extremist elements within the Palestinian community will continue to attack and murder pro-peace Palestinians and Israelis and the peace process.

It is equally possible that Israeli opposition to the peace process, and anti-government extremism, may grow in response to the transfer of territory in the West Bank and negotiations over the Golan, Jerusalem, and the future of the settlements.

At best, "peace" will involve new clashes and incidents of terrorism; it will be "peace with violence." More probably, there will be a long transition from "cold war" to "cold peace," and lingering uncertainty as to whether a "cold peace" will ever become a "warm" one. At worst, the situation may degenerate into a low to mid-intensity conflict between Israel and the Palestinians in which IDF security forces confront a new popular uprising (Intifada) or large scale Palestinian guerrilla warfare.

Normal measures of the conventional military balance have only limited meaning under such conditions. Conflicts in Afghanistan, Cambodia, Kashmir, Lebanon, Northern Ireland, the Sudan, Sri Lanka, Vietnam, and the Western Sahara have shown that long, bloody guerrilla wars and low level conflicts can be fought by small, poorly equipped extremist elements even when they face massively superior conventional armies. Even highly trained and well equipped Israeli forces never entirely succeeded in enforcing security during the Intifada, just as similarly trained and equipped British forces were never able to halt the violence in Northern Ireland.

Many low intensity wars have occurred where the guerrillas lacked broad popular support. In most cases, the military or paramilitary capabilities of guerrilla forces evolve during the conflict, adapting and re-adapting to the military and internal security techniques used to suppress them. Thus, the balance at the beginning of such a conflict is little indication of the balance that will exist at its end. The paramilitary and guerrilla organizations that exist at the start of such conflicts normally change radically in leadership, tactics, and equipment under the pressure of events.

Palestinian Paramilitary Groups

There are a wide range of Palestinian military and paramilitary forces. These forces include different factions with shifting alignments, almost all of which make grandiose claims about their active manpower, their combat equipment, and the size of their combat formations.[1]

Many of these are pro-peace forces, including some 16,500 to 18,000 police officers and security personnel controlled by the Palestinian Authority. In mid-1995, these forces included 7,000 men in the Public Security Force, 4,000 men in the Civil Police, 2,500 men in the Preventive Security Force, plus additional men in the Presidential Security, Military Intelligence, Coastal Police, and Civil Defense forces. Many of these personnel have been drawn from the Palestine National Liberation Army (PNLA).

Additional pro-Palestinian Authority forces include the security, military, and paramilitary elements of Fatah, Palestine Liberation Front (PLF), Arab Liberation Front (ALF), Popular Front for the Liberation of Palestine (PFLP), Democratic Front for the Liberation of Palestine (DFLP), and Palestine Popular Struggle Front (PPSF). Some forces like the Palestine National Liberation Army (PNLA) still exist as cadres, but much of their manpower has been incorporated in the forces of the Palestinian Authority.

Most of the pro–Palestinian Authority/pro-peace forces outside Gaza and Jericho have lost much of their strength and income since the Gulf War. Syria and the Lebanese Army partially disarmed many of the pro-PLO Palestinian factions in Lebanon in 1991 and took away their heavier arms like tanks, APCs, and artillery—although Syria and the Lebanese army left pro-Syrian factions like the PFLP-GC (General Command) alone. The Lebanese army has continued these efforts since 1991 and conducted new operations against the Fatah Revolutionary Council in 1994. Syria and Iraq maintain tight control over the operations and weapons of all Palestinian forces based on their territory.

Some Palestinian factions within the PLO, and most factions outside the PLO, oppose the peace process. At least ten organizations with some kind of military, paramilitary, or terrorist element have rejected the peace process and declared themselves part of the "opposition front" at a meeting in Damascus in September, 1992. While any list of the organizations that currently oppose the peace process tends to change with time, in 1996 this list included the Hamas-Islamic Resistance, elements of the Palestine Popular Struggle Front (PPSF), the Palestinian Islamic Jihad (PIJ), the Revolutionary Communist Party, DFLP, elements of the People's Liberation Front (PLF), al-Saiqa, and Fatah-Intifada. Other Palestinian forces not aligned with the PLO include forces belonging to the Fatah dissidents, Fatah Revolutionary Council/Abu Nidal Organization (FRC/ANO), Fatah Intifada (Abu Musa), Palestine Liberation Army (PLA) in Syria, PFLP-GC (General Command), and PFLP-SC (Special Command). Some of these forces are based in and under the direct control of Syria.

The current military strength of these various factions is difficult to estimate. Table 6.1 and Figure 6.1 provide a rough estimate of their manpower strength. Even where such units have significant manpower strength, however, they have little conventional military strength and cannot use most of the medium and heavy weapons (if any) they possess. Their capabilities are limited to terrorism, unconventional warfare, and low intensity combat in built-up areas and mountainous terrain. Figure 6.2 also shows that most such radical Palestinian forces have recently had low levels of activity of any kind. In fact, many such forces are now little more than political tools or ideological sinecures.[2]

Further, even if current estimates of such factions are reliable, they are only valuable as rough indicators of the kind of forces that might become involved in a future conflict. The key issue shaping this aspect of the Arab-Israeli military balance is not the current size and activity of Palestinian military and paramilitary forces. It is rather the future actions of various extremist groups that use terrorism and random violence, and the new forces that might emerge as a result of a breakdown of the peace process.

The Role of Hamas and the Islamic Jihad

There are, however, two Palestinian organizations that are particularly active in attacks on Israelis and pro-peace Palestinians and whose actions constitute a continuing threat to the peace process. Hamas and the Islamic Jihad continue to show that lightly armed insurgents inside the West Bank, Gaza, and Israel can conduct acts of terrorism and extremism and can strike successfully against their fellow Palestinians and the West, as well as Israel. While they have not yet been able to block the peace process, they have shown they can influence both its pace and Israeli support for the process.

A total of 140 Israeli civilians and soldiers were killed between the signing of the Declaration of Principles between Israel and the PLO on September 13, 1993, and September 13, 1995. These deaths included 27 civilians and soldiers in Judea, Samaria, and the Gaza Strip, and 62 civilians and 26 soldiers within the Green Line. Palestinian extremist groups killed a total of 73 Israeli soldiers during 1994 and wounded more than 100 additional Israelis—a slightly higher total than in 1993. At least 20 additional Palestinians were killed, and well over 100 were wounded. Hamas and Islamic Jihad were the source of virtually all of this violence.

TABLE 6.1   Military and Paramilitary Strength of Key Palestinian Factions
and the Hizbollah

PLO/Palestinian Authority
- 18,000 security and paramilitary pro-PLO forces enforcing security in Gaza and Jericho, including public security (7,000+), civil police (4,000+), preventive security (2,500+), general intelligence (3,000+), presidential security, military intelligence, coastal police, civil defense, and other. (45 APC, with more coming.) Small arms.
- Palestinian National Liberation Army (PNLA)/Al Fatah—5,000–8,000 active and semi-active reserves that make up main pro-Arafat force, based in Algeria, Egypt, Lebanon, Libya, and Jordan.
- Palestine Liberation Front (PLF)/Abu Abbas Faction—300–400 men led by Al-Abbas, based in Iraq.
- Arab Liberation Front (ALF)—300 men.
- Palestine National Salvation Front (PNSF)—1,000 man anti-Arafat, pro-Syrian force led by Khalid al-Fahum, based in Syria and Lebanon.
- Democratic Front for the Liberation of Palestine (DFLP)—400–600 men led by Naif Hawatmeh, which claims eight battalions and is based in Syria, Lebanon, and elsewhere.
- Popular Front for the Liberation of Palestine (PFLP)—800 men led by George Habash, based in Syria, Lebanon, West Bank, and Gaza.
- Palestine Popular Struggle Front (PPSF)—200–700 men led by Samir Ghawsha and Bahjat Abu Gharbiyah, based in Syria.
- Fatah Intifada—400 men led by Said Musa Muragha (Abu Musa).
- Popular Front for the Liberation of Palestine–General Command (PFLP-GC)—600 men led by Ahmad Jibril, based in Syria, Lebanon, and elsewhere.
- As-Saiqa—100–1,000 men in pro-Syrian force under Issam al-Qadi, based in Syria.

Anti-PLO
- Palestinian Islamic Jihad (PIJ)—250–350 men in various factions, led by Asad Bayud al-Tamimi, Fathi Shekaki, Ibrahim Odeh, Ahmad Muhana, and others.
- Hamas—military wing of about 300 men, based in the West Bank and Gaza.
- Hizbollah (Party of God)—about 3,000 men, Shi'ite fundamentalist, APCs, artillery, MRLs, ATGMs, rocket launchers, AA guns, SA-7s.
- SAIQA—led by Issam al-Khadi, 1,000 men, based in Syria.
- Fatah Revolutionary Council (FRC)/Abu Nidal Organization (ANO)—300 men led by Abu Nidal (Sabri al-Bana), based in Lebanon, Syria, and Iraq.
- Fatah Revolutionary Council (FRC)—Emergency Command (secessionists from Abu Nidal) with 150–200 men.
- Popular Front for the Liberation of Palestine–Special Command (PFLP-SC)—100 men led by Abu Muhammad (Salim Abu Salem).
- Palestine Liberation Army (PLA)—4,500 men, based in Syria.
- Black September 13—24 to 72 men led by Munir Makdah.
- Popular Front for the Liberation of Palestine–Special Command (Abu Muhammad) with 100 men.
- al-Fatah pro-Jordanian elements with 300 men.
- Palestine Revolutionary Army (PRA)—24 to 48 men, based in South Lebanon.

Source: Adapted from US Department of State, "Patterns of Global Terrorism, 1994," Washington, GPO, April, 1995, pp. 13–18, 20–69; IISS, *Military Balance, 1995–1996,* pp. 127, 135; and the Jaffee Center for Strategic Studies, *The Military Balance in the Middle East, 1993–1994,* pp. 393–402. Note that data for the IISS are taken from the country chapters. The JCSS data are taken from the summary tables on pages 479–509.

FIGURE 6.1   Anti-Peace Palestinian Armed Forces

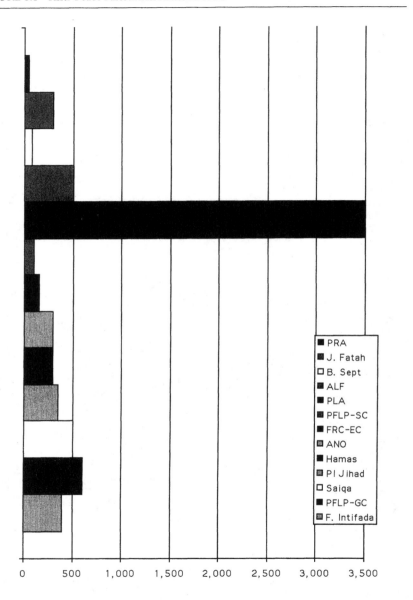

FIGURE 6.2   Arab-Israeli Casualties of Non-State Low Level Violence: 1994

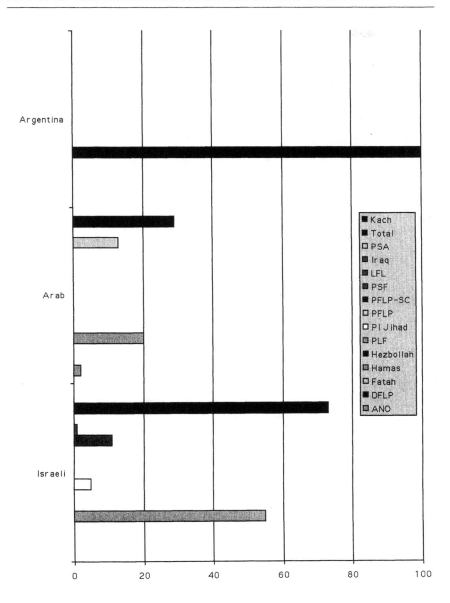

Hamas

The Hamas organization is the most politically powerful of these two organizations. Hamas is both an acronym for "Harakat Al-Muqawwama Al-Islamia"—Islamic Resistance Movement—and a word meaning zeal. Hamas has several other names, including the Islamic Stream ("Al-Tiar Al-Islami"), or the Islamic Trend ("Al-Athja Al-Islami"). Hamas is a radical Islamic fundamentalist organization which has stated that its highest priority is a Jihad (holy war) for the liberation of Palestine and the establishment of an Islamic Palestine "from the Mediterranean Sea to the Jordan River." Hamas has stated that the transition to the stage of Jihad "for the liberation of all of Palestine" is a personal religious duty incumbent upon every Muslim, and rejects any political arrangement that would relinquish any part of Palestine. Its central goal is the establishment of an Islamic state in all of Palestine.

Hamas first became active during the early stages of the Intifada. It emerged out of the religious-social "Al-Majama Al-Islami" (Moslem Brotherhood) association in the Gaza District. Many senior members of "Al-Majama" helped form Hamas, and used the existing infrastructure Al-Majama as a basis for semi-covert activity once the Intifada began. Hamas then expanded its activity into the West Bank and at least some cells in Israel proper, becoming the dominant Islamic fundamentalist organization in the occupied territories.

Hamas has changed its attitude toward Iran over time. Initially, it largely ignored or rejected the Iranian revolution as Shi'ite—although a few leaders of Al-Majama quoted leading Iranian revolutionaries—and focused almost exclusively on Sunni groups and issues. It also took a relatively ambiguous position on the Gulf War because of its dependence on rich Gulf donors and its rivalry with the PLO. Iran actively began to court Hamas after the Gulf War, and meetings took place between a Hamas delegation and Iran's foreign minister in October, 1992. While it is unclear just how much Iranian support Hamas actually obtained, Hamas did set up a small office in Iran and its leaders began to visit there regularly. The leaders of Hamas also began to meet regularly with the leaders of the Hizbollah in Lebanon. Iran seems to have begun to provide Hamas with up to several million dollars a year from 1993 onward, and some Israeli estimates go as high as $20 to $30 million. However, it is doubtful that Iran has provided large amounts of arms and military training. It is also doubtful that there is extensive cooperation between Hamas and Hizbollah in training or operations.[3]

Hamas's operation in Gaza and the West Bank currently consists of a combination of regional and functional organizations. It has several identical, parallel frameworks which operate in each region. Hamas has a well organized fund-raising apparatus in Gaza, the West Bank, and Jordan, as well as outside the region. It has a framework called "Dawa," literally "call" or "outreach," which engages in recruitment, distribution of funds, and appointments. It has another framework called security ("Amn"), which gathered information on suspected collaborators during the Intifada. This information was passed on to "shock committees," which interrogated and sometimes killed suspects. Amn is now a key element in Hamas's rivalry with the Palestinian Authority and in intelligence gathering operations.

The paramilitary elements of Hamas have played a major role in violent fundamentalist subversion and radical terrorist operations against both Israelis and Arabs. Its "shock troops" ("Al-Suad Al-Ramaya"—the "throwing arm") were responsible for popular violence during the Intifada, and still play a role in violent opposition to the peace process. Hamas also has two paramilitary organizations for more organized forms of violence. The first is the Palestinian Holy Fighters ("Al-Majahidoun Al-Falestinioun")—a military apparatus which includes the "Iz al-Din al Qassam Brigades." The second is the Security Section ("Jehaz Amn").

According to Israeli government sources, the "Al-Majihadoun Al-Falestinioun" was established by Sheik Ahmed Yassin in 1982. It procured arms and began to plan an armed struggle against both Palestinian rivals and Israel. This activity was uncovered in 1984, and Yassin was sentenced to 13 years in prison but was released shortly afterward as part of the Jibril prisoner exchange (May, 1985). Yassin then resumed his effort to set up a military apparatus. He began by focusing on the struggle against "heretics" and collaborators, in accordance with the view of the Muslim Brotherhood that Jihad should come only after the purging of rivals from within. At the same time, he prepared a military infrastructure and stockpiled weapons for war against Israel. Shortly before the outbreak of the Intifada, operatives were recruited to carry out the military Jihad and regular terrorist attacks. The new military apparatus carried out a large number of attacks of various kinds, including bombs and gunfire, mostly in the northern part of the Gaza District.

The Security Section ("Jehaz Amn") of Hamas was established in early 1983. Its function was to conduct surveillance of suspected collaborators and other Palestinians who acted in a manner which ran counter to the principles of Islam (drug dealers, sellers of pornography, etc.). In early 1987, it began to set up hit squads, known as "MAJD"—an Arabic acronym for "Majmu'at Jihad wa-Dawa"—Holy War and Sermonizing Group)—which became the operational arm of the Security Section. Its purpose was to kill "heretics" and collaborators. Yassin instructed the leaders of these sections that that they must kill anyone who admitted under interrogation to being a collaborator and reinforced this instruction with a religious ruling.

After the outbreak of the Intifada, Hamas began to organize military action against Israeli targets as well. The "MAJD" units then became part of the "Al-Majahadoun" network. At the same time, the military apparatus of Hamas underwent several changes as a result of preventive measures and exposure by the Israeli forces following major terrorist attacks. The military apparatus formed the "Iz al-Din al Qassam" Squads or "Brigades," which have been responsible for most of the serious attacks carried out by Hamas since January 1, 1992. These squads were formed out of dozens of proven personnel from Gaza who later began to operate in the West Bank as well. Palestinians from the West Bank were recruited to carry out attacks inside the Green Line. Since the peace accords, these groups have been formed into cells which sometimes recruit young Palestinians and form smaller cells to carry out attacks and suicide bombings.

During the Intifada, Hamas used its overt political operations to recruit members into the units which engaged in riots and popular violence. Those who distinguished themselves were then recruited into the military apparatus, which carried out attacks against Israelis and Palestinians.

While the source of some terrorist incidents is unclear, the military wing of Hamas (the Izz el-Din al-Qassam) claimed responsibility for the April 6, 1994, bus bombings in Afula and Hadera, which killed 14 Israelis and wounded nearly 75. It also claimed responsibility for the kidnapping of Israeli Corporal Nachshon Wachsman, the shooting of people on the streets of Jerusalem on October 9, a suicide bombing of a commuter bus in Tel Aviv on October 19 that killed 22 Israelis, an April 9, 1995, suicide bombing that killed seven Israelis and an American tourist, a July 24 suicide bombing on a commuter bus in Ramat Gan that killed 6 people, and an August 21 bomb explosion on a bus in Jerusalem that killed 5 and injured more than 100.[4] There is no way to know exactly how many Arabs Hamas has killed, but the Israeli government estimates that Hamas killed 20 Israelis and one Jewish tourist from the beginning of the Intifada (December 9, 1987) until December, 1992 and assassinated close to 100 Palestinians.

This violence has caused a considerable backlash within the Palestinian community and has given Hamas some reason to halt its violent actions. A combination of Palestinian desire for peace and the loss of jobs and income as a result of Israeli economic retaliation led to a steady drop in Hamas's public support. Public opinion polls show that support has dropped from nearly 40% in 1993 to 18% in June, 1995, and 11% in some polls in October, 1995. As a result, Hamas began to hold talks with the Palestinian Authority in the summer of 1995.[5]

There were reports in late 1995 that a meeting in Khartoum might have produced an accord between Hamas and the Palestinian Authority, and that Hamas might either convert to a peaceful political party or form such a party under a separate name. In October, 1995, the Palestinian Authority released Dr. Mahmoud al-Zahar—the main Hamas spokesman in Gaza—from three months in prison after Hamas indicated that it might become a peaceful political party.[6] Hamas was also allowed to resume the publication of its newspaper, although it declared in October, 1995 that its willingness to resume a dialogue with the Palestinian Authority did not mean it had rejected its armed struggle against the Jewish state.[7]

Hamas, however, has always maintained a distinction between the overt and covert aspects of activity of its various sections. Hamas could not be characterized as a purely terrorist organization during the Intifada, and cannot be characterized as a purely terrorist organization now, just because it opposes the peace process and the Palestinian Authority. It has always had strong civil elements which perform charitable roles and have little or no direct connection to violence. Even if Hamas makes a public commitment to peaceful political action, it may simply make its violent elements more covert without changing its real nature and behavior.

It is interesting to note, in this regard, that Hamas issued a leaflet after Rabin's assassination, "congratulating the Palestinian people for the assassination" and stating that "the assassination proves that the Zionists are not ready for real peace and the next period of time will prove the Zionists want the Palestinian to give up more and more . . . Our people have to be happy for the assassination of Rabin." Another leaflet issued shortly afterward called for a "serious national dialog" with the Palestinian Authority, but also announced that Hamas would not give up the "struggle against occupation."[8] Hamas also seems to have carried out two bloody suicide bombings on February 25, 1996, that were designed to break up the peace process, and that killed 27 and wounded 80 people.

Islamic Jihad

The Islamic Jihad movement has a somewhat different history and character from Hamas. Like Hamas, it began as an ideological element within Sunni Islam, primarily within the Moslem Brotherhood, and was formed in reaction to the Brotherhood's loss of militancy. It is committed to violence in the struggle to establish an "Islamic alternative." Like Hamas, its struggle is directed against both non-Muslims and Arab regimes which have "deviated" from Islam and which have attacked or suppressed the Moslem Brotherhood.

Islamic Jihad is not, however, simply a Palestinian group. Elements of the Islamic Jihad have appeared in almost all the Arab states and in some parts of the non-Arab Islamic world under various names. These groups have been influenced by the success of the revolution in Iran and by the growth of Islamic militancy in Lebanon and in Egypt. According to Israeli sources, the Palestinian factions of the Islamic Jihad are part of the Islamic Jihad movements which appeared in the Sunni part of the Arab world in the 1970s. These movements are characterized by their rejection of the Brotherhood's "truce" with most of the existing regimes in the Arab world. They see violence as a legitimate tool in changing the face of Arab societies and regimes.

Unlike the Islamic Jihad movements in Arab countries, the Palestinian factions of the Islamic Jihad see the "Zionist Jewish entity" embodied in the State of Israel as the foremost enemy and their primary target. They see "Palestine" as an integral and fundamental part of the Arab and Moslem world, where Muslims are "subjected" to foreign rule. The fact that Israel is seen as foreign and non-Moslem allows the Islamic Jihad to use different methods of resistance than those adopted by similar groups operating against Moslem and Arab regimes. The Palestinian Jihad calls for armed struggle against Israel through guerrilla groups composed of the revolutionary vanguard. These groups carry out terrorist attacks aimed at weakening Israel and "its desire to continue its occupation." These attacks lay the groundwork for the moment when an Islamic army will be able to destroy Israel in a military confrontation.

The Islamic Jihad movement is divided into factions, and the dominant faction that has emerged since the signing of the Declaration of Principles between Israel and the PLO is the one which was headed by Dr. Fathi Shekaki until his assassination in Malta on October 26, 1995. Shekaki had succeeded in pushing aside Abd al-Aziz Ouda, the co-founder of the organization and its spiritual leader.

Shekaki and Abed el-Aziz Ouda were both from Gaza, and founded their faction because of the influence of similar political groups in Egyptian universities. They began to coordinate similar groups in Gaza when they returned from their studies, and may have had some responsibility for the grenade attack on an Israeli army induction ceremony at the Wailing Wall in October, 1986, which killed 1 person and wounded 69. They were deported from Gaza to Lebanon in 1988. They then reorganized their faction to establish a military unit to carry out attacks against Israeli targets alongside the existing political unit. These forces seem to have played a role in the assault on an Israeli tourist bus in Egypt in February, 1990, that killed 9 Israelis and 2 Egyptians, and wounded 19. They also seem to have been responsible for killing 2 people and wounding 8 in a knifing attack in Tel Aviv in March, 1993.

Islamic Jihad has made no secret of its commitment to violence since the peace accords or of its close ties to Iran.[9] It has distributed propaganda material and tapes and used the mosques as centers of its activity. It has also created a newspaper called "Al-Istiqlal," which appears in the area under the jurisdiction of the Palestinian Authority, which is edited by Ala Siftawi. Until his assassination, Dr. Shekaki resided in Damascus, and his organization remains one of the ten Palestinian opposition factions based in Syria.

Shekaki often boasted of his ties with Iran—which, according to him, were strengthened following his first visit to Teheran in December, 1988. (He visited Iran again in October, 1993—following the signing of the Israeli–PLO peace accords.) Unlike Hamas, his faction also had close ties to the Hizbollah.[10] Shekaki praised the Islamic Republic and its political and spiritual support of the Palestinian people's efforts to continue the Jihad and to achieve independence. In 1994, he stated that Islamic Jihad did not receive Iranian military aid and did not have a base in Iran, but claimed that Iranian support for his organization and Hamas amounted to $20 million a year.[11]

Islamic Jihad intensified the tone of its anti-Israeli statements after the murder of Islamic Jihad activist Hani Abed in Gaza on February 11, 1994. Shekaki said: "The continuation of the jihad against the Zionist occupation is our primary concern and the center of our lives," and "We shall raise arms against the criminal Israelis wherever they may be in the autonomous territory and outside it. We have a new reason which justifies the continuation of our struggle." In another statement, he announced the establishment of a group of 70 people prepared to commit suicide "in order to carry out attacks against the occupation forces in the self-governing areas. Such attacks in the Gaza Strip will cease only when the Israeli settlements in the area will be disbanded . . . If this will occur, the suicide attacks will be transferred to other areas, because our fight against the occupation will continue."[12]

The Palestinian Islamic Jihad (PIJ)–Shekaki faction has killed at least 30 Israelis since the 1993 peace accords. It claimed responsibility for killing 2 Israelis at a bus stop in Ashdod in April, 1994 and for 17 other attacks on Israelis. These included killing an Israeli soldier on foot patrol in Gaza on September 4, 1994, and three Israeli officers in a suicide bombing at the Netzarim junction in the Gaza on November 11, 1994, a bombing that killed 20 Israeli soldiers and a civilian at a bus stop in Beit Lid near Netanya in central Israel on January 22, 1995. Both the Palestinian Islamic Jihad and Hamas claimed responsibility for a suicide bombing on April 9, 1995, where two Palestinians on buses blew themselves up near Kfar Darom, a Jewish settlement in the Gaza Strip. Seven Israeli soldiers and an American student were killed, and 40 other Israelis were wounded. Eleven other Israelis were hurt in two suicide bombings on November 1, 1995, that were conducted as revenge for Shekaki's assassination.

Other Patterns in Terrorist Activity

There have been other sources of low level violence, particularly along the Israeli-Lebanon border. The Hizbollah is a radical Shi'ite Islamic group which seeks to end the Israeli occupation of Lebanon, supports Iran, and denies Israel's right to exist. Most of their attacks are designed to drive Israeli forces out of Lebanon, but Hizbollah also fires rockets and artillery into Israel and occasionally attempts to attack targets in Israeli territory. For example, Israeli forces intercepted a team of four DFLP terrorists trying to infiltrate the border in March, 1994.

Clashes had continued to take place between the Hizbollah, Israeli forces, and the Israeli-backed South Lebanon Army ever since 1984. The Lebanese government has not disarmed the Hizbollah or been forceful in trying terrorists. Hizbollah artillery and rocket attacks have continued against Israel and Israel has continued to retaliate with air raids and land attacks on Hizbollah positions and towns in South Lebanon. The Hizbollah may also have played some role in the bombing of the Israeli Embassy in Buenos Aires, in terrorist activity in Thailand, and in the attack on the Argentine-Israeli Mutual Association (AMIA) in Buenos Aires on July 18, 1994.

Hizbollah may have carried out these attacks with Iranian assistance—although the evidence is uncertain and recent disclosures relating to the attack on the Argentine-Israeli Mutual Association have done more to implicate the Argentine military than outside groups. This uncertainty is a significant issue. As Figure 6.2 shows, the attack on the Argentine-Israeli Mutual Association was one of the bloodiest guerrilla attacks in 1994, and is a potential warning that such warfare does not have to be conducted inside the region.[13]

Jordan has allowed a number of Palestinian rejectionist groups to operate offices within Jordan. These have included the PFLP, PFLP-GC, DFLP, PIJ, and Hamas. Jordan has, however, restricted the actions of such groups. Jordan arrested 30 Palestinians, including 15 members of the Abu Nidal Organization (ANO), on February 25, 1994, and an Islamic extremist for stabbing tourists on February 27. Jordan declared Hamas to be an illegal organization in April and arrested another 25 Islamists, or Arab "Afghans," arrested during 1994 for planning the assassination of Jordanian officials. More than 20 other Palestinian Islamic extremists suspected of planning terrorist acts against Israel were arrested after Jordan signed a full peace treaty with Israel on October 26, 1994.

Other nations play a role in Palestinian violence. Iran has actively supported the Hizbollah, PIJ, and Hamas, and has some links to the Popular Front for the Liberation of Palestine (PFLP).[14] It continues to provide regular shipments of funds and arms to the Hizbollah. Syria has not permitted any Palestinian activity in the Golan, but it does support hard-line groups like the Palestine Liberation Front (PLF) (Abd al-Fatah Ghanim faction), Popular Front for the Liberation of Palestine–General Command (PFLP-GC), Popular Front for the Liberation of Palestine–Special Command (PFLP-SC), Hamas, and Palestinian Islamic Jihad. Iraq supports Palestinian extremist groups like the ANO and the Palestinian Liberation Front (PLF). It also permits Abu Abbas and Abu Ibrahim to live in Iraq. The Sudan and Libya also give these groups at least some support.[15]

Extremism breeds extremism. Figure 6.2 also reflects the fact that Baruch Goldstein, a Kach member, killed 29 Palestinian worshipers and wounded more than 200 in a Hebron mosque on February 25, 1994. Israel declared Kach and Kahane Chai to be terrorist organizations, and arrested 11 Jewish extremists for planning attacks on Palestinians in September, 1994.[16]

This, however, did little to halt the activities of Israeli extremists whose rhetoric grew progressively more violent as the peace accords were implemented. Their verbal and physical attacks have come to include Israel's leaders. Yigal Amir, an Israeli with ties to an extreme right-wing group, assassinated Israel's prime minister, Yitzak Rabin, on November 4, 1995. There have been many serious incidents of Israeli violence against Palestinians, and each new case of violence by one side tends to trigger even more violence and extremism by the other. Tomorrow's factions may prove to be more of a threat than any of the current factions listed in Table 6.1.

The Palestinian Authority Response

While the combined activity of Hamas and Islamic Jihad has scarcely amounted to low intensity conflict or threatened Israel in any military sense, it has had a massive impact on Israeli public opinion and has threatened to bring an end to the peace process. Terrorist attacks during 1993 and the first part of 1994 steadily shifted Israeli opinion against further withdrawals. On January 22, 1994, two bombs exploded at a bus stop at Beit Lid, killing 21 and wounding 60. The Palestinian Islamic Jihad claimed responsibility for the attack. On January 27, 3 Israelis were wounded by an unidentified assailant near Netzarim, in Gaza. On February 6, an unidentified gunman killed an Israeli in Gaza. On March 20, unidentified assailants fired on a bus near Kiryat Arba, killing 2 Israelis.

This violence escalated sharply in April, 1994. In early April, several Hamas members were killed in Gaza when a bomb they were making exploded prematurely. Then, on April 9, a suicide bomber linked to the Palestinian Islamic Jihad drove an explosives-laden car into a bus near Kfar Darom in Gaza, killing 7 Israelis and 1 American and wounding 34. Another attack on the same day near Netzarim left 11 Israelis wounded. Hamas claimed responsibility for this second attack.[17]

A US State Department investigation of these events concluded that "we have no information that incidents of terrorism were perpetrated or organized by PLO elements under Arafat's control during the period covered by this report." Further, Prime Minister Rabin stated during a speech on May 15, 1994, that "Fatah groups under the Palestinian Authority headed by Arafat have not taken part in any murderous terrorist attacks against Israelis."

The State Department investigation also concluded that Palestinian and PLO officials had denounced these acts of terrorism as they occurred. For example, Chairman Arafat telephoned Prime Minister Rabin to express his condolences in response to the Beit Lid attack on January 22, 1994, and called the attack a "criminal act that threatens the peace process." The planning minister of the Palestinian Authority, Nabil Sha'ath, called the act a "criminal deed which we resolutely condemn." The Health Minister of the Palestinian Authority reacted to the March 20, 1994, attack in Hebron by stating that the Palestinian Authority "shares the grief of the families" of the victims, and stressed that no terrorist attack would stop the peace process. The housing minister called the attack on civilians "deplorable." Arafat responded to the April 9 bombings in Kfar Darom and Netzarim by stating he would "make war on the perpetrators of terrorist attacks who seek to thwart the peace process."

Words, however, were not enough. Each attack by Hamas and Islamic Jihad undermined the peace process, and it took time for the Palestinian Authority to realize that it had to match its words with action. The particularly bloody terrorist incident on April 9, 1995, was a key catalyst in this process.[18] The Israeli response made it clear that the peace process could only continue as long as the Palestinian Authority improved the quality of its security options and was seen to publicly and constantly crack down on violent movements like Hamas and Islamic Jihad. Israel threatened to enforce prolonged travel bans in Gaza and West Bank that affected tens of thousands of Palestinian jobs and businesses—and even partial bans cost the Gaza at least $1.5 million a day.[19]

This Israeli response cost Hamas and the Palestinian Islamic Jihad a consider-able amount of popular Palestinian support because of the loss of jobs and trade. It also led the Palestinian Authority to take a much firmer line in reacting to at-tacks. Its security forces improved their cooperation with Israeli security forces, conducted ruthless interrogations and quick trials, and expanded their prisons. These actions reduced the number of terrorist incidents and weakened Islamic Jihad, which also lost some of its leaders to assassinations overseas. They also showed that the Palestinian Authority and PLO could crack down effectively on the Hamas and Islamic Jihad without losing significant public support or major reprisals.[20]

Although a number of reports have implied that the Palestinian Authority re-sponse was limited or inadequate, the US State Department investigation of Palestinian Authority actions describes these actions as follows.[21]

> Gaza security chief Nasser Yussef confirmed that he has been charged with develop-ing a plan of action to combat terrorism. Senior Palestinian Authority officials, in-cluding Arafat, have described steps the Palestinian police forces have taken to pre-empt terrorist attacks. Israeli Police Minister Shahal said February 5 that "there is information that the Palestinian police recently prevented several attacks." Arafat has said he is committed to end Hamas and Palestinian Islamic Jihad (PIJ) violence against Israelis whether in or launched from Palestinian Authority–controlled areas or the West Bank.
>
> In late January, the Palestinian police reportedly arrested a number of PIJ mem-bers implicated in the Beit Lid bombing. On February 8, the Palestinian police ar-rested a Hamas activist suspected of planning to explode a hand grenade in Tel Aviv. The police detained two other Gazans suspected of planning unspecified attacks. On February 9, the Palestinian police arrested several persons suspected of preparing a car bomb for detonation in Jerusalem. On February 14, Palestinian Authority secu-rity forces found and seized 200 kilograms of explosives.
>
> The police caught two individuals February 15 who were reportedly attempting to persuade a third man to carry out a suicide bombing. And in April, a potential suicide bomber recruited by Hamas was detained by the Palestinian police. His al-leged recruiter was sentenced to 15 years by the Palestinian Authority security court, according to a press report. The press also reported the Palestinian police arrest of eight Hamas militants and the seizure of weapons and explosives in a series of raids in late April. A Hamas spokesman confirmed the arrests. The State Department has been unable to verify all of these claims of preemption of terrorism. Nevertheless, we do have evidence that the Palestinian Authority is making a serious effort to prevent terrorist attacks and devoting more resources to preemption of violence.
>
> The Palestinian Authority routinely responds to terrorist incidents or attempts with widespread detentions of suspects followed by their release. Following the Jan-uary Beit Lid bombing, the Palestinian Authority detained more than 250 members of PIJ and Hamas for questioning. After a foiled truck bomb at Beersheba in March, the Palestinian Authority arrested more than 70 Islamic activists. The Palestinian Authority detained more than 300 PIJ and Hamas members after the April 9 bomb-ings in Gaza. As of late May, the Palestinian Authority says it still has 40 members of

Hamas in detention; local human rights groups place the number of opposition members currently in detention at 80–90. These security sweeps send a warning to those involved with terrorist groups that their actions are being monitored, and the interrogations are an important source of information.

During the period under review, the PLO has initiated prosecutions of those involved in terrorism. In February, Arafat established a "security court" system in Gaza, operating under civil law but presided over by security officers, to try those suspected of terrorism. The court began trying cases and handing down sentences after the April 9 attacks in Gaza. Nabil Sha'ath said in an April 12 interview that the security courts demonstrated a "new firmness in dealing with those who are planning to sabotage the peace process." Chairman Arafat said he is committed to continue use of the security courts.

The security court record of convictions includes: April 9—a PIJ member sentenced to 15 years for assisting a terrorist attack; April 10—a PIJ activist sentenced to life imprisonment for conspiring in the Beit Lid bombing; April 15—a PIJ member sentenced to 15 years; April 16—two Hamas members sentenced to two years for terrorist acts in which IDF soldiers were killed; April 17—a Hamas member sentenced to seven years for complicity in the pre-empted truck bomb near Beersheba; April 22—two Hamas members sentenced to four and seven years for recruiting minors to take part in suicide attacks against Israelis; April 23—two Hamas members were sentenced to 3 years for killing a Palestinian suspected of cooperating with Israel; April 24—two Hamas members sentenced to three years for the murder of a Palestinian believed to be cooperating with Israel. On April 26 the security court sentenced a PFLP member to one year in prison for his involvement with a group of boys caught with homemade explosives.

On April 30, two Gazans were sentenced to a prison term of unknown duration for smuggling arms; on May 1 an individual of unknown affiliation was sentenced to 12 years for arms smuggling; and on May 4 four residents of Beit Hanun were sentenced to 6 months for setting fire to Israeli fields. On May 13, the Palestinian police arrested Sayid Abu Musameh, the highest-ranking Hamas official detained by the Palestinian police to date. Abu Musameh was sentenced to two years in prison for seditious writing, incitement and tampering with security. Hamas spokesmen warned the PLO to stop its most recent crackdown in Gaza "before it was too late." On May 15, Prime Minister Rabin stated in a speech that "over the past four months we have seen the Palestinian Authority take clear-cut steps against the radical Islamic terrorist elements, against the Islamic Jihad and against Hamas."

On April 11, the Palestinian Authority announced that all weapons had to be registered by May 11. Palestinian Authority Justice Minister Frei Abu-Middein told a Jerusalem newspaper on May 7 that the Palestinian Authority had begun to collect illegal weapons and explosives in Gaza. He said the campaign to confiscate weapons would be stepped up after the May 11 (later extended to May 14) registration deadline. Police chief Ghazi al-Jabali stated publicly that the police would collect any unlicensed weapons after May 11. In a statement announcing the extension of the deadline, Palestinian Authority Justice Minister Frei Abu-Middein said that any citizen found in possession of unlicensed weapons would be prosecuted, with prison sentences ranging from six months to seven years. A Palestinian Authority security official said that 450 licenses have been issued to date. A sustained approach in this area would be another important indicator of the Palestinian Authority's commitment to a serious and structured approach to enhancing security.

Joint security patrols and district coordinating offices are the principal daily mechanism for coordination and cooperation between the Palestinian police and Israeli security forces. Reports from both Palestinians and Israelis indicate the level of cooperation is generally good. On May 14, Arafat announced that the Palestinian Authority had discovered 1,500 blank Israeli ID cards, which would allow the bearers free access to Israel, during a check on a Hamas hideout. The Palestinian police also found arms and explosives. Samples of the confiscated documents were passed to the Israeli security forces. Palestinian police routinely share intelligence information with Israeli security. However, the actual patrols have mixed results and are still largely dependent on individual personalities.

At their March 9 meeting at Erez, Chairman Arafat and Foreign Minister Peres agreed to establish a senior joint security committee to share intelligence and to broaden cooperation aimed at preventing terrorist attacks. This senior committee meets weekly, most recently at the level of Foreign Minister Peres and Nabil Sha'ath in Cairo. In a May 1 statement on behalf of Prime Minister Rabin, Israeli Environment Minister Sarid reflected favorably on the level of joint security cooperation with the Palestinian Authority. A senior Israeli official told US officials May 19 that the Palestinian police had accomplished much in a short time.

We remain very concerned about some aspects of the Palestinian Authority's performance on security matters. The Palestinian Authority claims to have turned over 20 prisoners to the Israelis without a formal request. Israel has reportedly made three formal and two informal requests for suspects believed to be within territory under the jurisdiction of the Palestinian Authority. These requests are under discussion between the parties in accordance with the Gaza/Jericho agreement. Israeli officials have stated that the number of police in Gaza and Jericho exceeds the numbers permitted in the Gaza/Jericho agreement. The parties are discussing this issue in the joint security committees. The Palestinian Authority has turned over to Israel a partial list of individuals currently serving in the Palestinian police and security forces.

In addition, the Palestinian Authority remains hampered by an inadequate legal system that has evolved insufficiently to provide due process. The police are also hindered by overlapping jurisdictions and unclear command structures. Clearly, these investigations, prosecutions and sentences demonstrate a greater seriousness on its part to punish terrorists. At the same time, the Palestinian Authority must approach the security issue in a way that is consistent with the rule of law. We have raised these concerns with the Palestinian Authority. On April 23, the Palestinian Authority Attorney General announced the Palestinian Authority would set up an appeals procedure for prisoners, including those convicted in security courts. The need to respect human rights is part of our ongoing dialogue with Palestinian Authority officials.

State Department officials and US intelligence experts indicate that the Palestinian Authority has continued to improve its performance since mid-1995. At the same time, Israeli officials remain far more critical and events have shown that the Palestinian Authority will take years to develop fully effective internal security forces.[22] A Palestinian suicide bomber blew up a bus in Tel Aviv and killed 6 Israelis and wounded 28 on July 24, 1995. A suicide bomber blew up a bus in Jerusalem, killing 4 Israelis and 1 American and wounding 100 people on August 21, 1995. Suicide bombers blew up a bus in Jerusalem and a soldier's hitchhiking post near Ash Keloa on February 25, 1996, killing 27 and wounding 80.

Palestinian security forces continue to have problems with internal discipline and there has been some infiltration by anti-peace elements. In addition, there is a significant risk that the loyalty of the security forces could be threatened or undermined by a collapse or delay of the peace process, being asked to take action that was too extreme, or by extreme Israel security actions which sharply infringed on Palestinian rights.

Creating effective security forces is anything but easy, and groups like Hamas, the Hizbollah, and Islamic Jihad know that bombings and killings produce dramatic swings in Israeli public opinion polls, polarize Israelis and Palestinians, and can affect elections. The Palestinian Authority must convert paramilitary elements that were anti-Israeli before the peace accords to an effective security force which can provide security and law enforcement for a secular Palestinian Authority. It must expand its capability to conduct joint patrols with Israeli security forces, prevent attacks on Israelis, disarm and suppress violent extremist movements like the Islamic Jihad, and prevent conflict between Palestinians.

The Palestinian Authority must deal with extremely difficult security problems where the risk of terrorist attacks and low intensity fighting between Palestinians—of a kind that already took place during the Intifada—is very real. It also faces the problem that its present political structure is built around the influence of one man—Yasser Arafat—who may or may not survive and who may or may not be able to make the difficult transformation from leader of an opposition in exile to someone who can both govern and be a statesman. Further, the Palestinian Authority's ability to enforce security measures is highly dependent on Palestinian public support, progress in the peace process, progress in reducing control over the Palestinians, and belief that the peace will bring jobs and economic development.

Conflict in Gaza

Some level of continuing violence is almost inevitable for years to come. Extremists will inevitably attempt to attack the peace process at its weakest link. This violence could be far worse, however, if the peace process fails, or if the Palestinian Authority and IDF cannot develop effective security measures. A new low level war might then result in fighting similar to, or more violent than, the Intifada.

The Security Problem in Gaza

Such a conflict could take a number of forms. Gaza is an area of about 380 square kilometers, sharing a 51 kilometer border with Israel, an 11 kilometer border with Egypt, and 40 kilometers of coastline.[23] As a result of the September 13, 1993, accords between Israel and the Palestinian Authority and the Cairo Agreement of May 4, 1994, it is divided into a mix of common roads, Israeli controlled entry points and roads, Israeli settlements, Palestinian Authority controlled areas, and other areas.[24]

Gaza has a Palestinian population of around 813,000 (July, 1995)—some of it sympathetic to religious extremist groups like Hamas, rather than the Palestinian Authority—and has around 4,800 Israeli settlers in 24 different settlements. Palestinian per capita income in the Gaza is only about $1,275, and a large percentage of the Palestinian residents of Gaza—well over 50%—have been dependent on aid since 1948. Unemployment and disguised unemployment in Gaza vary from 20% to 60%, depending upon political conditions. This unemployment is particularly high among young Gazans, who made up a large part of the total of 400,000 unemployed Palestinians on the West Bank and Gaza in late 1995.[25]

The Gaza has also been highly dependent on Israel in the past. Gaza provided most of the roughly 50,000 Palestinian workers who worked in Israel during 1994, and over 43% of all Gazan employment came from Israel during the peak employment year of 1992.[26] Israel has also accounted for about 90% of Gaza's external trade. This employment has dropped sharply since 1992, however, and was only about one quarter of its peak level in mid-1995. This was a major reason that total Palestinian unemployment was rising by 10% per year.[27]

Gaza has no natural resources and no significant internal industrial activity or exports except souvenir production, a few showpiece factories, and citrus fruits—many of which are grown by Israelis.[28] Its unemployment problems are certain to grow worse unless there is heavy outside investment and/or Gaza can maintain close economic ties to Israel. The Palestinian population growth rate has risen sharply since 1968, from 42 births per 1,000 to 51.6 in 1991. The Palestinian population growth rate was 4.55% in 1995, the total fertility rate was about 7.74 children per woman, and 52% of the population was under 15 years of age.[29]

Palestinian Security Forces in Gaza

The Palestinian Authority has absorbed much of the Palestinian personnel and administrative structures that worked in Gaza under the Israeli civil administration, and has steadily improved its administrative efforts in Gaza since 1993. It has shown that its security forces can become more effective.

The regular police force and the Palestinian Authority security forces initially were unprepared for their task and had little money and equipment. Key elements of the new security forces, like the Central Security Forces (CSF), were formed largely out of elements from the Palestinian Liberation Army (PLA) and Fatah forces, based throughout the world. These forces had little cohesion, little training for their new mission, and included a large number of men who were aging bureaucrats living on a PLO income rather than effective paramilitary personnel.

The regular police force combined volunteers from Gaza and the West Bank, including some former violent opponents of Israel like the Fatah Hawks and Black Panthers. The CSF forces were built up out of the Palestine National Liberation Army (PNLA) and various Palestinian paramilitary forces that existed in foreign countries. Some of the CSF forces received training in Jordan and Egypt and some of the civil police trained in Amman and Cairo, but these training efforts only involved limited numbers of personnel and were slow to develop. Many members of the civil police initially had little or no training. These problems were compounded by Arafat's insistence on personal direction of much of the effort, his use of overlapping and rival elements within the security forces, and long-standing rivalries within the various security and paramilitary forces within the PLO and Arafat's immediate entourage.[30]

Israel was able to rapidly adapt its forces to the problem of controlling Palestinian movement in and out of Gaza and securing its access to Gaza, key lines of communication, Israeli settlements, and mixed areas. At the same time, it had to develop and enforce extremely complex arrangements with the Palestinian Authority to define the right of hot pursuit and secure key roads inside Gaza as well as the perimeter of several key settlements.

Members of the IDF and Israeli security forces that dealt with the new Palestinian security forces initially had serious reservations about whether the Palestinians could become effective in maintaining civil order and conducting counter-terrorism operations. Over time, however, the various Palestinian security and police forces gained experience, improved their training and equipment, set up intelligence and informer networks, and improved their cooperation with Israel. This improvement was partly a response to the growing risk that tolerance of Palestinian terrorism would lead to a breakdown of the peace process. The Palestinian security forces only began to take decisive action after the April 9, 1995, suicide attack on Israelis. Nevertheless, the Palestinian security operation in Gaza and Jericho built up total forces of 9,000 regular police and 12,000 security police by late 1994, and demonstrated that a number of its cadres had at least moderate effectiveness.[31]

The new "Oslo II" peace accords signed by Israel and the Palestinian Authority on September 13, 1995, will further strengthen the role of the Palestinian security forces in Gaza. They allow the Palestinian Authority to deploy 18,000 men in Gaza out of a total security force of 30,000. This force may recruit up to 7,000 men from Palestinians abroad. It may be armed with rifles and pistols and possess a total of 7,000 light personal weapons. It can have 120 machine guns of .30 to .50 caliber and 45 wheeled armored vehicles.[32]

The new agreements between Israel and the Palestinian Authority also built on the experience gained since 1993. They will expand regional and district security liaison offices which are manned on a 24 hour basis and have special communications links. The agreements call for the sharing of intelligence, joint patrols on key roads, joint mobile units for rapid response to disturbances and terrorist attacks, and joint liaison bureaus at the key crossing points.

Future Military Clashes in Gaza

The Palestinian Authority security forces should be able to maintain a high degree of security in Gaza as long as they remain under the direction of leaders who support the peace process, and as long as most Gazans support the peace process or at least oppose violence. This situation could change, however, as a result of a breakdown in the peace process, the power struggle between the Palestinian Authority and Hamas, or the failure to develop the economy and improve living standards.

At some point in the future, Israel may be faced with a hostile Gaza under the control of hard-line Islamic extremists who are willing to fight a prolonged low level battle to drive Israel out and/or defeat the peace process. The Palestinian Authority could then become a hostile force or simply tolerate extremist military action using Palestinian areas as a sanctuary.

The IDF has the military strength to deal with this situation by re-securing the Palestinian areas in Gaza in a matter of days if it chooses to do so. It would, however, face political problems in dealing with world public opinion, and would have to be willing to take casualties in the process. These casualties could be serious if the IDF had to fight urban warfare in the middle of a hostile population and/or if the IDF had to confront most of the Palestinian Authority security forces. Such an initial victory might prove illusory, however, and lead to Gazans regrouping, reorganizing, and shifting to the kind of low level war that took place in Lebanon and Ulster.

If Israel had to defend the settlements in Gaza under such low intensity warfare conditions, the IDF would have to expand its presence to create a series of complex security zones and enforce a wide range of security measures to defeat violent elements within the Palestinian population in Gaza while pacifying the rest. It would probably also have to make further improvements to the security of key lines of communication and almost completely substitute low cost Asian workers like Thais for the Palestinians. It is striking that unemployment for Palestinians in Israel has already dropped from a peak of 115,600 in 1992 (36% of all Palestinian employment in 1992) to 47,000 in May, 1974, and that Israel had only issued a total of 27,000 Palestinian work permits as of May, 1995.[33]

The question for Israel would be how long this security effort would last and at what cost. The IDF and the Israeli General Security Services (GSS), or Shin Bet, have lost a considerable amount of their intelligence on Palestinian activities in Gaza, and the Palestinian towns and cities in Gaza could become places of refuge.[34] The security along the Gazan border with Egypt has deteriorated since the peace accords, and there are reports of "tunnels" and extensive arms smuggling. These reports may be exaggerated, but there does seem to be more unauthorized arms in Gaza than before and a considerable amount of military explosives.[35] Israel might be unable or unwilling to retake control of Palestinian population centers in Gaza, and the peace process has created a climate where extremists may be able to build up enough small arms, explosives, etc. to present major problems in terms of low intensity urban combat. This would almost certainly be the case if Arafat and the Palestinian Authority lost control of Gaza or the Palestinian Authority's security forces, or large elements of currently pro-PLO/pro-Palestinian Authority Gazans turned firmly against the peace process.

As a result, Israel might well choose to isolate Gaza from Israel, giving up at least the smaller settlements, using a secure perimeter to halt all traffic into Israel, and using Israel's control of water and power to exert some leverage on the Palestinian government in Gaza.

There is little doubt that Israel could create and maintain such a security zone and isolate Gaza. At the same time, Israel might then be confronted with the need to block the transfer of longer range weapons like artillery and mortars into Gaza from the coast. The political effects of such containment or "separation" policy could be extremely serious in terms of relations with Egypt, Jordan, other members of the Arab world, and Palestinians outside Gaza. A military solution based on treating Gaza as an isolated enclave would prevent another Intifada and would be less destabilizing than Israeli reoccupation of Gaza, but it would have serious political and strategic costs.

Conflict on the West Bank

The West Bank is much larger than Gaza, and has many more natural resources. It has 5,860 square kilometers and 5,640 square kilometers of land area. It has 307 kilometers of boundaries with Israel and a 97 kilometer border with Jordan.[36] This compares with an area of 20,700 square kilometers for all of Israel within its 1967 borders. The West Bank is also a significant military barrier to any attack from the East. Its north-south ridge may only reach heights of about 3,000 feet, but the Jordan River and Dead Sea descend 1,200 feet below sea level—resulting in an incline of 4,700 feet over a space of 15 miles. There are only five major east-west routes connecting the Mediterranean to Jordan, which makes any route of armored advance across the West Bank predictable and easier to target.[37]

The problem of maintaining security and reaching a secure peace for both sides is complicated by a greater intermingling of the two populations, population growth issues, problems in dividing key resources like water, problems in dealing with Israeli and Palestinian immigration, and greater difficulties in deciding how much territory will be traded for peace (an issue that includes Jerusalem).

There are different ways to count the number of Israelis involved. The CIA estimates that the total Palestinian population in the West Bank is around 1.5 million, with 122,000 Jewish settlers in 200 settlements and land use sites in the West Bank, and another 149,000 Jewish settlers in 25 areas in East Jerusalem. There are

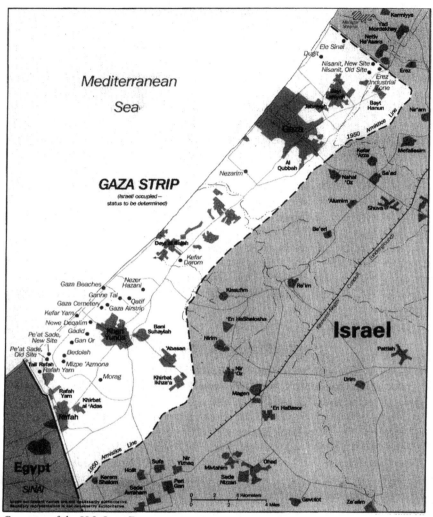

Courtesy of the U.S. State Department

another 865,000 Palestinians within Israel's 1967 boundaries—about 17% of the
total population. Israel normally refers to a total of 145,000 Jewish settlers, and Israeli government sources refer to a total of either 128 or 145 settlements in the
West Bank. This discrepancy in the two estimates occurs because Israel counts all
of Jerusalem as an integral part of Israel, while the CIA counts all Israelis and Israeli settlement areas outside Israel's 1967 boundaries as being in the Occupied
Territories.[38]

Major Security Issues on the West Bank

There are several major security issues affecting a final peace settlement dealing with the West Bank. Israel loses much of its present strategic depth if it returns all of the Occupied Territories. (It is only 14 kilometers wide from west to east in its narrowest area near Tel Aviv.) There are large Israeli settlements and landholdings in areas outside Israel's 1967 boundaries, and Israelis and Palestinians intermingle or live in close proximity in many areas. Such a settlement must also deal with demographics, water, the right of return, and Jerusalem.

The Palestinian fertility rate in the West Bank is lower than in Gaza—5.34 children per woman, but the annual growth rate is still 3.5%. More than half of the population is under 18. About 90.2% of the Palestinian population is Muslim, and 8.8% is Christian.[39] This young and rapidly growing population puts serious demographic pressure on any peace settlement and security arrangements. So do shifts in the religious composition of the population. There has been a steady emigration of Palestinian Christians to other countries. As a result, formerly Christian cities like Bethlehem are acquiring a Muslim majority, increasing the potential strength of Islamic extremists.

The Palestinian population on the West Bank currently has relatively low living standards. Per capita income is about $2,500—much higher than Gaza, but much lower than Israel's $14,000. While some figures put Palestinian unemployment as low as 12%, true unemployment and disguised unemployment on the West Bank can vary from around 20% to 50%, depending upon political conditions. After the first peace agreement, World Bank studies recommended a minimum of $1.35 billion in short term investment, and $1.6 billion in long term investment to improve living standards in the West Bank and Gaza over the next five years. Such investment would not, however, make more than a limited reduction in the gap between Palestinian and Israeli living standards and finding jobs and career opportunities for both older Palestinians and the large and volatile younger Palestinian population will still be a major problem.[40]

Control of the West Bank involves serious water issues. While various reports differ significantly over the amounts of water involved, a large system of mountain aquifers supplies both the West Bank and Israel's pre-1967 territory. This system of aquifers can supply about 970 million cubic meters of renewable water per year. It currently provides about 40% of the water Israel uses for agriculture and 50% of its drinking water—much of it for Tel Aviv and its suburbs.

While the West Bank has over 600 million cubic meters (21 billion cubic feet) of this water, much of it drains into Israel's pre-1967 boundaries and is easier to collect there. The Palestinian Authority has made claims for a total of roughly half of the entire 970 million cubic meters. However, virtually all of the water collected within Israel's pre-1967 boundaries goes to Israelis, and about 470–480 million cubic meters of the 600 million cubic meters' worth of water available from the mountain aquifers on the West Bank was used by Israel in 1994—about 80–83%.

About 50 million cubic meters of the 600 million cubic meters was given solely to Jewish settlers on the West Bank. Israelis use at least three times more water per capita than Palestinians.

In contrast, the entire Palestinian population was only given about 120–130 million cubic meters (4.2 billion cubic feet)—16% to 20%. This allocation forced many Palestinian villages on the West Bank to severely ration water, and 37% of the Palestinian villages were entirely without running water. Only a few Israeli and Palestinian towns had wells in addition to piped water.[41]

The allocation of West Bank water to the Palestinians will increase as part of the accords signed by Israeli and the Palestinian Authority in September, 1995, but the new allocation scarcely meets Palestinian demands and the control of water will remain a major security issue. Population growth is steadily reducing the amount of water per capita. Even if no outside immigration takes place, World Bank studies indicate that current population growth levels in Israel, Gaza, and the West Bank will restrict renewable water use for human consumption and light industrial needs by 2010.

Some experts have indicated that this problem could be solved by shifting water use away from agriculture, making better use of recycled water, and creating major new desalination plants. Other experts have claimed such shifts are costly and impractical for Israel. They could take up to a decade to accomplish, and could involve an investment in excess of $10 billion. The one thing that is certain is that the combination of water and security problems is likely to present major strategic complications well beyond the year 2000.

There are up to 1.5 million people outside the West Bank and Gaza who are registered as Palestinian refugees and who might claim the right of return. In 1995, this total included over 330,000 people in Lebanon (10% of the country's population with an annual growth rate of 2.9%), 310,000 people in Syria (2.3% of the country's population with an annual growth rate of 3.0%), and 1,100,000 people in Jordan (28% of the country's population with an annual growth rate of 3.6%). Many groups representing these refugees have long demanded the right of return and/or compensation from Israel, as have the registered refugees in the West Bank and Gaza. There are over 475,000 registered refugees in the West Bank and East Jerusalem (38% of the population with an annual growth rate of nearly 5.0%) and 586,000 registered refugees in Gaza (75% of the population with an annual growth rate of over 3.5%).[42]

Palestinian demographics are already a major burden for the West Bank and Gaza. They present potential security problems in terms of both military manpower and economic pressure. Projections by the US Census Bureau indicate that the total Palestinian population in the West Bank and East Jerusalem will increase from 1.2 million in 1995 to 1.4 million in 2000, 1.5 million in 2005, and 1.7 million in 2010. Similarly, the total Palestinian population in Gaza is projected to increase from 0.73 million in 1995 to 0.84 million in 2000, 0.95 million in 2005, and 1.1 million in 2010. The total Palestinian population in Lebanon is projected to increase from 0.39 million in 1995 to 0.46 million in 2000, 0.53 million in 2005, and 0.6 million in 2010.[43]

The total Palestinian population in Jordan is projected to increase from 1.9 million in 1995 to 2.3 million in 2000, 2.7 million in 2005, and 3.1 million in 2010. The total Palestinian population in Lebanon is projected to increase from 0.39 million in 1995 to 0.46 million in 2000, 0.53 million in 2005, and 0.6 million in 2010. The total Palestinian population in Syria is projected to increase from 0.36 million in 1995 to 0.41 million in 2000, 0.46 million in 2005, and 0.51 million in 2010.[44]

Even the most favorable outside projections of economic development in the region indicate that there is only a moderate chance that the living standards of the Palestinians already in East Jerusalem, the West Bank, and Gaza can be improved at a rate that will reduce the security problems inherent in the gap between their present per capita income and that of Israelis.[45] Any major immigration by Palestinians from outside the West Bank and Gaza would also sharply increase the water problem, while major immigration to Israel will also mean more competition for water.[46]

There are more immediate military and security problems for Israel. The Jordan River Valley forms a natural security barrier between Israel and Jordan and effectively acts as a giant anti-tank ditch. Giving up this defensive line affects the time Israel has to mobilize and its ability to ensure control over the West Bank in the event of a war, which is why Prime Minister Rabin stated that Israel would never do this in an October 5, 1995, speech to the Knesset shortly before his assassination.

Similarly, each sacrifice of control over the routes up the heights above the West Bank and down to Israel's pre-1967 territories reduces the ease with which the IDF can deploy, increasing the potential risk of a Jordanian, Palestinian, or Syrian force being able to deploy into the heights. Control of access of the heights above the Jordan River Valley also provides a major military advantage in terms of sensor coverage, warning, artillery operations, and armored warfare.

For these reasons, Israel seems likely to resist giving up control of the Jordan River area north of Jericho, positions on the heights on the West Bank that provide sensor and intelligence coverage of Jordan and the West Bank, and a substantial strip of the West Bank to the east of its 1967 boundary south of Tulkarm and north of Ramallah. Prime Minister Rabin indicated in his October 5, 1995, speech that Israel would retain a security border in the Jordan Valley, annex the west bank of the Jordan, and annex the settlement blocs of Ma'ale Adumim, Givat Zeev, and Gush Etzion around Jerusalem. This would put the homes of about 48,000 Jews, or one-third of the current settlers, under full Israeli sovereignty.[47]

Further, the final settlement negotiations that began in early 1996, mean Israel and the Palestinian Authority must publicly begin to come to grips with the issue of control over Jerusalem and the extent to which Israel will seek substantial adjustments in its pre-1967 boundaries. This issue alone is almost certain to lead to new incidents of violence on both sides. It may ultimately prevent a "final" peace settlement, and may lead to violence for years even if Israel and the Palestinian Authority agree to some formal settlement.

Israel now seems virtually certain to insist on undivided control over Jerusalem, although this can mean very different things. The Israeli government has not yet defined precisely how much of "greater Jerusalem" it will seek to retain. Prime Minister Rabin made it clear that he regarded control of Jerusalem as non-negotiable in a speech he gave on October 25, 1995, at Israeli's celebration of the 3,000th anniversary of King David's establishment of Jerusalem as the capital of Israel. He told an audience of Israeli lawmakers and leading Jewish figures that "there is only one Jerusalem. For us, Jerusalem is not a subject of compromise, and there is no peace without Jerusalem. Jerusalem . . . was ours, is ours, and will be ours forever . . ." This is a position that has since been endorsed by Prime Minister Peres, and is an issue where Israel has strong domestic US political support. On October 24, 1995, the US Senate voted 93 to 5 to move the US Embassy to Jerusalem by 1999.[48]

There are few indications that the Palestinians are willing to accept this Israeli position without some compromise. The problems in reconciling the Israeli and Palestinian positions are compounded by the fact that Jerusalem is not easy to define in either religious or geographic terms. The old city involves complex religious issues regarding the control of Jewish and Muslim holy places. The Jewish and Palestinian population of greater Jerusalem now extends far beyond the former administrative boundaries of Jerusalem and involves suburbs and settlements beyond the boundaries of several Palestinian cities.

"Jerusalem" is now a large area with very complex demographics. Metropolitan Jerusalem has a population of nearly half a million and spreads over more than 100 square kilometers (42 square miles) of hills and valleys.[49] East Jerusalem, in the West Bank, occupies about 67 square kilometers. In addition, the Israeli-occupied suburbs in the West Bank now extend beyond Ramallah and Bethlehem. There are four major Jewish settlement complexes in the greater Jerusalem metropolitan areas, including Betar-Gush Etzion-Tekoa in the south (16,713 Israelis), Ma'aleh Adumim-Mishor Adumim in the east (21,348 Israelis), Beit El-Kochav Ha Shahar in the north (7,573 Israelis), and Givon-Beit Horon in the west (17,644 Israelis). Israeli settlements as far away from the old city as Beit Shemesh in the west, Almog junction in the east, Ofra in the north, and Tekoa in the south are still within a 30 minute commute of modern Jerusalem.[50]

The Israeli definition of "Jerusalem" today is likely to be at least 60% larger than the Jerusalem of 1967, and the Israeli controlled area around Jerusalem could include much more territory. Many Israeli analysts believe it is likely to include a zone that begins at Gush Etzion in the south and extends north to Givat Ze'ev, and some Israelis have argued that it should extend to Beit El. This, however, means that any settlement involves municipal areas that will mix at least

160,000 Jews and 150,000 Palestinians and leave at least 64,000 Israelis in settlements in the greater Jerusalem area.[51]

It seems likely that Israel will seek to annex part of the West Bank along the upper part of the Jordan River and keep the Jordan River Valley as its security border. Even if it is willing to make some concessions in this regard, Israel is virtually certain to demand an agreement that limits the growth of Palestinian paramilitary capabilities to levels only slightly higher than those allowed in the new 1995 accords, and demand that no regular Palestinian or Jordanian military forces be permitted in the West Bank area or deployed closer to Israel than Jordanian forces are today. Israel will almost certainly demand that there be fixed force limitations, force deployment and disengagement agreements, limits on the nature and size of military exercises, and warning and pre-notification agreements. At the same time, the Palestinian entity is likely to seek the maximum amount of flexibility and sovereignty.[52]

Finally, Israel and the Palestinian Authority must resolve the issue as to whether the Palestinians are to become a fully independent and sovereign state. They must work with other Arab governments to resolve the rights and treatment of Palestinians outside the West Bank and Gaza. Any final decision regarding the political status of the Palestinian Authority means deciding on Palestinian statehood and the rights the Palestinians will have to develop military forces or paramilitary forces, and resolving the issue of whether there should be a confederation with Jordan—a decision with a major potential impact on the future role of the Jordanian military and Jordan's role in the peace process.

The New Security Arrangements on the West Bank

At the same time the Palestinians held their first successful election, the "final settlement" negotiations over Jerusalem and the rest of the West Bank began without incident. The new peace accords reached by Israel and the Palestinian Authority in September, 1995, have also made a substantial beginning toward dealing with some of these issues. The Palestinian Authority will have a new chief executive and an elected 82 member Palestinian Council.[53] It will have the power to tax, to zone land, to control some aspects of communications, to control local radio and TV broadcasts, to regulate many aspects of commerce, to issue passports, to have foreign currency reserves, to enter into some types of international agreements, and to set up courts and enforce their judgments over Palestinians.[54]

The new accords involve major trades of territory for peace on the West Bank that go far beyond the token control of Jericho the Palestinian Authority obtained in 1993. If their implementation proceeds as planned, the West Bank will be divided into three areas and the Palestinian Authority will gradually acquire control over seven largely Palestinian cities and some 450 Palestinian towns. According to the accords,

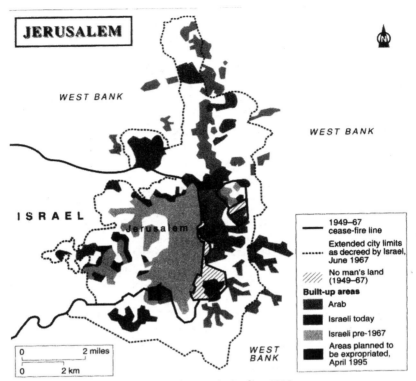

Copyright International Institute of Strategic Studies, 1995

- Area A includes Jenin, Nablus, Tulkarm, Kalkiylia, Ramallah, and Bethlehem. Special security arrangements will exist for Hebron, with one district largely under the authority of the Palestinian civil police and another—where the Israeli settlers live—under Israeli control. The new 82 member Palestinian Council will have full responsibility for internal security and public order, as well as full civil responsibilities.

- Area B comprises roughly 450 Palestinian towns and villages of the West Bank. In these areas, which contain some 68% of the Palestinian population, the Palestinian Council will be granted full civil authority as in Area A. As a result, the Palestinian Authority will have authority over nearly 98% of the Palestinian population. The Council will be charged with maintaining the public order, while Israel will have overall security authority to safeguard its citizens and to combat terrorism. This responsibility shall take precedence over the Palestinian responsibility for public order. Twenty-five Palestinian police stations, each with 25–40 civil police, will be established in specified towns and villages to enable the Palestinian Authority to exercise its responsibility for public order. These will include stations in Yamun, Meithalun, Kafr Ray, Jalqamus, and Burqin in the Jenin District; Asirat al-Shamaliyya, Talouza, Tell, Talfit, Tamun, and Aqraba in the Nablus District; Shuweika, Kafr Zibad, Anabta, and Illar in the Tulkarm and Qalqilya District; Tuqo'a in the Bethlehem District; and Yata, Dhahiriyya, Nuba, Dura, and Bani Na'im in the Hebron District. The agreement contains provisions fixing the number of police at each station and requiring that the movement of the Palestinian police in Area B be coordinated and confirmed with Israel.

- Area C comprises about 68% to 70% of the West Bank and includes unpopulated areas, Jewish settlements, future Jewish settlement areas, strategic roads, strategic high points along the West Bank hill ridge, and areas used by the IDF such as military depots, deployment areas, early warning and intelligence facilities, and training areas. Israel will retain full responsibility for security and public order. The Palestinian Council will, however, assume all those civil responsibilities not related to territory, such as economics, health, education, etc. in the parts of Area C that are eventually turned over to the Palestinian Authority.

Although this is specified in the accords, the IDF seems likely to retain the right to set up checkpoints and roadblocks around Palestinian cities and villages.

The new accords also call for the PLO to revoke those articles of the Palestinian Covenant calling for the destruction of Israel within two months of the inauguration of the Palestinian Council. The Security Annex of the accords specifies the commitment of Israel and the Palestinian Council to cooperate in the fight against terrorism and the prevention of terrorist attacks. It specifies that the Palestinian police is the only Palestinian Security Authority, that it will act systematically against all expressions of violence and terror, and will arrest and prosecute individuals suspected of perpetuating acts of violence and terror. It specifies that the Palestinian Council will issue permits in order to legalize the possession and carrying of arms by civilians and that any illegal arms will be confiscated by the Palestinian police.

According to the original schedule agreed to in September, 1995, the Palestinian Authority was to take over in Jenin on February 11, 1996, in Tulkarm on February 18, in Nablus on February 25, in Qalqilyah on March 3, in Ramallah on March 10, in Bethlehem on March 17, and in Hebron on March 24. The entire Israeli withdrawal was to be completed by March 24. In the course of these redeployments, additional parts of Area C were to be transferred to the jurisdiction of the Palestinian Council, so that by the completion of the redeployment phases Palestinian territorial jurisdiction would cover West Bank territory, except for areas where the jurisdiction is to be determined by the final status negotiations (settlements, military locations, etc.).[55]

This schedule has since been accelerated. Partly as a result of the assassination of Prime Minister Rabin, Israel has sped up its withdrawals from Jenin, Bethlehem, Tulkarm, Nablus, and Qalqilya. Virtually all of the transfers in Areas A and B were completed by early January, 1996.[56]

The accords allow the Palestinian Authority to have a total of six different security forces, including the Civil Police (Shurta), Public Security force, Preventive Security, Presidential Security Detail (Amn al-ri-asa), Intelligence, and Emergency Services. They also include small elements like the Maritime Police in Gaza.

Under the current accords, the Palestinian Authority can eventually deploy 12,000 men on the West Bank out of a total Palestinian Authority security force of 30,000 men—including the 18,000 men in Gaza. This force may have a total of 5,000 men recruited from Palestinians abroad. A total of 6,000 may be deployed initially to Area A and limited parts of Area B, with the other 6,000 to be deployed later. This force may have a total of 4,000 rifles, 4,000 pistols, 120 machine guns of .30 to .50 caliber, and 15 light unarmed riot vehicles. Under the initial deployment schedule, the Palestinian Authority can deploy up to 6,000 men, which will increase as it takes control over the seven largest Arab cities. The Palestinian Authority can deploy 1,000 men in the Jenin District, 400 men in the Tulkarm District, 1,200 men in the Nablus District, 400 men in the Qalqilyah District, 1,200 men in the Ramallah District, 850 men in the Bethlehem District, and 950 men in the Hebron District (including 400 men in the zone under Palestinian Authority control within the city limits). It can deploy up to 600 men in the Jericho District, which are counted as part of the 18,000 men who can be deployed in Gaza. Given past experience, Israel may agree to increase these totals, although not their heavy weapons and military capabilities.[57]

The agreements call for national, regional, and district security liaison offices which will be manned on a 24 hour basis and have special communications links. These agreements call for a Joint Security Committee (Joint Coordination and Cooperation Committee for Mutual Security, or JSC) with 5 to 7 members from each side, which must operate on the basis of agreement by both sides, and which will develop comprehensive plans for the transfer of regional authority. There will be Joint Regional Security Committees (JRSCs) for the West Bank and for Gaza, and joint District Coordination Offices (DCOs) for each district.

The DCOs will have six officers from each side, a commander, and five duty officers. They will coordinate affairs in the individual districts and report to the JRSCs and the JSC. They will direct the Joint Patrols and Joint Mobile Units that are to ensure "free, unimpeded, and secure movement" along key roads and provide a rapid reaction to any incidents. Each Joint Patrol will have an Israeli and a Palestinian vehicle with an officer and three guards. The JRSCs, DCOs, and joint patrols will share intelligence and support joint liaison bureaus at the key crossing points along the border with Jordan.

The accords specify that the IDF and Israelis will continue to move freely on roads in the West Bank and Gaza. In Area A, Israeli vehicles will be accompanied by joint patrols. Israelis may not, under any circumstances, be arrested or placed in custody by the Palestinian police, and may only be required to present identity and vehicle documentation. On roads that are jointly patrolled, any request for identification shall only be made by the Israeli side of a joint patrol. Both sides shall cooperate, lend assistance to one another in the search for missing persons, and share pertinent information.

The Palestinian and Israeli Security Problem

Both the Palestinian Authority and Israel will be forced to conduct aggressive countersecurity operations for years to come. These operations not only are the price for peace, they are essential to prevent any new crises and confrontations from escalating to large scale violence or war. At the same time, such operations can have a high price tag and present risks of their own.

Palestinian Authority Security Operations

The new peace accords offer the Palestinians effective self-rule, with good prospects of eventual statehood and/or confederation with Jordan. At the same time, they present a significant security problem that would be difficult for even the most sophisticated government and security force to deal with. A relatively small force will have to maintain total order among a population with significant elements that strongly oppose the peace process, deny the legitimacy of the Palestinian Authority and PLO, have experience in the use of violence, and have extensive cells of paramilitary extremists.

Establishing an effective security structure takes time and experience, and the Palestinian Authority lacks both. Further, it must demonstrate to Israel that it will act immediately and decisively to prevent violence and arrest and punish any terrorists while maintaining popular support and meeting the demands of public opinion and human rights activists.

No security force in history has been able to do a perfect job under similar circumstances. The British forces in Ulster are perhaps the most successful example of a security force working with similar problems. By and large, they did an excellent job of balancing the conflicting problems of effective security and a concern for human rights. At the same time, there were still many incidents of violence and terrorism, and many cases where the British used excessive force, abused human rights, and used extreme interrogation methods and torture.

It is scarcely surprising, therefore, that the Palestinian Authority faces similar problems. Some Israelis accuse it of being inefficient and tolerating terrorism. Some Palestinians accuse it of acting for Israel, and outsiders accuse it of violating human rights. For example, anti-peace American-Jewish groups have lobbied for a halt of all US aid to the Palestinian Authority on the grounds it has failed to fight terrorism, and right wing Israeli political leaders have threatened to shoot Palestinian policemen on sight. At the same time, the Palestinian Preventive Security forces have been accused of the arbitrary arrest and torture of Palestinians.

Further, this force is under the command of Colonel Jibril Rajoub who reports to Arafat, and Palestinian extremists have accused him of being "a big agent of the Israeli police."[58]

The Palestinian Authority security forces have emphasized security over human rights—in order to preserve the peace process. The three main Palestinian security forces already have six prisons. The civil police, under Nasir Yusef and Brigadier General Ghazi Jabali, has two prisons. The chief of the preventive security force in Gaza, Mohammed Dahklan, has two prisons. And the director of military intelligence, Mousa Arafat, has two prisons. Suspects in these prisons have been subject to long detentions without trial, and there are reports of torture and violent interrogations. For example, Mahmoud Zohhar, the chief spokesman of Hamas, was arrested in June, 1995 and held at the military intelligence prison at Saraya for 105 days. His head and beard were shaved, and there were reports he was beaten and had several broken bones.[59]

The Palestinian Authority security forces are likely to get better in the future, but there is no meaningful possibility that they can efficiently meet all of their conflicting political and security objectives. As a result, such accusations about ineffectiveness and/or human rights abuses are certain to continue, and such accusations will be justified on some occasions. The various Palestinian security forces are not an apolitical, high technology paramilitary force operating in a Western democracy. The West Bank and Gaza are not suburbs of Washington or London, and the situation forces painful trade-offs between counterterrorism and civil rights.

Critics of Palestinian Authority security forces must understand that there will be no peace or peace process if these security forces do not act ruthlessly and effectively. They must react very quickly and decisively in dealing with terrorism and violence if they are to preserve the momentum of Israeli withdrawal, the expansion of Palestinian control, and the peace process. They must halt civil violence even if this sometimes means using excessive force by the standards of Western police forces. They must be able to halt terrorist and paramilitary action by Hamas and Islamic Jihad even if this means interrogations, detentions, and rapid trials. If they do not, the net cost to both peace and the human rights of most Palestinians will be devastating.

Israeli Security Operations

The same requirements apply to Israeli security forces. They too must take quick and decisive counterterrorist action. Although these forces are under much tighter control, and are less prone to arbitrary human rights abuses, they will often have to choose between a strict interpretation of the law and effectiveness and do so with the knowledge that effectiveness is the price of any hope of maintaining Israeli political support for the peace process. More broadly, Israeli security forces must operate against extremist and terrorist forces that have learned to cloak their activities under "respectable" political cover, to deliberately manipulate the rhetoric of human rights and democracy, to manipulate human rights groups and the media, and to exploit every weakness in the law and legal procedures.

This is why Prime Minister Rabin described such Israeli security operations as "war without quarter" shortly before his assassination, and why Israeli counterterrorist activity is often swift and violent. It is why Israeli officials like Attorney General Michael Ben-Yair have stated publicly that security organizations like the Shin Bet have used extreme violence during interrogations and have sometimes killed those being interrogated.[60]

It is also an open secret that Israeli intelligence has assassinated terrorist leaders. A probable list of such assassinations includes:[61]

- April, 1973: Israeli commandos land on Beirut beach and drive into city to kill PLO officials Kamal Nasser, Mohmmed Najjar, and Kamal Adwan.
- January, 1979: PLO special forces head Abu Hassan, aka Ali Salameh, who was involved in 1972 Munich Olympics massacre of 11 Israelis, killed in car bombing in Beirut.
- July, 1979: Zuhayr Mohsen, PLO operations wing chief, killed in Cannes, France.
- December, 1979: Samir Tukan, second secretary in PLO office in Nicosia, Cyprus, and Abu Safawat, another top PLO official, are murdered.
- October, 1981: Majed Abu Sharar, head of the PLO information office, killed by bomb at Rome Hotel.
- June, 1982: PLO deputy Kamel Hussein killed by bomb in Rome.
- July, 1982: Fadel el-Daani, deputy of the PLO representative in France, killed by car bomb.
- August, 1983: Mamoun Muraish, aide to Abu Jihad, No. 2 in Yasser Arafat's Fatah movement, shot to death in car.
- June, 1986: Khaled Ahmed Nazal, of the Marxist Democratic Front for the Liberation of Palestine, gunned down at Cyprus hotel.
- October, 1986: Munzer Abu Ghazala, PLO navy commander, killed in Athens.
- February, 1988: Three senior PLO officers killed by car bomb in Limassol, Cyprus.
- April, 1988: Khalil al-Wazir, aka Abu Jihad, killed in his home in Tunis, Tunisia, by Israeli commandos.
- December, 1988: Israel kidnaps Hizbollah leader Jawad Kaspi from south Lebanon.
- August, 1989: Israeli commandos kidnap Hizbollah spiritual leader Sheik Abdul Karim Obeid from south Lebanon.
- February, 1992: Israeli helicopters kill Hizbollah chief Abbas Musawi, firing rockets at his car in south Lebanon.

- May, 1994: Mustafa Dirani, head of the Believers Resistance Group, kidnapped from home in Lebanon.
- October, 1995: Dr. Fathi Shakaki, head of Islamic Jihad, shot and killed in Malta by gunman on motorbike.

Two other Palestinians have sometimes been added to this list, although they seem to have been killed by Abu Nidal. These include Said Hamami, a top PLO official, who was murdered in London in January, 1978; and Nayim Kader, a PLO representative in Belgium, who was killed on a Brussels street in June, 1981.

Recent US State Department reporting on human rights provides further insight into this aspect of Israeli security operations, and gives what seems to be an accurate picture of the trade-offs Israel must make between security operations and human rights:[62]

Internal security is the responsibility of the General Security Service (Shin Bet), which is under the authority of the Prime Minister's office. The police are under the authority of a different minister. The Israel Defense Forces (IDF) is under the authority of a civilian Minister of Defense. It includes a significant portion of the adult population on active duty or reserve status and plays a role in maintaining internal security. The Foreign Affairs and Defense Committee in the Knesset reviews the activities of the IDF and Shin Bet.

Political killings in Israel are neither practiced nor condoned by Israeli authorities. In the context of extreme political tension between Israel and the Palestinians, intercommunal killings are often assumed to have a political motivation. In 1994 the number of such killings of Israelis committed in Israel rose to 52, as extremists on both sides sought to disrupt the peace process.

On April 6, a Palestinian car bomber in a suicide attack killed 7 and injured at least 50 at a bus stop in the Israeli city of Afula, and on April 13 a bomb in the central bus station in Hadera killed 5 persons and wounded as many as 20. On October 19, a suicide bomber aboard a Tel Aviv bus killed some 22 people and injured more than 40. Another suicide bomber killed himself and injured 12 at a Jerusalem bus stop on December 25. In other violence, a Jewish settler armed with an automatic rifle attacked a morning prayer service at the Ibrahim Mosque, also known as the Tomb of the Patriarchs, in the West Bank city of Hebron on February 25, killing at least 29 Arab worshippers.

Although Israeli laws and administrative regulations prohibit such practices, there are credible reports that security officers abuse Palestinian detainees. Incarceration facilities in Israel and the occupied territories are administered by either the Israeli Prison Service (IPS), the national police, or the Israel Defense Forces (IDF). Although conditions vary, all facilities are monitored by various branches of the Government, by members of the Knesset, the International Committee of the Red Cross (ICRC), and many human rights organizations, which have access to the prisons, police jails, and IDF camps.

Generally, inmates are not subject to physical abuse by guards, food is adequate, and prisoners receive basic necessities. However, security prisoners are subject to a different regime, even in IPS facilities, and as a class they are often denied certain privileges given to prisoners convicted on criminal charges. Overcrowding is the most severe problem in all facilities. IPS prisons conform to general international standards which permit inmates to receive mail, have televisions in their cells, and receive regular visits. Prisoners receive wages for prison work and benefits for good behavior. Many IPS prisons have religious and drug-free wards and educational and recreational program.

Police detention facilities are intended for pretrial detentions but are often used as de facto jails, holding detainees for several months because of court backlogs. Inmates are often not accorded the same rights and living conditions as prisoners in the IPS facilities. Some police detention facilities can fall below generally accepted minimum international standards.

Detention camps administered by the IDF are limited to male Palestinian security prisoners and are guarded by armed soldiers. The number of security prisoners dropped sharply in 1994, after the Government released over 5,400 Palestinian detainees. Conditions in the camps do not meet minimum international standards and threaten the health of the inmates. Many camps continue to house inmates in unheated tents, even in severe weather conditions. Family visits are restricted in the camps and recreational facilities are minimal. A petition to close the Ketziot detention camp, filed by a human rights organization before the High Court of Justice in 1993, was withdrawn in 1994. The number of detainees in the camp had decreased to about 820 by the end of the year, down from 4,900 in 1993.

Israeli law and practice prohibit arbitrary arrest or imprisonment. Writs of habeas corpus and other procedural and substantive safeguards are available. Defendants are considered innocent until proven guilty. However, a 1979 law permits administrative detention without charge or trial. The Minister of Defense may issue a detention order for a maximum of 6 months. Within 48 hours of issuance, detainees must appear before a district judge who may confirm, shorten, or overturn the order. If the order is confirmed, an automatic review takes place after 3 months. Administrative detention orders are renewable. Detainees may be represented by counsel and appeal detention orders to the Supreme Court. At detention hearings, the Government may withhold evidence from defense lawyers on security grounds. Moreover, a judge may postpone notification up to 15 days in national security cases.

After the Hebron massacre in February, the authorities placed under administrative detention several activists of the Jewish ultra-nationalist Kach and Kahane Chai Organizations. In September the authorities placed in administrative detention a number of Israelis, because the Government was concerned that they might commit terrorist acts. One of those arrested is a member of the IDF who is being tried by a military court.

The Government continues to hold nearly half of the Palestinian detainees from the occupied territories in detention centers in Israel. The transfer of prisoners from the occupied territories to Israel contravenes article 76 of the Fourth Geneva Convention. The Government acknowledges that it detains 11 Lebanese citizens and has provided information on the whereabouts of all but two of them. The disposition of their cases appears linked to government efforts to obtain information on Israeli military personnel believed to be prisoners of war or missing in Lebanon. Another

12 Lebanese prisoners, who had been detained after serving their sentences, are no longer in detention.

Security cases may be tried in either military or civil courts, and may be partly or wholly closed to the public. The Attorney General determines the venue in such cases. The prosecution must justify closing the proceedings to the public. Defendants have the right to be represented by counsel even in closed proceedings but may be denied access to some evidence on security grounds. Convictions may not be based on any evidence denied to the defense.

Although privacy of the individual and the home are generally protected by law, authorities sometimes interfere with mail and monitor telephone conversations. In criminal cases, the law permits wiretapping by court order; in security cases, the order must be issued by the Ministry of Defense. Under emergency regulations, authorities may open and destroy mail on security grounds.

The Government censors Arabic publications more strictly than Hebrew publications. In August the Ministry of the Interior closed the East Jerusalem weekly newspaper, Al-Bayan, because of the paper's alleged connections with the terrorist group Hamas. Authorities also prohibited the distribution of the PLO-affiliated Al-Awdah publication for several months.

Emergency regulations prohibit anyone from expressing support for illegal organizations. The Government occasionally prosecutes persons for speaking or writing on behalf of terrorist groups. Such actions are almost always directed against Israeli Arabs; no such cases were filed against Jews in 1994, but the Kach and Kahane Chai extremist organizations were banned under provisions of a 1948 anti-terrorism act.

The law and court rulings protect the rights of assembly and association. The Government may prohibit individuals from belonging to terrorist groups. After the Hebron massacre in February, the Cabinet invoked the 1948 Ordinance for the Prevention of Terror to ban the ultranationalist Kach and Kahane Chai organizations. The decision stipulated imprisonment for anyone belonging to, or expressing support for, either organization.

Citizens have the freedom of movement except in military or security zones or in instances where they may be confined by administrative order to their neighborhoods or villages. In 1994 the Government issued at least 40 orders limiting the movements of some Jewish settlers in the occupied territories.

In practice, Israeli Arabs are not allowed to work in companies with defense contracts or in security-related fields. The Israeli Druze and Circassian communities, at their initiative, are subject to the military draft, and some Bedouin and other Arab citizens serve voluntarily. Apart from Druze and Circassians, Israeli Arabs are not subject to the draft. Consequently, they have less access than other Israelis to those social and economic benefits for which military service is a prerequisite or an advantage, such as housing, new-household subsidies, and government or security-related industrial employment. Under a government policy whose implementation began in January, the social security child allowance for parents who have not served in the military will be increased over a 3-year period to equal the allowance of those who have served in the military.

Israeli Arabs may establish their own unions but have not done so. Palestinian trade unions in the occupied territories are not permitted to conduct activities in Israel. However, nonresident workers in the organized sector are entitled to the protection of Histadrut work contracts and grievance procedures. They may join, vote for, and be elected to shop-level workers' committees if their numbers in individual establishments exceed a minimum threshold. Palestinian participation in such committees is minimal. Labor laws apply to Palestinians in East Jerusalem and to the Syrian Druze living on the Golan Heights.

At the same time, the need for effectiveness does not condone Israeli security operations that needlessly violate human rights, or which punish large groups for the actions of individuals. Israel cannot hope for a stable peace if it ignores the need to preserve Palestinian dignity and create a security climate that promotes economic cooperation and an improvement in Palestinian living conditions.

Further, Israeli security forces can only have mid- and long-term effectiveness if they constantly consider the broader political implications of their actions, and remember that any excesses undermine outside support for Israel, breed Palestinian hostility and violence, and undercut Palestinian and Arab support for the peace process and Palestinian security operations.[63] In short, both Israeli and Palestinian security forces must try to walk the same narrow line in a climate of crisis and uncertainty in which neither can hope to be fully successful.

Both Israelis and Israel's supporters need to remember that Israeli terrorism is a problem as well as Palestinian terrorism. Israeli and pro-Israeli extremists operate in a climate where their verbal violence can be as deadly as the use of bombs and weapons. Israeli extremists use rhetoric that is as violent and extreme as that of the Palestinian extremists. They have charged leaders like Yitzak Rabin and Shimon Peres with "treason," and one of their members murdered Yitzak Rabin on November 4, 1995. They have threatened to kill Palestinians who interfere with their actions and drive them out of their homes or the entire West Bank. At least a few have beaten or murdered innocent Palestinians.

Groups like the Action Committee for the Abolition of the Autonomy Plan, Kach, Kahane Chai, Zu Artzenu, Eyal, radicals in the more extreme settlements such as Hebron and Kiryat Arba, and the more extreme members of settler groups not only commit occasional direct acts of terrorism, but they constantly and directly provoke extreme Palestinian actions. In the process, they have done just as much to kill their own countrymen as the Palestinians who have actually used a bomb or pulled the trigger. Unfortunately, there is little prospect that any Israeli government can bring a complete halt to such Israeli extremist activity, and there is equally little prospect that Israeli extremists will see that they have often played a direct role in terrorism.[64]

"Peace with Abuses" and "Peace with Violence"

A successful combination of peace negotiations and economic development may eventually bring a lasting peace to the West Bank and limit any violence to spo-

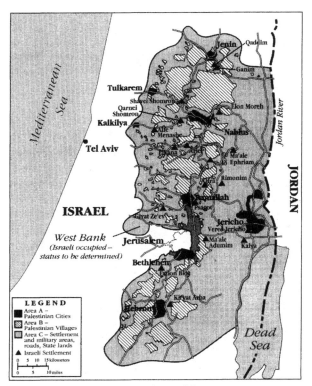

Courtesy of The Foundation for Middle East Peace

radic confrontations or civil unrest. It is almost certain, however, that the implementation of the existing accords, the negotiations for the final accords, and the implementation of any final accords will involve many further incidents of violence. Issues like the right of return, the future of Jerusalem, and the fate of the Israeli settlements are simply too controversial and too likely to provoke extremists on both sides. Even under the best conditions, there is little near term prospect that either Palestinians or Israelis can avoid living with "peace with violence" and "peace with abuses."

These are not easy realities to face. They mean that "peace with security" is at least a decade away—if this means peace with near perfect security. There also is no doubt that both Palestinian Authority and Israeli security operations will sometimes have a high price tag in terms of human rights, that they will sometimes involve torture and killings, and that they will sometimes alienate Palestinians and threaten the peace process they are intended to protect.

At the same time, the alternative is a collapse of the peace process and possibly another war. Every counterterrorist force that has ever succeeded has had to act decisively and sometimes violently. Effective counterterrorism relies on interrogation methods that border on psychological and/or physical torture, arrests and detentions that are "arbitrary" by the standards of civil law, break-ins and intelligence operations that violate the normal rights of privacy, levels of violence in making arrests that are unacceptable in civil cases, and measures that involve the innocent (or at least not proven directly guilty) in arrests and penalties.

The issue is not whether extreme security measures will sometimes be used or whether they are sometimes necessary. The issue is rather how many such acts occur, how well focused they are on those who directly commit terrorism, and how justified they are in terms of their benefits relative to their costs.

If Peace Should Fail: The Balance of Forces on the West Bank

As long as the peace negotiations continue and there is any progress in resolving the remaining issues, there is no reason to assume that sporadic violence will escalate to low intensity conflict or more serious forms of war. The balance of political power could, however, shift in favor of Palestinian or Israeli opponents of peace. This shift could result from a breakdown in the peace process over the issues discussed earlier; a shift in West Bank politics; the election of an "anti-peace," "hard-line," or more cautious Israeli government; and added violence and extremism in Israel. It could also result from Israeli security measures that alienated Palestinian support for the peace process or growing Palestinian unemployment and economic problems.[65]

Such developments could create a hostile or divided Palestinian Authority and one that tolerates the creation of significant extremist forces and cadres long before the situation leads to large scale violence. If this happens, the new peace accords will create some military risks for Israel—although much would depend on whether the Palestinian Authority tolerates or supports violence. Giving up control of the Arab cities and loosening controls over the border could give Palestinian extremists—like the military wing of Hamas and Islamic Jihad—the equivalent of sanctuaries and better access to weapons and explosives. It could increase the risk that Palestinian extremist groups outside the West Bank and Gaza—like those listed in Table 6.1—would supply and train new cadres of Palestinian forces before the control began.

Israeli officers and officials have also indicated that Israel will lose much of its intelligence gathering capability in giving up the Palestinian occupied areas on the West Bank, and may find it difficult to enforce the arrangements relating to the "transfer of suspects"—effectively making Palestinian Authority areas into refuges for hostile Palestinians. Lt. General Amnon Shahak, the Chief of Staff of the IDF, stated that the Oslo II accords would make an effective counterterrorist strategy "far harder than it is now, particularly in the field of intelligence." Brigadier General Ya'akov Amidror, the head of the analysis section of Israeli military intelligence, has said that "Israel's intelligence capability in the Gaza has dropped to zero, and a similar situation could develop in Judea and Samaria, when we transfer control to the Palestinian Authority."[66]

There already are examples of Palestinian extremists using the Palestinian Authority–controlled areas as a sanctuary. When two Israelis—Ohad Bachrach and Ori Shavord—were killed in the Wadi Kelt on July 18, 1995, the suspects—Yussef and Shaher Ra'ii—took refuge in Jericho. The Palestinian Authority claimed the two were imprisoned after a rapid trial and were not subject to a "transfer of suspects." At least one of the suspects may, however, have then been released from prison.[67]

The "institutionalized" nature of the peace settlement will also create growing political problems for Israel over time. The international community will grow used to treating the Palestinian Authority as "sovereign," regardless of its formal status. Time and this international acceptance of the new facts on the ground will make it progressively more difficult for Israel to intervene directly in Palestinian Authority–controlled territory, particularly as long as the Palestinian Authority or its successor officially appears to officially support the peace process. It will also take progressively more Palestinian provocation or risk to Israel before an Israeli government will be willing to act. This, in turn, means Israel will require progressively more warning indicators before it will act, or is willing to try to enforce all of the terms in the peace accords.

At the same time, it is unlikely that any Israeli government will ever take serious strategic risks simply because of international opinion. The new peace accords do offer Israel some military advantages. For example, Israel no longer has to maintain control within the Arab towns and cities that presented the greatest problems during the Intifada. Under many scenarios, the IDF could largely avoid involvement in such areas and concentrate on more orthodox military operations, like securing routes of communication, perimeter operations, and protecting the settlements. It could either shift the burden of counterterrorism and maintaining public order to the Palestinian Authority, or isolate Palestinian towns and cities until violence halted. This might well reduce the morale problems that arose in dealing with the kind of civil disorder that took place during the Intifada, as well as the problems of media exposure and public opinion.

Israel retains overwhelming military strength, and continues to control 70% of the actual land on the West Bank.[68] It retains military control over the Jordan River and a strong presence in the Jordan River area, in heavily Jewish areas near the Jordan River, near the Jerusalem Metropolitan District, and in areas near Israel's 1967 boundaries. It has significant security detachments in or near several key settlements—including Ariel, Beit El, Ma'alch Adumin, the Gush Etzion bloc, and Kiryat Arba (Hebron).

Israel is establishing an extensive net of new security roads that bypass Arab cities to help secure the settlements and allow the IDF to redeploy into the West Bank and reinforce its positions at the Jordan River. This road net raises questions about how many settlements will actually be withdrawn from the West Bank area, and the future of key areas of contention like Hebron. Hebron is now a city where 415–450 Israelis—including a number of radical Jewish militants—live in an overwhelmingly Palestinian city of 120,000 with a large number of Islamic fundamentalists.[69]

This situation is not likely to change even when a final settlement is negotiated. There is little doubt that Israel will insist on the near demilitarization of the Palestinian areas, and the Palestinians will have little incentive to try to create significant conventional forces. As a result, Israel will have the military ability to execute any combination of reoccupation, expulsion, separation, and security zone measures it desires—although scarcely without cost in terms of casualties or a negative reaction from world public opinion.[70]

Israel will retain powerful economic weapons. At least in the near term, it will retain control over movement, utilities, transport, and water. It will also be able to set the terms by which Palestinians can work in Israel. Further, Israel has already demonstrated that it can use low cost Asian and East European labor as a substitute for Palestinian labor. Israel issued labor permits to over 55,000 non-Palestinian foreign workers in 1994 and nearly 70,000 in 1995, versus less than 5,000 a year during 1992 and 1993. About 51% of these permits were for construction and 13.2% for agriculture—jobs Israel had previously given to Palestinians.[71] This shift in labor patterns will further reduce the kind of security problems Israel faced under the Intifada.

If peace does fail, a number of IDF planners believe that Israel could resecure the West Bank through a combination of added separation of Israelis and Palestinians, limited reoccupation of key areas, improved security measures, and economic and political pressures on the Palestinians. They believe that this would entail some Israeli casualties and some continuing low level problems with terrorism, but this might well be enough to restore something approaching a cold peace at a political, military, and economic cost that is actually lower than that of the Intifada.

There is no consensus among Israelis as to exactly what tactics Israel should employ in such a scenario. However, various Israeli experts have suggested the following possible approaches to dealing with such problems—many of which are based on the lessons of the Intifada:

- *Relying on the Palestinian Authority and peace process wherever possible*—Israel would not take preemptive action.
- *Isolating the Gaza*—Israel would seal the borders with Israel and use the crisis as a rationale to remove any remaining Israeli settlements in the Gaza. These settlements currently cost more to protect in military and economic terms than they contribute to the Israeli economy.
- *Ending any remaining dependence on Palestinian labor*—Israel would use labor permits largely as a political weapon, having imported Asian and East European labor as a substitute for Palestinian labor.
- *Removing or marginalizing small Israeli settlements in the middle of Palestinian populations that do not serve security purposes*—Like the Israeli settlements in Gaza, IDF experts feel many of these settlements are an expensive ideological liability.

- *Securing lines of communication*—Israel would fully secure its strategic lines of communication and major routes into the area, and use travel permits as a lever to push the Palestinian Authority to crack down on violence and extremism.
- *Using economic infrastructure as a lever*—Similarly, Israel would use international phone links, power generation, international postal services, external water flow, and similar levers to pressure the Palestinians into ending attacks on Israel.
- *Secure the perimeter of Palestinian cites and towns*—The IDF would stay out of populated areas wherever possible, but would seal off the perimeter of towns where violence took place and punish towns felt to be centers of violence or extremism.
- *Mobilize "border" defenses of Israel proper, the greater Jerusalem area, and Israeli settlements on the West Bank*—Israel would create strong security defenses that tightly controlled entry and movement into Israeli areas. It would seal off any Palestinian areas felt to be centers of violence and effectively halt all economic activity until such violence ceased. Such efforts would be highly selective and would seek to rely largely on nonviolent means.
- *Use trained security forces*—The IDF and security forces would avoid mass call-ups or the use of troops without special training. It would emphasize the identification and tracking of actual threats, the use of the GSS and Border Police, and officers and forces with counterinsurgency training. It would utilize the improved equipment it obtained during the Intifada.
- *Use non-intrusive surveillance methods*—Israel would use its UAVs and SIGINT capabilities to provide surveillance of Palestinian activity without sending IDF forces into Palestinian areas except to deal with known targets or in hot pursuit. Although Israel's network of informers and covert operatives in Palestinian areas has been sharply reduced, use would still be made of such techniques where possible.
- *Emphasize a willingness to continue the peace process and good relations with Arab states*—Israel would seek to politically and diplomatically isolate the violent and extremist elements within the Palestinians.
- *Reward Palestinians who support the peace process and/or are nonviolent*—Restrictions would be minimized in any area or case where the Palestinian Authority or some town or company did not present security problems. Labor permits and investment would be encouraged in such areas.

There is no way to predict the exact effectiveness of any given mix of such tactics, and hatred can be remarkably creative. It seems likely, however, that Israel would have least difficulty in fighting a low level terrorist or guerrilla war by relatively small extremist groups like Hamas and/or Islamic Jihad. This would be a conflict in which the IDF attempted to secure the countryside and the Jewish settlements while the Palestinian Authority attempted to secure the Arab cities and villages. Any such joint Israeli–Palestinian Authority action against extremists would involve a host of potential problems and frictions, but Israel and the Palestinian Authority should be able to establish security relatively quickly—or at least reduce extremist groups like Hamas and/or Islamic Jihad to minimal levels of violence.

The situation would be much worse if the Palestinian Authority security forces became hostile to Israel, divided, or tolerate large scale violence by others. The same would be true if the Palestinian people should violently reject the peace accords or react violently to a breakdown in the peace process. The resulting level of conflict would then be a function of (a) the level of arms and military supplies available to Palestinian forces, (b) the unity within the Palestinian side, (c) which key elements of the PLO and security forces of the Palestinian Authority joined the conflict, (d) the amount of territory already ceded to Palestinian control in the peace process, and (e) the level of violence Israel was willing to use in suppressing Palestinian attacks.

Such a conflict could range in intensity from a repeat of the Intifada to a serious low intensity war in which Israel would be forced to make extensive use of the IDF and use methods like reoccupation, expulsion, and/or creating security zones which isolated Israelis from the Arabs. Further, if the IDF was not content to isolate Palestinian cities and towns, such fighting could lead to bloody urban warfare. Much would then depend on just how much light weaponry the Palestinians were able to obtain before the fighting began, and the amount of anti-tank weapons, light artillery, and light anti-aircraft weapons they had available. Even a relatively limited number of such weapons could allow a Palestinian force to make the IDF fight some initial battles on a "house by house" basis.

The key "wild card" in such a conflict would be greater Jerusalem and those heavily populated areas where Israelis and Palestinians either intermingle or live in such close proximity that it would be difficult to separate them or isolate the Palestinians. This would require Israel to (a) rely on a combination of police and paramilitary operations on a community-by-community—and sometimes house-by-house—basis, (b) rely on curfews and strict limitations on local movement, (c) return to demolitions and limited expulsions, (d) suppress all signs of violence or protest with force, often deadly force, (e) hunt down and seize or kill suspected enemies, and/or (f) expel large blocs of Palestinians from such areas. Such tactics might cause further tension and conflict and lead to a broader breakdown of the peace process. There is, however, little doubt that Israel would use such measures in some mix, and that they would prove to be largely effective at least in the short run.

The worst case would be the kind of war that escalated to the point where it institutionalized the levels of hatred exhibited in Bosnia. Ethnic warfare might also possibly explode to a point so serious that the only solution available to the IDF would be a state of armed occupation in which the IDF had to occupy most Palestinian cities, react with extreme force, and deal with constant low level violence. Such a "reoccupation" would probably be far more costly than either the Intifada or the fighting on the West Bank during 1967. It might also lead to the equivalent of "ethnic cleansing" and Israeli security measures that would drive large numbers of Palestinians out of Israeli security zones or the Gaza and West Bank. A total breakdown of the peace process, combined with a hard-line Israeli government, could conceivably result in a more humane but very real form of "ethnic cleansing."

Each new level of conflict will also make it progressively harder to reach a "cold" or "warm" peace. Any major IDF fighting in the territories controlled by the Palestinian Authority is likely to force Arafat, the PLO, the Palestinian Authority, and its security forces to join in the conflict. Such a conflict would involve Hobson's choices for both Israel and moderate Palestinians, and choices which may become progressively more severe as the level of Palestinian autonomy increases. Each level of conflict will also be a test of the political costs Israel is willing to pay for giving up parts of the West Bank, and how long it is willing to fight a prolonged low level or anti-terrorist conflict that is much more violent than the Intifada.

The Role of Egypt, Syria, Jordan, Iran, and Hizbollah in a Conflict in Gaza or the West Bank

There is also the risk that Israeli action against large numbers of Palestinians in either Gaza or the West Bank might alienate world opinion, threaten Israel's peace with Egypt and Jordan, and block further progress in the peace negotiations with Syria. A conflict over and within Gaza would present problems for Egypt, although these might not be serious enough to affect the Camp David Accords.

A major struggle between Israel and Palestinians on the West Bank might well end the peace between Jordan and Israel. Such a war would almost certainly either derail the peace negotiations between Syria and Israel or end or suspend any agreement they had reached. It would also probably trigger new action by Iran and anti-Israeli/anti-peace Shi'ite extremists in Lebanon like the Hizbollah and Islamic Jihad. It also could make Israel's Arabs shift to a much more active political and military role in opposing Israel.

As a result, what might start as a low level war between Israel and Palestinian extremists could produce longer term and more serious shifts in the regional military balance. This escalation to involve Arab states would, in fact, almost certainly become the goal of Palestinian extremists if they were given the opportunity.

This does not mean that outside Arab support short of an attack on Israel would succeed in helping Palestinian extremists sustain a long-term, low-level war against Israel, or be able to give them enough additional military strength to force a better peace settlement. There are severe limits to how many arms or other forms of military support outside states could give to the Palestinian forces as long as Israel controlled the security of its borders and could seal off Gaza and access to the West

Bank. The Palestinian forces might, however, gain significant additional political leverage if they could broaden their struggle to include Israel's Arab neighbors, dominate the Palestinian community and defeat the Palestinian supporters of the peace process, and/or obtain major supplies of arms, money, and training from extremist nations and movements outside the West Bank and Gaza.

The Impact of the Peace Process on the Military Balance

The preceding contingency analysis assumes that Israel will not take existential risks and negotiate a peace that allows any Palestinian entity to create significant military forces or reach some confederate that would allow other Arab forces to operate from their territory. Nothing about Israel's history indicates that it would be foolish enough to take such risks. It also assumes that Israel will insist on prudent security measures as part of any final settlement.

As a result, trading territory for peace on the West Bank and Gaza, and trading political and military control of the Palestinian population for peace, will create only limited military risks. Every increase in Palestinian autonomy will create some new problems for Israeli internal security efforts and increase the risk that Palestinian action might interfere with Israeli military operations against an Arab state. However, there can be no peace without a steady strengthening of the Palestinian Authority, the Palestinians will not be able to challenge the IDF at any time in the foreseeable future, and the risks created by withdrawal will be partially offset by the increased separation of Israelis and Palestinians and by reducing the need to occupy Palestinian towns and cities.

The preceding contingency analysis is also a warning that Israeli military and internal security capabilities are not tools that can win a grand strategic victory without a peace settlement based on Palestinian dignity and economic development. Regardless of how many near term victories the IDF can win, true security ultimately requires both a stable peace settlement and security for Israeli and Palestinian alike. There will be endemic violence in the West Bank and Gaza until the peace process creates Palestinian political entities which support the peace process, can enforce internal security within Palestinian areas, and have the support of the vast majority of the Palestinian population. This, at best, will come only after a successful agreement on all of the final settlement issues to be agreed upon between 1996 and 1999, years in which Israelis and Palestinians may learn how to live together.

7

CASE TWO: A SYRIAN GRAB
FOR THE GOLAN

At this point in time, Syria presents the only major war fighting threat to Israel. Camp David, Jordan's peace with Israel, and Iraq's defeat in the Gulf War make the "Arab-Israeli Balance" largely a "Syrian-Israeli Balance." Barring some massive shift in the current political situation, neither Egypt nor Jordan has any reason to initiate a conflict with Israel, and neither would offer Syria significant support if a conflict did begin.

This Syrian-Israeli balance is summarized in Table 7.1, which shows both the International Institute for Strategic Studies (IISS) and Jaffee Center for Strategic Studies (JCSS) estimates of the forces involved. While most of the differences between the IISS and JCSS data are limited, they illustrate the range of uncertainty inherent in any effort to establish accurate "bean counts" of the balance. Figure 7.1 summarizes the IISS data in Table 7.1 in graphic form.

Comparing Total Syrian and Israeli Forces: Syrian Capabilities

While it is clear from Table 7.1 that Syria has built up massive military forces, it is also clear from any comparison of Table 7.1 with Tables 1.1 and 3.1 that such a balance is far less threatening to Israel than any comparison based on the strength of all the Arab "ring states." Further, the preceding analysis has shown that any purely quantitative comparison overstates Syria's war fighting capabilities. Syria's force structure and procurement planning seem to reflect many of the problems chronic in Soviet-bloc supplied forces in the Third World and many of the problems that limited Iraqi capabilities during the Gulf War. While Syria has improved some aspects of its air and land force equipment in recent years and some Syrian forces fought well in 1973 and 1982, its forces and weapons do not approach those of Israel in quality.

Syria has developed good land defenses on its side of the Golan, and many of its units in the area between Damascus and the Golan have considerable readiness and effectiveness. However, Syria has not come close to Israel in developing the kind of capabilities for combined operations that the IDF takes virtually for granted. Further, the previous data on arms transfers have shown that Syria faces massive problems in recapitalizing its present force structure, and cannot afford to either modernize its present forces at past rates or maintain and refurbish its existing pool of equipment without major increases in its military expenditures and arms imports.

Syria's greatest strength is its armored forces, but it has clearly emphasized quantity over quality. Although Syria now has a total of some 4,600 tanks, at least 1,200 of these tanks are in static positions or in storage. Roughly half are relatively low grade T-54s and T-55s, and only 1,400 are relatively modern T-72s. Even the T-72s lack the advanced thermal sights, fire control systems, and armor to engage the Israeli Merkavas and M-60s on anything like a 1:1 basis. The T-72 also performed surprisingly poorly in Iraqi hands during the Gulf War. Its armor did not prove to be as effective against modern Western anti-tank rounds as was previously expected, and its sensors and fire control systems proved inadequate for night and poor visibility combat and could not keep up with Western thermal sights in range and target acquisition capability.

Syria does have some 2,310 BMPs. These armored fighting vehicles can supplement and support Syria's tanks in combined arms combat and increase its potential ability to overwhelm unmobilized Israeli forces with sheer mass. Only about 60 of these BMPs are the more modern BMP-2, however, and nearly half of Syria's other armor consists of low grade BRDM-2 and BTR-40, 50, 60, and 152 reconnaissance vehicles and APCs. Even the BMP-2 has relatively light armor and retains many of the ergonomic problems in fighting from the vehicle and using its guns and anti-tank guided missile launchers as with the BMP-1. The BMP has only moderate ability to escort tanks in a combat environment where the opponent has modern sensors and anti-tank guided weapons.

US experts also believe Syria has made relatively limited progress in improving its combined arms and armored war fighting capabilities since 1982. They believe that Syrian exercise and command post training is weak above the battalion or regimental level, that Syrian tactics are rigid, and that Syrian reaction times are slow.

Syria can mass large numbers of towed artillery weapons and multiple rocket launchers, and this could have a major impact in an area like the Golan where ranges are relatively short and where Syria normally deploys much of its artillery in the area. At the same time, massed artillery fire has only limited lethality against well dug in defenses and armor, and Syria lacks the sensors and battle management systems to concentrate its artillery fire with great precision and rapid switch fires. Syria will also have problems in maneuvering its artillery. Only about 28% of Syria's artillery consists of modern self-propelled weapons.

Syria does have good physical defenses of its own positions on the Golan. It has spent decades improving terrain barriers and creating anti-tank barriers and ditches. At the same time, Syria's only modern third-generation anti-tank guided missile launchers consist of 200 Milans out of total holdings of some 5,500 anti-

TABLE 7.1   The Syrian-Israeli Balance—Part One

Category/Weapon	IISS		JCSS	
	Israel	Syria	Israel	Syria
Manpower				
Total Active	185,000	330,000	177,500	390,000
(Conscript)	138,500	–	–	–
Total Reserve	430,000	400,000	427,000	142,500
Total	615,000	730,000	604,500	532,500
Paramilitary	6,050	8,000	13,500	400,000
Land Forces				
Active Manpower	125,000	220,000	136,000	306,000
Reserve Manpower	365,000	100,000	363,000	100,000
Total Manpower	490,000	300,000	499,000	406,000
Main Battle Tanks	4,700	4,600	3,850	4,800
Total Other Armor	11,000	4,800	8,100	4,980
AIFVs	(350)	(2,300)	–	–
APCs/Recce/Scouts/Half-Tracks	(10,650)	(2,500)	–	–
ATGW Launchers	1005	5,050	–	2,000
Total Guns and Mortars			1,300	2,400
SP Artillery	1,150	470	–	–
Towed Artillery	500	1,630	–	–
MRLs	100+	480	–	–
Mortars	6,500	4,500+	–	–
SSM Launchers	20	46+	12	62
AA Guns	1010+	1,985	–	–
Lt. SAM Launchers	945	?		

The Syrian-Israeli Balance—Part Two

Air Forces				
Active Manpower	32,000	100,000	32,500	80,000
Reserve Manpower	55,000	92,000	54,000	40,000
Aircraft				
Total Fighter/FGA/Recce	453	440	742	515
Fighter	56	280	75	345
FGA/Fighter	325	0	663	170
FGA	50	154	–	–
Recce	22	6	–	–
AEW	4	0	–	–
EW	28	10	–	–
Maritime Reconnaissance (MR/MPA)	3	0	–	–
Tanker	5	0	–	–

TABLE 7.1   (Continued)

Category/Weapon	IISS		JCSS	
	Israel	Syria	Israel	Syria
Transport	40	29	93	23
Combat Training	60	91	–	–
Helicopters				
Attack	117	140	115	100
Other	160	110	138	185
Total	277	250	253	285
SAM Forces				
Batteries	20	99	–	108
Heavy Launchers	–	698	–	–
Naval Forces				
Active Manpower	6,600	6,000	9,000	4,000
Reserve Manpower	10,000	8,000	10,000	2,500
Total Manpower	16,600	14,000	19,000	6,500
Submarines	3	3	3	3
Destroyers/Corvettes				
Missile	3	0	0	0
Other	–	2	0	0
Missile Patrol	20	18	19	21
Coastal/Inshore Patrol	35	11	40	16
Mine	–	7	–	9
Amphibious Ships	1	3	–	–
Landing Craft	4	5	11	3

Source: Adapted from data provided by US experts, the IISS, *Military Balance, 1995–1996,* and the Jaffee Center for Strategic Studies, *The Military Balance in the Middle East, 1993–1994.* Note that data for the IISS are taken from the country chapters. The JCSS data are taken from the summary tables on pages 479–509.

tank guided missile launchers.[1] These relatively low grade anti-tank guided missile systems can hardly be ignored, but they greatly reduce the effectiveness of Syrian anti-tank forces both in the defensive mode and in providing mechanized infantry support for armored operations.

The Syrian Air Force and Air Defense Command have more severe problems. Syria's 20 Su-24s are its only truly modern attack fighters and they lack the avionics and precision all-weather strike capabilities of first-line Israeli attack aircraft. Similarly, Syria's 20 MiG-29s are its only modern fighters with advanced beyond-visual-range and look-down shoot-down capabilities, and Syria so far has shown little ability to use such aircraft effectively in training and simulated combat or to generate high sortie rates. The bulk of Syria's air defense fighters have poor look-down shoot-down capabilities and beyond-visual-range combat capability, and

FIGURE 7.1   Israel Versus Syria

Land Weapons

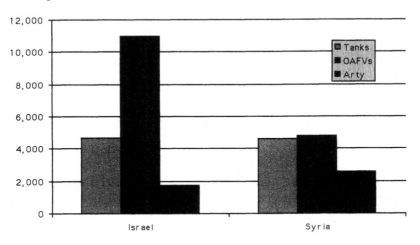

Air Forces

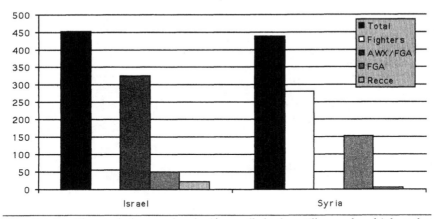

Note: Total Artillery includes towed and self-propelled tube artillery and multiple rocket launchers. Total air forces include only operational fixed wing fighter, fighter-attack, and reconnaissance aircraft in combat units, less aircraft in combat training units.

still operate largely using obsolete and electronically vulnerable ground controlled intercept (GCI) techniques.

Syria has also been slow to modernize its attack helicopter tactics. While Syria's attack helicopter tactics were successful in the 1982 war, they were successful largely because the IDF did not expect them and was often trying to rush its advances without adequate coordination. The IDF has now greatly improved its counterattack helicopter training and tactics and light air defense weaponry.

Syria has no airborne early warning and electronic intelligence and warfare aircraft which approach Israel's capabilities. Syria has vast holdings of land-based air defenses, but these consist largely of obsolescent SA-2, SA-3, SA-5, and S-6 surface-to-air missile systems and shorter range systems. Israel was able to defeat all of these systems in 1982, except for the SA-5, which was only deployed late in 1982 after the fighting.

Syria has not modernized its C^{4}I/BM system to anything approaching a high capability automated system, and virtually all of its systems require active radar to operate—which makes them very vulnerable to Israeli anti-radiation missiles, target location and identification systems, and electronic warfare capabilities. While such land-based air defenses can scarcely be disregarded, and are certain to both force Israel to conduct a massive air defense suppression campaign and fly attack missions that avoid or minimize exposure to surviving defenses. Syrian air defenses do not have the quality necessary to match their quantity.

It is uncertain how well Syria understands the technical limitations of its forces. While it has attempted to remedy many of its technical problems by procuring upgrades and supporting technology from the West, Syria has not done well in obtaining such technology or in negotiating recent arms agreements with Russia and other suppliers. As has been discussed earlier, Syria owes Russia roughly $7.5 billion for past arms purchases and a total of $11 billion for both its military and civil debt. There is little prospect that Russia will ever be paid, and Russia failed to fill a major arms deal in 1992 for some 24 MiG-29s, 12 Su-27s, 3 T-72s and T-74s, and an unknown number of SA-10 and SA-16 missiles because of Syria's lack of finances.[2]

Syria's economic liberalization may give it added resources to spend on arms, but it has yet to make such expenditures. Although Syrian reporting on military and security expenditures sharply understates the true scale of its expenditures, it does provide a rough indication of the trend in spending. According to Syrian reporting, Syrian military spending totaled about 35% of its budget in the early 1990s, but dropped to 25% during 1994 and 1995. The most recent Syrian reports indicate that military and security expenditures were allocated $960 million in 1995 out of a total budget of $3,888 million. Once inflation is considered, these expenditures were lower than in 1994 and significantly lower than in the early 1990s—when Syria had the benefit of concessional sales and aid from the former Soviet Union.[3]

This does not mean all arms transfers have halted. Syria may have signed a new cooperation agreement with Russia in April, 1994 for "defensive weapons and spare parts." There have been unconfirmed reports, which disagree with the analysis of US experts, that indicate Syria was able to spend some $1.4 billion on military modernization between 1992 and 1994 and will be able to begin full rate production of the North Korean Scud missile as early as mid-1996. There have also been unconfirmed reports that Syria negotiated with Russia in 1994 to buy 30 Su-24s, 50 MiG-29s, 14 Su-17s, 300 T-72s and T-74s, S-300 multiple rocket launchers (a Russian system similar to the MLRS), and SA-10 missiles.[4]

Even if most of these reports of new arms sales are true, they would still leave Syria with far fewer funds than it needs to recapitalize its current force structure to compete with Israel in modernization—perhaps with only about half the funds and projected deliveries necessary to replace its older land force equipment and aircraft. It would also take Syria some three to five years to fully absorb all of the new technology it needs, integrate it into effective combat systems, and retrain its forces—assuming it recognizes the need to do so. Barring massive outside aid, Syrian forces are almost certain to continue to go "hollow" for the foreseeable future, although moderate deliveries of advanced modern aircraft, tanks, and surface-to-air missile systems like the SA-10 could still help correct key Syrian weaknesses.

Further, Syria's technical limitations are compounded by a politicized and compartmented command structure, inadequate military pay, poor manpower management, poor technical training, poor overall training—particularly in realistic combat exercises—and aggressor training. Syrian forces have inadequate combat and service support, equipment for night and poor weather warfare, long range sensors and targeting systems, and mobile rapidly maneuverable logistics, recording, and combat repair capability. While individual Syrian officers have shown a keen understanding of many of these problems, Syria has never taken effective action to deal with them.

Comparing Total Syrian and Israeli Forces: Israeli Capabilities

Israel is not "ten feet tall" and faces qualitative problems of its own. Military spending has dropped from 19.1% of the GDP in 1982 and 11.2% in 1991, to well under 10% in 1995. Israel is attempting to convert its force structure to a smaller "peacetime" force that reflects its peace with Egypt and Jordan. It has reduced the number of men and women called up for conscript service and their period of service, and there are some reports it plans to cut its reserves from 430,000 in the mid-1990s to as few as 230,000.[5] These force cuts inevitably will increase Israel's vulnerability to saturation through sheer mass and raise questions about Israel's ability to fully mobilize against a Syrian surprise attack.

IDF experts feel that the improvement of intelligence capabilities and fighting in all-weather conditions of the kind Israel often encounters on the Golan are two of the highest priority lessons that Israel has drawn from the Gulf War.[6] At the same time, they indicate that Israel now needs to act on strategic warning at least 24 hours before a Syrian attack to mobilize and man its forward defenses, and needs 36 to 48 hours of reaction time to be fully effective. Israel miscalculated the compromises it could make in reducing the size and readiness of its reserve forces between 1970 and 1973, and it has been over 20 years since it faced the kind of challenge that forced it to fully mobilize under true wartime conditions and test its system *in extremis*—a "learning experience" that military history shows is inevitably more demanding than even the best peacetime exercises and training.

Israel also has recapitalization problems of its own. It has not been able to afford to convert its armor to a coherent force of first-line systems. Israel's 930 Merkavas and 750 M-60A3s are its only tanks which are likely to have a decisive "edge" over the T-72—although some analysts argue that its Magach 7s are equal to the M-60A3 in many areas. Roughly 1,390 of Israel's 3,895 tanks are relatively low grade Centurions, T-54s, T-55s, or T-62s.[7] Israel is expanding its Merkava force, but only at a rate of about 60 per year.

Israel has had to choose between funding improved tanks and funding improvements in other armored fighting vehicles. As a result, it has few modern AIFVs to supplement its tanks. It only has a small number of Nagmashots and Achzarits—although large numbers of its 6,000 M-113s have been converted from APCs to AIFVs. While Israel has built up a massive modern artillery force of some 1,284 self-propelled weapons and more than 100 modern multiple rocket launchers—and is acquiring the US MLRS—it is still dependent on large numbers of obsolete half-tracks for support vehicles and reserves.

While sea power is not likely to be a significant issue in any near term Arab-Israeli conflict—particularly one between Israel and Syria—Israel has also had to cut its procurement of new Sa'ar corvettes from eight to three and cut back substantially on its Barak ship defense missile, although these are armed with Harpoon and Gabriel ship-to-ship missiles.[8]

At the same time, the Israeli Air Force (IAF) is one of the most modern air forces in the world. It has systematically improved its conventional attack—or "soft strike"—capability since 1973, and it has many of the same advantages US air power enjoyed during the Gulf War, plus a wide range of subsystems and weapons tailored to deal with threats like Syria and the special conditions in its theater of operations. The IAF is in the process of being strengthened by the purchase of 20–24 F-15Is, 50 surplus USAF F-16s, additional AH-64s for a total force of 40, 10 Black Hawk helicopters, advanced new RPVs, and further Israeli upgrades of the F-4E into the Phantom 2000.[9]

Israel also has modern versions of the IHawk and three advanced Patriot surface-to-air missiles—and is the only country in the Middle East with the technical resources to steadily modernize and improve the capability of its electronic warfare and reconnaissance aircraft. At the same time, Israel has the C4I/BM, training, night warfare, electronic warfare, support, sustainability, and other specialized qualitative capabilities necessary to exploit the revolution in military affairs. Its superior technology is fully supported by superior tactics and training, and this gives it all of the qualitative advantages over Syria that were discussed earlier.

This mix of Israeli capabilities should allow Israel to decisively defeat Syria in any prolonged conflict in which Israel reacts to strategic warning. There are, however, alternative contingencies. They include a sudden or surprise Syrian attack through the Golan or a combined Syrian-Jordanian attack—which is discussed in the following section.

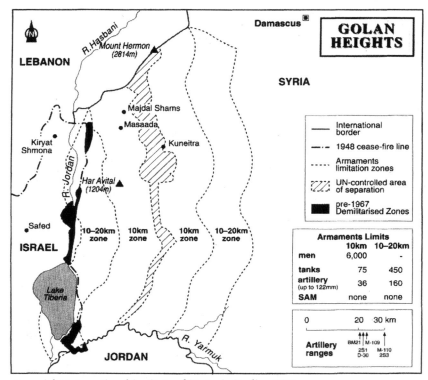

Copyright International Institute of Strategic Studies, 1995

An Attack Through the Golan Heights Before
a Peace Settlement with Syria[10]

The Golan Heights is one of the most critical strategic areas in the Middle East. It is a plateau that has about 1,150 square kilometers. It is roughly 67 kilometers long from north to south and a maximum of 25 kilometers wide from the buffer zone between Syrian and Israeli-occupied territory on the Golan to Israel and the Galilee. Prior to the 1967 war, the Syrian-Israeli border along the Golan was 76 kilometers long.[11]

Movement through the Golan area is limited by Mount Hermon in the north and by the Ruqqad and Yarmuk River wadis in the far south. In the south, it rises from below sea level at the Jordan River to 929 meters at Mount Faris and 780 meters at the plateau at Aniam, although the southern end sometimes slopes down to heights of 350–450 meters. The central Golan has a relatively gentle slope down toward Damascus, but it rises very sharply above the Sea of Galilee, Jordan River, and the surrounding land below Mount Hermon. In the space of less than 20 kilometers, it rises to 780 meters at Shaal and 1,204 meters at Mount Avital. In the north, it rises from 100 meters in Israel to peaks as high as 1,121 meters at

Mount Hermon, and 890 to 950 meters on the Golan plateau at Khan Arnabah. The Golan descends sharply to the Jordan River and the Huleh Valley and is difficult to approach through Jordan.

Movement through the Golan can occur through five main east-west routes, but each presents problems. The terrain on the Golan is relatively smooth at the top, but it is broken up with small volcanic cones that make natural sites for defensive positions and strong points. Israel occupies the key line of volcanic peaks to the west of Quneitra, and Israeli ground forces are deployed on the high ground on the Golan to the east of the line of volcanic mounds that defines the Golan watershed. This is the most favorable line of defense on the Golan, and Israel has created an extensive network of fire points, anti-tank obstacles, and mine fields. Syria has created a formidable series of fortified positions, fire points, mine fields, and anti-tank ditches and barriers on its side of the Golan.

Israeli analysts indicate that Israel's present borders on the Golan are highly defensible. In the south, the Yarmuk and Ruqqad river beds constitute a natural obstacle for armored combat vehicles and even for the movement of infantry forces. Observation posts and light forces are sufficient for the defense of this sector. In the eastern Golan, a chain of hills extending from Tel Saki near Ramat Magshimim to Mt. Hermon in the north forms a reasonable defense line. The IDF positions on these hills—Tel Faris, Bashanit ridge, Mt. Shipon, Mts. Avital, Bental, Hermonit, Mt. Odem, and Mt. Hermon—make it easy to detect any Syrian military effort and to respond to it rapidly. The topography permits a Syrian breakthrough at only two points: the Tel Faris area and the Quneitra area, and the Golan gives Israel strategic depth to defend the Huleh and Jordan Valleys.

The Golan has economic value as well. There are some 14,000 Jews settled on the Golan in 29 settlements and some 15,000 Druze.[12] It gives Israel de facto control over the headwaters of the Jordan and Sea of Galilee and access to the critical water resources in the region. Control of the Golan also affects control of the waters of the Hatzbani River and any diversion of the Banias River. As a result, any peace settlement must deal with both settlement and water issues in the area.

The Golan provides the IDF with excellent staging points for radars and observation points to cover Israel and Syria. Israel has observation points on Mount Hermon (1,121 meters) in the northwest, on the volcanic mound at Tel Avital (1,024 meters) in the central Golan, and on Tel Faris (929 meters) in the southern Golan. These posts not only provide a relatively clear picture of Syrian military activity near Israel, but the post on Mount Hermon provides surveillance of part of Lebanon.[13] The Golan is only 50 kilometers from Damascus, and Israeli sensors have a direct line of sight to downtown Damascus, as well as direct line of sight and line of sensor observation of threatening movements from Lebanon and Syria.[14] The Israeli signals and electronic intelligence sensors on the Golan are an integral part of Israel's early warning system and provide good intelligence coverage of much of Syria and some of western Iraq.

Israeli control of the Golan confronts Syria with the fact that Israel has a springboard to launch an attack into Syria, a platform for artillery and rocket attacks, and the ability to target movement and military positions from the Golan to Damascus. The Golan also provides Israel with an excellent platform for artillery and missile fire and for launching UAVs and other sensor systems that can be used in attacking Syria's land-based air defenses and air force.

Israel will have to give up these advantages if it withdraws from the Golan, and such a withdrawal would also increase Israel's vulnerability. The Golan is within 20 kilometers of Israeli cities like Tiberias and 60 kilometers of relatively obstacle-free terrain from Haifa and Acre. The Golan would be a good observation platform for Syria, which could locate visual and signals intelligence observation posts at Mount Herman, Tel al-Hara, Tel al-Sha'ar, and Tel al-Jalbiya. Syria could also use the Golan for artillery and missile attacks on northern Israel. Syria never repopulated its former provincial capital of Quneitra after the 1974 disengagement, but would not have to worry about Israeli fire on Syrian towns in the Golan.

Even if a peace agreement restricted Syrian deployments and created a demilitarized zone, the terrain would give Syrian ground forces an advantage in a "race for the Golan." Syrian armor could exploit the fact that the Syrian side of the Golan consists of relatively flat or smooth undulating terrain while the western "edge" of the Golan plateau rises in steep increments of hundreds of feet in something approaching a vertical "wall." This factor allows Syrian armor to descend the western edge relatively quickly, but makes it difficult for the IDF to use armor and infantry to fight its way up the "wall" to the heights. Further, if Syria were able to achieve a breakthrough and advance into the Galilee and then dig in, Syrian forces could prove costly to dislodge to defend—although there are only a limited number of routes Syria could take, and any advance along these routes and into the Huleh Valley would make Syrian forces vulnerable to Israeli air attacks.

Control of the Golan could give Syrian radar improved sensor coverage of Israel while greatly complicating the IAF's problems in air operations, in suppressing Syrian surface-to-air missiles, and in deploying radars to improve its air warning and control of Syrian fighter intercepts.

These differences in strategic vulnerability and relative advantage help explain why it is so difficult to reach a peace settlement and why Israel has insisted on maintaining Israeli-manned observation posts on the Golan. It also explains why any contingency analysis of a conflict on the Golan is highly dependent on whether a Syrian attack takes place before a peace settlement or after Syrian recovery of the Golan.

Much depends on whether a Syrian attack could take place with enough surprise or speed to prevent Israel from mobilizing before Syria might create new facts on the ground—seizing back the Golan or even penetrating into the Galilee and then using diplomatic pressure to reach a cease-fire. If Syria could attack before Israel mobilized and deployed, such an attack might initially make total national peacetime military strength or fully mobilized force ratios and capabilities moot.

As a result, the balance of forces each side could bring to bear in the critical 24 hour period before the attack began and after it commenced is a critical factor in assessing the Israeli-Syrian balance. The character and success of any such Syrian attack on the Golan would depend on its ability to conduct a massive sudden move under the cloak of weather or night or its ability to implement a political and military deception plan. Syria showed this all too clearly in 1973, when 1,400 tanks and 28,000 other weapons and vehicles launched a surprise attack against unprepared Israeli forces on the Golan and thrust 15 kilometers into Israeli territory.

The Israeli-Syrian disengagement agreement signed on May 31, 1974, limits the forces Israel and Syria can deploy in the Golan area. There is a 3–6 kilometer wide disengagement zone where no forces are permitted, except for a UN disengagement observer force (UNDOF) of 1,000–1,250 men. This force has been in place since 1974 and has manning from Austria, Canada, Finland, and Poland.

Israeli and Syrian forces are then separated by a 10 kilometer wide force limitation zone where each side can deploy a maximum of 6,000 soldiers, 75 tanks, and 36 short range howitzers (122 mm equivalent). There is third 10 kilometer wide force limitation zone where both sides are limited to 450 tanks and 162 artillery weapons with a range not exceeding 20 kilometers. Finally, each side is forbidden to deploy surface-to-air missiles closer than 25 kilometers from the disengagement zone.

Syria does, however, have large forces near the Golan area with an active strength of nearly 40,000 men. Although Syria would need sustained training and exercise activity to properly prepare its forces for a massive all-out attack, and some 48 to 72 hours of intensive mobilization and redeployment activity to properly support and sustain such an attack, it might still take the risk of attacking with the forces on hand and supporting them with follow-on echelons. Under these conditions, Syria could use its existing forces to attack with minimal warning and mass large amounts of artillery to support its armored advance.

The Syrian I Corps, which is headquartered in Damascus, has the 5th and 7th Mechanized Divisions in the Golan area, the 9th Armored Division in support, the 1st Armored Division northeast of Qatana, and the 569th Armored Division and a Republican Guards Division near Damascus. Three more armored divisions—the 11th, 17th, and 18th—are located in the general area between Homs and Hama.[15]

As will be discussed shortly, Syria could put simultaneous pressure on Israel by attacking across the Lebanese border with the 30,000 men it stations in the Beqa'a or using the 3,000 men in the Hizbollah.[16] Syria does have at least two high quality heavy divisions and three special forces regiments that performed well in 1982 and could bring two other heavy divisions to bear in support. It could reinforce such units relatively rapidly, although the readiness and training of many of these Syrian reinforcements would be limited. Virtually all heavy units in the Syrian army now suffer from a sustained lack of spare parts and outside support, a result of Syria's lack of funds and the breakup of the Soviet Union.

Such an attack would confront the IDF with a major threat, and much would depend on whether the IDF and Israeli Air Force reacted to initial warning indicators on a near "hair trigger" basis to prevent significant initial Syrian gains. The IDF has completely reorganized its defenses on the Golan since 1973 and has progressively improved these defenses ever since. Although the May 31, 1974, separation of forces agreement between Israel and Syria cost Israel about 600 square kilometers of territory on the Golan, particularly control over the dominant Bahta ridge line in the south and Rafid junction, Israel is also aided by the fact that it no longer is forced to split its forces to defend against both Egypt and Syria.

The IDF has deployed a wide range of all-weather sensors and can detect virtually any major Syrian movement in time to mobilize and react—although such indicators can never ensure that the IDF makes the right assessment of Syrian moves or whether its political leaders choose to react. It has built up major strong points in the Golan, specially tailored heavy armored brigades designed to blunt any initial attack, and improved its mining and artillery capabilities in the Golan. It has significantly improved its ability to rapidly reinforce its forward deployed forces and to provide artillery and rocket support. It has developed much stronger attack helicopter forces and fixed wing air capabilities that can attack Syrian armor with considerable precision and lethality even at night or in relatively poor weather. Israel has also improved its real- and near real-time long range surveillance and battle management capabilities.

Israeli coverage of Syria includes advanced airborne radar reconnaissance that extends north of Damascus from positions in Israeli air space, coverage from advanced RPVs which include electronic intelligence (ELINT) as well as imagery systems, airborne ELINT coverage capable of characterizing and precisely locating any Syrian electronic emitter including radars, and land-based sensors in the Golan and on Mount Hermon.

Any Syrian attack on the Golan would also involve the risk of strategic retaliation. Israel currently has so large a qualitative "edge" in air, precision attack, and electronic warfare capabilities that it could probably win air superiority in a matter of hours and break through part of Syria's land-based air defenses in a day. Israel could then strike high value targets in Syria with relative impunity in a conventional war—and Syria would only be able to launch limited numbers of air and missile attacks in retaliation.

Ever since 1973, the IDF has organized its targeting, battle management, and strike plans for both conventional and nuclear strategic strikes on key potential enemies. Israel gives high priority to destroying and suppressing the enemy's air and land-based air defense capability during the initial stages of the battle. The potential scale of Israel's success in suppressing Syrian air defenses in a future battle over the Golan is indicated by the fact that during the 1982 war, Israel essentially broke the back of the Syrian surface-to-air missile network in the Beka'a Valley in one day, on June 9. Israel shot down over 80 Syrian fighters, and only lost 1 A-4 in flying a total of over 1,000 combat sorties—including the sorties delivered against Syrian ground-based air defenses in the Beka'a. Israel also was able to devote an extraordinary percentage of its total sorties to the attack mission, although it should be noted that even in the 1973 war, some 75% of all IAF sorties were attack sorties.[17]

The IAF has learned from its mistakes in the 1973 and 1982 wars. It has steadily improved its coordination with the land forces in combined operations. It can do a much better job when coordinating the air-land battle in both tactical operations and at the strategic level. Its C⁴I and battle management systems may lack all the sophisticated technology and techniques used by US forces, but they are tailored to a unique area and set of missions and allow given assets to be used with great effectiveness.

The IAF is organized and equipped to use a combination of electronic intelligence aircraft, jammers, stand-off munitions, land-based strike systems, UAVs, and other countermeasures to suppress both Syrian and Jordanian air defenses. It has steadily improved its technology bases to reflect the lessons of the Gulf War, while Syria and Jordan have made virtually no significant improvement in their air defenses since the 1980s. As a result, the IAF could probably win immediate freedom of action over the Golan and West Bank, win air superiority over critical areas of Syrian and Jordan in 24–48 hours, and then maintain air supremacy over much of Syria and all of Jordan.

Israel has sufficient long range precision munitions, land-based missile and rocket systems, and UAVs to then use conventional weapons to cripple the power, water, refining, key communications and command centers, and critical industrial facilities of either or both confrontation states before the US or outside powers could intervene. If Israel were to launch such attacks on a surprise or preemptive basis, or do so before Syrian and/or Jordanian air forces were fully alert and dispersed, it would achieve nearly certain success. It would have a very high probability of success even against fully alert Syrian and Jordanian forces.

The IAF does, however, have certain basic operational constraints. The IAF cannot destroy the dispersed land forces of a major enemy like Syria within a short period, although it might be decisive in cooperation with the IDF in an air-land offensive. It can contribute to the land battle, but Syria's forces near the Golan are too close to the border and too large for any combination of interdiction bombing and close air support to act as a substitute for effective defensive action by the IDF's land forces.

The strength of the IAF is limited, and its ability to win rapid air supremacy and conduct strategic attacks would be radically different if it confronted both a hostile Syria and a hostile Egypt. The IAF cannot be used as flexibly in attacks on populated areas, and any effort to conduct precision bombing in urban warfare raises a serious risk of collateral damage. It cannot normally locate and destroy guerrilla forces or play a decisive role in low intensity conflict.

There are limits to its ability to exploit its capabilities. If the IAF is to minimize IAF losses and inflict maximum damage on Syria, it must achieve strategic surprise—either through preemption or deception. As Israel learned in 1982, it does not make sense to reveal its air defense suppression capabilities in limited attacks with limited objectives, and give an enemy time to improve its own defense and develop countermeasures. The most effective uses of Israeli air power involve massive, preemptive strikes on Syria's air defenses, ground-based air defenses, and missile delivery systems.

Such attacks, however, approach total war and risk Syrian escalation to biological and chemical weapons. They also require a level of Israeli strategic commit-

ment to achieving rapid strategic success that could force Israel to escalate to
weapons of mass destruction if conventional IAF attacks failed. Further, it involves sudden unilateral Israeli military action under conditions where Israel
must expect US and outside pressure to limit such military action.

On the one hand, the IAF operates under political conditions that deter large
scale action. On the other hand, the IAF operates under military conditions that
lead it toward sudden and massive escalation. This is particularly true if Israel
should seek any decisive victory over Syria or Iraq. It is unclear that Israel feels
that any land victory over Syria or Iraq would be sufficient to force Syria to accept
a peace or so weaken it that it could not recover as a threat in a few years.

At least some Israeli planners have argued since 1973—reinforced by Israel's
experience in 1982—that Israel must fight either very limited military actions or
strategically decisive ones. While Israel's current political leadership has no inten-
tion or desire to fight a strategically decisive war, it remains a future military possibility.

The existence of Israeli nuclear weapons would also probably succeed in deter-
ring Syrian use of biological and chemical weapons in response to conventional
strategic air attacks. While no IDF commander can dismiss worst case scenarios,
and the risk exists that Syria might use chemical weapons against the Golan and
chemically armed missile strikes against Israeli mobilization centers, the IDF
should be able to repulse any Syrian attack and inflict a devastating series of air,
rocket, and missile strikes on Syria within a 12–48 hour period.

Even so, Syria might still risk a limited war—if it felt it could achieve strategic
surprise and hold a significant amount of the Golan long enough for world opinion to bring a halt to fighting and use such "shock therapy" to achieve its goals in
the peace process. It seems unlikely that Syria would take such a risk without a su-
perpower patron to support it diplomatically, but it might try to use the threat of
escalation to chemical warfare as a substitute for outside diplomatic and military
support. Such an attack might also seem feasible if Syria felt it could attack Israeli
forces on the Golan before Israel could mobilize—as it did in 1973—and if it
could exploit world opinion to achieve a rapid cease-fire. Much of the Syrian
army is forward deployed and could rapidly mobilize and attack across the Golan
with roughly six armored division equivalents. This attack could potentially be
supported by a thrust through Jordan and/or Lebanon, although such a thrust is
now politically unlikely.

While Israel has greatly improved its defenses and fortifications on the Golan,
and Syria could not prevent Israel from retaliating with powerful air strike capabilities or hope to penetrate much beyond the Golan, Syria might still launch such an
attack in an effort to create new facts on the ground and create at least shallow defenses and emergency fortifications. Syria might also attempt to use such an attack
to alter the outcome of peace negotiations, to respond to a failure of the peace negotiations, or to exploit a peace agreement that disrupted or weakened the IDF
presence on the Golan without placing compensating limitations on Syria.

An Attack Through the Golan Heights After a Peace Settlement with Syria[18]

Any change in the military deployments on the Golan resulting from the peace process could also shift the balance between Israel and Syria. It is one thing to fight from prepared positions on the Golan, and another thing to fight up the Golan Heights against well positioned Syrian forces which would have time in which to create limited defensive barriers. The entire Golan is only 20–24 kilometers wide—and the terrain limits the potential combat area to about 240 square kilometers.

If Syria could succeed in advancing to the base areas it occupied on the edge of the Heights in 1967, it would have an altitude advantage of about 120 meters over the surface of the Sea of Galilee and about 100 meters over the heights of lower Galilee. Such a terrain advantage has lost some of its meaning in an era of high performance tanks, attack helicopters, attack aircraft, and artillery with beyond-visual-range precision fire capability, but dug in forces would still present problems for Israel and could not be dislodged without casualties.

Both military planning and peace negotiations must also take account of the fact that a Syrian attack through the Golan might also become more feasible as a result of future weapons transfers to Syria. Syrian armor would be considerably more effective if it were equipped with modern thermal sights, fire control systems, anti-armor rounds, and armor—although it is far from clear that any of the T-72s in Syria's inventory can currently be adapted to match the capabilities of the Merkava in any of these areas. A major improvement in target acquisition and fire management systems could also greatly improve the suppressive and direct fire capabilities of Syrian artillery.

Equally important, Syria might blunt some of the IAF's "edge" in the air if it could actually obtain its reported orders of 30–50 additional MiG-29s, 24–37 SU-24s, and the SA-10 surface-to-air missile and Israel did not react by strengthening its own forces. Deployment of an advanced heavy surface-to-air missile like the Russian SA-10 might significantly reduce the IAF's ability to rapidly suppress Syrian air defense capabilities and the ability of the Israeli Air Force to use attack aircraft and helicopters to halt Syrian armor—although Israel's anti-radiation missiles and stand-off precision guided weapons would still have considerable capability in destroying and suppressing land-based air defense weapons.

Giving up the Golan reduces the strategic threat Israel can pose to Syria, and increases the strategic risk to Israel. From a Syrian perspective, such a shift in the balance may be essential for a peace agreement or any concessions on arms control. Israel's positions on the Golan not only occupy Syria's territory, they do give Israel a major advantage in using artillery or missiles to attack Syria, in any land or helicopter assault on Syria, in providing intelligence coverage of civil and military developments from the Golan to Damascus, and in targeting Syrian forces and positions.

At the same time, if Syria could succeed in deploying forces to cover the entire Golan, it would then be only 52 kilometers from the Israeli port of Acre on the Mediterranean and 12 kilometers from the first major Israeli town at Safed. It would only be about 8 kilometers from the Israeli settlements in the northwest tip of Israel and 35 kilometers from Nazareth. Syria might also use its occupation of the Golan to try to reassert its claims to Lake Tiberius or to violate the force limitations in the vicinity of Damascus that are certain to be part of any peace agreement.

Syria also would not have to take such territory to increase its artillery threat to much of Northern Israel. Syria has large numbers of FROGs, and much of Syria's artillery and multiple rocket launchers have effective ranges up to 35 kilometers.[19] Syria can also target accurately against fixed targets at such ranges using RPVs. As a result, the Golan has potential military significance in allowing Syria to use artillery to attack Israel and increasing the risk of a surprise Syrian attack against the Galilee—although any such use of the Golan would be targetable by Israeli sensors and vulnerable to massive retaliation by Israeli air and artillery forces.

These issues have led those Israelis who oppose giving up the Golan to argue that there is no parallel between a peace settlement with Egypt and one with Syria. They argue that the Sinai demilitarization agreement had substantial security significance, with a depth of some 200–300 kilometers. This means that even if Egypt should violate the peace treaty, the IDF could immediately enter into a war of maneuver with air and surface forces and halt the Egyptians while they were still deep inside Sinai.

In contrast, these Israelis argue that even if the Golan Heights were fully demilitarized when they were handed over to Syria, and Syria agreed to demilitarize an additional 40 kilometer belt within its own territory, such force limitation measures would have little security value. They argue that the Syrian army would be capable of advancing rapidly on level ground and could move at least two to three divisions to the front overnight from their staging points in the Damascus area. They argue that Syria has developed commando units intended to occupy key junctions on the Golan Heights, with the objective of delaying Israel's reserve forces, and is capable of using Scud C missiles against Israel's reserve assembly and equipment storage areas and to significantly delay access to the front by reserve forces. This might allow Syria to penetrate into the Galilee and/or fully militarize the Golan, while the IDF would then have to respond by fighting back up the Golan Heights from its bases in the Huleh and Jordan Valleys, and do so in spite of decisive topographic inferiority.

They also argue that any agreements which attempt to treat Israel and Syria equally in defining the disengagement and force limitation zones could push the IDF into deploying outside of the Galilee and Samaria, creating major problems for Israel in responding to any Syrian build-up on the Golan. This leads many to argue that Israel must retain significant forces in the northern Galilee and its military camps and equipment and supply storage areas in the Jordan Valley.

Given such arguments, it is not surprising that Israeli experts also argue over how much of the Golan can safely be traded for peace. Some Israelis have argued for a compromise that would only give the four key Druze villages in the Golan and control of the volcanic peaks of Tel al-Aram and Tel Abu al-Nada (which overlook Quneitra) back to Syria. This compromise would allow Israel to keep its settlements and some strategic depth. Others have argued for a staged withdrawal from the Golan that would keep positions on the heights for a matter of years. Still others have said Israel might be able to withdraw completely in one step if such a withdrawal was coupled to clear limits on Israeli and Syrian deployments in the area, to "transparency" in terms of guaranteed warning of major movements and surveillance of preparations for a build-up in the rear, and to confidence building measures like limitations on military exercises and pre-notification of military movements.

US experts who have analyzed and modeled such conflicts, and many Israel military experts, sharply dispute this view. They feel that Syria would need at least 12 to 24 hours of very visible movement to move up bridging equipment, redeploy artillery batteries, move ammunition stores, redeploy forward air defense elements, and make armored units ready for combat, and that this process could take a matter of days. They believe there is little chance of Syria achieving surprise with any prudent warning and surveillance measures, and that Syria would take so long to mass and move its armored forces in the forward area that it would be very vulnerable to Israeli air attack, as well as attack using long range artillery weapons with "smart" anti-armor submunitions.

They believe that Syrian armor could not descend the Golan quickly in strength, and that the terrain would channel such a Syrian advance into natural killing grounds for the IDF. Further, the Huleh and Jordan River Valleys and the area above them would make excellent defensive barriers. They also feel that Israel can give up most or all of the Golan and still preserve most of its sensor and advanced attack capabilities. They also feel that the IAF has the capability to do decisive strategic damage to Syria's economy using conventional weapons, and that such strategic strikes would have a far greater deterrent effect than any attempt to fight back up the Golan. It is the latter view that seems most likely to be correct, given the acute weaknesses and problems in Syria's military capabilities.

These assumptions are based, however, on the condition that Israel attacks on strategic warning and reacts with massive and decisive force the moment Syria carries out any major deployment for attack or violation of any peace accords. This is a critical point, and one that needs to be understood by all concerned. Israel's defense after the return of the Golan will have to be based on preemption, and the need for immediate and decisive action grows with each improvement in Syrian readiness and pre-movement preparation. Further, the time-urgent need for decisive action increases in direct proportion to how much of the Golan that Israel gives up, and how many concession it makes on warning, demilitarization, and/or force limitations.

Creating a Secure Peace on the Golan

The fact that the IDF can still defend Israel effectively if it withdraws from the entire Golan is not a reason to withdraw, particularly at a time when Syria can put so little pressure on Israel to compromise. Withdrawal entails some risk to Israel even under the best of conditions, and these risks will increase sharply if Syria is not bound by detailed arms control agreements that:[20]

- Severely limit the number and type of military forces that Syria could deploy in the Golan,
- Allow Israel comparative freedom in building up its defenses and military forces below the Golan,
- Provide for sensor and warning systems that ensure Israel could detect any significant change in Syrian readiness and movement toward the Golan in near real time, and
- Place severe limits on Syrian exercise activity, mobilization, and large scale offensive training.

Syrian officers and arms control negotiators have not expressed detailed public opinions on Syria's perceptions of its military vulnerabilities. It seems highly likely, however, that Syria feels as threatened by the current status quo on the Golan as the IDF feels threatened by the prospects of withdrawal. It also seems likely that Syria has drawn its own lessons from the Gulf War, including its vulnerability to precision artillery fire and Israel's precision air attack capabilities and lack of night and poor weather warfare capability. If Israel feels threatened by surprise and mass, Syria may feel equally threatened by surprise and quality, and may well argue that some of the warning data and "transparency" Israel may want from a peace agreement translates into targeting data for an Israeli offensive against Syria.

Israeli and Syrian Positions

The full details of Israeli and Syrian negotiations over these issues have not been made public. However, several major issues have surfaced where their relative positions seem clear:[21]

- Israel is primarily concerned with military security and normalization of relations with Syria. Syria is primarily concerned with sovereignty and that any agreement be at least as favorable in terms of territory, timing, and other arrangements as the Israeli accords with Egypt over the Sinai.
- Syria's most important single demand is full Israeli withdrawal. Prime Minister Rabin unofficially indicated before his assassination that Israel was willing to fully withdraw, although this meant withdrawal to the international boundary and not the June 4, 1967, boundary—which would give Syria control of part of the eastern shore of Lake Tiberius. This is an Israeli

position that Prime Minister Peres supports but that Syria has so far rejected.[22]

- Israel is concerned with control of the ten meter strip along the eastern shore of Lake Tiberius that is part of the international boundary and gives it control over the entire lake. It is also concerned with the control of the eastern bank of the Jordan River and the flow of waters from the Banias River, which have an important impact on Israel's water supplies. Syria insists on Israeli withdrawal to exactly the same border that existed at the start of the 1973 war.

- Syria initially argued that all security arrangements on the Golan must be "reciprocal, balanced, and equal." In practice, this meant that any disengagement and forced limitation zones would be the same on both sides. Israel argued that the relative size of the zones should be 9:1 in Israel's favor. In June, 1995, Israel announced that Syria seemed to accept the idea that a settlement would have to recognize Israel's need to limit Syria's capability for sudden or surprise attack and would accept an asymmetry that was 5:3 in Israel's favor. However, Israel and Syria remain divided over the details of any such arrangements and such issues as the presence of Israeli inspection and warning posts on the Golan, other early warning systems, demilitarized areas, troop pullbacks, weapons deployment limits, and other security arrangements.

- Syria originally pressed for full Israeli withdrawal in six months while Israel pressed for a period of eight years. Syria has since asked for a complete one stage withdrawal in 18 months, while Israel is now pressing for a two stage withdrawal over three years and eight months—the same period Israel took to withdraw from the Sinai.[23]

- Israel pressed for Israeli warning posts on Syrian soil. Syria rejected such proposals and said that only aerial surveillance would be acceptable.

- Israel pressed for full normalization of relations after the first stage of its withdrawal—as was the case with Israel's peace treaty with Egypt—while Syria only agreed to full normalization after completed withdrawal. Syria seems to have accepted a compromise calling for low level relations after the first stage of withdrawal but not Israel's call for full peace.

Force Limitation Measures and Confidence Building Measures

While it is possible to discuss a long list of possible force limitation measures and confidence building measures that Israel and Syria might agree on to secure a peace agreement, such a discussion is moot. Israel has already developed a detailed list of options and negotiating measures, and Syria almost certainly has a list of its own.

What is clear is that such measures are necessary and that they reflect the geographic and strategic differences between the two parties. Further, it is clear that the strength of such measures will play a critical role in determining the extent to which Israel and Syria can cut military spending in the future, in reducing the incentive for preemption or a race for the Golan in a crisis, and in reducing the risk that peace on the Golan may become a political pawn in some unrelated Arab-Israeli crisis or confrontation.

Given Israeli planning to date, the key issues that are likely to emerge from this aspect of Israeli-Syrian negotiations over the Golan are the:

- Nature of the observation points, sensors, and transparency measures.
- Character and role of an international peacekeeping or observation force.
- Role of the US in securing the Golan.
- Choice of force limitations and their ability to secure against first strikes, preemption, and races to deploy into the area.
- Future disengagement and force separation agreements, and future of the Israeli-Syrian disengagement agreement signed on May 31, 1974, which establishes the present force limitation and disengagement zones.
- Limitations on exercises, redeployments, and other potentially threatening activities and related "transparency" measures.
- Joint military bodies and liaison groups, direct communications, and other measures designed to increase transparency and mutual confidence.
- Changes in military doctrine and technology designed to reduce the risk of attacks across the Golan.

Observation Points, Sensors, and Transparency

The transparency of any security regime will be critical, particularly to Israel. This has led many Israelis to argue that full withdrawal from the Golan would only be acceptable if Syria accepted Israeli observation posts on the Golan, and/or if the IDF was given major advances in weapons technology and new targeting and surveillance systems like the J-8 JSTARS. They feel that airborne platforms are not an adequate substitute for the permanent, line-of-sight SIGINT collection centers necessary to analyze Syrian VHF communications or to ensure reliable all-weather, day and night coverage. They believe that any international monitoring group might be infiltrated, deceived, or pressured to withdraw or limit its activities and that Syria might then wait some time to attack to restore an element of surprise.

There is some justification in these views. Virtually without exception, the proponents of airborne surveillance have made claims about cost, capability, reliability, and endurance which have proved to be untrue. This has been particularly true of claims made for aerostats and long-endurance UAVs. The Golan does present complex weather problems. Further, full "transparency" in intelligence collection and warning cannot depend on a narrow range of sensors. It requires a range of different collection assets and considerable human analysis and intervention.[24] More broadly, it is in both Israel's and Syria's interest that this transparency be as great as possible. The risk of misunderstanding is simply too great—given the cost of reacting or not reacting on a time-urgent basis and of not reacting with large amounts of force. Prestige and sovereignty make good ideological slogans, but avoiding an accidental war or destabilizing misunderstandings is far more important.

"Military science" is almost as uncertain an art as political science, and the fact that Israelis with years of military expertise differ over such issues is a reflection of valid uncertainty and the immense importance of the technical details of the security agreements that must underpin a Syrian-Israeli peace accord. There is no wrong or right view on such issues, and no perfect agreement will ever be possible.

At the same time, some Israeli experts believe that Israel could solve its problems with other means such as satellites or international observers. Israel is nearing the capability to launch satellites with electro-optical sensors and digital down-links. Israel used its three-stage Shavit launch vehicle to launch the Ofeq-3 from a secret launch site at the Palmachim test range near the coast south of Tel Aviv on April 5, 1995.

Israeli radio almost certainly exaggerated in claiming that the satellite could transmit imagery "that allows identification of license numbers in downtown Baghdad." In fact some reports indicate that only about 36 kilograms of its 225 kilogram weight was payload and the rest was structure. Nevertheless, the Ofeq 3 had a much larger payload than the Ofeq 2, and the IDF spokesman confirmed that the 495 pound satellite was in a low orbit that circled the earth every 90 minutes and covered Syria, Iran, and Iraq. It is scarcely coincidental that the Ofeq 3's orbit takes it almost directly over the Golan and Damascus, about 90 miles north of Tehran and 240 miles north of Baghdad.[25]

Some Israeli experts feel that a suitable verification regime should include a US monitoring unit with tailored sensors similar to the unit in the Sinai, unattended ground sensors, and tight restrictions on exercises. Others have indicated that a small international peacekeeping force would be adequate. Some Israeli experts argue for US aid in providing satellite intelligence systems, UAVs, attack helicopters, long endurance UAVs, aerostats, and other military and sensor assets that could compensate Israel for withdrawal from the Golan.

Syrian views on these issues are far less clear, partly because Syria has stressed sovereignty over the Golan and has not articulated its security views in detail. It does seem likely, however, that Syria is deeply concerned with the risk that some crisis might lead Israel to move its forces to the edge of the Golan, preemptively attack Syria, or overreact to Syrian actions and warning indicators. Transparency is ultimately as important to Syria as it is to Israel.

The Role of a Peacekeeping or Observer Force and the Role of the United States

The character and role of a peacekeeping or observer force on the Golan will be another important factor affecting contingency capabilities on the Golan. Neither Israel nor Syria has publicly indicated what kind of peacekeeping or observer force it would like to replace UNDOF, if any. The major options seem to be:

- Retain the UNDOF.
- Strengthen the UNDOF or some new multinational force to provide a much more capable observer force.
- Strengthen the UNDOF or some new multinational force to provide both a much more capable observer force and a force strong enough to act as a "tripwire" that would make any incursions across the Golan a clear act of international aggression.
- Strengthen the UNDOF or some new multinational force to verification functions that would ensure full inspection of Israeli and Syrian activity within the disengagement and force limitation zones and verification of confidence building measures.
- Strengthen the UNDOF or some new multinational force to add a combat force strong enough to delay or resist any incursions across the Golan.
- Formalize the US-Israeli strategic alliance.
- Any of these options could include strong Israeli and Syrian elements or liaison teams to strengthen Israeli and Syrian confidence in their effectiveness.
- These options could also be supported by dedicated intelligence assets, the use of high resolution commercial satellites, and/or guaranteed intelligence reporting by the US and Russia, or some other mix of countries.
- They could also be supported by a more formal set of bilateral security guarantees or alliance between the US and Israel, designed to give Israel guarantees of US support after it withdraws from the Golan.

US Presence in a Peacekeeping Force

There is no easy way to evaluate the merit or risk of having the US deploy a peacekeeping and warning force on the Golan as part of UNDOF or as the core of some replacement force. The fact that such US force might be at risk is scarcely a reason not to deploy it. In fact, the almost obsessive concern of some analysts with the risk of American casualties is almost an insult to the Americans who have volunteered for service in the armed forces or other hazardous duties overseas. The merit of the cause, and the capability to perform the mission, are more serious issues than the risk of casualties.

The UNDOF force has taken similar risks for more than twenty years, and such missions are typical of the peacekeeping missions other countries have manned for many years. Canada and Japan have already volunteered to send such forces to the Golan. Reaching an Israeli-Syrian peace accord and ensuring that Israel will have adequate warning are legitimate strategic interests of the US, and one where many members of the US military would volunteer to accept the risk. This is the position endorsed by Secretary of Defense William Perry and it seems to be correct.

At the same time, much will depend on exactly what type of US force is asked to perform a given function under a given peace agreement. For example, there seems little reason the US should not perform missions like manning observer and sensor posts on the Golan as a substitute for Israeli and Syrian forces, rein-forcing UNDOF, providing a US-only observer force, or heading a non-UN multinational force. All of these options might provide Israel with added confi-dence that such an observer force would remain in a crisis and provide full warn-ing and Syria with confidence that it would not face the risk of Israel overreacting or preempting.

One thing is clear, the US should strongly resist making any choices about whether to commit US personnel or forces in reaction to the arguments of hard-line Jewish Americans who attempt to use "scare tactics" in describing the risk to US forces. These arguments do not reflect legitimate concerns with military and political risks; they are simply a means of disguising the fact that they oppose the peace process and any Israeli withdrawal from the Golan. The US must judge the cost-benefits of a US role in the Golan on the basis of US strategic interests, but the choice of whether Israel should agree to a given peace is a choice that Israelis should make and not Jewish-Americans.

A US-Israeli Strategic Alliance

Somewhat similar issues apply to an Israeli request for a more formal alliance or set of security guarantees from the US of the kind that Prime Minister Peres has discussed in broad detail. Such an alliance could do a number of things to under-pin the peace process. Such an alliance could formally guarantee Israel:

- US presence in a peace monitoring force.
- US aid over a period of time long enough to ensure the IDF could adjust to withdrawal from the Golan.
- Rapid US resupply of Israel in the event of a conflict.
- US support in developing effective defensive counterproliferation capabili-ties—such as anti-tactical ballistic missile defenses and nuclear-chemical-bi-ological defense equipment.
- US intelligence support in key areas related to strategic and tactical warning, and real-time tactical intelligence support in the event of an attack on Israel.
- US guarantees to preserve Israel's air and naval lines of communication.

On the other hand, neither Israel nor the US should have any illusions about US ability to provide Israel with a substitute for strategic self-reliance. There are severe limits on what US power projection capabilities can do during the first hours and days of an attack on Israel. The US can provide Israel with powerful political-mili-tary support during a crisis and could play a major role in limiting any outside rein-forcement of Syria. However, it would take major US heavy combat units in place in Israel for the US to play a major role in opposing a massive Syrian advance.

A major US military presence in Israel would be extraordinarily expensive for the US, would potentially involve the US directly in every new crisis in the region, would probably alienate many friendly Arab states, would almost inevitably be less efficient than an integrated mix of IDF forces, would create inevitable C⁴I/BM problems in coordinating with Israeli forces, and would raise major potential problems in terms of when such a US force should engage in battle.

Token US forces would serve little purpose. Even a full US heavy brigade could only delay a Syrian advance, rather than halt one. The bulk of the defensive task would still fall on the IDF, and the IDF might well end in devoting resources to trying to protect the US force. The US could not deploy additional heavy land forces into Israel in less than several weeks. A limited US air presence would compete directly with the IAF for basing space and present serious C⁴I/BM problems. While the US could reinforce Israel relatively rapidly with air units, naval forces, and cruise missiles, this reinforcement would still not be a substitute for a strong IAF with a decisive technical edge.

There may be a case for a symbolic US combat presence if Israel should feel such symbolism was vital to the peace process, but the war fighting limits of such a US force must be kept carefully in mind. The tyranny of time and space precludes the US from providing security guarantees to Israel based on US reinforcement within the period of hours or days that would be necessary for such a force to have major contingency value. A strong IDF, supported by continued US aid, is a much more realistic alternative.

US "Extended Deterrence"

Similarly, proposals that the US provide Israel with an explicit or tacit guarantee of "extended deterrence" seem to have uncertain credibility and pose major problems in terms of implementation. It is virtually certain that Israel would massively retaliate in the event of any attack using weapons of mass destruction that threatened Israel's existence. Any such "guarantee" by the US would be far less credible and would present the problem that there is little chance the US would ever act preemptively or before it could fully characterize the nature of an attack on Israel.

Such a US guarantee would also present the problems that (a) Israel would probably have to receive massive damage before the US would act, (b) US retaliation would be uncertain in the case of ambiguous attacks on Israel or ones where the use of covert attacks made it difficult to immediately and conclusively identify the attacker, and (c) the US would be confronted with the political problems inherent in retaliating in punishment or revenge without a clear strategic objective which would undermine the credibility of US retaliation.

Including Arab States

There are political and grand strategic dangers in allying the US directly with Israel to the exclusion of Arab participants in the peace process like Egypt and Jordan. The US has spent nearly two decades convincing friendly Arab states that US ties to Israel can be compatible with US ties to friendly Arab states. These efforts have been vital both in allowing the peace process to move forward and in serving US strategic interests outside Israel.

Any US participation in the peace process that formalizes the US-Israeli strategic relationship in ways that favor Israel at the expense of Syrian security or favor Israel to the exclusion of proven friends like Egypt, will have a significant political and strategic price tag for both the US and Israel. As a result, any US participation in a peacekeeping force must be "neutral" to the extent it offers Syria guarantees that the US will provide Syria with strategic warning and that the US will act as a stabilizing presence that will help ensure there is no repetition of the Israeli adventurism that took place in 1982.

Similarly, any more formal US-Israeli strategic relationship must be explicitly linked to US military support only in the event of an attack on Israel or an imminent threat of attack, and serious consideration should be given to providing similar guarantees to Egypt, Jordan, and any other participant in the peace process who demonstrates a full commitment to peace, to confidence building measures and regional arms control efforts, and to eliminating terrorism and violent extremism. It is to every nation's interest that a peace agreement be based on a mix of self-reliance and regional security negotiations, and not on overexclusive strategic relationships or overdependence on the US.

The Lebanese Dimension[26]

While the Golan is the focus of the current Israeli-Syrian peace talks, Lebanon is now divided between a nation that is largely under Syrian control and a much smaller Israeli-controlled security zone in southern Lebanon along the Israeli border.[27]

Some discussions of an Israeli-Syrian peace agreement assume that Syria would either withdraw from Lebanon or restrict its military presence to the Beqa'a and positions far enough north of the Israeli border so that they would only pose a limited threat to Israel, and one that would not require any adjustment in the present deployment and strength of Israeli forces.

It is also possible, however, that the peace talks could fail and that Syria might then exploit its control of Lebanon to either broaden any attack on Israel or to use Lebanon for a proxy war—involving the Hizbollah. Further, it is possible that a peace agreement may leave Syria in tacit control of Lebanon—subject to some formal or informal agreement regarding the size, structure, and deployment of Syrian forces. There are now hundreds of thousands of Syrian workers and soldiers in Lebanon—which has a total native population of 3.7 million—and Syria is slowly integrating much of Lebanon into its economy.[28] Lebanon might prove to be a "sacrifice pawn" in Israeli-Syrian negotiations.

The Lebanese Military Forces

It is impossible to disregard the possibility that Lebanon's regular forces might eventually become a threat to Israel, but this seems so doubtful at the present time that it only merits limited contingency analysis. As has been noted earlier, Lebanon's regular military forces currently cannot be taken seriously as part of the Arab-Israeli balance. They total some 55,000 men on paper, but they are barely adequate for internal security purposes.

The Lebanese army is the only element of Lebanon's military forces that has any potential capability. On paper, it appears to have some war fighting capability. It has an authorized strength of about 53,000 men, and its order of battle has 11 regular infantry brigades, a Presidential Guard Brigade, a Ranger Regiment, 3 special forces regiments, an air assault regiment, and 2 artillery regiments. It also has 350 tanks—with an estimated 100 M-48A1 and M-48A5 tanks and 250 T-54 and T-55 tanks. It has 15–30 AMX-13 light tanks and 145 Saladin, Ferret, AML-90, and Staghound light armored reconnaissance vehicles. It has 550–595 APCs, including the operational portion of an inventory of 550 M-113s, 20 Saracens, 60 VAB-VCIOs, 24 VAB-VTTs, 70 AMX-VCI, and 15 Panhards. It has 140 towed artillery weapons, 30 multiple BM-11 and BM-21 rocket launchers, and 280 mortars. It has 20 BGM-71A TOW launchers, Milan and ENTAC anti-tank guided missiles, and large numbers of light anti-tank weapons and light air defense weapons.

However, Lebanon's "brigades" and "regiments" are often little more than battalion or company equivalents. Conscripts train for only one year. Career soldiers are still highly politicized, generally low in quality, and have limited training for anything other than defensive infantry combat. The Lebanese army's seemingly impressive equipment pool is worn, often obsolescent, and much of it is not operational.

Lebanon does have some excellent individual officers and some good combat elements, but it is only slowly emerging from the chaos of civil war. It is heavily under Syrian influence, but it is still heavily Christian and its heritage is one of incompetence, corruption, and ethnic division. It will be years before the Lebanese army can emerge as an independent fighting force that could engage Israeli or Syrian forces in anything other than well positioned defensive combat.

Lebanon has no real air force or navy. Its air force has 800 men on paper, but its real strength is much lower. It only has three worn, obsolete, low capability Hunter light attack aircraft and four SA-342 attack helicopters armed with obsolete short range AS-11 and AS-12 missiles. It has no significant surface-to-air missile defenses. The only significant assets of the Lebanese air force are its transport helicopters, which consist of about 16 UH-is, 4 AB-212s, 16 AB-205s, 6 SA-330s, 2 SA-318s, and 2 SA-319s. A substantial number of these helicopters need major overhauls or are only semi-operational.

The navy has 500 men based at Juniye, Beirut, and Tripoli. It has five worn, lightly armed Attacker-class inshore patrol craft, four Tracker-class inshore patrol craft, some other armed small craft, and two aging French Edic-class LCTs.

The Lebanese army is improving in some ways. It has played a steadily more important internal security role since the final battles of the civil war in October, 1990. It has deployed south from Beirut, and occupies Lebanese territory as far south as Sidon and Tyre, north to Tripoli, and in the Shuf Mountains. It has contained most militias to their local territory, and most are largely disarmed. Some militias have been integrated into the army, and most have turned over or sold their heavy weapons.

It is doubtful that Syria has any near term prospect of using regular Lebanese forces to support any attack through the Golan by attacking along Lebanon's 79 kilometer border with Israel. In fact, Syria would probably have to be desperate to do so since this could trigger mutiny by the Lebanese forces and lead to the breakup of Syrian influence and the Lebanese-Syrian treaty of friendship and co-operation of 1991—the arrangements which give Syria de facto control over all but southern Lebanon.

The Syrian Presence in Lebanon

The Syrian military presence in Lebanon is a different story. Syria has steadily im-proved its control of Lebanon since 1993. The number of Syrians working in Lebanon has steadily increased, as has the number of Lebanese involved with Syria. Most of Lebanon's warlords are now partially financed by Syria or are par-tially under Syrian control. Syria demonstrated its power in Lebanon in October, 1995 by unilaterally forcing Rafiq Hariri, the prime minister of Lebanon, and Nabih Berri, the speaker of the Lebanese parliament, to amend the constitution to allow the term of office of Lebanon's pro-Syrian president—Elias Hrawi—to be extended by three years.[29]

Syrian attitudes toward Lebanon were summarized with unusual frankness by Syria's vice president, Abdel-Karim Khaddam:[30]

> . . . the Lebanese don't want to work, they want a luxurious standard of living, they send their children to private schools, import maids and labor, evade taxes and du-ties, and then stand up and say the government is responsible for the budget deficit and the rise in the cost of living.

Syrian intelligence and security forces operate throughout most of Lebanon. Syria also has strong military forces in Beirut, just south of Beirut, in northern Lebanon, and in the Beqa'a Valley. This control is strong enough to allow Syria to maintain a force structure with a potential manning level of 30,000 to 40,000 men in Lebanon—although much of the Syrian military presence in Lebanon is now involved in control of Lebanon, black market operations, and/or quasicommer-cial activity, and current manning levels in Syria's combat forces are substantially lower than 30,000 men.[31]

Syria's force structure in Lebanon includes the headquarters of the II Corps at Shtawrah, a mechanized division headquarters, and the 62nd and 85th Mecha-nized Brigades. It has elements of the 51st Armored Brigade and a special forces division with four special forces regiments in the area around Beirut (including the 55th, 54th, 46th, and 35th regiments). Syria has the 44th Special Forces regi-ment near Shikka, the 53rd Special Forces regiment south of Halba and east of Tripoli, and the 804th and 41st Special Forces Regiments east of Juniyah. It has the

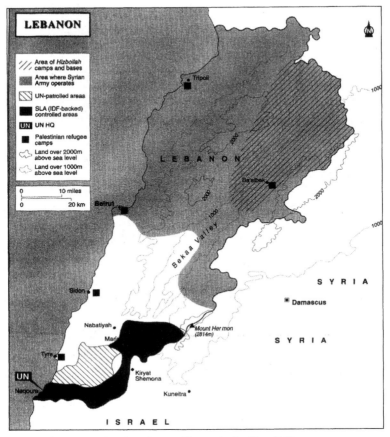

Copyright International Institute of Strategic Studies, 1995

18th Mechanized Brigade in the Beqa'a and the 556th Special Forces Brigade north of Rashayya. All of these forces are kept north of the 1976 "red line" that Israel and Syria agreed to in 1976, and which runs from Sidon to Jazzin through Rashayya. Syria also has the 13th Rocket Artillery Brigade and two artillery regiments. All of the Syrian forces near the coast are north of Ad Damur.[32]

Syria has established a large military infrastructure in Lebanon, although this structure is largely defensive and is not designed to supply and sustain heavy forces in a major attack on Israel. Syria could, however, drive toward Tyre and Sidon with little warning. It also could deploy three more divisions into the Beqa'a on relatively short notice, although it would take about 48 hours simply to move such units and about 96 hours to deploy them for any kind of attack. Even then, it would take substantially longer to assemble all combat elements in a properly organized attack-ready and sustainable position, and Syria would have to divert assets from forces it might use in attacking the Golan.

Such a Syrian attack might help divert Israeli forces from a Syrian attack across the Golan, but a sudden deployment would risk massive early losses. It would take weeks of concerted build-up and training effort for Syria to create a sustainable, integrated attack capability. Even then, Syrian forces would have to attack through relatively narrow corridors and across rough and easily defensible terrain without adequate air support and air defense capability.

The result of such a Syrian attack might delay or limit the scale of an Israeli victory on the Golan, but would have only limited impact unless Syria could achieve a massive degree of strategic surprise and Israel failed to mobilize and deploy. It could also turn into a "killing ground" for Israel. Syria would not be able to deploy fully integrated heavy surface-to-air missile defenses in less than six weeks to two months, and Israeli targeting capabilities and long range strike assets have improved strikingly since 1982.

In the near term, therefore, the risk of some Syrian thrust at Israel through Lebanon cannot be totally disregarded, but it would take fundamental changes in the nature of the Syrian presence to put serious pressure on the IDF. This situation could change, however, if Lebanon came under even more direct Syrian control and if Syria could gradually build up a mix of Syrian and Lebanese forces and infrastructure designed to support an attack. This would necessarily require the development of effective Lebanese forces. Syria could concentrate on using the Lebanese forces to create the infrastructure and support capabilities needed to sustain a Syrian attack and improving command and control assets and air defense capabilities in southern Lebanon. This would not materially affect the outcome of any war between Syria and Israel without a massive rebuilding of Syria's forces, but it would complicate Israel's defensive tasks and serve as a possible Syrian military alternative to demilitarization of the Golan.

The Hizbollah and Proxy Wars in Lebanon

Syria and Israel are already involved in a low level proxy war between the Syrian-Iranian backed Hizbollah and Islamic Jihad, and the Israeli backed South Lebanon Army (SLA). While Iran is sometimes given sole blame for foreign support of the Hizbollah, the flow of Iranian money and arms is only part of the story. The Iranian training and support effort only occurs through Syrian tolerance, and much of the support of the Hizbollah seems to come through Syrian front groups. Further, at least some arms and training are provided directly by Syria.[33]

The Hizbollah also forms a better core for Syrian action than the regular Lebanese military forces. The Hizbollah is an umbrella organization of various radical Shi'ite groups and organizations which largely support the Islamic extremist ideology of Khomeini. It was established following Israel's invasion of Lebanon in 1982 as an organizational body for Shi'ite fundamentalists. It was formed by religious clerics, who saw the adoption of Iranian doctrine as the solution to Lebanon's political problems and who saw the use of armed force and terrorism as a legitimate means of attaining political objectives.

Iran sent Revolutionary Guards to assist these clerics in the establishment of a revolutionary Islamic movement in Lebanon in 1982, with the understanding that this movement would participate in the "Jihad" against Israel. These Revolutionary Guards forces are centered in the area of Ba'albek in the northern Beqa'a Valley and still aid the Hizbollah in maintaining a training apparatus throughout the Shi'ite villages in Lebanon and their surroundings, as well as in some training outside of Lebanon.

Since that time, the Hizbollah has established an extensive military network in the Ba'albek area with Iranian and Syrian assistance. Once the IDF withdrew from Lebanon in 1985, the Hizbollah established storage depots for weapons, recruited more activists and fighters, and broadened its base of support through the donation of money, equipment, medical supplies, etc. Its militias spread into the Shi'ite neighborhoods in southern and western Beirut as well as into southern Lebanon. Thousands of Hizbollah activists and members are now located in the Beqa'a valley, Beirut, and southern Lebanon. These areas also offer a base for the recruitment of additional activists and fighters among the local Shi'ite populations.

The Hizbollah's principal goal remains the establishment of a pan-Islamic republic headed by religious clerics. Its political platform, which was published in February, 1985, sees the establishment of an Islamic republic as the only type of regime which can secure justice and equality for all of Lebanon's citizens. It also supports the fight against "Western imperialism" and its eradication from Lebanon, and sees conflict with Israel as a central concern. This opposition not only affects the IDF presence in Lebanon, but calls for the complete destruction of the State of Israel and the establishment of Islamic rule over Jerusalem.

The Hizbollah supports the use of terrorism against its enemies as a legitimate weapon of the weak and oppressed against strong aggressors. It actively carries out attacks against IDF and SLA forces and extends the conflict into Israeli territory. Since the signing of the "Ta'if Agreement" in 1989, however, it has been forced to conform to Syrian dictates. In return, Syria has tolerated the continuation of Hizbollah attacks in south Lebanon and has allowed the Hizbollah to maintain its military forces. Syria has prevented the Lebanese government from disarming Hizbollah, using the pretext of opposing the Israeli occupation.

In recent years, the Hizbollah has used cover names such as "Islamic Jihad," "The Revolutionary Justice Organization," and "The Islamic Resistance." It has carried out a series of high profile attacks against Israeli targets in southern Lebanon and American and Multinational Forces targets in Lebanon. These attacks became more intensive in the late 1980s, demonstrating steadily better planning, especially immediately prior to the opening of the peace process. Israel estimates that the Hizbollah was responsible for 19 attacks in 1990, 52 attacks in 1991, 63 attacks in 1992, and 158 attacks in 1993. During the course of "Operation Accountability" in 1993, Hizbollah forces fired hundreds of Katyusha rockets into the Security Zone and Israeli territory, and they have kept up their pressure on the South Lebanon Army and the Israeli forces in Lebanon and on Israel's northern border in 1994 and 1995. Hizbollah attacks killed 21 Israeli soldiers in 1994 and 22 in the first ten months of 1995.[34]

The Hizbollah and Islamic Jihad now have full-time forces that total about 2,500–3,000 men, but can mobilize larger numbers. These forces are equipped with some armored fighting vehicles and artillery weapons, and with large numbers of light weapons, including AT-3 anti-tank guided missiles and anti-aircraft guns. They are deployed in the Beqa'a and in southern Lebanon in the Shi'ite areas near the zone occupied by the Israeli controlled and supported South Lebanon Army.

Hizbollah forces have repeatedly attacked the SLA and fired rockets and artillery across the border with Israel. They have been responsible for attacks on Israeli civilians and attacks both inside and outside the region. They have steadily improved in tactical skill and experience. Unlike the various Palestinian paramilitary forces, the Hizbollah forces have gained significant military experience and have developed an effective training, intelligence, and command and control base.

The Hizbollah forces do not currently present any regular military threat to the IDF. They have not proved effective in infiltrating into Israel, and they are restricted largely to sporadic artillery and rocket attacks on Israeli territory. They have, however, learned to set up effective ambushes of IDF and South Lebanese Army forces and to rapidly disperse in the face of Israeli air or ground attacks. This has often forced Israel to reply with air or artillery attacks against Shi'ite villages. One such IDF operation in 1993 killed 130 Lebanese civilians and created thousands of refugees, although the IDF has since improved its intelligence and targeting to focus more on Hizbollah facilities.[35]

The Hizbollah also presents problems in negotiating and enforcing a peace agreement that includes Lebanon. One critical issue will be whether the Hizbollah feels committed to its ideological opposition to Israel's existence or will accept a peace agreement that results in Israel's withdrawal from southern Lebanon. The Hizbollah has already shown that it can negotiate with Israel under some circumstances. In 1993, it accepted an agreement negotiated by US Secretary of State Warren Christopher in which the Hizbollah and Israel agreed not to attack each other's population centers in areas around the Israeli security zone. This agreement has sharply cut the number of attacks on Shi'ite villages and the Israeli towns in the northern Galilee, although there have been some violations.[36] It also has done nothing to prevent the war of ambush and counterambush and assassination discussed earlier.

Much also depends on whether Syria can fully control the Hizbollah if Syria reaches a peace agreement with Israel and Syria is willing to exercise such control. Most experts currently believe that Syria can exercise such control over the Hizbollah if it chooses to do so. They believe that Syria can exercise similar control over the other militias in Lebanon, including other Shi'ite militias like Amal.

It is not clear, however, that Syria could continue to extend such control if it reached a peace agreement with Israel—or if it ever proved willing to remove its military forces from Lebanon.

Syria also has the option of building up the Hizbollah, or supporting increased Hizbollah activity, to try to divert Israeli forces from the Golan or pin some units down in southern Lebanon. It could use the Hizbollah to put pressure on Israel while Syria maintains the status quo on the Golan or participates in a peace agreement. As long as Syria can maintain some degree of plausible deniability, it can make at least some use of the threat from the Hizbollah. Further, if a catastrophic breakdown should occur in the peace talks, Syria might be able to both expand the Hizbollah and use at least some elements of the 2,000 men in the Amal's militia. These forces could not invade Israel or even hope to maintain a successful pattern of infiltration, but they could conduct more low level attacks across the border and outside the region and present an additional security problem.

Finally, it is possible that Iran and Syria might split over a peace settlement with Israel and that Iran might try to use the Hizbollah to break up or resist the peace process. It is not clear whether Iran has the leverage to do so, particularly since Syria has considerable influence over the Hizbollah and controls the Amal— which might counterbalance any extremist Shi'ite forces. Nevertheless, this is one more risk in an already long list.

The Israeli Security Zone and the South Lebanon Army

In contrast, Israel controls a roughly 10 kilometer deep "Security Zone" just north of its border with Lebanon. This zone is bordered on the north by the UNIFIL peacekeeping area, but UNIFIL has little or no effectiveness. Israel controls this Security Zone using a combination of IDF forces and Israeli intelligence units, and what has always been little more than a mercenary Lebanese force. The supposedly "Christian" South Lebanese Army has been under the direction of Israeli-paid Christian warlords, but its forces have always been largely Muslim and many have been Shi'ite. They have worked for Israeli pay and privileges and have never represented any significant political force in Lebanese politics.

The South Lebanon Army (SLA) now has about 2,500 men—many of which are Shi'ite or Druze. It is now almost solely funded, equipped, and trained by Israel. It has some 30 T-54 and T-55 tanks; some M-113s, BTR-50s, and BTR-60s; and D-30 122 mm, M-46 130 mm, and M-1950 155 mm artillery weapons. It could not function or survive for more than a few weeks without cadres of Israeli advisors and intelligence officers, military support from the IDF, and IDF funds.

The South Lebanon Army is still useful in containing the Hizbollah and in supporting Israel in low level security operations, but it lacks the motivation and capability to be used in more serious military operations. Its morale has also declined significantly in recent years, and it has increasingly been infiltrated by the Hizbollah. In spite of continuing efforts to purge the SLA by Israeli intelligence, it has become steadily more difficult for Israel to conduct operations involving the SLA that are not fully reported in advance to the Hizbollah—a major factor in the Hizbollah's ability to ambush IDF and SLA forces or avoid their attacks.

These changes in the South Lebanon Army have increased the casualties of the roughly 1,000 men that the IDF keeps in the zone, and which have totaled some 347 killed over the last 10 years. This has led some Israelis to argue that Israel would be better to withdraw behind the border and abandon the SLA and security zone. Others feel, however, that this would simply allow the Hizbollah to move rocket launchers and artillery closer to the border and improve its infiltration efforts, and might prompt Syria to risk moving units further south. These latter arguments seem likely to keep Israel in Lebanon for the near term, but it is clear that the SLA is far less of an asset than in the past.[37]

Syria, Israel, Lebanon, and the Peace Process

This mix of Syrian and Israeli capabilities presents significant problems in defining peace and arms control options. The Lebanese problem is not a critical aspect of the Syrian-Israeli balance but it cannot be ignored. The use of proxy forces presents special problems for arms control, particularly since even low level terrorism and violence can have a major political impact. Similarly, the presence of Syrian forces in Lebanon confronts Israel and Syria with the need to negotiate a peace that at least tacitly considers Syria's future role in Lebanon.

It is possible that the threats Lebanese factions pose to Israel are low grade enough to be ignored or finessed in any initial peace or arms control agreement over the Golan and even a full Israeli-Syrian peace. It seems likely, however, that it will take a much more active international peacekeeping force to enforce any peace agreement than the present UN peacekeeping force in the area.

The current force is called the UN Interim Force in Lebanon (UNIFIL) and was established in March, 1978 to monitor the Israeli withdrawal from Lebanon after an attack on Palestinian forces. The nine country force is now renewed by the UN Security Council every nine months and operates in a 10 mile wide belt across southern Lebanon. The force has an authorized strength of about 6,000 men, but now has about 5,000. It has six infantry battalions—with one battalion each from Fiji, Finland, Ghana, Ireland, Nepal, and Norway, plus support elements from France, Italy, Norway, and Poland. There is also a small contingent of 70 men from the UN Truce Supervision Organization (UNTSO) which acts as the Observer Group Lebanon. This force was originally established in 1948 to observe the application of the 1949 Arab-Israeli armistice agreements.[38]

UNIFIL's forces have always suffered from the classic limitations of a small peacekeeping force that has no enforcement or peacemaking mission. It lacks the military capability and intelligence data to enforce the separation of the various sides. Further, they have had to operate in a relatively narrow area without a clearly defined force limitation and disengagement zone and without the full support of Israel and Syria. They have never been able to seriously limit the actions of the Hizbollah or the South Lebanon Army and have not had any impact on Israeli and Syrian operations.

An effective peacekeeping force might well need brigade-sized combat elements with real "teeth," superior mobility and firepower to any local militias, and the support of modern intelligence and sensor systems. There may also be a need for well-defined disengagement and force limitation zones in southern Lebanon to replace the South Lebanon Army and to integrate the operations of any peacekeeping force on the Golan with the one operating in Lebanon.

The broader question is whether Syria will give up de facto control of Lebanon for peace, or whether such a peace will formally or tacitly recognize Syria's "special role" in that country. Syrian withdrawal from Lebanon is essential if Lebanon is to emerge as a truly independent state. At the same time, Lebanon remains more a group of warlords and ethnic-religious factions than a country. It is all too possible that Syrian withdrawal from Lebanon could trigger a new round of fighting between these factions and lead to attacks by some factions on Israel.

In contrast, if Syria does remain in Lebanon, its control over Lebanon may slowly become de facto annexation. Further, any peace agreement between Israel and Syria must then take account of the risk Syria's remaining military presence in Lebanon poses to Israel. This means a peace agreement may require arms control arrangements that consider Syria's ability to attack through Lebanon and/or explicitly limit both Syrian deployments in Lebanon and Israel's support of the South Lebanon Army. Such arrangements would have to formalize the present agreements that limit the presence of Syrian forces in southern Lebanon and add limits on the total size of Syrian forces in Lebanon. They would not have to be as formal or carefully defined as a peace on the Golan, but they could involve some of the same verification and disengagement issues. They may prove to be anything but easy to negotiate.

8

CASE THREE: THE COLLAPSE OF THE PEACE PROCESS AND CONFLICT BETWEEN ISRAEL AND JORDAN

A conflict between Jordan and Israel is substantially less likely than a conflict between Israel and Syria. Jordan showed little interest in risking strategic attacks or further losses of territory after 1967. The threat of Israeli intervention helped keep Syria from intervening in Jordan's battle with the Palestinians in 1970, and although Jordan sent a brigade to help Syria in 1973, it took no action across its border. Under some conditions, it is even possible that Jordan and Israel might cooperate in dealing with any post-Asad rebirth of a Syrian threat to Israel or would cooperate to put down an Islamist extremist-led conflict on the West Bank.

Jordan signed a peace accord with Israel on July 25, 1994, called the Washington Declaration. This agreement has led to a rapid normalization of Jordanian-Israeli relations, is leading to important further changes in Jordan's forces, and is leading both nations to adopt new confidence building measures. Article 3 of the Washington Declaration has led Jordan and Israel to resolve their remaining differences over the border between Jordan and Israel's defense lines in Israel and on the West Bank. It has led to agreement on the use of air space, water, and the delimitation of their boundary in the Gulf of Aqaba. Article 4 not only calls for the adoption of bilateral confidence building measures, but regional efforts. It formalizes the long-standing tacit agreement between the two countries to avoid the use of force, suppress terrorist and extremist activity, and avoid the support of hostile third parties or groups. It precludes Jordan and Israel from allowing third party military forces or groups on their soil that "adversely prejudice the security of the other Party." It has led Jordan and Israel to establish strong liaison groups to deal with security issues and cooperate in the Multilateral Working Group on Arms Control and Regional Security (ACRS).

Jordan has little to gain from war and much to lose. King Hussein has no near term prospect of being able to integrate the Palestinians in the West Bank and Jerusalem into Jordan, and Jordan is extremely vulnerable to Israeli air and artillery attacks. As the previous analysis has shown, Jordan suffered severely from its support of Iraq during the Gulf War and a corresponding lack of external military aid. Jordan has lost the roughly $200 million in Saudi aid, and $50 million in Kuwaiti aid, it received before the Gulf War and has had no way to pay for the roughly $160–$170 million in annual imports it needs to keep its US supplied equipment running.[1] It is also at least possible that Israel and Jordan might actually cooperate against the Palestinians in some future contingency where the Palestinians threatened the Hashemite dynasty.

Nevertheless, it is still possible to visualize conditions under which Jordan might go to war with Israel. There are three primary forms that such a conflict could take: support of Palestinian forces, a unilateral attack on the West Bank, and joint action with Syria in an "Eastern Front."

Jordanian Support of Palestinian Forces in the West Bank, Jerusalem, and Israel

The first type of conflict—which would involve the least risk for Jordan—would be a low level conflict in which Jordan actively and covertly supported Palestinian attacks on Israel, but did not overtly use its military forces. Jordan has not acted as a sanctuary for hostile Palestinian elements since 1970, but some radical collapse of the peace process or series of violent clashes between the IDF and Palestinians might create political conditions which undermined the peace process. Jordan might then be willing to provide bases, training facilities, and arms to Palestinian extremists on the West Bank. Such Jordanian support for a low intensity war in the West Bank might significantly complicate Israel's internal security problems.

Jordan could also escalate its involvement in such a conflict by sending in cadres of lightly armed special forces from the Jordanian army under civilian cover. Such Jordanian covert forces would be easier for Israel to identify than native Palestinians, but would have far more training than the Palestinians. They could make a significant contribution to any Palestinian military effort that involved urban warfare or terrorism that required high levels of discipline and technical expertise. Cadres of trained advisors and troops have played a significant role in previous guerrilla and low level wars—often under conditions where they preserved "plausible deniability." Such a use of Jordanian forces would allow Jordan to exploit its strengths—a highly trained and well disciplined army—with less risk than other uses of Jordanian forces.

At the same time, Israel has established a secure perimeter along the border with Jordan in the past, and the terrain favors such a security perimeter as long as a Palestinian entity does not exist on the West Bank which cannot be cut off from Jordan. Israel can also retaliate with the kind of air and artillery strikes it has used against the Hizbollah in Lebanon and retaliate economically by sealing off the border between Jordan and Israel. Anything but very low level covert Jordanian support of a Palestinian conflict would be detected by Israel in a matter of hours or days, and would also present major problems in terms of US reactions and those of other states. Jordan would risk serious problems in terms of access to foreign investment, trade, loans, and aid.

As a result, low level Jordanian support of Palestinian military efforts does not seem likely to have any significant effect on the military balance unless the Palestinian entity on the West Bank becomes so strong that Israel can no longer secure the present border with Jordan, the final settlement talks between Israel and the Palestinians fail after the Palestinian Authority has established full control over most Palestinian population centers, or a hard-line Israeli government comes to power that halts the peace process.

Under these conditions, the IDF might take time to reestablish a firm control over movements from Jordan into the West Bank and might be unable to deal with any covert Jordanian presence on the West Bank. Even so, such a contingency is something of a contradiction in terms. Israel is only likely to give up its ability to secure the border after it secures and tests a "warm peace" with both Jordan and its Palestinians. Further, Jordan's current regime is unlikely to cooperate with any Palestinian entity that falls under Islamist extremist or other radical control because such an entity would be as much of a threat to Jordan as it would to Israel.

Jordanian "Rescue" of Palestinians in the West Bank: Jordanian Re-Occupation of the West Bank

The second contingency would be a crisis-driven Jordanian intervention in the West Bank. Such a contingency is extremely unlikely under current conditions. It would either require Israel to abandon the peace process so catastrophically that Jordan would feel compelled to go to the aid of the Palestinians or require a massive change in the character of Jordan's government. Even then, Jordan would only be willing to take risks of this kind if it was dominated by Islamic extremists, or extreme Israeli provocation threatened Jordan's existence. This would effectively require Israel to conduct a massed forcible expulsion of the Palestinians living in the West Bank. Such events are conceivable, but they presently strain the limits of political credibility.

If such a battle did occur, Jordan would almost certainly lose decisively during the first day or days of combat. Jordan's forces are well trained and disciplined, with some of the best officers, NCOs, and career troops in the developing world. They have significant defensive capability against limited to mid-intensity Israeli attacks that attempt to move across the Jordan and up the East Bank. Jordanian forces have also performed well in exercises with US troops, such as the desert warfare exercises the US and Jordan conducted during August, 1995.[2]

Jordan could only attack across the Jordan, however, by moving virtually all of its land forces down to the East Bank. This would provide clear strategic warning and allow Israel to use its air force extensively with only limited resistance by the

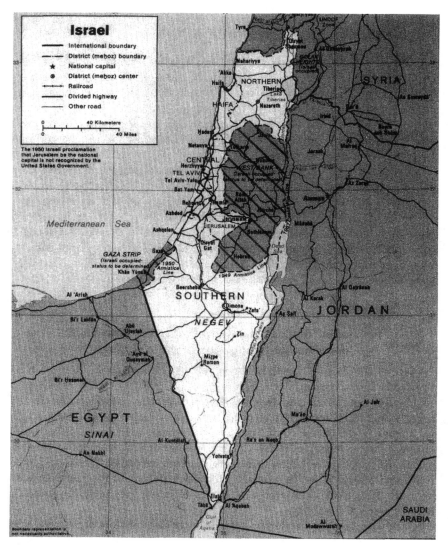

Courtesy of the U.S. State Department

Jordanian air force and ground-based air defenses. Jordanian land forces would then have to fight their way across the Jordan and up the West Bank in the face of overwhelming Israeli superiority in the air, a high level of Israeli superiority on the ground, and Israeli ability to exploit a wide range of defense barriers.

Table 8.1 and Figure 8.1 show that Israel has overwhelming numerical superiority against Jordan—as well as the massive qualitative superiority discussed ear-

FIGURE 8.1   Israel Versus Jordan

Land Weapons

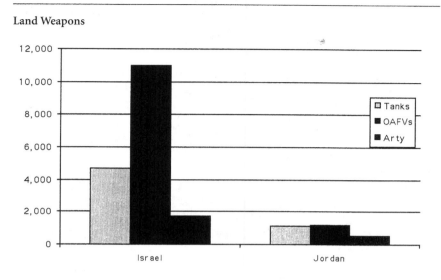

Air Forces

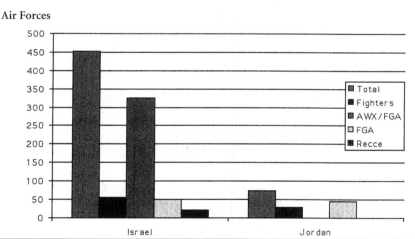

Note: Total Artillery includes towed and self-propelled tube artillery and multiple rocket launchers. Total air forces include only operational fixed wing fighter, fighter-attack, and reconnaissance aircraft in combat units, less aircraft in combat training units.

lier. As the previous discussion has shown, Jordan has also faced an economic crisis since 1990 that has severely limited its ability to maintain its military forces, much less increase them. As a result, Israel's superiority is steadily increasing and it would now take at least several years of massive aid to Jordan to reverse the situation.

TABLE 8.1   The Jordanian-Israeli Balance—Part One

Category/Weapon	IISS		JCSS	
	Israel	Jordan	Israel	Jordan
Manpower				
Total Active	172,000	110,000	177,500	90,000–100,000
(Conscript)	138,500	–	–	–
Total Reserve	430,000	35,000	427,000	60,000
Total	615,000	145,000	604,500	150,000–160,000
Paramilitary	6,050	10,000	13,500	200,000–250,000
Land Forces				
Active Manpower	125,000	95,000	136,000	80,000–90,000
Reserve Manpower	365,000	35,000	363,000	60,000
Total Manpower	490,000	125,000	499,000	145,000
Main Battle Tanks	4,700	1,141	3,850	1,067
Total Other Armor	11,000	1,200	8,100	1,565
AIFVs	(350)	(50)	–	–
APCs/Recce/Scouts/ Half-Tracks	(10,650)	(1,150)	–	–
ATGW Launchers	1005	640	–	–
Total Guns and Mortars	–	–	1,300	450
SP Artillery	1,150	390	–	–
Towed Artillery	500	160	–	–
MRLs	100+	0	–	–
Mortars	6,500	750	–	–
SSM Launchers	20	0	12	0
AA Guns	1010+	360	–	–
Lt. SAM Launchers	945		–	–

The Jordanian-Israeli Balance—Part Two

Air Forces				
Active Manpower	32,000	8,000	32,500	9,700
Reserve Manpower	55,000	–	54,000	–
Aircraft				
Total Fighter/FGA/ Recce	453	75	742	10
Fighter	56	30	75	–
FGA/Fighter	325	0	663	103
FGA	50	458	–	–
Recce	22	0	–	–

TABLE 8.1   (Continued)

Category/Weapon	IISS		JCSS	
	Israel	Jordan	Israel	Jordan
AEW	4	0	–	–
EW	28	0	–	–
Maritime Reconnaissance				
(MR/MPA)	3	0	–	–
Tanker	5	0	–	–
Transport	40	9	93	18
Combat Training	60	14	–	–
Helicopters				
Attack	117	24	115	23
Other	160	24	138	30+
Total	275	48	253	53+
SAM Forces				
Batteries	20	14	–	14
Heavy Launchers	–	80	–	–
Naval Forces				
Active Manpower	6,600	600	9,000	400
Reserve Manpower	10,000	0	10,000	0
Total Manpower	16,600	600	19,000	400
Submarines	3	0	3	0
Destroyers/Corvettes				
Missile	3	0	0	0
Other	–	0	0	0
Missile Patrol	20	0	19	0
Coastal/Inshore Patrol	35	7	40	12
Mine	–	0	–	–
Amphibious Ships	1	0	–	–
Landing Craft	4	3	11	–

Source: Adapted from data provided by US experts, the IISS, *Military Balance, 1995–1996,* and the Jaffee Center for Strategic Studies, *The Military Balance in the Middle East, 1993–1994.* Note that data for the IISS are taken from the country chapters. The JCSS data are taken from the summary tables on pages 479–509.

Jordan has been forced to put about 270 of its 1,141 main battle tanks in storage, and its first-line tanks now consist of 218 M-60A1/A3 conversions, supported by 360 much less capable Khalid (Chieftain) tanks. Its other armored fighting vehicles consist of 19 aging Scorpions, 150 obsolete (and sometimes inoperable) Ferrets, and 35 BMP-2s. It has converted some of its roughly 1,000 M-113s from APCs to AIFVs, but a substantial number of the rest of its M-113s are not fully operable.[3]

Jordan does have 390 relatively modern US-made self-propelled artillery weapons and 160 towed artillery weapons, but it cannot support most of its artillery with advanced target acquisition, fire and battle management, and counter-battery capabilities. It is well armed with modern TOW and Dragon anti-tank weapons, but these are more valuable in the defense than attack.

Jordan has significant numbers of AA guns—including 44 ZSU-23-4 radar guided guns—and 100 self-propelled SA-8s and SA-13s and 240 SA-16 man-portable surface-to-air missile launchers, but these are only capable of protecting ground troops at low altitudes. Jordan's IHawk missile launchers are obsolescent Mark II versions which would take $100 million to fully modernize, and which are fixed and vulnerable to Israeli low altitude attacks, using anti-radiation missiles (ARMs), and electronic countermeasures.[4]

Jordan's air force is now limited to roughly 75 fully operational combat aircraft, and only 30 Mirage F-1s out of this total have significant air-to-air combat capability—although its F-5E-IIs may be upgraded as a result of a recent agreement with Singapore. Even the Mirage F-1 aircraft cannot hope to engage IAF F-16s and F-15s with any success, and Jordan lacks any form of AEW aircraft and its ground-based air battle management capabilities have severe technical limitations. Jordan does have 24 AH-1S attack helicopters, but these could not fly evasive attack profiles over most of the border with Israel and would be highly vulnerable.[5]

Accordingly, Jordan does not have the kind of forces that could securely move down to the Jordan River through narrow and predictable routes, cross a relatively open river plain averaging about 30 kilometers wide with a water barrier in the middle, and fight through Israeli forward defenses and then up in the heights on the West Bank. Only a few roads go down the 900 meters from the heights above the East Bank and the 400–600 meters up from the Jordan River. Israel can also couple its advantage in modern RPVs, reconnaissance and strike aircraft, and AEW to extraordinarily short flight times from Israel to land targets moving through the West Bank. Flight times vary from two to five minutes once an aircraft is airborne, and Israel has demonstrated excellent capabilities to surge high sortie rates and manage large numbers of sorties.

The only area where the Jordanian army could hope to take advantage of rough terrain is in the far northwestern part of Jordan at the junction of the Yarmuk and Jordan Rivers, just south of Lake Tiberius. The Jordanian heights of Umm Qays also overlook Lake Tiberius and the Galilee and would allow Jordan to use its artillery against targets in Israel. This, however, is an area where there are no easy routes up and down the heights and where Israel has excellent surveillance capabilities. The Yarmuk River is also a significant terrain barrier with only a few crossing points, and any attack through Irbid that involved armored or mechanized forces would be very vulnerable to air power, systems like the MLRS, and attack helicopters.

The Jordan River Valley becomes progressively harder to fight across at any point about 10 kilometers south of the junction between the Yarmuk and Jordan

Rivers. It opens up into a plain 5 to 40 kilometers wide. Israel is geographically vulnerable through the Beit Shean or Jezreel Valley, but forces attacking in this direction also become vulnerable to Israeli air and armor and it would take Jordan days to mass a sustainable force to launch such an attack, and at least six hours to cross the terrain and river barrier.

The distances involved are short by the standards of most wars, but they are still long enough for Israel to employ air power with great effect. It is roughly 40 kilometers from Irbid to Beisan/Beit Shean, 85 kilometers from Jerash to Irbid, 55 kilometers from Salt to Amman, 55 kilometers from Amman to Jericho via the King Hussein Bridge, and 45 kilometers by the King Abdullah Bridge. The southern route along the Dead Sea is 100 kilometers from Amman, and the route to Eilat through Aqaba and Maan is 130 kilometers.

There is also little prospect of sudden major quantitative or qualitative improvements in Jordanian forces. Jordan has had to cut its armed forces from 130,000 troops in 1991 to 98,600 troops in 1996. It has severe parts and/or munitions shortages for its tanks, TOW ATGMs, US supplied trucks, and 58 F-5E/F fighters, and is trying to sell its 200 oldest M-48 tanks.[6] It has been seeking new combat aircraft for more than a decade and still has no immediate prospects of major deliveries.

Although Jordan has begun to restore its military relations with the West and moderate Arab states and is seeking major amounts of aid from the US as a result of its peace agreement with Israel, it still has no funds to buy major amounts of new armor and high technology artillery and air defense equipment. Jordan is seeking totals of surplus equipment as high as 36–72 F-16s and 200 M-1A2s, but it will at best take several years before Jordan gets such aid, and it is unlikely that Jordan will get all the aid it desires.[7] As a result, much of the new equipment Jordan does obtain is likely to do more to offset the impact of Jordan's steady aging of its existing inventory of major combat weapons than increase Jordan's offensive power against Israel.[8]

Arms Control and Security Implications

Israel can scarcely ignore Jordan's capabilities in structuring its peace and security agreements with the Palestinians or arms control negotiations. At the same time, Israel can scarcely ignore Jordan's participation in the peace process and cooperation with Israel in bilateral and regional arms control efforts.

Jordan cannot by itself pose anything approaching an existential threat to Israel. Jordan's present and projected forces do not force Israel to seek the same kind of complex security arrangements it insisted upon in reaching a peace settlement with Egypt, and is certain to insist upon in reaching a peace settlement with Syria. Both nations are faced with the need to maintain strong deterrent and defensive capabilities relative to the other in spite of their peace agreement, but Jordan is far more of a problem for arms control in terms of its potential impact in combination with other Arab states than as an independent military power.

If anything, Jordan has become so weak that this threatens its ability to maintain armed forces which can firmly deter any pressure from Iraq and Syria. Jordanian self-sufficiency and self-reliance are also critical to obtaining Jordanian public support for the peace process and convincing the Palestinian Authority that Jordan can be a strong partner in any regional security arrangements.

There is a good case for providing Jordan with enough military equipment and aid to ensure that it can play its proper role in preserving regional stability and securing its peace settlement with Israel. There is an equally good case for ensuring that Jordan has enough military prestige to allow Jordanian military forces to act as substitutes for Palestinian forces. Such prestige is essential to underpin Jordan's monarchy and create a climate for some form of federation or confederation between Jordan and a Palestinian entity.

9

CASE FOUR: A JORDANIAN-SYRIAN ALLIANCE—THE EASTERN FRONT

The final contingency that might involve Jordan in any near term conflict is a Jordanian alliance with Syria, or the creation of some broader Arab "Eastern Front." The possible total forces that could be drawn upon in such contingencies are shown in Table 9.1 and summarized in Figure 9.1, but such comparisons again list total potential forces, and not the forces that would actually be deployed in war.

In practice, there seems to be little real-world political prospect that Jordan and Syria could fight in any integrated way or even under an effective joint command. They are not standardized, do not have interoperable land or air forces, and have no joint training. Rather than achieve any military synergy, they might actually add to the qualitative problems of each separate force by leaving gaps in capability or creating coordination problems.

At the same time, Jordan does have a 238 kilometer border with Israel. Even if Jordan did nothing more than deploy in ways that forced the IDF to deploy and the IAF to keep assets in reserve, this might assist Syria in a grab for the Golan. Syria could also reduce the IDF's concentration of force if Jordan gave Syrian troops free passage, and Syria could deploy armor reinforced with heavy mobile air defenses to attack through northern Jordan. Syria could also expand the area of attack by striking across the Lebanese border from positions in the Beqa'a.

The main problem Israel would face in this contingency is that it would increase the strain on the IDF in deploying across a broader front. At the same time, the Syrian-Jordanian forces would not have a significant probability of defeating Israel, and Syrian-Jordanian movements would be even more exposed to Israeli air attack than a concentrated Syrian movement through the Golan, and have significantly less heavy surface-to-air missile protection. Any Syrian-Jordanian attack would require significant political changes in Jordanian-Syrian relations and long preparation to be effective. As a result, any military advantages to the Arab side might well be offset by the added strategic warning and preparation time provided to the IDF.

TABLE 9.1   Israel Versus Jordan and Syria: The "Eastern Front" Balance—Part One

	IISS		JCSS	
Category/Weapon	Israel	Jordan and Syria	Israel	Eastern Front*
Manpower				
Total Active	185,000	440,000	177,500	–
(Conscript)	138,500	–	–	–
Total Reserve	430,000	130,000	427,000	–
Total	615,000	445,000	604,500	–
Paramilitary	6,050	18,000	13,500	–
Land Forces				
Active Manpower	125,000	315,000	136,000	532,000
Reserve Manpower	365,000	120,000	363,000	160,000
Total Manpower	490,000	445,000	499,000	692,000
Main Battle Tanks	4,700	5,741	3,850	7,400
Total Other Armor	11,000	6,000	8,100	8,550
AIFVs	(350)	(2,350)	–	–
APCs/Recce/Scouts/Half-Tracks	(10,650)	(3,650)	–	–
ATGW Launchers	1005	5,690	–	–
Total Guns and Mortars	–	–	1,300	3,400
SP Artillery	1,150	860	–	3,750
Towed Artillery	500	1,790	–	–
MRLs	100+	480	–	–
Mortars	6,500	1,158+	–	–
SSM Launchers	20	46+	12	95
AA Guns	1010+	1,985	–	–
Lt. SAM Launchers	945	900+	–	–

Israel Versus Jordan and Syria: The "Eastern Front" Balance—Part Two

Air Forces				
Active Manpower	32,000	108,000	32,500	146,000
Reserve Manpower	55,000	92,000	54,000	40
Aircraft				
Total Fighter/FGA/Recce	453	515	742	827
Fighter	56	310	75	460
FGA/Fighter/Bomber	325	0	663	367
FGA	50	199	–	–
Recce	22	6	–	–
AEW	4	0	–	–
EW	28	10	–	–

TABLE 9.1   *(Continued)*

Category/Weapon	IISS Israel	IISS Jordan and Syria	JCSS Israel	JCSS Eastern Front*
Maritime Reconnaissance				
(MR/MPA)	3	0	–	–
Tanker	5	0	–	–
Transport	40	38	93	83
Combat Training	60	105	–	–
Helicopters				
Attack	117	164	115	190
Other	160	134	138	235
Total	277	298	253	425
SAM Forces				
Batteries	20	113	–	135
Heavy Launchers	–	778	–	–
Naval Forces				
Active Manpower	6,600	6,600	9,000	13,500
Reserve Manpower	10,000	8,000	10,000	2,500
Total Manpower	16,600	14,600	19,000	16,000
Submarines	3	3	3	9
Destroyers/Corvettes				
Missile	3	1	0	10
Other	–	2	0	3
Missile Patrol	20	18	19	45
Coastal/Inshore Patrol	35	18	40	25
Mine	–	7	–	17
Amphibious Ships	1	3	–	–
Landing Craft	4	8	11	11

*The JCSS calculation for the Eastern Front includes all Syrian, Jordanian, and Palestinian forces plus 3 brigades, 4 FGA squadrons, 1 transport squadron, and 1 helicopter squadron from Saudi Arabia; 1 fighter squadron from Kuwait; 5 divisions, 100 combat aircraft, and 5 SSM launchers from Iraq; 3 armored brigades, 3 mechanized brigades, 20 SSM launchers, 2 combat aircraft squadrons, 1 attack helicopter squadron, and the entire navy of Libya and some land weapons systems from Iran.

Source: Adapted from data provided by US experts, the IISS, *Military Balance, 1995–1996,* and the JCSS, *The Military Balance in the Middle East, 1993–1994.* Note that data for the IISS are taken from the country chapters. The JCSS data are taken from the summary tables on pages 479–509.

FIGURE 9.1   Israel Versus Jordan and Syria

Land Weapons

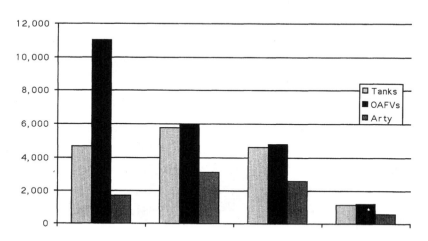

Air Forces

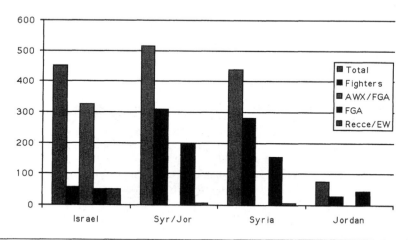

Note: Total Artillery includes towed and self-propelled tube artillery and multiple rocket launchers. Total air forces include only operational fixed wing fighter, fighter-attack, and reconnaissance aircraft in combat units, less aircraft in combat training units.

Such a large scale Syrian-Jordanian attack might also remove many of the constraints Israel might have in terms of launching strategic attacks on Jordan and Syria. It would be closer to all-out war, and Israel might well preempt or strike at critical economic targets in a systematic effort to force early conflict termination. It is also unlikely that the US would attempt to exercise any major restraint on Israel in making such attacks as long as Israel was directly threatened.

As for the broader "Eastern Front" contingency shown in Table 9.1, it is difficult to see this contingency as anything other than game-theoretic. The Jordanian-Israeli peace treaty forbids the kind of Iraqi-Jordanian joint exercises and Iraqi movements to Jordan that took place before the Gulf War. Iraq might deploy significant land and air forces at some indefinite point in the future, but any such attack in the near term would be likely to trigger US intervention with air strikes and cruise missile strikes. Iran is highly unlikely to cooperate with Iraq or deploy significant forces. Saudi Arabia, the other Gulf states, Libya, and the other Maghreb states have only made token deployments in the past Arab-Israeli conflicts and seem even less likely to make significant military contributions today. The force ratios in the "Eastern Front" columns of Table 9.1 cannot be ignored— quantity does influence combat—but the current trends in the balance make it less, not more, relevant to possible war fighting contingencies.

There is one final caution, however, that must be applied to all of the Jordan versus Israel scenarios that have just been examined. It is dangerous to examine military balances in terms of "probable" wars. Little about the history of the twentieth century indicates that war is the product of calmly planned grand strategy or processes of escalation based on rational ladders of escalation. At the same time, any of these conflicts would be a tragedy for both Jordan and Israel. A Jordanian war with Israel would probably be devastating for Jordan, in spite of the considerable professionalism of Jordan's military forces. Such a war would, however, complicate Israel's military problems, and Jordanian support of Palestinian forces in the West Bank might put considerable strain on the IDF and Israel's economy.

This, in turn, affects the problem of arms control in the region. No agreement related to the Golan can totally ignore Jordan's potential, any more than it can ignore the risk of attacks through Lebanon and the Beqa'a Valley. This does not mean that such agreements must explicitly take account of this risk. It might well be possible to create arms control agreements that dealt with these issues through tacit understandings about the risks involved, and such agreements might also aid in developing arms control options that reflected Israel's different perception of the risks from Jordan and Syria. At the same time, it is equally possible that Israeli and Syrian perceptions could differ fundamentally on this issue: that Israel would insist on considering the Jordanian threat and Syria would see the balance purely in terms of the threat posed by Israel.

10

CASE FIVE: ISLAMIC UPHEAVAL— EGYPTIAN CRISIS WITH ISRAEL

It is even harder to structure a current war fighting contingency between Egypt and Israel than it is to structure one involving Jordan. Like Jordan, Egypt has a moderate secular government. Egypt has fully adhered to its peace with Israel, has demonstrated its commitment to peace during several crises between Israel and its other Arab neighbors, and has helped lead other Arab states into the peace process. It joined the UN Coalition in liberating Kuwait, is heavily dependent on US aid, and has gained every strategic advantage from peace that it was denied as the result of war.

Egypt seems likely to stick to its commitment to peace as long as it retains a moderate secular government, and there seems to be steadily less prospect that Islamic extremists will come to power. Egypt has done a far better job of reestablishing its internal security than Algeria, and has sharply reduced the capability of its extremists to threaten its armed forces.

Such a contingency also presents the problem that many of Egypt's best educated military officers would strongly resist any such shift in Egypt's strategic position, and that an Islamic takeover could only take place after a massive disruption of Egypt's officer corps of the kind that crippled Iran's forces after the fall of the Shah. Egypt's secular government is one of the best institutionalized in the Middle East, and its military forces not only lead its government but have shown a consistent commitment to peace.

There is, however, at least some possibility that Egypt's economic and political problems could eventually lead to the kind of political upheaval that could bring an extremist Islamic government to power. This might conceivably be triggered by a combination of a cut-off or major reductions in US aid, the collapse of Egypt's international credit position, the rise of other Islamist extremist governments, or some catastrophic breakdown of the peace process followed by extreme Israeli use of force against the Palestinians.

Further, a conflict with even a secular Egyptian government might take place if some future US administration or Congress halted or sharply reduced aid, or if some other crisis in the Arab world forced Mubarak or his successor to take a much more strident line over problems in the peace process or issues like Israel's possession of nuclear weapons. Egypt might also alter the balance without attacking, if it responded to some crisis in the peace process by remilitarizing part or all of the Sinai—perhaps over an issue like Jerusalem. Such cases seem unlikely, but not impossible.

Egyptian War Fighting Strengths

There is no doubt that Egypt retains formidable military forces. Table 10.1 shows the present total strength of Egyptian and Israeli forces, and Egypt has near parity with Israel in land forces. It is acquiring a force of several hundred M-1A1 Abrams tanks. It has over 1,600 M-60 tanks and roughly 1,100 are modern M-60A3s. Egypt may be heavily dependent on other aging and obsolescent Soviet-supplied armored fighting vehicles, many of which are inoperable or incapable of sustained combat, but it has nearly 1,900 M-113 APCs, including a number of M-113 type combat vehicles.

Egypt is still largely dependent on towed Soviet artillery weapons, which it never effectively organized and equipped for effective BVR targeting, counterbattery fire, and rapid shifts of mass fire. It does, however, have 200 modern M-109A2 155 mm self-propelled artillery pieces, and AN/TPQ-37 counterbattery radars, RPVs, and RASIT artillery support vehicles to support this artillery force in maneuver warfare. It has large numbers of advanced US TOW anti-tank guided weapons (including the TOW-2A, which has a significant capability against reactive armor), many mounted on M-901 armored vehicles. It has truly massive numbers of short range air defenses, including over 100 radar guided ZSU-23-4s, 46 modern surface-to-air missile fire units, and thousands of manportable surface-to-air missiles.[1]

Egypt has the only air force in the Arab "ring states" with large numbers of modern fighters capable of advanced strike/attack missions and BVR/look-down shoot-down air-to-air combat. These combat aircraft holdings include 25 F-4Es, over 140 operational F-16As and F-16Cs, over 70 Mirage 5s, and 16–18 operational Mirage 2000s. Egypt is scheduled to receive significant additional deliveries of F-16s. Egypt is the only Arab air force with AEW aircraft and some modern electronic warfare, intelligence, and reconnaissance aircraft—including 5 E-2Cs, 2 CH-130Es, and 4 Beech 1900s. It also has modern self-propelled versions of the IHawk surface-to-air missiles.[2]

As has been discussed earlier, Egypt has significant force improvements under way. It is currently scheduled to receive a total of 190 F-16s and 12 AH-64s. Although its plans to produce the M-1A1 in Egypt have run into trouble, it is still scheduled to produce substantial numbers of additional M-1A1s, and is seeking to upgrade its low quality Fahd-30 AIFVs with BMP-2 turrets. Egypt is obtaining British aid in upgrading the ammunition for its 500 T-62 tanks and US aid in up-

TABLE 10.1   The Egyptian-Israeli Balance—Part One

	IISS		JCSS	
Category/Weapon	Israel	Egypt	Israel	Egypt
Manpower				
Total Active	185,000	440,000	177,500	435,000
Total Reserve	430,000	245,000	427,000	695,000
Total	615,000	685,000	604,500	1,126,000
Paramilitary	6,050	374,000	13,500	13,000
Land Forces				
Active Manpower	125,000	310,000	136,000	320,000
Reserve Manpower	365,000	150,000	363,000	600,000
Total Manpower	490,000	460,000	499,000	920,000
Main Battle Tanks	4,700	3,450	3,850	2,750
Total Other Armor	11,000	4,870	8,100	4,400
AIFVs	(350)	(280)	–	–
APCs/Recce/Scouts/Half-Tracks	(10,650)	(4,590)	–	–
ATGW Launchers	1,005	2,340	1,600–1,800	–
Total Guns and Mortars	–		1,300	2,200
SP Artillery	1,150	200	–	–
Towed Artillery	500	1,100	–	–
MRLs	100+	340	–	–
Mortars	6,500	3,700	–	–
SSM Launchers	20	0	12	24
AA Guns	1010+	1,677	–	–
Lt. SAM Launchers	945+	2,200	–	–

The Egyptian-Israeli Balance—Part Two

	IISS		JCSS	
Air Forces				
Active Manpower	32,000	110,000	32,500	95,000
Reserve Manpower	55,000	90,000	54,000	80,000
Aircraft				
Total Fighter/FGA/Recce	453	487	742	474
Fighter	56	340	75	318
FGA/Fighter	325	0	663	139
FGA	50	121	–	
Recce	22	20	–	
AEW	2	5	–	
EW	28	10	–	
Maritime Reconnaissance (MR/MPA)	3	2	–	
Tanker	5	0	–	

TABLE 10.1 *(Continued)*

Category/Weapon	IISS		JCSS	
	Israel	Egypt	Israel	Egypt
Transport	40	32	93	47
Combat Training	60	70	–	
Helicopters				
Attack	117	99	115	80
Other	160	113	138	117
Total	277	212	253	197
SAM Forces				
Batteries	20	38+	–	122
Heavy Launchers	–	738	–	–
Naval Forces				
Active Manpower	6,600	20,000	9,000	16,000
Reserve Manpower	10,000	14,000	10,000	15,000
Total Manpower	16,600	34,000	19,000	31,000
Submarines	3	3	3	8
Destroyers/Corvettes				
Missile	3	4	0	4
Other	–	1	0	1
Missile Patrol	20	26	19	22
Coastal/Inshore Patrol	35	18	40	87
Mine	–	8	–	11
Amphibious Ships	1	3	–	–
Landing Craft	4	16	11	17

Source: Adapted from data provided by US experts, the IISS, *Military Balance, 1995–1996,* and the Jaffee Center for Strategic Studies, *The Military Balance in the Middle East, 1993–1994.* Note that data for the IISS are taken from the country chapters. The JCSS data are taken from the summary tables on pages 479–509.

grading its submarines. It has the technology to make Fuel-Air-Explosive (FAE) weapons, although it is not clear it has done so.

Egypt has also sought large amounts of 19 different items of surplus military equipment from the US, including 865 M-60A3 tanks, 1,512 M-113s, 94 M-88 tank recovery vehicles, 12 IHawk III surface-to-air missile batteries, 237 Stinger launchers, 2 Knox-class frigates, 25 fast attack boats, 24 C-130 transports, and 2 KC-135 tankers. While such requests are unlikely to be fully met, Egypt did get 2 leased FF-1052 frigates and 6 excess SH-2 helicopters in 1994.[3]

These force improvements are giving Egypt more defensive strength than it has had at any time since 1973, and reinforce the already high level of deterrence it maintains against any Israeli attack. While such an Israeli attack is even more im-

FIGURE 10.1 Israel Versus Egypt

Land Weapons

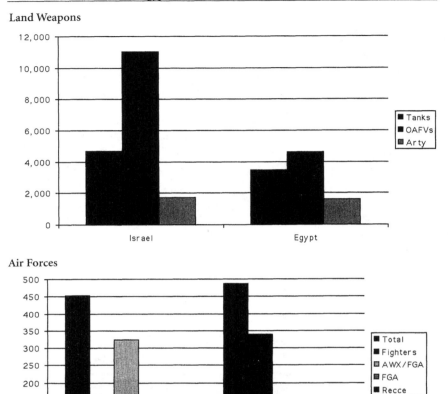

Air Forces

Note: Total Artillery includes towed and self-propelled tube artillery and multiple rocket launchers. Total air forces include only operational fixed wing fighter, fighter-attack, and reconnaissance aircraft in combat units, less aircraft in combat training units.

probable than an Egyptian attack on Israel, this deterrent and defensive strength is important both in terms of Egyptian perceptions and those of over moderate and friendly Arab states. It demonstrates that Egypt's support of the peace process does not mean the acceptance of strategic inferiority, that it does not mean acceptance of the kind of Israeli "edge" that gives Israel offensive freedom of action as distinguished from defensive security, and that Arab strategic alliances with the US can involve parity in technology transfer.

Egyptian War Fighting Liabilities

At the same time, Egyptian forces have all of the qualitative weaknesses which have been discussed earlier, and much more limited offensive capabilities. Even if a revolution could occur in Egyptian politics without disrupting the capability of the Egyptian armed forces, any near term Egyptian land attack on Israel would have to redeploy massive armored and mechanized forces across the Suez and through the Sinai, and do so without anything approaching the required major support and staging facilities in the Sinai.

Egypt would have powerful war fighting liabilities in such an attack. The Egyptian army has not modernized its infrastructure, support, and sustainment capabilities near the Suez Canal in ways that allow it to efficiently mobilize and assemble a massive armored force that can rapidly thrust across the Sinai and then sustain itself in intense combat. It has emphasized acquisition and modernization over overall readiness and sustainment, and it is much better postured to defend in depth than to attack in a massive war of offensive maneuver.

Egypt is gradually refocusing some aspects of its military structure to emphasize force quality rather than force quantity, and is giving more emphasis to im-

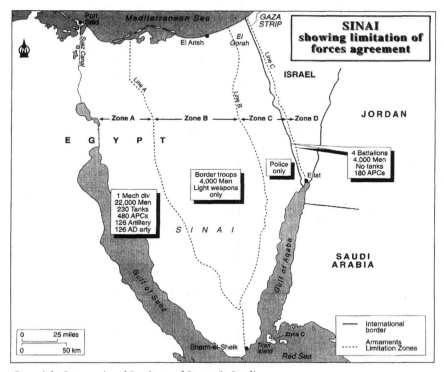

Copyright International Institute of Strategic Studies

proving "intangibles." At the same time, it still places its primary weight of effort on obtaining more advanced combat aircraft, M-1 tanks, other armored fighting vehicles, and self-propelled artillery forces—regardless of its ability to use these effectively in combat and sustain them in high intensity warfare.

Egypt still needs to make major improvements in its manpower quality, change many of its training methods above the brigade and squadron level, and allocate funds to buy the high technology equipment necessary to support more advanced training methods. Egypt is substantially less capable of modernizing its entire force structure with currently foreseeable Egyptian military budgets and US aid than Israel.

As has been discussed earlier, Egypt has also weakened itself by overextending its force structure. It tries to support far too large a land force structure at the cost of relying on low quality conscripts, poor training for most of its forces, and increasingly underpaid officers and other ranks.[4] About 60% of Egypt's total inventory of major land combat weapons consists of obsolete and badly worn Soviet-bloc systems supplied in the late 1960s, and none of its Soviet-bloc inventory was supplied after 1974. At least one-third of its 3,450 tanks are obsolete to obsolescent Soviet-bloc types, only 200 of which have had any real upgrading. Only 220 of its present holdings of AIFVs are BMP-1s and have significant war fighting capability—although some 600 YPR-765s are being delivered. Only about half of its 4,590 APCs are combat effective types. Ironically, the Egyptian army could be much more effective if it concentrated its manpower and training resources on much smaller and better equipped forces. It could also use the resulting savings in military spending either to improve its readiness and sustainment or for economic development.

The Egyptian air force could do a better job of supporting a land attack than the Syrian or Jordanian air force, and some Egyptian squadrons have excellent pilots. However, the 487 combat aircraft in the Egyptian air force include over 40 low quality PRC-made J-6s and 60 J-7s, and over 90 worn-out Soviet-bloc MiG-21s.[5] The EAF has not done well in bringing its Mirage 5s up to a high degree of combat readiness. The operational readiness of many of its 65 SA-342K armed helicopters is limited, and the HOT weapons suite on this aircraft has significant operational limitations.

Egyptian land-based air defense capabilities are also much more effective as a static defense in depth than in protecting Egyptian offensive operations. While Egypt has some 738 heavy surface-to-air missile launchers, 570 are obsolete SA-2s and SA-3s, and only 72 are IHawks. Egypt cannot project large mobile land-based surface-to-air missile forces without having to operate individual fire units outside the full sensor and C4I/BM capabilities of its central air defense command and control system. It would have to support its advancing land forces with individual surface-to-air missile units which would become progressively more vulnerable to the IAF as they moved across the Sinai. Unless Egypt had months in which to build up its forces near Israel's border, they would become progressively more vulnerable to air attack in terms of both Israel's ability to rapidly suppress Egyptian air defenses and target and attack Egyptian land units.[6]

Egypt cannot threaten Israel from the sea. The Egyptian navy has some capable vessels, but its navy has had limited recent modernization and its training and sustainability have been poorly funded. The Egyptian navy is slowly modernizing some of its combat vessels, but its present readiness and combat capability are limited.

Egypt would be vulnerable to Israeli air attacks and armored maneuver—and Israel could probably break through Egypt's air defenses to launch significant strategic air attacks with conventional weapons. Unless Israel passively allowed Egypt to redeploy in the Sinai and did not react with its own deployments, the result could be a relatively intense conflict, but it would also be one which Israel would be likely to win relatively quickly and decisively, and Egypt might again be confronted with the loss of the Sinai and Suez.

Even if some radical political upheaval did occur, Egypt's dependence on US aid would also create major problems for Egypt. Egypt's current modernization plans and resources will not allow Egypt to modernize at a scale that can offset its severe problems in maintaining its current force structure. New US aid and deliveries will simply not be large enough to compensate for Egypt's problems with its aging Soviet-bloc and European-supplied equipment, and currently programmed modernization seems unlikely to alter the current qualitative balance between Egypt and Israel. Egypt would also face an immediate cut-off of US aid and resupply if it should come under extremist Islamist rule, and this would present major near term problems in Egypt's effort to support US-supplied systems as well as probably lead to an immediate internal economic crisis.

An Egyptian-Israeli Conflict and the Geography of the Sinai

The geography of the Sinai is another factor that must be considered in assessing any Egyptian-Israeli contingency. Unlike Israel's boundaries with Gaza, Jordan, Lebanon, Syria, and the West Bank, the force limitations in the Sinai affect a relatively large territory. The Sinai is defined by the Suez Canal, the Mediterranean Sea, the Gulfs of Suez and Aqaba, and the border with Israel. The distances are about 190 kilometers from the Suez Canal to the Israeli border, about 145 kilometers along the Suez Canal and the Great Bitter Lakes, and about 370 kilometers from the coast of the Mediterranean down to the southernmost tip of the Sinai. The terrain is very barren and rugged.

Movement through the Sinai is limited in ways which increase the difficulty in moving forces and sustaining them and increase their vulnerability to air attack. There are only a limited number of roads through the Sinai. The main roads go along the northern coast and through two passes, the Giddi in the north and Mitla in the south. The two passes are about 20 kilometers apart. The Mitla pass is about 32 kilometers long and the Giddi pass is about 29 kilometers long. The

Mitla pass is more open and has relatively wide slopes. The Giddi pass has rough terrain and narrows down to as little as 100 meters. South of these passes, the terrain becomes very rugged and large scale armored movements become very difficult. The north coast road is vulnerable to air and land attacks. The ocean blocks northern movement and extensive southern movement is highly restricted by "seas of sand." Further, Egypt's border with Israel is far from most Israeli population centers, and the Negev Desert gives Israel strategic depth.

The paved and graded roads in the north central Sinai are channeled through the Giddi and Mitla passes, and bypassing them is difficult. This makes them the preferable route for large mechanized forces, and such movements involve hundreds of armored vehicles and nearly 600 support vehicles for each heavy division. Combat and service support units must also accompany combat units to sustain them in combat and provide artillery support, and most Egyptian support vehicles are wheeled rather than tracked. This further limits the areas in which they can move and makes the passes more important. Further, unless Egypt moves its heavy land-based air defenses forward to create the kind of defensive belt it had near the Suez in 1970–1973, its forces would be exposed to the IAF— which would be far more effective against armor than in any previous Arab-Israeli conflict.

Even if a new Islamic government should come to power in Egypt, or Egypt should by driven to attack by some breakdown in the peace process or new Arab-Israeli crisis, Egypt would lack the ability to conduct an effective surprise attack across the Sinai, and any build-up in its capabilities for such an attack would give Israel ample strategic warning. Further, Egypt could only prepare for such an attack and execute it by violating an international treaty and risking the almost certain loss of US aid.

Arms Control in the Sinai

It is also important to remember that the Sinai is the site of one of the world's most successful arms limitation agreements and peacekeeping operations. Long before the Egyptian-Israeli peace treaty, Egypt and Israel reached two different disengagement agreements and agreed to the deployment of a small multinational monitoring force in the key passes in the Sinai.

When Egypt and Israel reached a full peace treaty on March 26, 1979, the treaty called for the withdrawal of all Israeli forces from the Sinai and demarcated the Sinai into military zones. Annex I, Article VI of the treaty proposed that UN forces and observers supervise these security arrangements, and the US made a commitment during the Camp David negotiations to ensure the establishment of an acceptable alternative force if the UN failed to agree on such a force. In the months that followed, the UN Security Council did fail to agree on the proposal to establish UN forces and observers, and reported this lack of agreement on May

18, 1981. As a result, Egypt and Israel agreed to a protocol to their peace treaty on August 3, 1981, which established a Multinational Force and Observers (MFO).

Since that time, the MFO has enforced the following provisions of the peace treaty:[7]

- There are four force limitation and disengagement zones in the Sinai that progressively limit the size of Egyptian forces in the Sinai relative to the distance from the Israeli border.
- Egyptian forces in Zone A, which extends 50–60 kilometers from the Suez Canal, are limited to one mechanized division (consisting of three mechanized brigades and one armored brigade) with up to 230 tanks, 126 artillery weapons, 126 anti-aircraft guns, a very limited number of surface-to-air missiles, and limits on other material.
- Egyptian forces in Zone B, which extends to the east of Zone A for 100–130 kilometers, are limited to four border battalions with light weapons.
- Zone C extends from Zone B to the international border with Israel, and is 16 to 30 kilometers wide. Only UN forces and Egyptian police units may be in this zone. The Egyptian police are limited to light weapons.
- Zone D is a narrow strip several kilometers wide on the Israeli side of the border. The Israeli forces in this zone are limited to four infantry battalions and may not include tanks, artillery, or surface-to-air missiles other than portable weapons.
- No Egyptian overflights or reconnaissance flights may take place east of Zone A and no Israeli flights may take place west of Zone D.
- Egypt may only operate early warning systems in Zone A, and Israel may only operate them in Zone D.

These arrangements divide each side's forces by roughly 150 kilometers and place significant limits on Egypt's logistic and support capabilities in the Sinai, land-based air defenses, and air power. These limitations mean that the bulk of Egypt's ground forces are located on the other side of the Suez Canal and are a minimum of 210 kilometers from the Israeli border. They place powerful restrictions on Egypt's ability to conduct a surprise attack, or even to prepare for such an attack without major preparations and taking actions that would give Israel extensive strategic warning. They also effectively remove any major incentive for Israel to preempt in a crisis, and prevent any surprise Israeli land attack on Egypt.

Since 1982, the MFO has enforced these provisions of the treaty by manning observation posts in the Sinai, conducting ground and air surveillance, and conducting naval patrols in the Straits of Tiran. The MFO has also used sensors and has been supported by US intelligence data. In 1995, there were eleven countries in the MFO, each with its own participation agreement. The MFO consisted of roughly 2,000 men, of which nearly half were US soldiers.[8]

While there have been minor technical violations of the zone agreements, Egypt and Israel have complied with the limitations in the Egyptian-Israeli peace treaty ever since Israel withdrew from the Sinai on April 25, 1982.[9] As a result, the MFO and the force limitation agreements of the Egyptian-Israeli peace treaty create significant obstacles to both an Egyptian attack on Israel and an Israeli attack on Egypt. They also serve as a useful precedent for an Israeli-Syrian agreement— although the Golan and Lebanese border areas have far less strategic depth and the terrain and distance from Israel's major mobilization areas make it far more difficult for air and land forces to disrupt an offensive.

Egypt's Impact on Peace Negotiations and Arms Control

Egypt's conventional capabilities are so large that no Israeli planner can afford to ignore them in any arms control agreement and/or view the Arab-Israeli balance solely in terms of Syria and Jordan. They are strong enough to give Egypt powerful defensive and deterrent capabilities. They do not, however, represent the kind of threat that requires Israel to take any additional military measures or consider them in reaching the kind of peace agreement with Syria discussed earlier.

Israel must consider Egyptian capabilities in structuring Israeli-Syrian and Israeli-Jordanian disengagement, deployment, warning, and force limitation agreements but has no need to make this consideration an explicit part of such agreements. It can create arms control agreements with Jordan and Syria that deal with the contingency threat posed by Egypt through tacit understandings about the risks involved. In fact, such bilateral agreements may be easier to negotiate in ways that reflect Israel's perception of the different levels of risk from Egypt, Jordan, and Syria than broader multilateral agreements.

Once again, Israel and a key neighbor are likely to have very different perceptions of risks that could present serious problems in structuring and agreeing upon an arms control agreement. Major arms reductions would force Israel to consider the full range of threats from the Arab "ring states" while Egypt might have different perceptions of the risk posed by Israel and insist on some form of near parity.

11

CASE SIX: A BROAD ISLAMIC UPHEAVAL—EGYPT, JORDAN, AND SYRIA ARE JOINED BY OTHER ARAB STATES

Table 11.1 illustrates a "worst case"—a more modest and slightly more credible version of the force comparisons shown in Table 1.1. Any conflict involving this array of Arab forces, however, would probably require the systematic breakdown of the entire peace process, the conversion of all the Arab "ring states" into aggressive powers interested in war fighting capability, and a level of unity the Arab world never approached in any of the previous Arab-Israeli wars.

It is also important to note that while Israel can deploy most of the forces shown in Table 11.1 in actual combat, the Arab states cannot. Only about half of the forces shown for Egypt and Syria could be committed in any strength without a massive military build-up over a period of at least nine months to a year. It is credible that such forces might be supplemented by other Arab forces and by a Palestinian force that simultaneously engaged the IDF in low intensity combat, but any major reinforcements are unlikely.

Nevertheless, the force ratios shown in Table 11.1 cannot be dismissed in any assessment of the current trends in the balance. A conventional Arab-Israeli conflict is inherently asymmetric in one critical grand strategic dimension. Israel's existence can be threatened; that of its Arab neighbors cannot. There are powerful negative political and military trends affecting the Arab-Israeli peace process—as well as positive ones—and the kind of contingency reflected in the forces in Table 11.1 might emerge over a period of five to ten years—coupled to significant transfers of new weapons and technology to Egypt, Jordan, and/or Syria of the kind that could overcome many of the technical limitations in these forces.

A multi-front war of this kind would put severe strains on Israel—even allowing for the fact that the level of political change necessary to make such a worst case alignment of an Arab force possible would probably give Israel several years of strategic warning to make crash improvements in its own war fighting capabil-

TABLE 11.1 The Arab-Israeli Balance: Forces by Country in the Arab-Israeli "Ring States"—Part One

Category/Weapon	Israel	Total Arab	Syria	Jordan	Egypt	Lebanon
Manpower						
Total Active	185,000	935,000	330,000	110,000	440,000	55,000
Total Reserve	430,000	680,000	400,000	35,000	245,000	0
Total	615,000	1,615,000	730,000	145,000	685,000	55,000
Paramilitary	6,050	405,000	8,000	10,000	374,000	13,000
Land Forces						
Active Manpower	125,000	678,000	220,000	95,000	310,000	53,000
Reserve Manpower	365,000	280,000	100,000	30,000	150,000	0
Total Manpower	490,000	958,000	320,000	125,000	460,000	53,000
Main Battle Tanks	4,700	9,541	4,600	1,141	3,450	350
AIFVs	350	2,680	2,300	50	280	50
APCs/Recce/Scouts/Half-Tracks	11,000	9,090	2,500	1,150	4,590	850
ATGW Launchers	1,005	8,050	5,050	640	2,340	20
SP Artillery	1,150	1,060	470	390	200	0
Towed Artillery	500	3,040	1,630	160	1,100	150
MRLs	100+	850	480	–	340	30
Mortars	6,500	9,230+	4,500+	750	3,700	280
SSM Launchers	20	46+	46+	0	0	0
AA Guns	1010+	4,242	1,985	360	1,677	220
Lt. SAM Launchers	945	3,100+	?	900+	2,200	–

The Arab-Israeli Balance: Forces by Country in the Arab-Israeli "Ring States"—Part Two

	Israel	Total Arab	Syria	Jordan	Egypt	Lebanon
Air Forces						
Active Manpower	32,000	218,800	100,000	8,000	110,000	800
Reserve Manpower	55,000	182,000	92,000	0	90,000	0

Aircraft						
Total Fighter/FGA/Recce	453	1,005	440	75	487	3
Fighter	56	650	280	30	340	0
Fighter/FGA	392	0	0	0	0	0
FGA	50	323	154	45	121	3
Recce	22	26	6	0	20	0
AEW	4	5	0	0	5	0
EW	28	20	10	0	10	0
Maritime Reconnaissance						
(MR/MPA)	3	2	0	0	2	0
Tanker	5	0	0	0	0	0
Transport	40	70	29	9	32	0
Combat Training	60	177	91	14	70	2
Helicopters						
Attack	117	267	140	24	99	4
Other	160	261	110	24	113	14
Total	277	528	250	48	212	18
SAM Forces						
Batteries	20	151+	99	14	38+	0
Heavy Launchers	–	1,516	698	80	738	0
Naval Forces						
Active Manpower	6,600	27,100	6,000	600	20,000	500
Reserve Manpower	10,000	22,000	8,000	–	14,000	0
Total Manpower	16,600	49,100	14,000	600	34,000	500
Submarines	3	6	3	0	3	0
Destroyers/Corvettes Missile	3	4	0	0	4	0
Other	–	3	2	0	1	0
Missile Patrol	20	44	18	0	26	0
Coastal/Inshore Patrol	35	45	11	7	18	9
Mine	–	15	7	0	8	0
Amphibious Ships	1	6	3	0	3	0
Landing Craft	4	26	5	3	16	2

Source: Adapted from IISS, *Military Balance, 1995–1996.*

ities. Israel cannot fight on all its borders at once. Israel does not have the numbers to concentrate decisive force simultaneously against Egypt, Jordan, and Syria. At the same time, Israel can use its short lines of communication to redeploy forces quickly and effectively, and can exploit any major gap in the timing of attacks on its northern and southern borders. Israel also can shift air power very quickly from one front to another, and the IAF is far more capable of attacking armor and ground forces than it was in 1973 or in 1982.

The practical question would be the extent to which Arab forces could act in unison and put maximum strain on Israel's defense capabilities. It would be the level of coordination and interoperability Arab forces developed in building up for such an attack, and the level of technology and weapons transfers they received, that would determine the degree of Arab success.

Several factors will be critical in determining whether Arab forces can collectively erode Israel's qualitative "edge":

- The level of improvement in advanced interceptors, AEW aircraft, electronic warfare, and air-to-air missiles.
- The level of improvement in self-propelled advanced surface-to-air missiles such as the SA-10.
- The improvement of tank capabilities to match the IDF in range, all-weather-night combat, and rate of engagement capability.
- The number of advanced anti-tank weapons with third or fourth generation guidance systems and the ability to defeat advanced armor.
- Shifts in artillery equipment to provide advanced BVR and counterbattery targeting capability, more lethal rounds, and an MLRS-like capability, coupled to advanced C⁴I/BM capabilities to use advanced targeting systems and to mass and switch fires.
- Shifts in armored infantry fighting vehicle capabilities to provide better support for armor.
- Improvements in attack helicopter capability to provide better sensors and targeting capability, all-weather-night operations capability, and effective long-range anti-armor capability.
- Improved air attack forces capable of stand-off precision attacks on IDF armor and aircraft shelters.
- Cruise missile or similar precision conventional strike capability against strategic targets in Israel.

All of these developments are possible over a period of time—and some are planned. It is important to note, however, that they will only be effective to the degree that the Arab forces in each country go beyond the "glitter factor" of acquiring new systems and transform them into an integrated set of sub-systems that can support combined operations and match new technology with new tactics and new training methods.

The peace process could also weaken Israeli capabilities to fight in such a contingency if such a peace collapsed after Israel had withdrawn from most of the West Bank and the Golan. As has been discussed earlier, trading territory for war is different from trading territory for peace.

At the same time, territory alone is not the issue. A Palestinian Authority armed with a few light armored vehicles and small arms cannot threaten Israel militarily or play a major role in reducing Israel's ability to defend at the West Bank or prevent a Syrian drive around the Golan. This would require Palestinian forces to be large enough and well armed enough to seriously limit the mobility of Israeli armor and pose a threat to the Israeli air force.

At a minimum, this would require the Palestinian forces to have large numbers of guided anti-tank weapons, mines, and modern light surface-to-air missiles like the Stinger or SA-14/SA-16. Even then, such a force would be largely defensive and could only harass and delay Israeli forces, not challenge them in any form of prolonged combat. While such Palestinian forces might be able to fight effectively in urban warfare, Israel would have little reason for house to house fighting in most contingencies or even to enter most Arab cities, and could rapidly overrun such Palestinian forces in the field, near roads, or in small towns.

The Palestinian forces could only be more effective if they could acquire substantial amounts of artillery, armor, and anti-aircraft weapons and delay the IDF long enough for Syria and Jordan to massively reinforce the Palestinian forces, or pose enough of a threat on the West Bank to pin down a large amount of Israel's ground forces and limit its capabilities against other Arab armies. Palestinian forces are unlikely to have these capabilities until well after the final peace negotiations are completed, and even then it seems unlikely that Israel would accept such a level of armament or ignore any change in the combined capabilities of Palestinian and other Arab forces.

A peace that restored the Golan to Syria, created a sovereign or near sovereign Palestinian entity, created free right of passage between Jordan and the Palestinian entity, *and* did not involve substantial arms control measures would create more risks for Israel—particularly if Israel did not react preemptively to any significant Arab build-up on its new borders. Such a peace would improve Syria's military position in the Golan, potentially ease Jordanian deployments on the West Bank, and create a potential terrorist or unconventional warfare threat to Israel's mobilization centers, air bases, and other critical facilities and to Israel's roads and lines of communication. A simultaneous uprising in the West Bank, Gaza, and Jerusalem during a major Arab attack might then complicate IDF mobilization and movements and seriously weaken Israel's defensive capabilities.

At the same time, such a peace seems remarkably unlikely. Israel will not give up the Golan casually or ignore the need for warning, disengagement arrangements, new rapid reaction contingency capabilities, or the need to act upon strategic warning. A war that involved a "race for the Golan" in which Israel and Syria raced to redeploy forces would not expose the IDF to major interference

FIGURE 11.1   Israel Versus Egypt, Syria, Jordan, and Lebanon

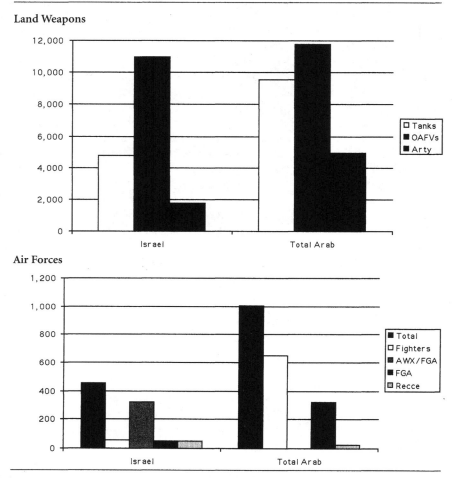

Land Weapons

Air Forces

Note: Total Artillery includes towed and self-propelled tube artillery and multiple rocket launchers. Total air forces include only operational fixed wing fighter, fighter-attack, and reconnaissance aircraft in combat units, less aircraft in combat training units.

from any Palestinian uprising. Syria's advantage in distance and terrain would be offset by Israel's superior air and precision weapons delivery capabilities, and Syria would find it difficult to either sweep around the Golan through Jordan or penetrate down through the Golan and achieve any significant gains in the Galilee.

The risks posed by a Syrian attack from the Golan are much more an argument for coupling arms control and security measures to a peace settlement than argu-

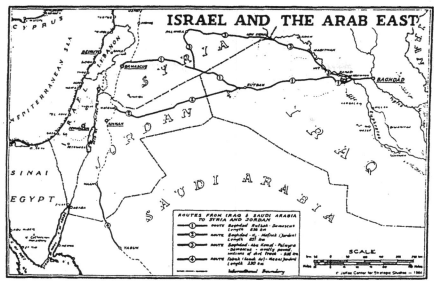

Copyright Jaffee Center for Strategic Studies

ments against a peace settlement. While some increase in military risk may be inevitable during some stages of the peace process, there is no inherent reason that arms control cannot make a peace as secure or substantially more secure than the present status quo. In fact, measures that reduced the costs of military forces and arms imports offer a potential way of providing the kind of "peace dividend" that may be necessary to secure the peace process. Such arms control options are an important part of the current peace negotiations.

There is no way to anticipate the success of the linkage between arms control and the peace process at this time, or the extent to which confidence building measures and constraints on exercises and deployments can be coupled to actual reductions in military forces and changes in military technology. This linkage will, however, be a critical factor in determining the shifts in the military balance. The preceding analysis indicates that Israel's "edge" is not sufficiently large to secure the peace process militarily without arms control or to preserve the current level of deterrence of war.

Finally, it is important to note that Israel is not bound to defend against such a "worst case" Arab attack on Arab terms. Israel can launch strategic conventional strikes against critical economic and leadership targets, attacking the nation rather than the nation's forces. Israel's nuclear forces would also act as a significant deterrent at some point to any Arab exploitation of the force ratios illustrated in Table 11.1, even if Arab forces could win an initial conventional victory on at least one front. Israel's existential vulnerability gives Israeli nuclear escalation growing credibility at the point where Arab forces begin to win a decisive conventional victory. Similarly, such an Arab victory becomes steadily more likely to trigger massive US intervention of some kind and diplomatic initiatives by other states. There are important limiting factors on Arab military success, even if Israel should be defeated. It is far from clear that even a worst case Arab attack—under worst case conditions—could ultimately be exploited to the point of a successful end game.

12

CASE SEVEN: LIBYAN, IRANIAN, AND IRAQI CONVENTIONAL FORCES

There is often a difference between perceptual threats and war fighting threats. As has been discussed earlier, this has been a key reason that Israelis have tended to see the military balance in terms of large parts of the entire Arab world, and have often exaggerated the kind of forces Arab states outside the region can bring to bear against Israel.

Tables 12.1 and 12.2 provide further insight as to this Israeli perspective. They do not make any attempt to portray the balance in war fighting terms. They rather show the size of Israel relative to the total military demographics of the greater Middle East and the total military forces of all the countries involved. It should be clear from the preceding analysis that such comparisons of military demographics have only a very limited impact on the military balance—largely because the states in the region are far more limited by the number of troops they can pay for, train, equip, and support than they are by their total manpower pool. Similarly, most of the forces shown in Table 12.2 have absolutely no military relevance to the Arab-Israeli balance. They cannot be deployed to fight against Israel in any combat effective form. They represent the impact of arms races and conflicts between Arab, North African, and Gulf states that have nothing to do with Israel. And they include the forces of many nations that recognize Israel's right to exist or have never played a role in past Arab-Israeli conflicts.

There are, however, three nations on these two tables which do merit further discussion: Libya, Iran, and Iraq. There is no question that Libya, Iran, and Iraq have large inventories of conventional weapons. At the same time, such a contingency does not seem to have great near term relevance to the Arab-Israeli balance.

Libyan Capabilities

Libya has military forces with an active strength of 80,000 men. It has a large inventory of combat equipment, including 2,200 tanks and over 410 combat aircraft. However, Libya has never created effective land and air forces and cannot

TABLE 12.1   The "Perceptual Balance": Military Demographics of the Greater Middle East (1996)

Country	Total Population	Males Reaching Military Age Each Year	Males Between the Ages of			Males Between 15 and 49	
			13 and 17	18 and 22	23 and 32	Total	Medically Fit
Israel	5,443,000	45,839	266,000	262,200	476,800	1,310,000	1,073,000
Egypt	62,360,000	648,724	3,264,000	2,739,600	4,650,200	16,113,000	10,456,000
Jordan	4,100,900	45,494	246,400	232,600	410,000	981,004	699,891
Lebanon	3,696,000	—	197,000	198,200	361,200	858,000	534,000
Syria	14,284,000	159,942	869,600	702,400	1,075,000	3,440,030	1,928,000
Iran	64,625,000	615,096	3,844,400	3,159,000	4,828,600	14,630,000	8,704,000
Iraq	20,644,000	229,015	1,293,000	1,063,000	1,562,600	4,627,000	2,598,000
Bahrain	575,900	4,346	25,600	20,800	40,800	210,725	117,414
Kuwait	1,817,000	16,710	102,000	78,400	140,800	610,205	363,735
Oman	2,125,000	26,065	105,600	83,400	127,800	520,428	294,993
Qatar	544,000	3,915	21,200	17,600	38,800	219,442	115,013
Saudi Arabia	18,730,000	164,220	1,128,400	907,400	1,396,200	5,304,000	2,950,000
UAE	2,924,600	19,266	82,600	72,000	140,400	1,072,300	584,000
Algeria	28,539,000	313,000	1,796,400	1,551,800	2,416,200	7,125,000	4,373,000
Libya	5,248,000	54,676	312,400	262,200	389,000	1,131,175	673,000
Mauritania	2,263,000	—	123,000	108,000	161,600	484,000	236,000
Morocco	29,169,000	324,000	1,599,600	1,439,400	2,314,800	7,307,000	4,637,000
Tunisia	8,880,000	93,601	499,000	450,400	786,400	2,295,000	1,318,000
Chad	5,586,000	54,945	333,000	282,200	454,600	1,307,000	680,000
Djibouti	421,300	—	34,400	29,000	46,400	101,385	59,357
Eritrea	3,579,000	—	209,800	175,800	267,800	—	—
Ethiopia	55,979,000	566,000	3,165,200	2,633,400	3,979,400	12,658,000	6,669,976
Somalia	73,478,000	—	507,600	407,800	608,400	1,737,000	972,000
Sudan	30,120,000	314,000	1,683,000	1,400,000	2,113,000	6,807,000	4,185,000
Yemen	14,728,000	181,057	800,400	707,800	1,120,400	3,135,600	1,771,226

Source: Adapted by Anthony H. Cordesman, CIA, *World Factbook, 1995* and IISS, *Military Balance, 1995–1996.*

TABLE 12.2 The "Perceptual Balance": Military Forces of the
Greater Middle East (1996)

Country	Total Active Manning	Total Active Army Manning	Tanks	OAFVs	Artillery	Combat Aircraft	Armed Helicopters
Israel	185,000	125,000	4,700	11,350	1,750	449	117
Egypt	450,000	320,000	3,450	4,870	1,640	564	99
Jordan	110,000	95,000	1,141	1,200	550	82	24
Lebanon	55,000	43,000	350	900	180	3	4
Syria	330,000	315,000	4,600	4,800	2,580	579	140
Iran	513,000	450,000	1,440	1,065	2,948	295	100
Iraq	382,500	350,000	2,900	4,400	1,980	353	120
Bahrain	10,700	8,500	106	281	58	24	10
Kuwait	16,600	10,000	220	329	40	76	16
Oman	43,500	25,000	91	76	102	46	0
Qatar	11,100	8,500	24	238	40	12	20
Saudi Arabia	105,500	70,000	1,055	2,900	498	295	0
UAE	70,000	65,000	133	964	172	97	42
Algeria	127,700	105,000	960	1,495	716	170	60
Libya	80,000	50,000	2,210	2,620	1,170	417	52
Mauritania	15,560	15,000	35	105	75	7	0
Morocco	195,500	175,000	524	1,344	370	99	24
Tunisia	35,500	27,000	84	382	117	32	7
Chad	30,350	25,000	60	63	7	4	0
Djibouti	9,600	8,000	0	31	6	0	0
Eritrea	39,000	39,000	–	–	–	–	–
Ethiopia	120,000	115,000	350	200	300	22	18
Somalia	35,000	35,000	–	–	–	–	–
Sudan	118,500	115,000	320	732	1,137	50	2
Yemen	39,500	37,000	1,125	1,140	727	69	8

Note: Totals count all equipment, much of which is not operational. They should not be confused with estimates of operational equipment holdings. Light tanks are counted as OAFVs.
Artillery counts towed and self-propelled tube weapons and multiple rocket launchers, but
not mortars. Only combat aircraft in combat, COIN, or OCU units are counted, not other
trainers or aircraft.

Source: Adapted by Anthony H. Cordesman, CIA, *World Factbook, 1995* and IISS, *Military
Balance, 1995–1996.*

use its aircraft and major land weapons effectively. Most of its already limited military capabilities have degenerated steadily since the breakup of the Soviet Union
and Warsaw Pact, and the imposition of the UN sanctions.

A combination of wretched organization and training, a cut-off of most arms
imports, and cutbacks in military spending has meant its forces have gone from

terrible to worse. At least 60% of Libya's tanks and combat aircraft are in storage or have negligible operational capability. Libya has virtually ceased modernizing many of its conventional weapons and has lacked organized flows of spare parts and force-wide maintenance efforts.

Most of Libya's operational armor and combat aircraft have little or no sustainable combat capability. Its active forces have only token levels of combined arms training, and Libya is little more than a massive military parking lot. It might be able to transfer some arms to other Arab forces and deploy a few ships and combat aircraft, but it could not deploy or sustain combat effective formations. In fact, the cost to any host Arab nation of supporting Libyan reinforcements would probably be far greater than their military value.

Iranian Capabilities

Iran is slowly rebuilding its forces and is acquiring modern T-72 tanks and combat aircraft like the MiG-29 and Su-25. Since the end of the Iran-Iraq War, Iran has obtained hundreds of modern T-72 tanks and it is seeking hundreds more. It is acquiring self-propelled artillery and more modern armored fighting vehicles. It is building up a significant force of Su-24 strike aircraft, with better avionics and range-payload capabilities than the Russian medium bombers of the 1960s, and MiG-29s with advanced beyond-visual-range combat capability. It has acquired SA-5 and SA-6 missiles to supplement its US-supplied IHawks. It is acquiring advanced air-to-surface and air-to-air missiles, and more advanced radars and command, control, communications, computer, and intelligence (C^4I/BM) systems.

Iran has acquired two relatively advanced conventional submarines with wire guided torpedoes and "smart" mines. It has acquired more advanced anti-ship missiles which can attack ships virtually anywhere in southern Gulf waters from relatively small ships, from land positions near the Straits of Hormuz, and from the islands it seized in the lower Gulf. It now has large numbers of smart non-magnetic mines that include types that can be moored in shallower waters, and "bounding mines" that can rise from the bottom to attack ships in deep channels. Iran is also steadily receiving additional advanced versions of the Scud that can attack targets across the Gulf and has ordered the No Dong missile, which has nearly twice the range of the Scud C and can reach targets deep into the southern Gulf.

In early 1996, Iran had about 397,000 full time actives in its regular forces, plus 350,000 men in its reserves. The IISS also estimated that it had 120,000 men in its Islamic Revolutionary Guards Corps (Pasdaran Inquilab), 200,000 in its Basiij (Popular Mobilization Army), 45,000 in its internal security forces, and around 12,000 men in an Iranian trained and funded Kurdish Democratic Party militia.[1] A combination of the regular and Revolutionary Guards forces would give Iran about 513,000 full time actives—a small fraction of Iran's potential manpower strength.

Iran had an inventory of around 1,440 tanks in early 1996—reflecting a rise of some 200 tanks over 1994, 400 over 1993, and 520–580 tanks over 1992.[2] Iran seems to have about 1,000–1,250 operational armored personnel carriers and armored infantry fighting vehicles, and 2,700–3,000 medium and heavy artillery weapons and multiple rocket launchers. The Iranian air force and air defense force had around 30,000 men, a total inventory of around 260–300 combat aircraft, and 30 Improved Hawk fire units (150+ launchers), 50–55 SA-2 and HQ-23 (CSA-1) launchers (Chinese-made equivalents of the SA-2), and 25 SA-6 launchers. The air force also had three Soviet-made long range SA-5 units with a total of 10–15 launchers—enough for six sites.

The scale of Iranian capabilities and the Iranian build-up has, however, often been exaggerated. Iran has spent far less on arms imports in recent years than it did during the Iran-Iraq War. Iran has not come close to being able to replace its losses of land force equipment during the final battles of the war in 1988—losses which US experts estimate reached 40–60% of its entire inventory of armor and artillery. Much of its remaining inventory of land and air weapons is now 15–25 years old, has been severely worn in combat, and has lacked any orderly maintenance and modernization since the fall of the Shah.

Iran also has no strategic mobility or meaningful power projection capability, and its equipment and command and control assets are not interoperable with the equipment and systems of any Arab "ring state." Once again, any limited Iranian reinforcements would probably cost an Arab host nation far more in support effort than their military effectiveness would be worth.

As a result, it is Iran's ties to Islamic extremist movements like Hams, the Islamic Jihad, and the Hizbollah which pose the greatest threat to Israel and the peace process. Iran does have the ability to support an unconventional war against Israel, even though it presents little near term threat of being able to deploy significant effective conventional military forces.

Iraqi Capabilities

Iraq has been a major threat to Israel in the past. It deployed a total of four brigades against Israel by the end of the 1948 war, which fought in Samaria. It deployed a reinforced division, composed of an armored brigade, a mechanized brigade, and two infantry brigades in 1967—as well as a Palestinian contingent. This force only failed to engage Israeli land forces because the lead Iraqi mechanized brigade was badly hurt by the IAF while it was still on the East Bank.

Iraq deployed several divisions and significant air power in 1973. This Iraqi force played a significant role in limiting the IDF advance toward Damascus and might have been far more effective if Iraq had been better able to move and sustain its forces and Syria had provided more effective overall C⁴I and battle management assistance. Iraq acquired enough tank transporters and logistic equipment, and improved its infrastructure in western Iraq, to the point where it could have rapidly moved and sustained four divisions in a conflict with Israel by the mid-1980s. Iraq also began to exercise air units and small land headquarters units in Jordan before the Gulf War, although Jordan is now forbidden to allow the deployment of Iraqi forces on Jordanian soil as part of its peace agreement with Israel.

Iraq is still a major power by regional standards. It is a nation with nearly 382,000 active troops and a 350,000 man army. It has some 2,200–2,700 tanks, 700–900 BMP-1/BMP-2 armored infantry fighting vehicles, 1,500 armored reconnaissance vehicles, 2,000 APCs, 230 self-propelled and 1,500 major towed artillery weapons, 250 multiple rocket launchers and FROG rockets, and thousands of light surface-to-air missiles and anti-aircraft guns. It is a nation that still retains roughly 350 combat aircraft—including 1 Su–24 and some MiG–29s, large numbers of armed helicopters, and extensive surface-to-air missile defenses.

Nevertheless, Iraq's capabilities to intervene in an Arab-Israeli conflict are now limited. Iraq suffered massive losses during the Gulf War—losing 40–60% of its inventory of armor, artillery, and aircraft—and often many of its most advanced systems. While Iraq has rebuilt and reorganized its forces since 1991, these efforts have not come close to offsetting the damage inflicted by the Gulf War. Iraq also now deploys much of its army where it can deal with the threat from Iran and internal security missions against its Kurds and Shiites. It has had steadily growing problems with morale and desertions, and at least some senior officers have been involved in coup attempts.

While Iraq has extensively reorganized its Republican Guard and conventional forces since the Gulf War, it has had no major new arms imports. This has had a steadily more serious impact on Iraq's readiness. Iraq never developed an effective large scale maintainable support system before the Gulf War. It relied on vast imports of new weapons and parts to substitute for effective support, logistic, and maintenance capabilities. Its expansion of its military industries since the Gulf War have not been able to correct these problems, and it lacks the capability to provide large numbers of heavy weapons or technically sophisticated equipment and parts. Iraq has been unable to import the new technology it needs to react to any of the major lessons of its defeat in the Gulf War. Its air force and air defense forces have had very limited training, and much of its land forces have been tied up in operations in the marshes or in securing the perimeter of the Kurdish security zone.[3]

These problems do not mean that Iraq could not deploy several heavy divisions or several squadrons of combat aircraft to Syria or Jordan. It has the infrastructure in western Iraq and the tank transporters necessary to move at least two divisions relatively quickly. Any such deployments, however, would force Iraq to deploy several of its best divisions if they were to be effective, and this might affect Saddam Hussein's security. Such a deployment would also require a sudden political rapprochement between Saddam Hussein and Hafaz Asad and/or King Hussein—a now unlikely contingency. Even then, such Iraqi deployments would have limited sustainability and real-world combat power, would present many of the same battle management and coordination problems that arose in 1973, and could not obtain effective air cover and support from the Iraqi air force.

Iraq may well reemerge as a threat to Israel once current sanctions are lifted, and it has the opportunity to fully rebuild its forces. This, however, will require several years at a minimum, and much will depend on Iraq's political leadership and policies at this point and whether it chooses to thrust itself back into the Arab-Israeli confrontation, as well as deal with its problems in the Gulf.

The Impact of Libyan, Iranian, and Iraqi Conventional Capabilities

Libyan and Iranian conventional capabilities cannot be totally disregarded, and Iraq may pose a more significant mid-term threat. Israel must consider these threats in its military and arms control planning—at least on a contingency basis. At the same time, the current threat of any major deployment of conventional forces by radical states outside the region seems very limited, and it does not seem meaningful to attempt detailed contingency analysis. If such nations pose a near term threat, it is more likely to come in the form of unconventional warfare or aid to a ring state in acquiring or using weapons of mass destruction.

The practical problem for both Israel and its immediate Arab neighbors is not so much the near term war fighting threat from Libya, Iran, and Iraq, but rather their potential impact on arms control. Arms control agreements between Israel and its neighbors cannot be based simply on current capabilities. It takes years to build up military forces and war fighting capabilities, and Israel must consider this in reviewing any agreement that ignored threats from states outside the region—particularly Iraq. Further, the more Israel cuts its forces, the more limited Iraqi reinforcements might influence war fighting or crisis outcomes since they will be large relative to Israel's remaining capabilities.

This problem will not be an easy issue for Israel and its Arab neighbors to deal with. Syria sees Iraq as a potential threat—as well as a possible ally—and would have to consider Iraq in developing its arms control positions. Jordan cannot ignore the Iraqi threat, and Egypt has regional concerns about Iran's intentions and capabilities. At least in the near term, the "greater Middle East" may present more risks and problems for the Arab-Israeli military balance than it does economic or political opportunities.

13

CASE EIGHT: DETERRENCE FAILS— A MAJOR USE OF WEAPONS OF MASS DESTRUCTION

All of the previous seven contingencies are limited in the sense that they are unlikely to escalate to levels of conflict which threaten the existence of one or more states, or produce massive civilian casualties. The slow proliferation of weapons of mass destruction does, however, pose a growing risk of wars that could threaten the major population centers of Israel and its Arab neighbors, and even the existence of Israel and any Arab state that became involved in a large scale exchange using biological or nuclear weapons.

Israeli Weapons of Mass Destruction

A rough estimate of the trends in the acquisition of weapons of mass destruction and long range delivery systems that affect the Arab-Israeli balance is shown in Table 13.1. The most important single fact reflected in these data is that Israel is the only state in the region that currently has nuclear weapons. Many US experts believe that Israel has at least 50 to 90 plutonium weapons and could have well over 135, provided that it was forced to use the normal amount of plutonium in such weapons.[1] A few experts estimate Israel may have over 200 weapons.[2]

If the Vanunu disclosures are correct, Israel may also have the capability to boost the yield of its fission weapons to yields in excess of 100 kilotons, reduce the amount of material it required per bomb, or even build a fusion weapon.[3] As a result, Israeli stockpiles may have included some highly efficient weapons by the early 1980s, as well as other enhanced yield weapons with variable yields of up to 100 kilotons or more.[4]

As for the current details of Israel's nuclear facilities, they seem to include:[5]

- Major nuclear research facilities at Soreq and Negev;
- Uranium phosphate mining in the Negev near Beersheeba;
- Yellowcake production in two plants at Haifa;

TABLE 13.1   The Race for Weapons of Mass Destruction

Algeria

Delivery Systems
- 10 Su-24 long range strike aircraft.
- 40 MiG-23BN fighter ground attack aircraft.
- Tube artillery and multiple rocket launchers.

Chemical Weapons
- Possible development. No evidence of deployed systems.

Biological Weapons
- Some early research activity.
- No evidence of production capability.

Nuclear Weapons
- Deliberately sought to create a covert nuclear research program under military control with Chinese support. Exposure to public opinion and Western objections and economic/political crisis have largely halted further progress.

Libya

Delivery Systems
- Al-Fatih missile with 300–450 mile range reported to have been under development with aid of German technical experts, but no signs of successful development.
- FROG-7 rocket launchers with 40 kilometer range.
- Deployed 80 Scud B launchers with 190 mile range in 1976, but could not successfully operate system. Many of the launchers and missiles sold to Iran.
- Purchased SS-N-2C and SSC-3 cruise missiles. Little operational capability.
- Pursued other missile development programs with little success.
- Tu-22 bombers with minimal operational capability.
- Su-24 long range strike fighters. These are operational and have limited refueling capability using C-130s.
- Operational Mirage 5D/DE and 10 Mirage 5DD fighter ground attack aircraft.
- Mirage F-1AD fighter ground attack aircraft.
- MiG-23BM Flogger F and 14 MiG-23U fighter ground attack aircraft.
- Su-20 and Su-22 Fitter E, J. F fighter ground attack aircraft.
- Tube artillery and multiple rocket launchers.

Chemical Weapons
- May have used mustard gas delivered in bombs by AN-26 aircraft in final phases of war against Chad in September, 1987.
- Nerve and mustard gas production facilities in an industrial park at chemical weapons plant at Rabta. This plant can produce both the poison gas and the bombs, shells, and warheads to contain it. Are probably two other research/batch production facilities. Plant seems to have started test runs in mid-1988.
- Additional chemical weapons plant in construction in extensive underground site south of Tripoli.
- Several thousand tons of chemical munitions, chemical bombs and rockets with mustard gas, and possibly nonpersistent nerve gas.

TABLE 13.1   *(Continued)*

- Unconfirmed reports of shipments of chemical weapons to Syria and Iran do not seem valid.
- Very low quality weapons designs with poor fusing and lethality.

Biological Weapons
- Some early research activity.
- No evidence of production capability.

Nuclear Weapons
- Has sought to create a development and production capability, but no evidence of any real progress or success.

Egypt

Delivery Systems
- Cooperation with Iraq in paying for development and production of "Badar 2000" missile with a 750–1,000 kilometer range. This missile is reported to be a version of the Argentine Condor II or Vector missile. Ranges were reported from 820–980 kilometers, with the possible use of an FAE warhead. Egyptian officers were arrested for trying to smuggle carbon materials for a missile out of the US in June, 1988. Covert US efforts seem to have blocked this development effort.
- Cooperation with Iraq and North Korea in developing the Saqr 80 missile. This rocket is 6.5 meters long and 210 mm in diameter, and weighs 660 kilograms. It has a maximum range of 50 miles (80 kilometers) and a 440 pound (200 kilogram) warhead. Longer range versions may be available.
- Has developed plant to produce an improved version of the Scud B, with North Korean cooperation.
- Scud B launch units with approximately 100 missiles with 300 kilometer range.
- FROG-7 rocket launch units with 40 kilometer range.
- AS-15, SS-N-2, and CSS-N-1 cruise missiles.
- F-4E fighter ground attack aircraft.
- Mirage 5E2 fighter ground attack aircraft.
- Mirage 2000EM fighters.
- F-16A and 80 F-16C fighters.
- Multiple rocket launcher weapons.
- Tube artillery.

Chemical Weapons
- Produced and used mustard gas in Yemeni civil war in 1960s, but agents may have been stocks British abandoned in Egypt after World War II. Effort was tightly controlled by Nasser and was unknown to many Egyptian military serving in Yemen.
- Completed research and designs for production of nerve and cyanide gas before 1973.
- Former Egyptian minister of war, general Abdel Ranny Gamassay stated in 1975 that "if Israel should decide to use a nuclear weapon in the battlefield, we shall use the weapons of mass destruction that are at our disposal."

TABLE 13.1   *(Continued)*

- Seems to have several production facilities for mustard and nerve gas. May have limited stocks of bombs, rockets, and shells.
- Unconfirmed reports of recent efforts to acquire feed stocks for nerve gas. Some efforts to obtain feed stocks from Canada. May now be building feed stock plants in Egypt.
- Industrial infrastructure present for rapid production of cyanide gas.

Biological Weapons
- Research and technical base.
- No evidence of major organized research activity.

Nuclear Weapons
- Low level research effort. No evidence of more than basic research since the 1960s.

Israel

Delivery Systems
- New IRBM/ICBM range high payload booster in development with South Africa. Status unknown.
- Up to 50 "Jericho I" missiles deployed in shelters on mobile launchers with up to 400 miles range with a 2,200 pound payload, and with possible nuclear warhead storage nearby. Unverified claims that up to 100 missiles are deployed west of Jerusalem.
- Jericho II missiles now deployed, and some were brought to readiness for firing during the Gulf War. These missiles seem to include a single stage follow-on to the Jericho I and a multistage longer range missile. The latter missile seems to have a range of up to 900 miles with a 2,200 pound payload, and may be a cooperative development with South Africa. (Extensive reporting of such cooperation in press during October 25 and 26, 1989.)
- Jericho II missile production facility at Be'er Yakov.
- A major missile test took place on September 14, 1989. It was either a missile test or failure of Ofeq-2 satellite.
- Work on development of TERCOM type smart warheads. Possible cruise missile guidance developments using GPS navigation systems.
- F-15, F-16, F-4E, and Phantom 2000 fighter-bombers capable of long range refueling and of carrying nuclear and chemical bombs.
- Lance missile launchers and 160 Lance missiles with 130 kilometer range.
- MAR-290 rocket with 30 kilometer range believed to be deployed.
- MAR-350 surface-to-surface missile with range of 56 miles and 735 pound payload believed to have completed development or to be in early deployment.
- Israel seeking super computers for Technion Institute (designing ballistic missile RVs), Hebrew University (may be engaged in hydrogen bomb research), and Israeli Military Industries (maker of "Jericho II" and Shavit booster).

Chemical Weapons
- Mustard and nerve gas production facility established in 1982 in the restricted area in the Sinai near Dimona. May have additional facilities. May have capacity to

TABLE 13.1   *(Continued)*

produce other gases. Probable stocks of bombs, rockets, and artillery.
- Extensive laboratory research into gas warfare and defense.
- Development of defensive systems includes Shalon Chemical Industries protection gear, Elbit Computer gas detectors, and Bezal R&D air crew protection system.
- Extensive field exercises in chemical defense.
- Gas masks stockpiled and distributed to population with other civil defense instructions during Gulf War.
- Warhead delivery capability for bombs, rockets, and missiles, but none now believed to be equipped with chemical agents.

Biological Weapons
- Extensive research into weapons and defense.
- Ready to quickly produce biological weapons, but no reports of active production effort.

Nuclear Weapons
- Director of CIA indicated in May, 1989 that Israel may be seeking to construct a thermonuclear weapon.
- Estimates of numbers and types of weapons differ sharply.
- At least a stockpile of 60–80 plutonium weapons. May have well over 100 nuclear weapons assemblies, with some weapons with yields over 100 kilotons and some with possible ER variants or variable yields. Stockpile of up to 200–300 weapons is possible.
- Possible facilities include production of weapons grade plutonium at Dimona, nuclear weapons design facility at Soreq (south of Tel Aviv), missile test facility at Palmikim, nuclear armed missile storage facility at Kefar Zekharya, nuclear weapons assembly facility at Yodefat, and tactical nuclear weapons storage facility at Eilabun in eastern Galilee.

Missile Defenses
- Patriot missiles with future PAC-3 upgrade to reflect lessons of the Gulf War.
- Arrow 2 two stage ATBM with slant intercept ranges at altitudes of 8–10 and 50 kilometer speeds of up to Mach 9, plus possible development of the Rafale AB-10 close in defense missile with ranges of 10-20 kilometers and speeds of up to Mach 4.5. Tadiran BM/C4I system and "Music" phased array radar. Israel plans to deploy two batteries of the Arrow to cover Israel, each with four launchers, to protect up to 85% of its population.[270]

Advanced Intelligence Systems
- The Shavit I launched Israel's satellite payload on September 19, 1989. It used a three stage booster system capable of launching a 4,000 pound payload over 1,200 miles or a 2,000 pound payload over 1,800 miles.
- Ofeq 2 launched in April, 1990—one day after Saddam Hussein threatens to destroy Israel with chemical weapons if it should attack Baghdad.
- Launched first intelligence satellite on April 5, 1995, covering Syria, Iran, and Iraq in orbit every 90 minutes. The Ofeq 3 satellite is a 495 pound system launched using the Shavit launch rocket, and is believed to carry an imagery system. Its orbits pass over or near Damascus, Tehran, and Baghdad.[271]

TABLE 13.1   *(Continued)*

Syria

Delivery Systems
- Four SSM brigades: 1 with FROG, 1 with Scud Bs, 1 with Scud Cs, and 1 with SS-21s.
- New long range North Korean Scud Cs, with ranges of up to 600 kilometers and possible nerve gas warheads, now being deployed. Seems to have 6–12 launchers deployed.
- May be converting some long range surface-to-air and naval cruise missiles to use chemical warheads.
- 18 SS-21 launchers and at least 36 SS-21 missiles with 80–100 kilometer range. May be developing chemical warheads.
- Up to 12 Scud B launchers and Scud B missiles with 310 kilometer range. Believed to have chemical warheads.
- Short range M-1B missiles (up to 60 mile range) seem to be in delivery from PRC.
- SS-N-3 and SSC-1b cruise missiles.
- 20 Su-24 long range strike fighters.
- 30-60 operational MiG-23BM Flogger F fighter ground attack aircraft.
- 20 Su-20 fighter ground attack aircraft.
- 60-70 Su-22 fighter ground attack aircraft.
- 18 FROG-7 launchers and rockets.
- Negotiations for PRC made M-9 missile (185–375 mile range).
- Multiple rocket launchers and tube artillery.

Chemical Weapons
- Major nerve gas and possible other chemical agent production facilities north of Damascus. Two to three plants.
- Unconfirmed reports of sheltered Scud missiles with Sarin or Tabun nerve gas warheads deployed in caves and shelters near Damascus.
- Shells, bombs, and nerve gas warheads for multiple rocket launchers.
- FROG warheads under development.
- Reports of SS-21 capability to deliver chemical weapons are not believed by US or Israeli experts.
- Israeli sources believe Syria has binary weapons and cluster bomb technology suitable for delivering chemical weapons.
- Experts believe has stockpiled 500 to 1,000 metric tons of chemical agents.

Biological Weapons
- Extensive research effort.
- Probable production capability for anthrax and botulism and possibly other agents.

Nuclear Weapons
- Ongoing research effort.
- No evidence of major progress in development effort.

Iran

Delivery Systems
- Has new long range North Korean Scuds—with ranges near 500 kilometers. May manufacture missiles in Iran in future, possibly as cooperative effort with Syria.
- Probably has ordered North Korean No Dong missile which can carry nuclear and

TABLE 13.1   *(Continued)*

biological missile ranges of up to 900 kilometers. Can reach virtually any target in Gulf, Turkey, and Israel, although CIA now estimates deliveries will only begin in 1997–1999.[272]

- Su-24 long range strike fighters with range-payloads roughly equivalent to US F-111 and superior to older Soviet medium bombers.
- Has recently bought CSS-8 surface-to-surface missiles from China with ranges of 130-150 kilometers.
- Used regular Scud extensively during Iran-Iraq War. Has 6–12 Scud launchers and up to 200 Scud B (R-17E) missiles with 230–310 kilometer range. Scud missiles were provided by Libya and North Korea.
- May have placed order for PRC made M-9 missile (280–620 kilometer range). More likely that PRC is giving assistance in missile R&D and production facilities.
- Iranian made IRAN 130 rocket with 150+ kilometer range.
- Iranian Oghab (Eagle) rocket with 40+ kilometer range.
- New SSM with 125 mile range may be in production, but could be modified FROG.
- F-4D/E fighter bombers with capability to carry extensive payloads to ranges of 450 miles.
- Can modify HY-2 Silkworm missiles and SA-2 surface-to-air missiles to deliver weapons of mass destruction.
- Large numbers of multiple rocket launchers and tube artillery for short range delivery of chemical weapons.
- Experimenting in cruise missile development.

Chemical Weapons
- At least two major research and production facilities.
- Made limited use of chemical weapons at end of the Iran-Iraq War.
- Began to create stockpiles of cyanide (cyanogen chloride), phosgene, and mustard gas weapons after 1985. Includes bombs and artillery.
- Production of nerve gas weapons started no later than 1994.

Biological Weapons
- Extensive laboratory and research capability.
- Weapons effort documented as early as 1992.
- Bioresearch effort sophisticated enough to produce biological weapons as lethal as small nuclear weapons.
- Seems to have the production facilities to make dry storable weapons. This would allow it to develop suitable missile warheads, bombs, and covert devices.
- May be involved in active weapons production, but no evidence to date that this is the case.

Nuclear Weapons
- In 1984, revived nuclear weapons program begun under Shah.
- Received significant West German and Argentine corporate support in some aspects of nuclear technology during the Iran-Iraq War.
- Limited transfers of centrifuge and other weapons related technology from PRC, possibly Pakistan.

TABLE 13.1   *(Continued)*

- Stockpiles of uranium and mines in Yazd area.
- Seems to have attempted to buy fissile material from Khazakstan.
- Russian agreement to build up to four reactors, beginning with a complex at Bushehr—with two 1,000–1,200 megawatt reactors and two 465 megawatt reactors—and provide significant nuclear technology.
- Chinese agreement to provide significant nuclear technology transfer and possible sale of two 300 megawatt pressurized water reactors.
- No way to tell when current efforts will produce a weapon, and unclassified lists of potential facilities have little credibility. We simply do not know where Iran is developing its weapons.
- IAEA has found no indications of weapons effort, but found no efforts in Iraq in spring of 1990. IAEA only formally inspects Iran's small research reactors. Its visits to other Iranian sites are not thorough enough to confirm or deny whether Iran has such activities.
- Timing of weapons acquisition depends heavily on whether Iran can buy fissile material—if so, it has the design capability and can produce weapons in 1–2 years—or must develop the capability to process plutonium or enrich uranium—in which case, it is likely to be 5–10 years.

Iraq

Delivery Systems
- Prior to the Gulf War Iraq had extensive delivery systems incorporating long range strike aircraft with refueling capabilities and several hundred regular and improved, longer range Scud missiles, some with chemical warheads. These systems included:
  - Tu-16 and Tu-22 bombers.
  - MiG-29 fighters.
  - Mirage F-1, MiG-23BM, and Su-22 fighter attack aircraft.
  - A Scud force with a minimum of 819 missiles.
  - Extended range Al-Hussein Scud variants (600 kilometer range) extensively deployed throughout Iraq.
  - At least 12 Al-Abbas missiles (900 kilometer range) deployed at three fixed sites in northern, western, and southern Iraq. Al-Abbas can reach targets in Iran, the Persian Gulf, Israel, Turkey, and Cyprus.
  - Long range superguns with ranges of up to 600 kilometers.
- Iraq also engaged in efforts aimed at developing the Tamuz liquid fueled missile with a range of over 2,000 kilometers and a solid fueled missile with a similar range. Clear evidence that at least one design was to have a nuclear warhead.
- Iraq attempted to conceal a plant making missile engines from the UN inspectors. It only admitted this plant existed in 1995, raising new questions about how many of its missiles have been destroyed.
- Iraq produced or assembled 80 Scud missiles in its own factories. Some 53 seem to have been unusable, but 10 are still unaccounted for.
- Had designed work under way for a nuclear warhead for its long range missiles.
  - The Gulf War deprived Iraq of some of its MiG-29s, Mirage F-1s, MiG-23 BMs,

TABLE 13.1   *(Continued)*

and Su-22s. Since the end of the war, the UN inspection regime has also destroyed many of Iraq's long range missiles.

- Iraq, however, maintains a significant delivery capability consisting of:
  - HY-2, SS-N-2, and C-601 cruise missiles, which are unaffected by UN cease-fire terms.
  - FROG-7 rockets with 70 kilometer ranges, also allowed under UN resolutions.
  - Multiple rocket launchers and tube artillery.
  - Some portion of 12-20 Scud launchers.
  - Iraq claims to have manufactured only 80 missile assemblies, 53 of which were unusable. UNSCOM claims that 10 are unaccounted for.
  - US experts believe Iran may still have components for 80–150 missiles.
- In addition, Iraq has admitted to:
  - Manufacturing a few of its own Scuds.
  - Developing an extended range variant of the FROG-7 called the Laith. The UN claims to have tagged all existing FROG-7s to prevent any extension of their range beyond the UN imposed limit of 150 kilometers for Iraqi missiles.
  - Experimenting with cruise missile technology.
  - Flight testing Al-Hussein missiles with chemical warheads in April, 1990.
  - Initiating a research and development program for a nuclear warhead missile delivery system.
  - Conducting research into the development of Remotely Piloted Vehicles (RPVs) for the dissemination of biological agents.
  - Attempting to expand its Ababil-100 program designed to build surface-to-surface missiles with ranges of 100–150 kilometers.
  - Starting an indigenous 600 mm supergun design effort.
  - Starting additional long-range missile programs, with ranges of 900, 2,000, and 3,000 kilometers.
- US and UN officials conclude further that:
  - Iraq is concentrating procurement efforts on rebuilding its ballistic missile program using a clandestine network of front companies to obtain the necessary materials and technology from European and Russian firms.
  - This equipment is then concealed and stockpiled for assembly concomitant with the end of the UN inspection regime.
  - The equipment clandestinely sought by Iraq includes advanced missile guidance components, such as accelerometers and gyroscopes, specialty metals, special machine tools, and a high-tech, French-made, million-dollar furnace designed to fabricate engine parts for missiles.
  - Jordan found that Iraq was smuggling missile components through Jordan in early December, 1995.
- US satellite photographs reveal that Iraq has rebuilt its Al-Kindi missile research facility.
- Iraq retains the technology it acquired before the war and evidence clearly indicates an ongoing research and development effort, in spite of the UN sanctions regime.
- The fact the agreement allows Iraq to continue producing and testing short range missiles (less than 150 kilometer range) has meant it can retain significant missile efforts.

TABLE 13.1 *(Continued)*

Chemical Weapons
- In revelations to the UN, Iraq admitted that, prior to the Gulf War, it:
  - Maintained large stockpiles of mustard gas and the nerve agents Sarin and Tabun.
  - Produced binary Sarin filled artillery shells, 122 mm rockets, and aerial bombs.
  - Manufactured enough precursors to produce 500 tons of the nerve agent VX. These precursors included 65 tons of chlorine and 200 tons of phosphorous pentasulfide and di-isopropylamine.
  - Tested Ricin, a deadly nerve agent, for use in artillery shells.
  - Had three flight tests of long range Scuds with chemical warheads.
  - Had large VX production effort under way at the time of the Gulf War. The destruction of the related weapons and feedstocks has been claimed by Iraq, but not verified by UNSCOM.
- The majority of Iraq's chemical agents were manufactured at a supposed pesticide plant located at Muthanna. Various other production facilities were also used, including those at Salman Pak, Samara, and Habbiniyah. Though severely damaged during the war, the physical plant for many of these facilities has been rebuilt.
  - Iraq possessed the technology to produce a variety of other persistent and non-persistent agents.
- The Gulf War and subsequent:
  - UN inspection regime may have largely eliminated these stockpiles and reduced production capability.
  - US experts believe Iraq has concealed significant stocks of precursors. It also appears to retain significant amounts of production equipment dispersed before or during Desert Storm and not recovered by the UN.
- Iraq has developed basic chemical warhead designs for Scud missiles, rockets, bombs, and shells. Iraq also has spray dispersal systems.
- Iraq maintains extensive stocks of defensive equipment.
- The UN maintains that Iraq is not currently producing chemical agents, but the UN is also concerned that Iraq has offered no evidence that it has destroyed its VX production capability and/or stockpile.
- Further, Iraq retains the technology it acquired before the war and evidence clearly indicates an ongoing research and development effort, in spite of the UN sanctions regime.

Biological Weapons
- Systematically lied about biological weapons effort until 1995. First stated that had small defensive efforts, but no offensive effort. In July, 1995, admitted had a major offensive effort. In October, 1995, finally admitted major weaponization effort.
- Iraq has continued to lie about its biological weapons effort since October, 1995. It has claimed the effort is headed by Dr. Taha, a woman who only headed a subordinate effort. It has not admitted to any help by foreign personnel or contractors. It has claimed to have destroyed its weapons, but the one site UNSCOM inspectors visited showed no signs of such destruction and was later said to be the wrong site. It has claimed only 50 people were employed full time, but the scale of the effort would have required several hundred.

TABLE 13.1 *(Continued)*

- The August, 1995 defection of Lt. General Hussein Kamel Majid, formerly in charge of Iraq's weapons of mass destruction, revealed the extent of this biological weapons program.
- Reports indicate that Iraq tested at least 7 principal biological agents for use against humans.
  - Anthrax, Botulinum, and Aflatoxin known to be weaponized.
  - Looked at viruses, bacteria, and fungi. Examined the possibility of weaponizing Gas Gangrene and Mycotoxins. Some field trials were held of these agents.
  - Examined foot and mouth disease, haemorrhagic conjunctivitis virus, rotavirus, and camel pox virus.
  - Conducted research on a "wheat pathogen" and a mycotoxin similar to "yellow rain" defoliant.
  - The "wheat smut" was first produced at Al Salman, and then put in major production during 1987–1988 at a plant near Mosul. Iraq claims the program was abandoned.
- The defection prompted Iraq to admit that it:
  - Imported tons of growth media for biological agents obtained from three European firms. According to UNSCOM, 17 tons remain unaccounted for.
  - Imported type cultures which can be modified to develop biological weapons from the US.
  - Created at least five primary production facilities including the Sepp Institute at Muthanna, the Ghazi Research Institute at Amaria, the Daura Foot and Mouth Disease Institute, and facilities at Al-Hakim, Salman Pak, and Taji. According to UNSCOM, weaponization occurred primarily at Muthanna through May, 1987 (largely Botulinum), and then moved to Al Salman (anthrax). In March, 1988 a plant was open at Al Hakim, and in 1989 an Aflatoxin plant was set up at Fudaliyah.
  - Manufactured 6,000 liters of concentrated Botulinum toxin and 8,425 liters of anthrax at Al-Hakim during 1990; 5,400 liters of concentrated Botulinum toxin at the Daura Foot and Mouth Disease Institute from November, 1990 to January 15, 1991; 400 liters of concentrated Botulinum toxin at Taji; and 150 liters of concentrated anthrax at Salman Pak. Produced 1,850 liters of Aflatoxin in solution at Fudaliyah.
  - Produced 340 liters of concentrated clostridium perfringens, a gangrene-causing biological agent, beginning in August, 1990.
  - Produced 10 liters of concentrated Ricin at Al Salam. Claim abandoned work after tests failed.
- Extensive weaponization program:
  - Conducted field trials, weaponization tests, and live firings of 122 mm rockets armed with anthrax and Botulinum toxin from March, 1988 to May, 1990.
  - Total production reached at least 19,000 liters of concentrated Botulinum (10,000 liters filled into munitions); 8,500 liters of concentrated anthrax (6,500 liters filled into munitions); and 2,500 liters of concentrated Aflatoxin (1,850 liters filled into munitions).

TABLE 13.1   *(Continued)*

- Weaponized at least three biological agents for use in the Gulf War. The weaponization consisted of 100 bombs and 15 missile warheads loaded with Botulinum; 50 R-400 air-delivered bombs and 10 missile warheads loaded with anthrax; and 16 missile warheads loaded with Aflatoxin, a natural carcinogen. The warheads were designed for operability with the Al-Hussein Scud variant. A total of at least 166 bombs were filled with some biological agent.
  - Developed and stored drop tanks ready for use for three aircraft or RPVs with the capability of dispersing 2,000 liters of anthrax. Development took place in December, 1990. Claimed later that tests showed were ineffective.
- The UN claims that Iraq has offered no evidence to corroborate its claims that it destroyed its stockpile of biological agents after the Gulf War. Further, Iraq retains the technology it acquired before the war and evidence clearly indicates an ongoing research and development effort, in spite of the UN sanctions regime.
- UN currently inspects 79 sites—5 used to make weapons before war; 5 vaccine or pharmaceutical sites; 35 research and university sites; 13 breweries, distilleries, and dairies with dual-purpose capabilities; 8 diagnostic laboratories.
- Retains laboratory capability to manufacture various biological agents including the bacteria which cause anthrax, botulism, tularemia, and typhoid.
- Many additional civilian facilities capable of playing some role in biological weapons production.

Nuclear Weapons
- Inspections by UN teams have found evidence of two successful weapons designs, a neutron initiator, explosives and triggering technology needed for production of bombs, plutonium processing technology, centrifuge technology, Calutron enrichment technology, and experiments with chemical separation technology.
  - Iraq used Calutron, centrifuges, plutonium processing, chemical defusion, and foreign purchases to create new production capability after Israel destroyed most of Osiraq.
  - Iraq established a centrifuge enrichment system in Rashidya and conducted research into the nuclear fuel cycle to facilitate development of a nuclear device.
- After invading Kuwait, Iraq attempted to accelerate its program to develop a nuclear weapon by using radioactive fuel from French and Russian built reactors. It made a crash effort in September, 1990 to recover enriched fuel from its safeguarded reactor at the Tuwaitha site.
- Iraq conducted research into the production of a radiological weapon, which disperses lethal radioactive material without initiating a nuclear explosion.
  - Orders were given in 1987 to explore the use of radiological weapons for area denial in the Iran-Iraq War.
  - Three prototype bombs were detonated at test sites—one as a ground level static test and two others dropped from aircraft.
  - Iraq claims the results were disappointing and the project was shelved but has no records or evidence to prove this.
- UN teams have found and destroyed, or secured, new stockpiles of illegal enriched

TABLE 13.1   *(Continued)*

---

material, major production and R&D facilities, and equipment—including Calutron enriching equipment.

- UNSCOM believes that Iraq's nuclear program has been largely disabled and remains incapacitated.
- Iraq, however, still retains the technology developed before the Gulf War, and US experts believe an ongoing research and development effort continues in spite of the UN sanctions regime.

Source: Prepared by Anthony H. Cordesman, Co-Director, Middle East Program, CSIS.

- Yellowcake production at a phosphate plant in southern Israel;
- Uranium purification (UO_2) and conversion (UF_6) and fuel fabrication at Dimona;
- Experimental pilot-scale centrifuge and laser enrichment facilities at Dimona;
- A five megawatt research reactor fueled with highly enriched uranium called the IRR-1 at Nahal Soreq;
- The IRR-2 at the Negev Nuclear Research Center in Dimona (which has anywhere from 40 to 150 megawatts of capacity);
- A major plutonium reprocessing facility at Dimona;
- Hot cell facilities and pilot-scale plutonium extraction facilities at Nahal Soreq and in the Negev;
- Heavy water production at Rehovot;
- Lithium-6 production for tritium and/or lithium deuteride at Dimona (possibly decommissioned);
- A pilot plant for extracting uranium from phosphates at the Negev Center; and
- Facilities at Kefar Zekhara, Eliabun, and Tel Nof for the storage of nuclear missiles and weapons.

Many of the details of Israel's potential nuclear weapons delivery systems are as uncertain as the details of its nuclear weapons. Israel is not a signatory to the Non-Proliferation Treaty and the only facility where it permits IAEA inspection is the IRR-1.[6] However, Israel has had long range strike fighters since it first acquired nuclear weapons, and some reports indicate that it had nuclear capable F-4 units deployed at the Tel Nof air base by the late 1960s.

Israel can now deliver nuclear weapons with its F-4Es, F-16s, and F-15s, and has the technology to adapt air-to-surface missiles like the Popeye to carry nuclear warheads with ranges in excess of 30 miles—although there is no evidence that it has done so.[7] It can refuel its strike aircraft with KC-130 and B-707 tankers and give its strike aircraft the range to launch missions of over 1,500 kilometers. Israel's strikes on Iraq and Tunisia have shown that it can execute long range missions with great military skill. Israel also has excellent electronic warfare capabilities and can provide excellent fighter cover using its F-15s and special purpose aircraft. A small number of Israeli attackers could probably penetrate the air defenses of virtually any nation in the region.[8]

There are convincing indications that Israel has deployed nuclear armed missiles on mobile launchers. Most outside sources call the first of these missiles the "Jericho I," but Israel has never publicly named its long range missile systems.[9] The current deployment of the "Jericho I" force is unclear, although one source indicates they may be deployed in the Hirbat Zachariah, in the Judean Mountains southwest of Jerusalem. It does seem likely that Israel has now deployed about 50–100 of these missiles. Another source claimed in 1985 that they were deployed on mobile erector launchers in the Golan and on launchers on flat cars that could be wheeled out of sheltered cases in the Negev, but there are no reports of when such deployments took place, and other reports indicate such missiles are located at sites west of Jerusalem. The number that are on alert, command and control and targeting arrangements, and the method of giving them nuclear warheads have never been convincingly reported.[10]

Israel has also gone far beyond the Jericho I in developing long range missile systems.[11] It has developed much longer range systems that outside analysts often call the "Jericho II" and has probably deployed these systems. The tests of these longer range missiles seem to have begun in the mid-1980s and may have involved both an improved single stage missile and a multistage missile. According to some reports, the new single stage missile uses strap down inertial guidance and was first tested in mid-1986 in a launch over the Mediterranean that reached a range of 288 miles (460 kilometers). It also seems to have been tested in May, 1987. A flight across the Mediterranean reached a range of some 510 miles (820 kilometers), landing south of Crete.[12]

The "Jericho II" seems to be a three stage missile that had its first tests in 1988.[13] A more publicized test occurred on September 14, 1989. Israel launched a missile across the Mediterranean that landed about 250 miles north of Benghazi, Libya. The missile flew over 800 miles, and US experts felt it had a maximum range of up to 900–940 miles (1,450 kilometers)—which would allow it to cover virtually all of the Arab world and even the southern USSR.[14] This same booster may have been the focus of cooperative Israeli–South African missile development and testing that was disclosed in 1989, but there are some indications that both the booster and any Israeli–South African cooperation may have focused on satellite launches.[15]

Some sources feel that 30–50 of these multistage missiles may have already been deployed, and a number believe that some were armed with nuclear weapons and brought to alert during the Gulf War. If so, these missile capabilities could change the balance of power in the Middle East. While the "Jericho I" missile could probably only cover Syria, Jordan, Lebanon, and upper Egypt, this may mean that the first of the "Jericho II" missiles already has the range to cover all of

Egypt, eastern Libya, all of Iraq, the western part of Iran, the upper Sudan, Saudi Arabia east of Riyadh, and Turkey. Arab countries would be extremely vulnerable to strikes on key cities. A single high yield weapon of 100 kilotons or more could effectively destroy a Syrian city like Damascus, Aleppo, or Homs; a Jordanian city like Amman, Irbid, or Zarqa; an Iraqi city like Baghdad, Basrah, or Mosul; a Libyan city like Tripoli or Benghazi; or most of the larger Egyptian cities of Cairo, Alexandria, or Gaza. A 20 kiloton to 50 kiloton weapon could destroy any other city in the region, as well as any major air base.[16]

As Table 13.1 shows, Israel seems to have other weapons of mass destruction. Israel seems to have revitalized its chemical warfare facilities south of Dimona in the mid-1980s, after Syria deployed chemical weapons and Iraq began to use these weapons in the Iran-Iraq War. Israel may now have production facilities for at least two types of chemical weapons and seems to have stepped up its studies of biological weapons as well as chemical ones. According to one interview with an Israeli source, Israel has mustard gas, persistent and nonpersistent nerve gas, and may have at least one additional agent. Israel has at least one major biological research facility with sufficient security and capacity to produce biological weapons.[17]

Israel is the only Middle Eastern state that seems likely to acquire its own imagery and targeting satellite.[18] It also is the only Middle Eastern state that can combine the development of offensive missiles with missile defense. Israel already has Patriot defenses whose anti-tactical ballistic missile (ATBM) defenses have been sharply upgraded since the Gulf War, and which will be further enhanced by the PAC-3 upgrade. It is also developing its own ATBM defenses.

Israel has advanced beyond its initial design and test phase for the Arrow-1, and is now beginning a test program for the Arrow-2 that will last until 1998. The Arrow-2 uses a two stage solid rocket and is designed to be fired in two missile salvos to intercept first at a target altitude of around 50 kilometers with a back-up intercept at an altitude of 8–10 kilometers. These intercept heights have been chosen to minimize any risk of collateral damage from a surviving or damaged warhead. The Israeli system is currently planned to be deployed in two sites near Tel Aviv and Haifa which will cover up to 85% of Israel's population. Each battery will have four missile launchers. Israel has not yet decided on the kill mechanism to be used with each missile warhead, but seems to have decided on the "Music" phased array radar system for use in both early warning and intercept guidance. There will also be a Tadiran manufactured C⁴I/BM unit attached to each battery.[19]

Syrian Weapons of Mass Destruction

Israel does not, however, have any monopoly on weapons of mass destruction. As Table 13.1 also shows, Egypt, Iran, Iraq, Libya, and Syria have significant capabilities that could threaten Israel, and Syria's capabilities could be critical in a future conflict.

Syria has made considerable progress in acquiring weapons of mass destruction since the mid-1970s. Syria has never shown a serious interest in nuclear weapons, although it did seek to buy two small research reactors from the PRC in 1992—including a 24 megawatt reactor—and purchased a small 30 kilowatt research reactor from the PRC in 1991. It allowed inspection by the International Atomic Energy Agency for the first time in February, 1992.[20] It does, however, deploy sheltered missiles, armed with chemical warheads, as a means of both countering Israel's nuclear forces and maintaining its rivalry with Iraq.

Syria obtained the FROG 7 in 1972, and the Scud B missile as early as 1974, but Syria does not seem to have given these missile forces a major role until Israel's invasion of Lebanon in 1982. In the ensuing fighting, Syria lost much of its air force in two brief clashes with Israeli fighters and saw Israel suppress its land-based air defenses in Lebanon in a matter of hours. This persuaded Syria that surface-to-surface missiles were a potential means of overcoming Israel's advantage in the air, and furnished a means of attacking Israel's air bases and mobilization centers.

Syria reorganized its surface-to-surface missile brigades. It obtained the SS-21, or Scarab, in 1983 and steadily improved the readiness and effectiveness of its missile units. In late 1994, Syria had a force of 18 SS-21, 18–24 FROG-7, and 18–36 Scud B surface-to-surface missile fire units, plus additional Sepal SS-1B and SSC-3 coastal defense missile fire units.[21]

Syria probably acquired limited stocks of mustard gas shortly before or after the October War in 1973. It was only after Syria's clashes with Israel in 1982, however, that Syria seems to have started a major effort in chemical and biological warfare. As is the case with missiles, Syria saw weapons of mass destruction as a way of countering Israel's advantages and as a means of maintaining its status relative to its other regional military rivals.

Syrian troops steadily increased their NBC training after 1982, and Syria began to give chemical warfare training a serious priority. More significantly, Syria started a crash effort to produce nerve gas—setting up at least two major chemical weapons plants. US experts indicated in 1984 that Syria had begun manufacturing and deploying nonpersistent nerve and other gases in 1982 or 1983. By the late 1980s, Syria seems to have been operating two, and possibly three, facilities for the production of chemical weapons. One seems to be the CERS Institute, which may also play a role in biological warfare research. Syria is stockpiling nerve gas and other chemical agents, including nonpersistent nerve gases like Sarin (GB) and persistent nerve gas agents like VX. A full list of the kinds of chemical weapons Syria may have developed is shown in Table 13.2.

Syria was also caught smuggling feedstocks from Russia in 1993 and 1994. It obtained 1,800 pounds of feedstocks for nerve gas in 1993 and attempted to smuggle out another 11,000 pounds in 1994. Ironically, the Russian responsible for the smuggling was General Anatoly Kuntsevich, once President Yeltsin's chief military liaison officer for chemical disarmament.[22]

Syria has also developed biological weapons, although it does not seem to have attempted to produce or stockpile them. It established at least one major biological warfare facility, and possibly two. One facility seems to exist near the Syrian coast and another facility may have been built underground. According to Israeli sources, Syria was able to produce botulin or ricin toxins in 1991, and probably anthrax as well.[23] A list of the kinds of biological weapons Syria may have developed is shown in Table 13.3.

As for delivery systems and weapons, Syria may have modified a variant of the Soviet ZAB series incendiary bomb to deliver such chemical agents, and may have modified the PTAB-500 cluster bomb to carry chemical bomblets. Syria has probably developed chemical artillery shells and may be working on chemical rounds for its multiple rocket launchers. Syrian FROG missiles also seem to have been given chemical warheads, although there is no precise way to date when they acquired them. Syria modified its Scud missiles to deliver chemical weapons no later than 1987.[24] In fact, a number of experts believe some Syrian surface-to-surface missiles armed with chemical weapons began to be stored in concrete shelters in the mountains near Damascus and in the Palmyra region no later than 1986, and that plans have long existed to deploy them forward in an emergency since that date.[25]

Putting chemical warheads on the Scud missile would give Syria a relatively effective weapons system, although such a weapon would have nothing like the lethality of Israel's nuclear weapons. For example, if Syria copied the Soviet designs for chemical warheads for the Scud—designs which the USSR seems to have made available to a number of Third World states in the late 1970s—and successfully produced an agent as lethal as the VX chemical warhead used on the Soviet version of the Scud missile, it would then have an 884 mm warhead weighing 2,170 pounds, of which 1,200 pounds would consist of chemical agent. The warhead would be fitted with a variable time fuse, and the agent would be dispersed by a bursting charge located along the center axis of the warhead.

Syria currently has 90–200 Scud B missiles, and the resulting combination of the Scud B, a modern warhead, and a stable nerve gas agent would be a much more lethal system than the conventional Scud warheads Iraq fired against Israel in 1991. The missile would have a range of approximately 260–300 kilometers and a CEP of around 300 meters. Assuming a burst altitude of 1,100 meters, a ground wind speed of 3 feet per second, and worst case conditions, the warhead could produce a contaminated area that would cover a band about 0.53 kilometer wide and 3.5 kilometers long—beginning about 1 kilometer from the burst. Assuming a flat plain and no protection, up to 50% of the exposed personnel would be casualties. This is a very impressive lethal area, and a VX nerve agent might remain lethal for several days. It is important to note, however, that this lethal area calculation does assume exposed personnel, a flat plain, and optimal delivery conditions. Real-world lethality might be only 5% to 20% as high, although this would still halt military activity in many targets.[26]

TABLE 13.2   Major Chemical Agents That May Be in Syrian Forces—Part One

NERVE AGENTS: Agents that quickly disrupt the nervous system by binding to enzymes critical to nerve functions, causing convulsions and/or paralysis. Must be ingested, inhaled, or absorbed through the skin. Very low doses cause a runny nose, contraction of the pupil of the eye, and difficulty in visual coordination. Moderate doses constrict the bronchi and cause a feeling of pressure in the chest, and weaken the skeletal muscles and cause fibrillation. Large doses cause death by respiratory or heart failure. Can be absorbed through inhalation or skin contact. Reaction normally occurs in 1–2 minutes. Death from lethal doses occurs within minutes, but artificial respiration can help and atropine and the oximes act as antidotes. The most toxic nerve agents kill with a dosage of only 10 milligrams per minute per cubic meter, versus 400 for less lethal gases. Recovery is normally quick, if it occurs at all, but permanent brain damage can occur.

> Tabun (GA)
> Sarin (GB)—nearly as volatile as water and delivered by air. A dose of 5 mg/min/m3 produces casualties, a respiratory dose of 100 mg/min/m3 is lethal. Lethality lasts 1–2 days.
> Soman (GD)
> GF
> VR-55 (Improved Soman)—a thick oily substance which persists for some time.
> VK/VX—a persistent agent roughly as heavy as fuel oil. A dose of 0.5 mg/min/m3 produces casualties, a respiratory dose of 10 mg/min/m3 is lethal. Lethality lasts 1–16 weeks.

BLISTER AGENTS: Cell poisons that destroy skin and tissue, cause blindness upon contact with the eyes, and can result in fatal respiratory damage. Can be colorless or black oily droplets. Absorbed through inhalation or skin contact. Serious internal damage if inhaled. Penetrate ordinary clothing. Some have delayed and some have immediate reaction. Actual blistering normally takes hours to days, but effects on the eyes are much more rapid. Mustard gas is a typical blister agent and exposure of concentrations of a few milligrams per meter over several hours generally at least causes blisters and swollen eyes. When the liquid falls onto the skin or eyes it has the effect of second or third degree burns. It can blind and cause damage to the lungs, leading to pneumonia. Severe exposure causes general intoxication similar to radiation sickness. HD and HN persist up to 12 hours. L, HL, and CX persist for 1–2 hours. Short of prevention of exposure, the only treatment is to wash the eyes, decontaminate the skin, and treat the resulting damage like burns.

> Sulfur Mustard (H or HD)—a dose of 100 mg/min/m3 produces casualties, a dose of 1,500 mg/min/m3 is lethal. Residual lethality lasts up to 2–8 weeks.
> Distilled Mustard (DM)
> Nitrogen Mustard (HN)
> Lewisite (L)
> Phosgene Oxime (CX)
> Mustard Lewisite (HL)

TABLE 13.2 *(Continued)*

CHOKING AGENTS: Agents that cause the blood vessels in the lungs to hemorrhage and fluid to build up until the victim chokes or drowns in his or her own fluids (pulmonary edema). Provide quick warning though smell or lung irritation. Can be absorbed through inhalation. Immediate to delayed action. The only treatment is inhalation of oxygen and rest. Symptoms emerge in periods after exposure of seconds up to 3 hours.

    Phosgene (CG)
    Diphosgene (DP)
    PS Chloropicrin
    Chlorine Gas

BLOOD AGENTS: Kill through inhalation. Provide little warning except for headache, nausea, and vertigo. Interfere with use of oxygen at the cellular level. CK also irritates the lungs and eyes. Rapid action and exposure either kill by inhibiting cell respiration—casualties will either die within seconds to minutes of exposure or recover in fresh air. Most gas masks have severe problems in providing effective protection against blood agents.

    Hydrogen Cyanide (AC)—a dose of 2,000 mg/min/m3 produces casualties, a
        respiratory dose of 5,000 mg/min/m3 is lethal. Lethality lasts 1–4 hours.
    Cyanogen Chloride (CK)—a dose of 7,000 mg/min/m3 produces casualties, a
        respiratory dose of 11,000 mg/min/m3 is lethal. Lethality lasts 15 minutes to 1
        hour.

Major Chemical Agents That May Be in Syrian Forces—Part Two

TOXINS: Biological poisons causing neuromuscular paralysis after exposure of hours or days. Formed in food or cultures by the bacterium clostridium Botulinum. Produce highly fatal poisoning characterized by general weakness, headache, dizziness, double vision and dilation of the pupils, paralysis of muscles, and problems in speech. Death is usually by respiratory failure. Antitoxin therapy has limited value, but treatment is mainly supportive.

    Botulin toxin (A)—six distinct types, of which four are known to be fatal to man.
        An oral dose of 0.001 mg is lethal. A respiratory dose of 0.02 mg/min/m3 is also
        lethal.

DEVELOPMENTAL WEAPONS: A new generation of chemical weapons is under development. The only publicized agent is perfluoroisobutene (PFIB), which is an extremely toxic, odorless, and invisible substance produced when PFIB (Teflon) is subjected to extreme heat under special conditions. It causes pulmonary edema or dry-land drowning when the lungs fill with fluid. Short exposure disables and small concentrations cause delayed death. Activated charcoal and most existing protection equipment offer no defense. Some sources refer to "third" and "fourth" generation nerve gases, but no technical literature seems to be available.

TABLE 13.2   *(Continued)*

CONTROL AGENTS: Agents which produce temporary irritating or disabling effects when in contact with the eyes or inhaled. They can cause serious illness or death when used in confined spaces. CS is the least toxic gas, followed by CS and DM. Symptoms can be treated by washing of the eyes and/or removal from the area. Exposure to CS, CN, and DM produces immediate symptoms. Staphylococcus produces symptoms in 30 minutes to 4 hours, and recovery takes 24–48 hours. Treatment of Staphylococcus is largely supportive.

> Tear: Cause flow of tears and irritation of upper respiratory tract and skin. Can cause nausea and vomiting:
> Chlororacetophenone (CN)
> O-Chlorobenzyl-malononitrile (CS)
> Vomiting: Cause irritation, coughing, severe headache, tightness in chest, nausea, vomiting:
> > Adamsite (DM)
> > Staphylococcus

INCAPACITATING AGENTS: Agents which normally cause short term illness and psychoactive effects (delirium and hallucinations). Can be absorbed through inhalation or skin contact. The psychoactive gases and drugs produce unpredictable effects, particularly in sick small children, the elderly, and individuals who already are mentally ill. In rare cases they kill. In others, they produce a permanent psychotic condition. Many produce dry skin, irregular heartbeat, urinary retention, constipation, drowsiness, and a rise in body temperature, plus occasional maniacal behavior. A single dose of 0.1 to 0.2 milligram of LSD-25 will produce profound mental disturbance within a half hour that lasts 10 hours. The lethal dose is 100 to 200 mg.

> BZ
> LSD
> LSD Based BZ
> Mescaline
> Psilocybin
> Benzilates

Adapted from Matthew Meselson and Julian Perry Robinson, "Chemical Warfare and Chemical Disarmament," *Scientific American,* Vol. 242, No. 4, April, 1980, pp. 38–47; "Chemical Warfare: Extending the Range of Destruction," *Jane's Defense Weekly,* August 25, 1990, p. 267; Dick Palowski, *Changes in Threat Air Combat Doctrine and Force Structure,* 24th edition, Fort Worth, General Dynamics DWIC-01, February, 1992, pp. II-335 to II-339; U.S. Marine Corps, *Individual Guide for NBC Defense,* Field Manual OH-11-1A, August, 1990; and unpublished testimony to the Special Investigations Subcommittee of the Government Operations Committee, US Senate, by Mr. David Goldberg, Foreign Science and Technology Center, US Army Intelligence Center, on February 9, 1989.

TABLE 13.3   Major Biological Weapons That May Be in Syrian Forces: Part One

Disease	Infectivity	Transmissibility	Incubation Period	Mortality	Therapy
Viral					
Chikungunya fever	high?	none	2–6 days	very low (–1%)	none
Dengue fever	high	none	5–2 days	very low (–1%)	none
Eastern equine encephalitis	high	none	5–10 days	high (+60%)	developmental
Tick borne encephalitis	high	none	1–2 weeks	up to 30%	developmental
Venezuelan equine encephalitis	high	none	2–5 days	low (–1%)	developmental
Hepatitis A	–	–	15–40 days	–	–
Hepatitis B	–	–	40–150 days	–	–
Influenza	high	none	1–3 days	usually low	available
Yellow fever	high	none	3–6 days	up to 40%	available
Smallpox (Variola)	high	high	7–16 days	up to 30%	available
Rickettsial					
Coxiella Burneti (Q-fever)	high	negligible	10–21 days	low (–1%)	antibiotic
Mooseri	–	–	6–14 days	–	–
Prowazeki	–	–	6–15 days	–	–
Psittacosis	high	moderate-high	4–15 days	mod-high	antibiotic
Rickettsi (Rocky Mountain spotted fever)	high	none	3–10 days	up to 80%	antibiotic
Tsutsugamushi	–	–	–	–	–
Epidemic typhus	high	none	6–15 days	up to 70%	antibiotic/vaccine
Bacterial					
Anthrax (pulmonary)	mod-high	negligible	1–5 days	usually fatal	antibiotic/vaccine
Brucellosis	high	none	1–3 days	–25%	antibiotic
Cholera	low	high	1–5 days	up to 80%	antibiotic/vaccine
Glanders	high	none	2–1 days	usually fatal	poor antibiotic
Meloidosis	high	none	1–5 days	usually fatal	moderate antibiotic
Plague (pneumonic)	high	high	2–5 days	usually fatal	antibiotic/vaccine
Tularemia	high	negligible	1–10 days	low to 60%	antibiotic/vaccine
Typhoid fever	mod-high	moderate-high	7–21 days	up to 10%	antibiotic/vaccine
Dysentery	high	high	1–4 days	low to high	antibiotic/vaccine

Major Biological Weapons That May Be in Syrian Forces: Part Two

Disease	Infectivity	Transmissibility	Incubation Period	Mortality	Therapy Fungal
Coccidioidomycosis	high	none	1–3 days	low	none
Coccidiodes Immitis	high	none	10–21 days	low	none
Histoplasma					
Capsulatum	–	–	15–18 days	–	–
Norcardia Asteroides	–	–	–	–	–
*Toxins**					
Botulinum toxin	high	none	12–72 hours	high neuromuscular paralysis	vaccine
Mycotoxin	high	none	hours or days	low to high	?
Staphylococcus	moderate	none	24–48 hours	incapacitating	?

*Many sources classify as chemical weapons because toxins are chemical poisons.

Adapted from Report of the Secretary General, Department of Political and Security Affairs, *Chemical and Bacteriological (Biological) Weapons and the Effects of Their Possible Use*, New York, United Nations, 1969, pp. 26, 29, 37–52, 116–117; *Jane's NBC Protection Equipment*, 1991–1992; James Smith, "Biological Warfare Developments," *Jane's Intelligence Review*, November, 1991, pp. 483–487.

The Scud B does, however, have important range limitations. It has a maximum range of about 290 kilometers, and can only cover Israeli targets deep in the south of Israel (as far south as Halserim air base and Dimona) from vulnerable forward positions. This seems to have led to its deployment in sheltered locations near Damascus and this may have aided Israel's ability to track and target Scud B unit movements—although firing the Scud B at such short ranges might complicate Israel's detection and tracking problems in using theater ballistic missiles for defense.

The SS-21s in Syrian hands do not have chemical warheads and Syria would find it difficult to develop such a capability without Soviet support. The problems of developing and testing an advanced missile warhead are beyond current Syrian capabilities. Given the accuracy of the SS-21, there is at least some long term risk that Syria could eventually fire nerve agents successfully at Israeli air bases, C⁴I sites, Dimona, and mobilization centers—and seriously degrade Israeli conventional and nuclear capabilities.[27]

This may help explain why Syria has sought longer range missiles that will give it the range to attack any target in Israel from sites as far away from Israel as possible—particularly the reserve assembly areas for Israel's ground forces, Israel's air bases in the south, and its nuclear facility at Dimona—although the Dimona complex may be too well sheltered for attack by missiles with anything other than nuclear or advanced penetrating warheads of a kind that Syria is unlikely to acquire in the near future.[28]

From 1984 onward, Syria tried unsuccessfully to buy more SS-21s and the SS-12 or SS-23 missile, from the USSR. It was particularly interested in the SS-23, which has a 500 kilometer range, and which could have hit targets throughout Israel and Jordan and much of Iraq. It is clear that both President Asad and the Syrian defense minister actively sought such missiles, and they may even have asked for SS-25 ICBMs once it was clear that the USSR would agree to the INF treaty. The USSR, however, refused to provide any of these systems.[29]

Syria then sought M-9 missiles from the PRC. Reports surfaced in August, 1989 that Syria ordered the new M-9 IRBM from the People's Republic of China.[30] While the PRC denied this, and the M-9 missile is still in development, it would meet many Syrian needs. It has a range in excess of 370 miles (600 kilometers), a projected CEP of around 600 meters, and a payload of 500 kilograms. There have also been reports that the PRC sold Syria the M-1B missile, with ranges of 50 to 60 miles, in March, 1990.[31] The PRC is developing two other long range mobile surface-to-surface missiles—the M-11 and the M-12—and Syria may have an interest in these systems as well. Syria purchased 30–90 tons of solid rocket fuel from the PRC in 1991.[32]

Syria did succeed in obtaining substantial deliveries of North Korean "Scud-C" missiles. These deliveries began on March 13, 1991, when a freighter called the Al-Yarmouk docked in Syria. Two more deliveries took place in 1991. When the US protested such shipments in February, 1992, North Korea shifted freighter movements to route them through Iran. The first such shipment took place when the North Korean freighter Dae Hung Ho reached Iran in March, 1992, and missile parts and manufacturing equipment were then airlifted to Syria.

Up to 50–80 missiles and 15–20 launchers have been delivered since 1992, and the first two Syrian tests of the missile took place in early August. These missiles give Syria a weapon with an estimated range of 500–600 kilometers, a CEP of around 650–850 meters, and a payload of 450–600 kilograms. Syria has cooperated with Iran in importing these systems, and both countries seem to be interested in manufacturing the missile as well as importing it. According to some reports, Syria is building two missile plants near Hama, about 110 miles north of Damascus. One is for solid fueled rockets and the other is for liquid fueled systems. North Korea may be providing the equipment for the liquid fuel plant.[33]

The "Scud C" offers Syria significant advantages in addition to longer range. While the North Korean missile is generally referred to as a "Scud C," the name may be highly misleading. The original Scud A was first seen in 1953 and entered service in 1954. The improved Scud B, with a range of 300 kilometers, entered service in 1965, and the "Scud C," with a range of 450 kilometers, was deployed in 1968. It is likely that the North Koreans have redesigned the now obsolete Soviet missile and have either extended the single stage liquid propelled motor or have added strap on boosters. It is nearly certain that they have improved the fusing options, strap down inertial guidance system, and the reliability of the Scud's jet vane course correction system. These improvements are likely to produce a system not only superior to the Soviet Scud—which was being replaced by the SS-23 before the INF Treaty—but one that has a higher payload, more accuracy, and more reliability than any Iraqi Scud variant.[34]

It is also likely that North Korea has made improvements over the Soviet MAZ-583 eight wheeled transporter-erector-launcher, the refueling process and ZIL-157 propellant tanker, and the command vehicle. There may also be improved position establishing and meteorological gear. If so, the set up time for a Scud unit being moved to a new position could be cut from a minimum of 45–60 minutes to as few as 15–20 minutes. This not only would greatly reduce the probability of detection and vulnerability to attack, but greatly improve operational accuracy. Commercially available Global Positioning Gear could further improve Syria's capabilities, particularly if reports of European GPS gear with military accuracies of 10 meters are true.

The new North Korean missile gives Syria the capability to strike at any part of Israel as well as its other neighbors, and Syria has long range drones that can assist in targeting such missiles. It can cover all 11 of Israel's air bases, all of the 15-odd main armories for Israel's armored forces, and all major reserve force assembly areas.[35] The new missiles have better range-payload, reliability, and accuracy than the extended range Scuds that Saddam Hussein used in the Gulf War. Most experts also believe that these missiles will be armed with nerve gas warheads—joining the large number of sheltered Scud missiles with nerve gas warheads that Syria already deploys. The possibility of biological warheads cannot be dismissed, although Syria is more likely to use the latter weapons in bombs or covert delivery systems.

While any use of such missiles would risk Israeli nuclear retaliation, some Israeli experts have suggested that Syria might risk limited strikes against Israeli air bases and mobilization assembly sites as part of a surprise attack on the Golan. Such an attack would not be designed to threaten Israel's existence or to capture the Galilee, but would rather attempt to establish new facts on the ground so rapidly that outside powers would force a cease-fire before Israel could counterattack and under conditions where it could not risk massive retaliation. Other Israeli experts believe that Syria will try to use its chemically armed missiles as a deterrent to Israeli strategic strikes and to allow it to attack the Golan using its armored forces without fear of massive Israeli retaliation. Such scenarios would certainly involve massive risks for Syria but cannot be dismissed. In fact, some Israelis argue that Syria's efforts to double its T-72 force with new purchases from the Russian Republic and Czechoslovakia could support this contingency.[36]

Experts on the Syrian force do, however, raise questions about the extent to which Syria's missiles will be survivable even after Syria fully deploys its North Korean missiles. Some experts feel that Syria has a first strike or preemptive force and must use its missiles the moment that it feels they are under attack. Others feel it would use some of its FROGs and Scuds on Israeli air bases, command centers, and mobilization staging areas, while holding others in reserve. Either tactic could be extremely destabilizing in a Syrian-Israeli conflict.

Syria may also have tried to convert some of its SA-2 surface-to-air, SSC-1B, and SS-C-3 coastal defense missiles to deliver chemical agents.[37] This illustrates major potential problems in controlling missile technology. While the SA-2 Guideline is now an obsolete surface-to-air missile, it weighs 2,360 kilograms and is a fairly large system. The Soviet versions had nuclear warheads and a 130 kilogram high explosive warhead. The slant range of the missile in the air intercept mode is about 50 kilometers, although the system would probably be accurate to over 100 kilometers in the surface-to-surface mode. It is not an ideal system for use against surface targets by any means and would require substantial modification. It has been deployed in such large numbers, however, that Syria and many other nations might find it attractive.

The SSC-1B Sepal is a relatively modern cruise missile by Third World terms and entered Soviet service in 1970. It has a range of 450 kilometers and a warhead of up to 1,000 kilograms. While it receives little attention, it is a large 5,400 kilogram missile with radio command mid-course guidance, a radio altimeter to control altitude, command guidance at long ranges, and terminal active radar guidance. It can fly at preset altitudes from surface skimming to 3,000–5,000 meters. It is designed for attack against ships, and the Soviet version has a 100–200 kiloton nuclear warhead. Its guidance system and accuracy make it difficult to modify for attacks on land targets that are much smaller than a large military base or small town, but its large warhead lends itself to chemical use against such area targets. Syria has several SSC-1B units, which normally have 16–18 missiles per battalion.

The SS-C-3 is another coastal defense missile based on the Styx. It is a modern system that was first deployed in Soviet forces in 1985. It has a much shorter range than the SS-C-1B. Its maximum range is only 80–90 kilometers and its warhead is unlikely to exceed 500 kilograms, although Soviet versions with yields of 1 to 200 kilotons have been reported. It uses inertial mid-course guidance (a programmed auto pilot with precision accelerometers), and uses a mobile launcher based on the Soviet MAZ-543 8X8 all terrain vehicle. It is specifically designed for export and has not been deployed with Soviet forces. It is normally used as a sea skimmer against naval targets, but can evidently be set for a high altitude cruise phase with accuracy sufficient to hit a small town or large air base. While converting such a system to chemical warheads would not normally be cost effective, the resulting system would be relatively mobile and easy to deploy. The possibility cannot be totally dismissed.

Further, Syria is slowly acquiring a significant long range air strike capability. It already has at least 20 Su-24 strike attack aircraft and Russia seems to be in the process of delivering more. The exact performance of the export version of the Su-24 is unclear, and its avionics seem to be far less advanced than the Soviet version. Nevertheless, it is probably still a precision all-weather or night attack capable aircraft with some similarities to the F-111 or Tornado. It has a powerful pulse Doppler radar and is capable of very low altitude penetrations. It is a two seat aircraft with a weapons/navigation officer sitting next to the pilot, may be fitted with FLIR and electro-optical aids, and has good inertial navigation capabilities. The Soviet version has a moderate to good ECM/ECCM suite and radar homing/warning. It has the range/payload to attack Israel by flying around or through Jordan, or over the Mediterranean and from the south. It is a heavy aircraft which weighs 64,000 to 87,000 pounds loaded. It is a swing wing aircraft with speeds of Mach 2.4 when clean of external munitions. Its LO-LO-LO combat radius with an 8 ton bomb load is 322 kilometers (200 miles). Its range with a 2.5 ton bomb load is 1,800 kilometers (1,115 miles). Its ferry range is about 6,400 kilometers (4,000 miles).[38]

While it is tempting to focus on missile systems, a well designed Syrian air raid on a city like Tel Aviv, saturating Israel's air defenses with other aircraft, and then raiding with Syria's total inventory of Su-24s, might be able to deliver a considerable payload. Such an attack could be particularly lethal if that payload were toxins or biological weapons rather than nerve gas. At the same time, it should be noted that a ship that took advantage of favorable winds, while sailing off the coast of Israel, could cover an area of up to several hundred square miles simply by releasing anthrax spores or some similar biological agent in a covert delivery mode.

Egyptian Weapons of Mass Destruction

Egypt has some long range missile capability, although it is unclear if such weapons have chemical warheads. Egypt has had FROG-7 and Scud B missiles since the 1960s, and these remain operational in spite of the fact that former president Sadat severed military relations with the USSR in 1974. Egypt retains two active surface-to-surface missile regiments with 12 FROG-7 free rocket launchers and has a regiment with at least 9 Scud B guided missile launchers.

Egypt has developed an improved and domestically produced version of the FROG called the Saqr 80. This rocket is 6.5 meters long, 210 mm in diameter, and weighs 660 kilograms. It has a maximum range of 50 miles (80 kilometers) and a 440 pound (200 kilogram) warhead. It is a TEL (transporter-erector-launcher) mounted system, and can be mounted on both wheeled and tracked vehicles. Egypt uses an RPV with the system for long range targeting. A variant is being studied that would hold four rockets per vehicle instead of the usual one. Egypt reports two types of conventional warheads for the Saqr 80—one with 950 AP/AT bomblets and one with 65 anti-tank mines, and that it is developing an automatic survey and fire control system for the rocket. The Saqr 80 could, however, easily be used to deliver chemical weapons.[39]

Although the Scud Bs Egypt received in 1973 would normally have become inoperable due to age and lack of service, Egypt seems to have carried out a successful reverse engineering program and is attempting to mass produce its own version of the missile. Egypt also seems to be building an improved version of the Scud B, using technology obtained with North Korean assistance.[40] While the Scud B missile is normally credited with having a range of 190 miles (300 kilometers) and a 2,200 pound (1,000 kilogram) warhead, some sources claim that the range and warhead size of the improved Egyptian version of the Scud may be closer to that of the Iraqi Al Hussein, and the range may be 30% to 50% greater than that of a normal Scud.[41]

Egypt's most ambitious missile program has been the Condor. During the mid-1980s, Egypt began a covert program with Argentina and Iraq, in which Egypt and Iraq paid Argentina to develop the "Badar 2000" long range missile and provide suitable production equipment. The Badar 2000 was based on the Argentine Condor II or Alacran missile and was a solid fuel system with ranges from 480 to 1,000 kilometers and warheads of 500 to 1,000 kilograms.[42] There is little doubt that the Badar 2000 was intended to use chemical warheads or other weapons of mass destruction.

Quiet US pressure on Argentina and Egypt and key supplier countries helped kill the Argentine and Egyptian efforts, although Iraq kept up work on the program. At the same time, it is unclear how well the program would have progressed without such US pressure. Argentina never operationally tested the Condor II, and there is some question as to Argentina's ability to provide the proper technical skills to develop such a system. According to some reports, a major program evaluation in 1988 revealed major technical problems in the original design, and Argentina may have decided to shift its efforts to a missile with a range of only 200 kilometers.

Other reports indicate, however, that the basic design was successful and that the US only succeeded in persuading Argentina to halt the program once its military government fell after a disastrous defeat in the Falklands. These sources also indicate that the US only succeeded in persuading Egypt to give up the program after President Mubarak was embarrassed by the arrest of the Egyptian officers attempting to smuggle missile technology out of the US.[43]

There are unconfirmed reports that Egypt has renewed its effort to develop and produce improved versions of the Scud since Israel's testing of the "Jericho II" missiles.[44] In June, 1990, there were also reports that Egypt had reached an agreement with the People's Republic of China to update Egypt's Saqr rocket factory to produce newer anti-aircraft missiles, the DF-4 Silkworm anti-ship missile, an improved version of the Scud, and three types of long range Saqr surface-to-surface rockets.[45] The deal was reported to include an improved version of the DF-4, with its range extended from 50 to 90 nautical miles, and a DF-5 missile with a range of 170 miles. The regular DF-4 has a 1,000 pound warhead and can be used in a surface-to-surface as well as an anti-ship mode.[46]

Egypt has been capable of delivering chemical weapons since the late 1950s, and may have acquired British stocks of mustard gas that Britain failed to remove from inventories it deployed in the northern desert in World War II. Egypt began low level research efforts to develop long range guided missiles and nuclear weapons in the 1950s. Egypt has had the capability to produce its own mustard gas and other chemical weapons since the early 1960s, and it used poison gas in its battles against the royalist faction in North Yemen in the period before its 1967 conflict with Israel.

Egypt has had large stockpiles of chemical defense equipment since the late 1960s—and substantial amounts of this equipment were captured during the fighting in October, 1973. Egypt almost certainly had stockpiles of mustard gas at the time and was probably producing limited amounts of nonpersistent nerve gas. Egypt has also been less reticent about its possession of chemical weapons in the past. The former Egyptian minister of war, General Abdel Ranny Gamassay, stated in 1975 that "if Israel should decide to use a nuclear weapon in the battle-field, we shall use the weapons of mass destruction that are at our disposal."[47] In spite of the dramatic changes in its relations with Israel, and careful observance of its peace treaty, Egypt seems to have continued some production of chemical agents after the Camp David accords as well as maintained small stockpiles of chemical bombs and other chemical weapons.

While Egypt does not appear to have developed the massive chemical weapons production and delivery capabilities of states like Iraq, Syria, and Libya, it does seem to have stepped up its research effort since gas began to be used extensively in the Iran-Iraq War. Egypt probably retains the capability to produce mustard gas, nonpersistent nerve gas, and perhaps to produce persistent nerve gas as well. Egypt was caught attempting to import the feedstock for nerve gas from Canada during 1988. Egypt has also placed highly specialized orders of fumigants, pesticides, arsenic, and strychnine for what seems to be use in a major poison gas production facility near or at the Beni Suef Air Base south of Cairo.[48]

Egypt also seems to have expanded its chemical weapons plant at Abu Zabaal, north of Cairo, and improved chemical weapons production equipment from firms like Krebs A. G. of Zurich, Switzerland. Egypt is believed to have approached Krebs in 1985, shortly after Iraq began to make large scale use of chemical weapons in the Iran-Iraq War. Krebs built a plant for the El Nasr Pharmaceutical Plant at Abu Zabaal to make phosphorous trichloride, a basic chemical that can be used for both insecticides and chemical weapons. Krebs also was active in designing a phosphorous pentasulfide plant for Iran that seemed to be linked to Iran's chemical weapons efforts.[49]

Although President Mubarak has categorically denied that Egypt has chemical weapons and a new long range missile development effort, there are reasons to question such denials. Israeli sources believe that Egypt may be building new chemical weapons feedstock plants north of Cairo and developing the capability to produce nerve and mustard gases without dependence on imports of precursor chemicals.

Egypt also seems to have carried out extensive research on biological weapons, but there are few indications it has attempted to manufacture biological agents or load weapons with such agents. There have been rumors that Egypt is seeking to develop advanced chemical and biological warheads for its missile systems and modern binary chemical bombs, and may be reviving its nuclear weapons research effort. If such Egyptian efforts exist, however, they are sufficiently covert so that few experts believe Egypt has gone beyond the research phase.

There is no significant evidence of any serious Egyptian nuclear weapons development effort since the late 1970s. Most US experts believe that Egypt has made no effort to invest in the required production technology and that it fully complies with the IAEA.

Libyan, Iranian, and Iraqi Weapons of Mass Destruction

Table 13.1 shows that other nations outside the region are also developing significant capabilities to develop weapons of mass destruction. At the same time, Table 13.1 shows that the present capabilities of such forces should not be exaggerated. Libya currently has no meaningful means of using weapons of mass destruction in war fighting, although it might transfer chemical agents to an extremist group or conduct "suicide" air raids on Israel using its Su-24s.

Iran lacks a long range delivery system capable of meaningful coverage of Israel, although it could potentially stage strike aircraft and Scuds through Syria or Jordan. At present, it does not seem to have highly effective chemical weapons or to have deployed significant numbers of biological weapons, and could not add significantly to Syrian capabilities. This situation will change, however, if Iran gets the No Dong or M-9 missile and/or develops an advanced air refueling capability and improves the quality of its chemical and biological weapons.

The situation will also change radically if Iran acquires nuclear weapons, and it seems firmly committed to doing so. It is not possible to confirm any specific Iranian sites, but it is clear that Iran is developing the capability to exploit its uranium resources in Yazd Province and has experimented in uranium enrichment and centrifuge technology at the Sharif University of Technology in Tehran. It may also have conducted research into plutonium separation. It has a small 27 kilowatt Chinese-supplied neutron source research reactor and subcritical assemblies with 900 grams of highly enriched uranium at its Esfahan Nuclear Research Center. This Center also has a heavy water zero-power reactor, a light water subcritical reactor, and a graphite sub-critical reactor. The Center may also have experimented with some aspects of nuclear weapons design. Iran has an Argentine-fueled, 5 megawatt, light water, highly enriched uranium reactor operating at the University of Tehran. Iran has also demonstrated that it is capable of copying the sheltering and satellite deception techniques used by Iraq before the Gulf War.[50]

Iran has sought to purchase power reactors from Russia. It has been denied Russian centrifuge technology as the result of US negotiations with Russia, but Iran signed a $1 billion agreement with Russia on January 8, 1995, to build at least one reactor at Bushehr—about 730 miles south of Tehran. Bushehr is the site of two incomplete reactors started by Siemens in 1976. Work halted there in 1979 with the fall of the Shah. Construction of the main buildings and steel containment vessel for one reactor had reached 85% of completion and construction for the other was partially finished, but both reactors were damaged during the Iran-Iraq War. As a result, Russian plans to build a VVER-1000 power reactor at the site can do little more than attempt to make use of the remaining buildings to the extent permitted by the fact that the VVER-1000 is physically very different from a Siemens 1,300 megawatt reactor.[51]

Russia has already deployed some 150 technicians at the reactor site, however, and plans major shipments of material in 1995. The reactor is scheduled to be completed by the year 2000, and Russia will train some 500 Iranian technicians. There are some uncertainties as to whether Russia will take back the plutonium-bearing spent fuel in the reactor, although recent reports indicate that it may do so.[52] Iran has shown an interest in another VVER-1000 reactor at Bushehr in purchasing two V-213 VVER 440 power reactors and in purchasing another large research reactor. Iran has already expressed an interest in buying two 300 megawatt pressurized water nuclear reactors from China similar to the Chinese plant at Zhejiang.[53]

These Iranian plans to buy reactors make virtually no economic sense in a country with vast supplies of natural gas that it can use to generate electricity at 18% to 20% of the cost of nuclear electricity under the most favorable conditions, and which still underprices oil to the point where the increase in domestic consumption is cutting into its export capacity. Iran could also reject IAEA safeguards once its reactor or reactors are complete and use such reactors to produce plutonium.

The IAEA regularly inspects declared Iranian sites and has made two special visits to suspect sites in February, 1992 and October, 1993. The IAEA, however, only formally inspects declared facilities with declared nuclear material. Its visits to other facilities have not involved the kind of intrusive inspection that does more than simply determine whether a major physical facility exists dedicated to weapons use. As a result, IAEA efforts to date can neither confirm nor deny the existence of a nuclear weapons program.

Iran officially continues to deny it is seeking nuclear weapons, and reports by various Iranian opposition groups that Iran has developed a $10 billion plan to acquire nuclear weapons seem little more than rumors.[54] Nevertheless, most US and other Western experts believe that Iran has an active nuclear weapons program. They believe that Iran now has all the basic technology to build a bomb and has a low to moderate level weapons design and development effort.[55] They indicate that no major weapons material and production effort has been detected, but that Iran has imported the technology for such a program, has sought enrichment and plutonium processing technology from nations like the PRC and Russia, and has attempted to buy highly enriched material from Asiatic republics of the former Soviet Union such as Khazakstan. They feel that Iran is at least three to five years away from acquiring a long range missile system, and five to nine years away from acquiring a nuclear device—but that Iran could probably develop a gun or simple implosion type of nuclear weapon in 9 to 48 months if it could buy fissile material.

Iraq currently has only a limited potential capability to recover its past ability to produce nuclear weapons.[56] It has lost most of its capability to deliver chemical and biological weapons and there is no immediate evidence it has improved the effectiveness of its low lethality weapon and warhead designs. Iraq is, however, still devoting resources to biological, chemical, and nuclear research efforts. It retains significant technology and much of the chemical and biological weapons equipment it dispersed before and during Desert Storm. It also retains a long range air strike capability and probably retains some Scud and improved Scud missile assemblies. Iraq currently lacks the capability to deliver high lethality strikes against Israel, although Table 13.4 and Figures 13.1, 13.2, and 13.3 show that even relatively low performance chemical and biological weapons would still have a substantial killing effect.

In short, the immediate threat posed by the capabilities of nations like Libya, Iran, and Iraq does not immediately alter the regional military balance, but the steady process of proliferation does. Israel can neither plan on the basis that such nations will radically change their behavior in the near term nor ignore the risks they pose to its arms control planning. Further, Egypt, Jordan, and Syria also face the problem that the regional balance of power will shift, and that Libya, Iran, and Iraq presently have regimes which will attempt to exploit any shift in their favor in ways which may threaten Egyptian, Jordanian, and Syrian interests.

The War Fighting Implications of Weapons of Mass Destruction

As a result, Israeli, Egyptian, and Syrian holdings of weapons of mass destruction—along with those of Iran, Iraq, and Libya—have important implications for arms control and peace process issues. They are making fundamental changes in the potential scale and intensity of a future conflict, and are extending the zone of Arab-Israeli conflict to include radical states armed with weapons of mass destruction like Iran, Iraq, and Libya. They also are creating the capability to conduct a fundamentally different level of warfare. Destructive as conventional wars may be, the process of creeping proliferation summarized in Table 13.1 is occurring in states that are relatively fragile when several of the most lethal types of weapons of mass destruction can destroy their major cities and kill a significant portion of their total population.

There is no easy way to translate this potential destructiveness into the analysis of specific contingencies for war fighting. Israel has never announced any specific doctrine of strategy for using its weapons of mass destruction, Egypt continues to deny it has such weapons, and Iran, Iraq, and Libya have either denied capability or made generalized threats to use such weapons in ways that tell little about their doctrine. Syria has never officially discussed its war fighting doctrine.

In fact, it is questionable that Egypt, Iran, Iraq, and Libya as yet have any detailed war fighting doctrine for using weapons of mass destruction against Israel. Egypt almost certainly sees its limited contingency capabilities largely as a deterrent against a type of war with Israel which is already so unlikely that it would take a major change in the political situation, and months or years of Egyptian effort to produce chemical and biological weapons and train for their use, before it would be a serious risk.

Iran and Iraq may be more significant threats in the future, but they currently lack the ability to deliver significant numbers of weapons against Israel. Iran and Iraq could conduct small one-way air strikes with chemical or biological weapons or use a civilian ship, civil aircraft, or proxy force to attempt the covert delivery of such weapons, but the probable lethality of such strikes would currently be so limited that Iran and Iraq would have to risk national destruction for what would probably prove to be little more than mass terrorism and the provocation of an Israeli nuclear strike.

Libya has only a token capability to deliver chemical and possibly crude biological weapons. It could conduct very small one-way air strikes with chemical or biological weapons or it could again use a civilian ship, civil aircraft, or proxy force to attempt the covert delivery of such weapons, but Libya's capabilities are far weaker than those of Iran and Iraq. The current Libyan threat is much more one

TABLE 13.4   The Comparative Effects of Biological, Chemical, and Nuclear Weapons Delivered Against a Typical Urban Target in the Middle East

Using missile warheads: Assumes one Scud sized warhead with a maximum payload of 1,000 kilograms. The study assumes that the biological agent would not make maximum use of this payload capability because this is inefficient. It is unclear this is realistic.

	Area Covered in Square Kilometers	Deaths Assuming 3,000–10,000 people per Square Kilometer
Chemical: 300 kilograms of Sarin nerve gas with a density of 70 milligrams per cubic meter	0.22	60–200
Biological: 30 kilograms of anthrax spores with a density of 0.1 milligram per cubic meter	10	30,000–100,000
Nuclear:		
One 12.5 kiloton nuclear device achieving 5 pounds per cubic inch of overpressure	7.8	23,000–80,000
One 1 megaton hydrogen bomb	190	570,000–1,900,000

Using one aircraft delivering 1,000 kilograms of Sarin nerve gas or 100 kilograms of anthrax spores: Assumes the aircraft flies in a straight line over the target at optimal altitude and dispensing the agent as an aerosol. The study assumes that the biological agent would not make maximum use of this payload capability because this is inefficient. It is unclear this is realistic.

Clear sunny day, light breeze

Sarin Nerve Gas	0.74	300–700
Anthrax Spores	46	130,000–460,000

Overcast day or night, moderate wind

Sarin Nerve Gas	0.8	400–800
Anthrax Spores	140	420,000–1,400,000

Clear calm night

Sarin Nerve Gas	7.8	3,000–8,000
Anthrax Spores	300	1,000,000–3,000,000

Source: Adapted by the author from Office of Technology Assessment, *Proliferation of Weapons of Mass Destruction: Assessing the Risks*, US Congress OTA-ISC-559, Washington, August, 1993, pp. 53–54.

that Qaddafi might take extreme risks for ideological reasons that would provoke Israel into a massive response and destabilize the regional political situation, than a military threat to Israel in serious war fighting terms.

Syria is the only Arab state that actively deploys weapons of mass destruction against Israel. It does not, however, conduct large scale land warfare or combined arms training to simulate the use of chemical weapons, provide intensive small unit and squad training, or deploy the equivalent of a chemical corps in peacetime. It could almost certainly use its artillery and aircraft to deliver chemical weapons against tactical targets, but it is very poorly prepared to actually fight such a conflict, and it is unlikely that it could use such weapons with great effectiveness.

Syria seems to use its chemical weapons, and any biological weapons, principally as a deterrent to Israel's use of nuclear weapons and as a threat to fixed Israeli military installations and populated areas in order to deny Israel a potential nuclear monopoly. It places a heavy emphasis on having sheltered mobile missiles and the ability to survive conventional Israeli attacks, but there is no reliable unclassified description of Syrian C^4I/BM, deployment plans, doctrine, tactics, or strategy. Some Syrians have privately discussed using "volleys" of biologically or chemically armed missiles to deter or retaliate against any Israeli use of nuclear weapons, but it is unclear that Syria could rapidly deploy enough missiles to fire "volleys," or that they could survive deployment.

Some experts also question the quality of Syrian warhead and bomb design, Syria's ability to get anything approaching maximum lethality from missile weapons or bombs under operational circumstances, and its ability to conduct a large scale attack in which it achieves high overall lethality. They feel that Syria has not yet demonstrated such sophistication, or even its possession of advanced fusing, in its conventional air weapons. Other experts believe that Syria may have had access to Russian and Iranian designs and significant technical assistance from China and North Korea.

Israel seems to have a much more sophisticated attack capability ranging from the ability to employ tactical weapons to the ability to target and destroy any long range enemy area target or population center. It does not conduct extensive offensive chemical warfare training or seem to conduct more than limited defensive biological warfare training. If it has stocks of tactical chemical and biological weapons, it seems to reserve these for deterrent or demonstrative use against enemy forces and possibly to avoid leaving a "gap" between the use of conventional and nuclear weapons. Israel is also capable of retaliating against the use of limited chemical or biological attacks with strategic conventional bombing that could rapidly do major damage to enemy C^4I/BM capabilities, leadership facilities, utilities and water, and critical economic targets. It can almost certainly do more damage to any Arab neighbor using conventional weapons than that neighbor can currently do using chemical weapons.

Israel almost certainly has the nuclear capability to destroy the key population centers of any combination of enemies and effectively destroy them as modern states. If Israel used its full capabilities, it could probably do enough damage to delay the recovery of such states by a decade or more and to destroy their present political, ethnic, and economic structure beyond the capability to recover in anything approaching its current form. At the same time, Israel almost certainly brings the same sophistication in its C⁴I/BM capabilities, targeting, and doctrine for nuclear warfare that it does to conventional air warfare. Further, Israel's large number of survivable weapons gives it the option of attacking a wide range of area targets like air bases and enemy rear areas without sacrificing its capability to destroy urban areas.

This aspect of Israeli capabilities is not fully understood by many Arab analysts, although it is probably understood by senior Arab commanders. Some Arabs discount Israeli nuclear capabilities on the grounds that Israel would not use nuclear weapons because it is too small and Arab targets are too close. In fact, Israel has had full access to the unclassified US literature on employing large numbers of theater nuclear weapons near friendly forces in Europe, and Israeli officers have participated in tactical nuclear exercises with US officers.

Israel is almost certainly able to fully target Syrian, Jordanian, and Egyptian air bases and rear assembly areas, and to avoid any significant risk of fall-out through a combination of varying weapons yield, varying the height of burst, and timing attacks according to accurate weather models. Israel could easily target 20–30 theater nuclear weapons on Syria, Jordan, or both; deliver them over a relatively short period; and do so safely—barring unusual weather conditions. Alternatively, Israel has the sophistication to vastly increase the killing effect of its nuclear weapons by using ground bursts to maximize fall-out and by taking advantage of prevailing weather conditions to expand the lethal "footprint" of that fall-out.

The only meaningful uncertainty affecting Israel's technical ability to use nuclear weapons relatively close to Israel is whether it would use tactical nuclear weapons near actual Israeli military operations. Some analysts feel that the IDF has tactical nuclear artillery shells for this purpose. It seems doubtful, however, that the IDF has more than remote contingency plans to use nuclear weapons in this way. It simply does not face sufficient risk to rely on nuclear weapons for minor tactical purposes and it can achieve far more damage far more safely by targeting further to the rear.

It is important to note that Israel's political and military leaders almost certainly see weapons of mass destruction primarily as a deterrent, and would only employ them in the event of an existential threat to Israel's security or to destroy an enemy that used weapons of mass destruction against it. Every aspect of Israel's current doctrine, force structure, and training indicates that it places primary reliance on conventional weapons. There is no evidence of any major IDF effort to organize or train personnel to use weapons of mass destruction, and

FIGURE 13.1   The Relative Killing Effect of Chemical Versus Biological Weapons of
Mass Destruction Using a 1,000 Kilogram Bomb or Missile Warhead

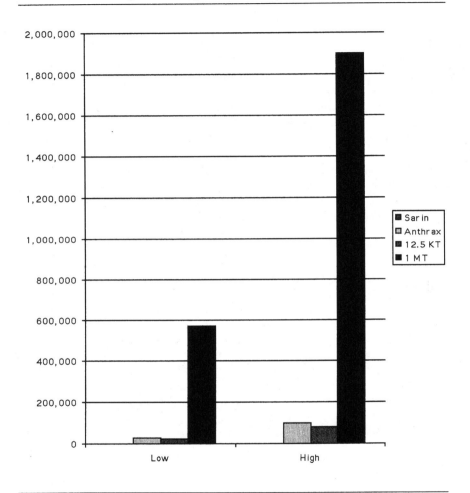

large scale training and organization would be essential if Israel was planning to
use such weapons at lower levels of conflict.

There is, however, one significant uncertainty affecting Israeli use of nuclear
weapons on at least a demonstrative basis. It is unlikely that Israel would tolerate
any major use of weapons of mass destruction on its civilian population or which
led to high casualties, and it is uncertain that it would tolerate such attacks on the
IDF. While Israel's reaction would almost certainly be highly contingency specific

FIGURE 13.2   The Relative Killing Effect in Numbers of Dead from Biological Versus Chemical Weapons with an Optimal Aerosol Delivery

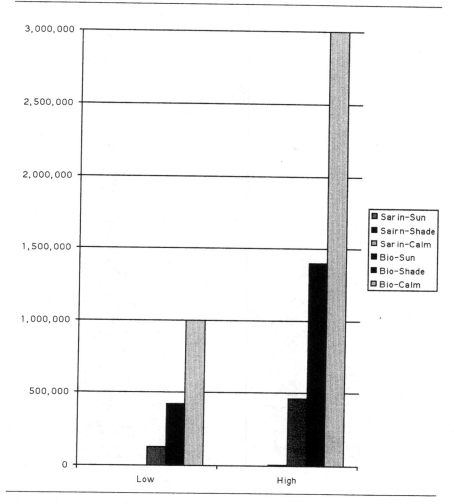

and depend on the leadership of Israel at the time, Israel seems unlikely to "ride out" more than very limited uses of weapons of mass destruction against Israeli targets. Further, the retaliatory capabilities of present threats are so limited that it could escalate with relative military impunity, and would have relatively little to fear in terms of lasting reactions from world opinion if it did so as long as its attacker was clearly perceived to have used weapons of mass destruction first and to have done so aggressively.

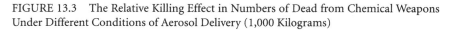

FIGURE 13.3   The Relative Killing Effect in Numbers of Dead from Chemical Weapons
Under Different Conditions of Aerosol Delivery (1,000 Kilograms)

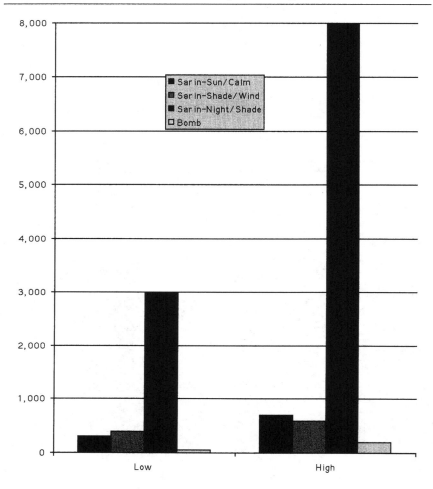

The Evolving War Fighting and Arms Control Implications
of Weapons of Mass Destruction

The uncertainties and risks just discussed will grow steadily worse as proliferation
proceeds and as the civil technology base of the region grows more sophisticated.
There is no way to translate such mid to long term shifts into detailed changes in
the war fighting capabilities that have just been discussed. Table 13.4 and Figures

13.1, 13.2, and 13.3 do, however, show that weapons of mass destruction are likely to increase steadily in lethality.

War fighting and arms control planning must take these differences into consideration, as well as the potential interactions between using one or more different types of weapons of mass destruction. Figures 13.1, 13.2, and 13.3 show, for example, that chemical weapons may be weapons of mass destruction, but they do not have anything approaching the destructive power of biological and nuclear weapons.

Increasing capabilities to deliver chemical weapons cannot be disregarded—particularly if an attacking state should use aircraft or cruise missiles to deliver such weapons in aerosol form rather than in the far less lethal form resulting from ballistic missile attacks. Chemical weapons could still radically alter the nature of the escalation and targeting in a future Arab-Israeli conflict. At the same time, they cannot threaten the survival of states in their current form.

In contrast, the potential threat from biological weapons makes them a true weapon of mass destruction. As Table 13.4 and Figure 13.2 show, biological weapons can be as destructive as small nuclear weapons, and all of the countries listed in Table 13.1 have made biological weapons efforts.

Further, covert delivery of such weapons is by far the most lethal way of using them. It is one of the ironies of biological warfare that it takes an extraordinarily advanced ballistic missile warhead and internal weapons system to disseminate a survivable and fully lethal biological agent over a wide area at the right height. At the same time, Figures 13.2 and 13.3 show that crude unconventional delivery systems can be very effective in delivering highly lethal biological weapons strikes.

The US, for example, experimented during the Cold War with particulate matter the same size and weight as anthrax spores. It delivered such spores from commercial vessels moving along the coast of New Jersey and in "terrorist" attacks sprinkling the spores over commuters rushing home through Grand Central Station in New York. Both dissemination systems were very effective and would have produced very high death rates. Both would have required human intelligence to prevent them or identify the attackers. Metal detectors and other technological means would not have been effective, and most conventional anti-terrorist protective measures would have failed.

It is also important to note that the lethality estimates shown in Table 13.4 and Figures 13.1, 13.2, and 13.3 understate the potential risks from biological and nuclear weapons. They assume that the biological agent will be no more lethal than anthrax, but most Middle Eastern states are nearing the capability to produce and weaponize more lethal agents, and will probably acquire them at some point between 2000 and 2010 as part of the advances they are making in light manufacturing, food processing, pharmaceutical production, and civil biological research and biotechnology.

These lethality estimates also only consider prompt casualties (death within 24–48 hours) from nuclear weapons. The longer long term deaths which would result from fall-out after a ground burst, particularly if weather data were used to ensure the prevailing wind patterns carried fall-out over additional urban areas, could more than double the casualties shown for a small fission weapon. Nations that can develop 12.5 kiloton weapons may well be able to get yields at least twice as high, and Israel may have boosted weapons with yields approaching 100 kilotons. Equally important, many Arab cities have large areas with population densities some 5 to 10 times higher than those assumed in these estimates—which are based on Western cities rather than Arab cities. The same lethality in weapons of mass destruction might easily kill three to five more times as many people in a city like Cairo than in a city like Tel Aviv.

If these lethality data are combined with the information on national military efforts in Table 13.1, they show that the Middle East is already committed to a pattern of proliferation that will allow Israel and its neighbors to engage in a spectrum of conflicts ranging from the most advanced weapons available to crude unconventional weapons, and from localized attacks to weapons delivered over an area from Iran to Libya.

This process of proliferation also varies sharply in character. It involves nations in producing both weapons of mass destruction requiring massive production facilities and weapons which are remarkably easy to produce in small facilities and conceal. It involves developing weapons which lend themselves to models of deterrence, defense, and retaliation close to those that shaped the US-Russian balance during the Cold War, and weapons which lend themselves to covert use—which might make it impossible to conclusively identify a given attacker.

There is also no way to know how each nation will develop a war fighting doctrine, war plans, safety procedures, leadership control procedures, release doctrine and procedures, targeting doctrine and capabilities, civil defense capabilities, and damage estimation and assessment capabilities over time. It seems unlikely that most leadership elites will consider major existential risks or behave recklessly except under extreme crisis conditions.

At the same time, the region is filled with leaders who believe in personal rule, are impatient with technical details, and may be poorly prepared for crises when they do occur. The region's military experts also tend to be far more interested in acquiring new weapons than the details of employing them, and it may be very difficult for many countries to estimate weapons reliability and effects—particularly when weapons development is covert. Restraint and rational deterrence in peacetime could quickly turn into uncontrolled escalation in a major crisis—particularly if leaders were confronted with the perceived need to preempt or a "use or lose" contingency.

The effects of any such use of biological and nuclear weapons should not be exaggerated. Egypt, Iran, Iraq, Israel, Libya, and Syria are not literally "one bomb" states. A single nuclear device could not destroy a majority of the population except under worst case conditions and under conditions where increases in the long term death rate were included in the estimate of casualties along with short term deaths within a 48 hour to seven day period.

At the same time, it is one thing to have a nuclear weapon and another to actually use it on population centers or a national capital. As has been mentioned earlier, Egypt, Iran, Iraq, Israel, Libya, and Syria are "few bomb" states. A nuclear or highly lethal biological attack on the capital and major population of any of the states just listed could destroy its current political leadership, much of its economy, and a great deal of the state's cohesion and national identity. Recovery would be questionable, and the social and economic impact of any such strike would last a decade or more.

The Arms Control Implications of Weapons of Mass Destruction

Advances in technology will present growing problems for arms control at every level. While there have been no breakthroughs in the production of fissile material, there is a vast amount of fissile material in the former Soviet Union, and more and more countries could produce an aircraft-deliverable nuclear device in a matter of a few months or years if they could buy weapons grade material.

The very nature of biotechnology means all of the countries in the Middle East are steadily acquiring the capability to make extremely lethal, dry storable biological weapons, and do so with fewer and fewer indicators in terms of imports of specialized technology, with more use of dual-use or civilian production facilities, and in smaller spaces. In most cases, their civil infrastructure will provide the capability to create such weapons without dedicated major military imports.

Long range ballistic missile systems are being deployed in Iran and Syria as well as Israel; better strike fighters with performance capabilities superior to yesterday's bombers are becoming commonplace. The kind of cruise missile technology suited to long range delivery of both nuclear and biological weapons against area targets like cities is becoming available to nations like Egypt, Iran, Iraq, Israel, and Syria. While improved air defenses and theater ballistic missile defenses—such as Patriot, Arrow, and THAAD—offer a potential countermeasure to such delivery systems, the peace process also will create more open borders and more civilian commercial traffic of a kind that makes it easier to use unconventional delivery means.

All of these developments have inherently uncertain war fighting and arms control effects. Nations that are just beginning to acquire a few nuclear weapons or serious biological weapons tend to see wars involving such weapons in terms of threats to enemy population centers and have little option other than to strike or concede if intimidation fails. They also tend to try to keep their capabilities covert and remove them from their normal political decision-making process. This can lead to rapid massive escalation or surprise attacks—particularly if a given side fears preemption, structures its forces to launch under attack, and/or seeks to strike before its opponent can bring its retaliatory forces and air and missile defenses to full readiness. Fewer weapons do not mean greater stability and security, and they almost inevitably mean countervalue targeting.

On the other hand, more weapons are hardly better. As the East-West arms race has shown, there is no logical stopping point. Broadening the number and type of weapons to allow strikes against military targets creates an incentive to be able to strike as many targets as possible. Obtaining the option to strike at tactical military targets lowers the threshold of escalation and may lead a given side to be more willing to attack. Reducing the vulnerability of steadily larger inventories of weapons and delivery systems may lead to a loss of control or more lethal plans to preempt or launch under attack. Larger forces potentially increase the risk that weapons directed against military targets will hit population centers, and while the Middle East may not be filled with "one bomb" states, it is definitely filled with "few bomb" states. Further, a state under existential attack by one neighbor may lash out against other states—a pattern Iraq has already exhibited by launching missile attacks against Israel during the Gulf War.

One should not exaggerate the importance of these "worst case" risks or their probability. Such possibilities do not alter the basic rules of rationale behavior. They do not lead rational and moderate leaders to take existential risks or escalate to genocidal conflicts. At the same time, it is difficult to say that they lead to predictable crisis behavior or escalation ladders. Further, they create problems in terms of establishing any clear arms control or war fighting doctrine that determines how the potential possession and use of given types of weapons of mass destruction—like chemical weapons—relate to the use of biological weapons and nuclear weapons. Even if regional leadership elites had large cadres of experts and took them seriously, there would still be no "rules" for dealing with different mixes of different types of weapons of mass destruction—particularly since it is remarkably difficult to predict the exact damage any given use of such weapons will have against a given target.

One cannot, for example, talk about Israeli nuclear strategy and then ignore the potential response in terms of Arab use of biological weapons. One cannot talk of potential uses of nuclear and biological weapons against military targets and be certain they will not produce massive collateral damage. One cannot talk about careful and rational decision makers who may use a weapon with unintended effects or whose perceptions of risk may be totally asymmetric.

It is also difficult to talk about plans and doctrine when most Middle Eastern states have only begun to think about the war fighting capabilities of the systems they or their neighbors are acquiring, and when perceptions and risk taking may change rapidly if a nation comes under actual attack or is faced with a decision to preempt or launch under attack that must be taken within hours, minutes, or seconds. Few chess players voluntarily engage in simultaneous games of Russian roulette.

At present, Israel's monopoly of nuclear weapons and the uncertainties in using biological weapons in war—where there are no precedents nations can use to judge deterrent and war fighting effects—seem to act as a stabilizing factor and deterrent. In some ways, they may also act as an incentive to the Arab states to seek arms control, for limitations on technology transfer, and for voluntary restraint and confidence building measures. Israel's possession of nuclear weapons also, however, acts as an incentive to Arab states to acquire more sophisticated weapons of mass destruction. So do the tensions between key states like Iran and Iraq. Weapons of mass destruction are the ultimate "wild card" in the trends in the Arab-Israeli military balance, and if such a card should ever be played, there is no way to predict its short and long term effects.

In short, the growth of existential risks involving unpredictable patterns of escalation using different weapons of mass destruction presents steadily more serious problems for arms control. Fewer weapons almost inevitably mean counter-value targeting against population centers, and this scarcely means that fewer weapons are safer. If the number of weapons is more than zero, it is generally better to have a significant number of survivable weapons.

At the same time, the covert nature of proliferation makes it almost impossible for any nation to be sure its opponent has actually reduced its weapons to zero, and the very nature of biotechnology means that no presently conceivable arms control regime can deny states in the region a steadily growing "break out" capability to build and use bioweapons capable of decimating an opponent's capital city, potentially disrupting its government, and threatening its existence as a state.

These risks are a critical—if not fatal—problem with global arms control regimes like the Nuclear Non-Proliferation Treaty and Biological Weapons Convention and are a serious problem with the Chemical Weapons Convention. Such regimes are inherently incapable of solving the "Nth Weapon" problem, and while they may be politically comforting, they cannot offer military security. If there is any hope for effective arms control, it must involve regional arms control measures that affect all forms of weapons of mass destruction, and which rely either on some level of possession to stabilize deterrence or on extremely intrusive technical means and unimpeded, sudden challenge inspection. Even then, it is far from clear that any regional arms control agreement can offer absolute assurance, no matter how many countries may be included or how demanding the proposed inspection system may be.

14

ANALYTIC AND POLICY IMPLICATIONS

There are obvious dangers in trying to summarize the complex dynamics of military developments in the Arab-Israeli balance and their impact on the peace process. As is often the case, the "devil is in the details." The previous analysis has shown that there is a wide range of problems and potential sources of conflict that can suddenly escalate into crises and conflicts.

At the same time, the analysis has also revealed a number of broader trends in the balance. It has shown that the conventional military balance is far more stable than it has been in the past, with strong elements of self-stabilizing deterrence. It has also shown, however, that a number of other trends are considerably more threatening—particularly the risks of low intensity combat between Israelis and Palestinians and the use of weapons of mass destruction. These trends have a number of important implications for policy and arms control.

Self-Stabilizing Deterrence

The current military balance between Israel and its immediate neighbors is remarkably stable. While it is possible to postulate a Syrian surprise attack that might achieve limited initial gains or a breakdown in the peace process, Israel retains a major defensive "edge" in tactics, technology, and training. This Israeli conventional superiority translates into a strong deterrent against war, gives Israel the defensive strength to risk trading territory for peace, and acts as a strong incentive for the Arab states to pursue the peace process.

At the same time, Israel's conventional edge does not extend to providing the kind of offensive superiority that allows it to threaten or intimidate its Arab neighbors. The cost of offensive operations would be far greater to Israel than they could be worth, and Egypt has strong defensive capabilities.

The Nations Outside the Peace Process

This conventional stability is the product of forces that cannot be easily reversed. The nations outside the peace process have been sharply affected by the end of the

Cold War, the outcome of the Gulf War, UN sanctions, and their own political, strategic, and military incompetence.

While military expenditures and arms transfers are only one set of measures of military capability, the previous analysis has shown that they can provide a good picture of the overall trends in military effort. Syrian military expenditures in constant dollars have dropped by about 40% since the mid-1980s. This drop in the dollar value of Syrian military spending has occurred in spite of significant Syrian economic growth, and Syrian military expenditures have dropped from a peak of 23% of GDP in the mid-1980s to less than 25% in 1995.[1]

Equally significant, deliveries of arms imports to Syria dropped from $5.2 billion in 1993 dollars during the four year period of 1987–1990, to $1.4 billion during 1991–1994—only 27% of the previous four year total. New Syrian arms import agreements have dropped even more. New agreements during 1991–1994 were only worth 17% of the value of the new agreements Syria signed during 1987–1990. Syria has effectively had to abandon the search for conventional parity with Israel, and even if it could obtain massive new orders of arms, it would now take close to half a decade for Syria to build back to the level of relative military capability it had in the mid-1980s.[2]

The Gulf War has shown the depth of the political divisions between Iraq and Syria, and the Coalition victory resulted in the destruction of about 40% of Iraq's major ground force weapons and the loss of many of its best combat aircraft. Since 1990, an import dependent and inefficient Iraqi military machine has been without arms imports. In fact, deliveries of new conventional arms have dropped in value from $16.6 billion during 1987–1990 to nearly zero during 1991–1994. Iraq has lost the imports it needs to sustain military operations and make up for its lack of effective organization and support capability. Iraq has lacked the ability to import the technology it needs to react to the lessons of the Gulf War, and will need years to "recapitalize" its conventional forces once the UN lifts its sanctions.[3]

Libya never made effective use of its massive arms imports during the 1970s and 1980s, and its forces have been little more than a large military "parking lot." In recent years, however, Libya has failed to spend the money necessary to maintain and modernize its past imports. Libyan arms imports declined from $3.2 billion annually in current dollars in the early 1980s to around $700 million in the late 1980s. They dropped to less than $400 million in 1990, and averaged around $125 million annually during the four year period of 1991–1994. As a result, Libya has made no significant improvements in conventional military technology and its conventional military capabilities are declining from "parking lot" to "junkyard."[4]

Lebanon remains a military cipher, and one where the real issue is the future of Israeli and Syrian occupation and their proxies like the South Lebanon Army and Hizbollah. Lebanon can be the scene of conflict, but the only military threat it poses is to itself.

The Nations Inside the Peace Process

The previous analysis has shown that the nations that already participate in the peace process—Egypt, Israel, and Jordan—have been affected by a very different mix of trends. The net effect of these trends has been to create further momentum behind self-stabilizing deterrence.

Egypt has benefited from loan forgiveness and massive amounts of US grant aid. The end result is that part of Egypt's force structure consists of modern, US-equipped units with improved tactics, training, and sustainability. Egypt's F-16s, E-2Cs, M-60s, and M-1s give it great defensive strength. This defensive strength is reinforced by its possession of the Improved Hawk, the Sinai accords and MFO, and strategic depth.

At the same time, Egypt has cut its real, domestically funded military spending by about 40% since the mid-1980s.[5] These cuts have saved Egypt money, but they have made it even more difficult for Egypt to sustain its inflated military force structure than in the past and have reduced its offensive capabilities. About 35% to 40% of Egypt's force structure now consists of low grade Soviet- and European-equipped forces with obsolete equipment. Money and manpower that could have been allocated to high quality units and economic development have been wasted on these units, which have negligible value in offensive operations.

Egypt has also emphasized modernization over improvements in its infrastructure and sustainment capabilities. It is not organized to project forces across the Sinai and provide its armored maneuver forces with effective air defenses. At the same time, the Sinai accords and MFO do as much to prevent Egypt from being able to achieve strategic surprise in an attack on Israel as they do to limit Israeli offensive capabilities against Egypt.

Jordan is now a full partner in the peace process, and its military capabilities have been crippled by a lack of modernization since the early 1980s and by the near cut-off in military and economic assistance that followed the Gulf War. Jordan has been forced to make major cuts in both its military expenditures and arms imports. Jordan's military expenditures in 1993 were only 60% of its expenditures in 1987, as measured in constant 1993 dollars.[6] Jordan's arms imports totaled only about $100 million during 1991–1994 versus a total of $800 million during 1986–1990. This latter total compares with arms transfers worth at least $4.3 billion for Israel and $4.8 billion for Egypt.[7] As a result, Jordan has not been able to maintain its past force levels, and its rates of modernization and recapitalization are so low that they are beginning to seriously undermine Jordan's military forces and strategic credibility.

Israel has cut real defense spending by about 40% since the early 1980s. Israel, however, has had the benefit of massive amounts of grant US aid. It has received $9.0 billion in US FMF aid in the last five years, and it has had billions of dollars' worth of additional ESF aid and $2 billion annually in loan guarantees. It also compares with a total of $6.5 billion in FMF aid for Egypt.

Israel has received about 40% more FMF aid than Egypt and it can use such aid far more efficiently. Egypt has had to buy fully assembled arms and support packages under the US FMS aid program, or has had to pay for facilities to assemble US weapons in Egypt. This has meant that much of the money Egypt spends under FMS goes to spares, special equipment, and overhead, and its weapons facilities have raised the unit cost of the arms that Egypt assembles above the unit cost of fully assembled US weapons.

In contrast, Israel can buy US weapons on a commercial basis and provide its own support packages, and its industries are so efficient that they can provide about 40% value added to the weapons components and technology Israel buys from the US. Israel has also benefited from free or low cost technology transfers, special pricing arrangements, and Israeli military sales to the US. As a result, the net value of a given dollar's worth of FMF aid to Israel is about 50% higher than to any other Middle Eastern country.

Equally important, the preceding analysis has shown that Egypt and Israel are the only nations affecting the Arab-Israeli conventional balance that have been able to buy the kind of advanced technology and weapons necessary to react to the lessons of the Gulf War and take advantage of the "revolution in military affairs." While weapons numbers are still important, they are no longer the key measure of military strength. It is the ability to exploit technology in a fully integrated "system of systems"—and to support this technology with new C^{4}I/BM, training, munitions, joint operations, and sustainment capability—that will shape conventional war fighting capability in the late 1990s and early 2000s.

Israel has had further advantages that have improved its defensive capabilities. It has been able to exploit technology with its own industrial base. Unlike Egypt, it has not had to convert from a Soviet-bloc supplied force structure. It has focused on the tactics, training, infrastructure, and sustainment capabilities necessary to fully exploit modern technology while Egypt has concentrated on procurement. As a result, Israel's defensive "edge" has steadily improved, while US arms and technology transfers to Egypt have ensured that Egypt has no reason to feel threatened or discriminated against.

In contrast, Syria has had to rely largely on aging Soviet-bloc designed weapons, has lacked the money and access to technology to modernize and restructure its forces, and has often chosen force quantity over force quality. Iraq and Libya have been largely frozen in military technology for half a decade. Jordan has lacked the money to compete.

The Self-Stabilizing Aspects of the Regional Conventional Arms Race

The end result of these trends is a remarkable level of conventional military deterrence that supports the peace process, with little chance of sudden destabilizing changes. The nations in the region also are already taking a "peace dividend"—although one that events have forced on Iraq, Jordan, Lebanon, and Libya, and one that has been financed by the US in the cases of Egypt and Israel. Only regional arms control can ensure that this situation will not be reversed in the mid to long term, but the destabilizing arms race and delicate conventional balance that have shaped security developments in the region from the end of World War II to the early 1990s no longer exist.

Beyond Conventional Deterrence

Conventional deterrence, however, is only part of the story. The military balance and the peace process are being affected by other military trends and some of these trends are far less reassuring than those that shape the conventional balance. These trends include issues like the future of the Palestinians and Jordan, the need for a full Israeli-Syrian peace agreement, the problem of weapons of mass destruction, the role of US security guarantees, and the need for US aid.

The Impact of Low Intensity Combat and the Palestinian Problem

Any analysis of the military balance that focuses solely on conventional war fighting ignores the risk that a breakdown of the peace process could transform the kind of conflict that took place during the Intifada into a far more serious level of low intensity or unconventional war. Israel is not Ulster, Vietnam, or Afghanistan, but the issue of Israel's security may still be determined as much by its internal security, and the security of any Palestinian entity, as by the balance of military forces.

This risk is a warning that efforts to find the proper balance between the security efforts of Israel and the Palestinian Authority security, and efforts to enhance Palestinian dignity and provide the Palestinians with economic aid, is absolutely critical. Palestinian political development, jobs, and living conditions may be unfamiliar measures of the military balance, but they are critical measures in securing a peace. They may ultimately prove to be far more important than numbers of tanks and aircraft or arms control reductions, and they already have a higher immediate priority for policy planning. The human dimension of Israeli and Palestinian security is the most important single factor threatening Arab-Israeli strategic stability in the near and mid term.

The Impact of Jordan

The peace process and regional stability are also dependent on giving Jordan added military self-reliance and self-stability, and on a consistent effort to help Jordan develop its economy and to broaden regional economic cooperation among Jordan, the Palestinian Authority, and Israel.

Jordan does not require massive amounts of new arms or military aid. The Jordanian five year plan discussed earlier is relatively modest and should meet Jordan's needs. Further, the Jordanian five year plan offers a new opportunity for Jordanian-Israeli cooperation in areas like their F-16 programs. Unthinkable as it may have been a few years ago, Jordan and Israel are already beginning to cooperate in ways that go beyond mere confidence building measures and are beginning to shape their military planning in ways that deliberately secure their peace agreement.

At the same time, the Jordanian military and the Jordanian people need to be shown that peace does not come at the expense of self-reliance or dignity and more is involved than arms transfers and military aid. As is the case with the Palestinians, Jordan's role in the military balance is dependent on internal security, and internal security is dependent on economic development.

These broader aspects of "human factors" are just as important in dealing with Jordanian security as they are in dealing with the Palestinian Authority, and it will be as important to ensure that the living standards of Jordanian Palestinians are improved as it will be to improve the living standards of Palestinians in Gaza and the West Bank.

The Impact of Syria, the Golan, and Lebanon

The present military balance and peace process can achieve considerable success even if Syria and Lebanon do not reach a peace agreement with Israel. At the same time, there can be little progress in conventional arms reductions, and Israel and Syria will continue to compete in acquiring weapons of mass destruction. Equally important, there will always be some risk of war, Syria and Iran will continue to use proxies to attack Israel, Syrian-backed Arab extremists will continue to challenge Israel's right to exist, and there will be little hope that Lebanon can regain its independence.

Reaching a full peace settlement does, therefore, have a high priority. At a minimum, this requires an Israeli-Syrian peace treaty, an agreement that transfers the Golan to Syria in return for normalization, and an effective arms limitation agreement. Ideally, it will mean Israeli, Syrian, and Iranian withdrawal from Lebanon and at least the beginning of a broad regional dialogue on the problem of weapons of mass destruction.

The Impact of Weapons of Mass Destruction

The trends in the regional acquisition of weapons of mass destruction are almost directly opposed to the trends in the conventional balance. Israel's nuclear monopoly acts as both a destabilizing factor in its relations with Egypt and an essential deterrent in dealing with threats from Iran, Iraq, and Syria. Egypt continues to make covert efforts to acquire long range missiles and chemical and biological weapons—partly for reasons of status and partly to create its own deterrent. Opponents of the peace process like Iran, Iraq, Libya, and Syria continue to make significant efforts to acquire or maintain their capability to manufacture and deliver such weapons.

Technology transfer is increasing the risks involved. New long range missiles and strike aircraft are being transferred to Iran and Syria. There now is little prospect that UNSCOM can deny Iraq the ability to produce biological and nerve gas weapons within a matter of months after the time the UN loses the right to conduct sudden intrusive inspection. Iran and Syria have biological and chemical weapons development and production efforts that are not subject to control, and Libya continues to expand its chemical weapons production efforts. Iran is seeking nuclear weapons, new biological technologies continue to increase the lethality of such weapons while making arms control more difficult, regional powers are steadily improving their ability to manufacture the precursors for chemical weapons, and cruise missile technologies are becoming more widely available.

There is no stable pattern of deterrence based on long, practical political and military experience. Strategy, doctrine, war planning, and targeting are secret national concerns—to the extent they yet exist or exist in a carefully structured form. Conflicts outside Israel and the Arab "ring states" can suddenly involve Israel and/or its neighbors with little warning and in highly unstable and confusing contingencies. A crisis between Israel and Syria involving such weapons would give both sides significant potential incentives to preempt, launch under attack, or massively escalate.

There are significant incentives for cheating on arms control treaties and uncertain capabilities to verify such cheating. Further, as long as weapons of mass destruction are not constrained, it will be tempting for nations like Syria to try to compensate for conventional weakness by increasing their holdings of such weapons, or for nations like Egypt to covertly try to compensate for Israel's nuclear monopoly by acquiring weapons of mass destruction.

The Impact of the Peace Process on the Strategic Role of the United States

The peace process also creates the dilemma that it increases Israel's reliance on its strategic relationship with the US while it simultaneously increases the impact of the limitations of US military power projection capabilities. Israel's sacrifice of territory for peace means it needs every security guarantee the US can provide in securing the peace and helping Israel defend itself, but makes it progressively harder for the US to deploy decisive amounts of force in time to affect the balance in a sudden or surprise conflict.

Unlikely as such a contingency may be in political terms, a Syrian or broader Arab attack on Israel could be prepared and executed in a matter of a few days. US naval and air deployments could react in such a time frame, but they would face important limits. The US could provide Israel with important aid in the first days of such an attack. It could secure the seas around Israel. Depending on US deployments at the time, the US could probably provide one or two carriers' worth of air reinforcements, limited numbers of land-based fighter and fighter-attack aircraft, support from long range bombers, and support with cruise missiles.

Much, however, would depend on US carrier and naval deployments at the time of such an attack, and on whether the US was involved in other contingencies. Israeli basing and C⁴I/BM capabilities already are nearly saturated by the IAF, and Israel would find it difficult to base and protect land-based US air reinforcements. There is little prospect the US could deploy land forces until such a conflict was over. It would take a minimum of a month to deploy even one heavy division in sustainable combat-ready form. Even if the US provided prepositioned land force equipment, US forces would take at least 7–10 days to marry up the required manpower with the prepositioned equipment and longer to deploy in a coherent combat capable form—and this would depend on their movement and equipment being secure from attack.

These problems are not arguments against US reinforcement of Israel, or an Arab ally, in an ultimate crisis. Control of the seas, air space to the west of Israel, the threat of US strategic retaliation with conventional air power and cruise missiles, limited US air reinforcements, and US resupply of Israel could be critical in some contingencies. At the same time, they indicate that Israel's security must ultimately rest on strong IDF forces and not on US security guarantees.

These problems also indicate that any US presence on the Golan must be limited to a peacekeeping mission rather than a peace enforcement mission. Given the massive forces available to Israel and Syria, a US flag is not a secure deterrent unless it is backed by US forces in place. If Israel is to emerge from the peace process with the same level of deterrence and defense capabilities it has today, the IDF must be strong and effective enough to be largely self-reliant. Israel, its Arab neighbors, and future arms control efforts must accept this reality.

The Impact of US Aid

The US needs to accept the fact that continued US aid to Israel and Egypt and increased US aid to Jordan and the Palestinians are essential aspects of regional stability and the peace process. Both regional stability and peace require that Israel have enough US military aid to be able to sustain its defensive "edge."

Maintaining this "edge" is necessary to ensure Israeli public support for the peace process, encourage Arab states to fully accept the peace process, ensure that Israel does not revert to a reliance on preemption or strategic conventional attacks, and ensure Israel does not increase its reliance on deterrence using weapons of mass destruction. Having such an "edge" is also likely to be an essential precursor to Israeli willingness to negotiate conventional arms reductions and make any serious efforts toward creating a Weapons of Mass Destruction Free Zone or placing limits on its nuclear capabilities.

At the same time, US aid is equally important in ensuring Egyptian support for the peace process and Egyptian confidence that Israel's defensive "edge" has not become a destabilizing offensive superiority. The US must demonstrate that Israel's security does not come at the expense of its Arab allies or the sacrifice of Arab strength and dignity. It must support Jordan and the Palestinian Authority through the difficult transitions still to come.

This scarcely means the US should be the only source of aid to the region, and the US should do everything possible to encourage conventional arms reductions as an alternative to military assistance. At the same time, there is no short term substitute for US aid, and US military assistance to Israel, Egypt, and Jordan will continue to play a critical role in ensuring regional stability and supporting the peace process.

Implications for Arms Control

These conflicting trends have important implications for arms control. On the one hand, there is little urgency in seeking near term reductions in conventional forces. In fact, ongoing military aid and weapons transfers will be needed if Israel is to have the security to give up the Golan, if Egypt is to complete its ongoing conversions to US supplied equipment, and if Jordan is to correct its major military weaknesses. The priority is to preserve and enhance the deterrence and defensive capabilities that underpin the peace process.

At the same time, there is a clear priority for other forms of conventional arms control:

- Israel and Syria must reach an agreement on force limitations and confidence building measures in the Golan—probably one that involves some form of multinational peacekeeping force. The details of such an agreement involve such vital national interests that they can only be shaped by Israel and Syria, and their mutual acceptance of an agreement they have both negotiated is more important than its precise form. At the same time, such an agreement will almost certainly require strong international support and some degree of US aid in terms of intelligence, warning, and verification.
- There is an equal need to reinforce the stabilizing trends in the conventional balance with confidence building measures, added transparency, and expert dialogue. This is necessary to reduce exaggerated Israeli concerns with the Arab threat and Egyptian and other Arab perceptions that Israel's defensive "edge" can somehow be translated into offensive dominance. More broadly, the region may not be able to simultaneously implement a peace process and reduce its conventional arms, but it does eventually need to reduce military spending and focus on economic development. Reaching agreement on major conventional arms reductions may well take a decade and it is scarcely too early for Israel and its neighbors to begin the process of planning and analysis, which is an essential precondition to structuring arms reduction agreements.

- There is a need for outside suppliers to carefully consider the implications of any transfers to nations outside the Arab-Israeli peace process. There are a number of critical technologies and weapons systems that can affect the present trends in the conventional balance. These weapons and technologies include (a) advanced electronic warfare capability; (b) advanced AWACS or AEW aircraft; (c) advanced surface-to-air missiles like the SA-10; (d) improved combat aircraft and air munitions for precision strike and beyond-visual-range combat; (e) advanced tanks and other armor with thermal sights, improved fire control, more lethal rounds, and spaced armor; (f) third or fourth generation anti-tank weapons; (g) large numbers of advanced infrared SHORADS; and (h) MLRS-like artillery weapons and advanced artillery fire control and targeting systems. Unless some qualitative limits are placed on such transfers to nations like Syria, Iran, Iraq, and Libya, the Middle East arms race is certain to continue and even accelerate in certain key areas.
- There is a need to find regional approaches to the problem of dealing with extremism and terrorism that can further limit the ability of outside powers and individuals to support Palestinian and Israeli extremists and to improve cooperation among Israel, Jordan, and the Palestinian Authority. Security operations will inevitably be dominated by local security forces and human intelligence, but it may be possible to provide outside assistance in technology and in controlling technology transfer that will both improve security and reduce the need for intrusive security measures. Improved cooperation and dialogue may also find ways to improve security operations while simultaneously improving the treatment of Palestinians and reducing the barriers to Israeli-Palestinian economic cooperation.

Finally, arms control must begin to deal with the problem of proliferation. This requires all of the nations involved in the peace process to look beyond the issue of the Nuclear Non-Proliferation Treaty and focus on the regional problem of all forms of weapons of mass destruction.

Egypt and the other Arab nations involved in the peace process need to recognize the difficulties Israel faces in dealing with any arms control effort that focuses solely on Israel's nuclear capabilities. Any negotiation that focuses on Israel's nuclear weapons without including Egyptian, Iranian, Iraqi, Libyan, and Syrian weapons of mass destruction singles out Israel's nuclear forces at a time when the capabilities of hostile neighboring states are growing and are subject to no—or temporary and uncertain—control.

The threat posed by Syrian, Iranian, and Iraqi biological and chemical warfare capabilities, coupled to the threat posed by Iranian and Iraqi long range missiles and aircraft, is not one Israel can ignore. They will soon approach the lethality of small nuclear forces if they do not have this lethality already. If Israel brings its nuclear advantage to the conference table, Israeli nuclear capabilities may be constrained or reduced, while rogue states in the region can steadily increase the risk of nuclear-biological-chemical attacks on Israel.

Further, moderate Arab states need to take a more realistic view of exactly who threatens whom. Israeli nuclear capabilities are presently only a game-theoretic threat to Egypt, Jordan, and the moderate Gulf states. In contrast, Syrian, Iranian, and Iraqi weapons of mass destruction provide these nations with political status and leverage against their Arab neighbors and create a considerably higher risk that moderate Arab states will become involved in actual war fighting contingencies.

If there is a way out of these problems, it seems to lie in a much broader approach to controlling weapons of mass destruction that clearly links regionwide progress in controlling nuclear weapons to regionwide progress in controlling chemical and biological weapons and long range delivery systems. President Mubarak has advanced similar ideas in talking about a zone free of weapons of mass destruction, and such broader efforts could be made part of the existing Arms Control and Regional Security (ACRS) process if they defined the region to consider Iran, Iraq, and Libya as well as the states now in the ACRS process, and the risk of the transfer of related weapons and technology from outside the region. Attempting to focus on some particular agreement—such as the NPT—may suit the political passions of the moment, but it is scarcely a realistic solution for enhancing regional security.

This, however, means that Israel must recognize that such negotiations are necessary and that only a solid framework of arms control measures, coupled to a solid peace, can begin to provide security for both Israel and its Arab neighbors against weapons of mass destruction. At some point, Israel must emerge from the nuclear closet and begin to provide its Arab neighbors with data on its forces and capabilities, just as they must begin to be frank about their biological, chemical, and missile programs.

Unfortunately Egypt, Israel, Jordan, and other moderate Arab states will need to consider the very real possibility that no amount of arms control negotiations may be able to stuff the genie of proliferation back into the bottle. In an ideal world, the Middle East should be free of weapons of mass destruction. In the real world, some mix of arms control and active counterproliferation measures may be the best that the nations in the peace process and ACRS can achieve.

There are obvious dangers in a Middle East where only extremist regimes have weapons of mass destruction, or where the only barrier to such a monopoly by extremists is arms control agreements where extremist regimes will find it far easier to cheat than moderate states. At least in the mid term, the nations in the peace process may find it equally necessary to cooperate in active counterproliferation efforts like air and missile defense. Egypt and Israel, in particular, may also find they have more to gain from a mix of such cooperation and efforts to structure regionwide arms control agreements that can be verified and secured than from squabbling over issues like the NPT.

15

SOURCES AND METHODS

The previous text has stressed the fact that many of the statements and statistics in this book are highly uncertain. Middle Eastern governments go to great effort to conceal the nature of virtually every aspect of their national security activity, and the various unclassified sources available differ in many details.

Sources

It was possible to visit Egypt, Israel, Jordan, and Syria at various times during the preparation of this book and to talk to Egyptian, Israeli, Jordanian and Syrian experts. Some provided detailed comments on the text. Interviews also took place with experts in the United States, United Kingdom, France, Switzerland, and Germany. Portions of the manuscript were circulated for informal review by officials and diplomats in several of the countries covered in the book, and some chapters were modified extensively in response. No such interviews or comments are referenced, however, unless those concerned specifically gave their permission, and no source is quoted by name. As a result, many of the sources shown in the notes are supplemented by interviews and comments that cannot be referenced or attributed.

Data are drawn from a wide range of sources but involve many detailed judgments by the author in reconciling different reports and data. In some cases, there was no "right" source, but one source was chosen for the sake of comparability and consistency. The *CIA World Factbook* was often chosen over other international data sources simply because it offered the most consistent basis for obtaining directly comparable data.

The sources for data on arms control are explained in depth in Chapter 2, along with the reasons for choosing given sources. The military manpower, force strength, and equipment estimates used throughout the book were made by the author using a wide range of sources, including computerized databases, interviews, and press clipping services.

Many key force strength statistics are taken from the latest edition of the International Institute for Strategic Studies *Military Balance* (IISS, London), in this case the 1995–1996 edition. Extensive use has also been made of the annual editions of the Jaffee Center for Strategic Studies, *The Military Balance in the Middle East* (JCSS, Tel Aviv), especially the 1993–1994 edition (the latest edition available in 1995) and working materials from the coming edition. Other sources include the *Military Technology "World Defense Almanac for 1994–1995,"* published in early 1995; computerized material available in NEXIS; and the latest annual editions of various Jane's reference books. There were, however, many cases in which US government experts sharply differ from the figures available in these sources and seem to have convincing reason to do so. Their estimates were used where unclassified data were available.

Military data were also estimated using computer printouts from the United States Naval Institute database and from the DMS/FI Market Intelligence Reports database. Extensive use has also been made of media sources, including Internet material, translations of broadcasts, newspapers, magazine articles, and similar materials. These are referenced in most cases, but some transcribed broadcasts and much of the Internet material did not permit detailed attribution.

The Internet and several on-line services were also used to retrieve data on US and Israeli government reporting and policy, descriptions of the details of the peace agreements, and examinations of Arab and Palestinian positions. Since most of the databases involved are dynamic and either change or are deleted over time, there is no clear way to footnote much of this material. Recent press sources are generally cited, but are often only part of the material consulted.

Virtually all of the sources drawn upon in writing this analysis are at least in partial conflict. They do not provide any consensus over demographic data, budget data, military expenditures and arms transfers, force numbers, unit designations, or weapons types. While the use of computer databases allowed some cross-correlation and checking of such sources, the reporting on factors like force strengths, unit types and identities, and tactics often could not be reconciled, and citing multiple sources for each case is not possible.

Mapping and location names also presented a major problem. The author used US Army and US Air Force detailed maps, commercial maps, and in some cases commercial satellite photos. In many cases, however, the place names and terrain descriptions used in the combat reporting by both sides, and by independent observers, presented major contradictions that could not be resolved from available maps. No standardization emerged as to the spelling of place names. Sharp differences emerged in the data published by the US and Israeli governments, and private reporting reflects a complete lack of progress in reconciling the conflicting methods of transliterating Arabic and Hebrew names into English.

The same problem applied in reconciling the names of organizations and individuals—particularly those being transliterated from Arabic. It again became painfully obvious that no progress is being made in reconciling the conflicting methods of transliterating Arabic and Hebrew names into English. A limited effort has been made to standardize the spellings used in this text, but many names are tied to relational databases where the preservation of the original spelling is necessary to identify the source and tie it to the transcript of related interviews.

Methods

In most cases, the author adjusted figures and data on a "best guess" basis, drawing on some thirty years of experience in the field. In some other cases, the original data provided by a given source were used without adjustment to ensure comparability, even though this leads to some conflicts in dates, place names, force strengths, etc. within the material presented—particularly between summary tables surveying a number of countries and the best estimates for a specific country in the text. In such cases, it seemed best to provide contradictory estimates to give the reader some idea of the range of uncertainty involved.

Most of the value judgments regarding military effectiveness are made on the basis of American military experience and standards. Although the author has lived in the Middle East and worked as a US advisor to several Middle Eastern governments, he feels that any attempt to create some Middle Eastern standard of reference is likely to be far more arbitrary than basing such judgments on his own military background.

Finally, this book deliberately focuses on military capabilities, security issues, and the military aspects of arms control. It is only indirectly concerned with politics and economics. It also deliberately focuses on the details of security issues. It is intended primarily to help provide technical background for those who must assess the military balance, and its implications for peace negotiations and arms control, rather than provide policy recommendations.

Notes

Chapter One

1. These estimates are extrapolated from the population growth data on the Arab-Israeli ring states in the *CIA World Factbook, 1995,* and from the military expenditure and arms import data over the preceding decade in ACDA, *World Military Expenditures and Arms Transfers, 1993–1994,* Washington, GPO, 1995.

Chapter Two

1. CIA, *World Factbook, 1995;* World Bank, *Claiming the Future: Choosing Prosperity in the Middle East and North Africa,* Washington, World Bank, 1995, pp. 114–115.

2. CIA, *World Factbook, 1995;* World Bank, *Claiming the Future: Choosing Prosperity in the Middle East and North Africa,* Washington, World Bank, 1995, pp. 114–115.

3. CIA, *World Factbook, 1995;* World Bank, *Claiming the Future: Choosing Prosperity in the Middle East and North Africa,* Washington, World Bank, 1995, pp. 114–115.

4. The Jaffee Center for Strategic Studies provides useful data on foreign advisors and sources of military aid, but does not estimate arms transfers.

5. The author has estimated the data for Lebanon for 1985–1989. ACDA did not report any figures.

6. The reader should examine Tables IV and V in ACDA, *World Military Expenditures and Arms Transfers, 1993–1994,* Washington, GPO, 1995. To take only one example out of many, ACDA reports in Table IV that the US delivered $11.7 billion worth of weapons during 1991–1993 versus $3.6 billion for Russia/Soviet Union. These figures indicate that the US provided 3.25 times more weapons than the USSR. If one looks at the data on actual arms transfers to the Middle East in Table V, however, Russia provided slightly more tanks, 2.7 times more artillery weapons, 2.4 times more supersonic combat aircraft, and 2.1 times more helicopters. The only categories where the US led in weapons transfers were in APCs and light surface-to-air missiles.

7. *Defense News,* September 4, 1995, p. 14.

8. World Bank, *Claiming the Future: Choosing Prosperity in the Middle East and North Africa,* Washington, World Bank, 1995, pp. 100–101.

9. World Bank, *Claiming the Future: Choosing Prosperity in the Middle East and North Africa,* Washington, World Bank, 1995, pp. 114–115.

10. *Jane's Defense Weekly,* July 12, 1995, p. 19.

11. US Department of State, *Congressional Presentation, Foreign Operations, Fiscal Years 1988, 1990, 1994, 1995,* Department of State, Washington, DC; Source: Adapted from US

Defense Security Assistance Agency (DSAA), "Foreign Military Sales, Foreign Military Construction Sales and Military Assistance Facts as of September 30, 1994," Department of Defense, Washington, 1995.

12. Israeli Finance Ministry, November, 1995.

13. US Department of State, *Congressional Presentation, Foreign Operations, Fiscal Years 1988, 1990, 1994, 1995*, Department of State, Washington, DC; Source: Adapted from US Defense Security Assistance Agency (DSAA), "Foreign Military Sales, Foreign Military Construction Sales and Military Assistance Facts as of September 30, 1994," Department of Defense, Washington, 1995.

14. Richard F. Grimmett, *Conventional Arms Transfers to the Third World, 1986–1993*, Washington, Congressional Research Service, 94–612F, July 29, 1994; Richard F. Grimmett, "Conventional Arms Transfers to Developing Nations, 1987–1994," CRS 85–862F, Washington, Congressional Research Service, August 4, 1995; and Richard F. Grimmett, "Conventional Arms Transfers to Developing Nations, 1987–1994," CRS 85–862F, Washington, Congressional Research Service, August 4, 1995, pp. 57 and 68.

15. United Press International, November 5, 1992, BC Cycle.

16. Conversations with World Bank experts, *Middle East Economic Digest*, September 20, 1995, pp. 10–11.

17. *Jane's Defense Weekly*, July 12, 1995, p. 19.

18. *Jane's Defense Weekly*, July 12, 1995, p. 19.

19. Clyde R. Mark, "Israel: US Foreign Assistance," Congressional Research Service, CRS-IB85066, May 18, 1995; Clyde R. Mark, "Middle East and North Africa: US Aid FY1993, 1994, and 1995," CRS 94–274F, March 28, 1994; "Congressional Presentation for Foreign Operations, FY1996," US Department of State, 1995.

20. Clyde R. Mark, "Middle East and North Africa: US Aid FY1993, 1994, and 1995," CRS 94–274F, March 28, 1994; "Congressional Presentation for Foreign Operations, FY1996," US Department of State, 1995.

21. Although scarcely without problems. The Clinton Administration sought $999 million in debt forgiveness in 1994, with the rest of the debt to be canceled over the next two years. The Congress barely approved the program, slowed down the initial rate of forgiveness, and full debt forgiveness will not take place until 1996. *Jane's Defense Weekly*, July 12, 1995, p. 19.

22. US Department of State, *Congressional Presentation, Foreign Operations, Fiscal Years 1988, 1990, 1994, 1995*, Department of State, Washington, DC.

23. Based on interviews in Jordan and with US government experts.

24. Discussions with US officials, *Defense News*, October 2, 1995, p. 4; *Jane's Defense Weekly*, July 1, 1995, pp. 20–21.

25. *Jane's Defense Weekly*, September 30, 1995, p. 19.

Chapter Three

1. Additional data are estimated using Schlomo Gazit, ed., *The Middle East Military Balance, 1993–1994*, Jaffee Center for Strategic Studies, Tel Aviv, 1994; and Military Technology, *World Defense Almanac, 1994–1995*, Bonn, Monch Publishing Group, Issue 1, 1995. Material has also been drawn from computer printouts from NEXIS, the United States Naval Institute data base, and from the DMS/FI Market Intelligence Reports database.

Weapons data are taken from many sources, including computerized material available in NEXIS, and various editions of *Jane's Fighting Ships* (Jane's Publishing); *Jane's Naval Weapons Systems* (Jane's Publishing); *Jane's Armor and Artillery* (Jane's Publishing); *Jane's Infantry Weapons* (Jane's Publishing); *Jane's Military Vehicles and Logistics* (Jane's Publishing); *Jane's Land-Base Air Defense* (Jane's Publishing); *Jane's All the World's Aircraft* (Jane's Publishing); *Jane's Battlefield Surveillance Systems* (Jane's Publishing); *Jane's Radar and Electronic Warfare Systems* (Jane's Publishing); *Jane's C3I Systems* (Jane's Publishing); *Jane's Air-Launched Weapons Systems* (Jane's Publishing); *Jane's Defense Appointments & Procurement Handbook (Middle East Edition)* (Jane's Publishing); *Tanks of the World* (Bernard and Grafe); *Weyer's Warships* (Bernard and Grafe); and *Warplanes of the World* (Bernard and Grafe).

Other military background, effectiveness, strength, organizational, and history data are taken from Anthony H. Cordesman, *After the Storm: The Changing Military Balance in the Middle East*, Boulder, Westview, 1993; and *Weapons of Mass Destruction in the Middle East*, London, Brassey's/RUSI, 1991; Anthony H. Cordesman and Abraham Wagner, *The Lessons of Modern War, Volume I*, Boulder, Westview, 1989; the relevant country or war sections of Herbert K. Tillema, *International Conflict Since 1945*, Boulder, Westview, 1991; Department of Defense and Department of State, *Congressional Presentation for Security Assistance Programs, Fiscal Year 1996*, Washington, Department of State, 1992; various annual editions of John Laffin's *The World in Conflict* or *War Annual*, London, Brassey's, and John Keegan, *World Armies*, London, Macmillan, 1983; "The IDF's Security Principles," Office of the IDF Spokesman, April, 1995; and Scotty Fisher, "Country Briefing Israel," *Jane's Defense Weekly*, February 18, 1995, pp. 29–38.

2. Interviews with Jordanian and US officials. *Jane's Defense Weekly*, July 12, 1995, p. 19.

3. For an interesting argument that currently planned cuts mean a shift toward a more full time professional, or "peacetime," Israeli army, see Stuart A. Cohen, "Studying the Israel Defense Forces: A Changing Contract with Israeli Society," BESA Center for Strategic Studies No. 20, Ramat Gan, Israel, Bar-Ilan University, 1995.

4. "The IDF's Security Principles," Office of the IDF Spokesman, April, 1995, and Scotty Fisher, "Country Briefing Israel," *Jane's Defense Weekly*, February 18, 1995, pp. 29–38.

5. *Defense News*, April 3, 1995, p. 3, October 30, 1995, p. 4; *Chicago Tribune*, January 4, 1993.

6. "The IDF's Security Principles," Office of the IDF Spokesman, April, 1995, and Scotty Fisher, "Country Briefing Israel," *Jane's Defense Weekly*, February 18, 1995, pp. 29–38.

7. *Jane's Intelligence Monthly*, Volume 7, Number 6, pp. 261–264, and Volume 7, Number 7, pp. 299–304.

8. *Jane's Defense Weekly*, April 15, 1995, p. 20.

9. *Defense News*, April 10, 1995, p. 24.

10. Both sides have long had some artillery weapons with such ranges. The difference is improvements in targeting, extended range projectiles, and projective lethality that give such weapons significant effectiveness.

11. "The IDF's Security Principles," Office of the IDF Spokesman, April, 1995, and Scotty Fisher, "Country Briefing Israel," *Jane's Defense Weekly*, February 18, 1995, pp. 29–38; *Jane's Defense Weekly*, November 4, 1995, p. 8.

12. *Jane's Defense Weekly*, November 28, 1987, p. 1239; Rafael briefing sheet; manufacturer offprint of "Rafael: Lessons of Combat" from *Military Technology*, May, 1991.

13. Tamir Eshel, "Israel's Defense Electronics," *Defense Electronics*, October, 1991, pp. 87–90.

14. Dick Pawloski, *Changes in Threat Air Combat Doctrine and Force Structure, 24th Edition*, Fort Worth, General Dynamics DWIC-91, February, 1992, pp. II–199 to II–211.

15. *Jane's Defense Weekly*, February 2, 1990, pp. 200–203.

16. *Jane's Defense Weekly*, February 2, 1990, pp. 200–203; *Air Force*, November, 1991, p. 50; *Jane's Defense Weekly*, June 24, 1989, p. 1324; *Aviation Week*, June 28, 1993, pp. 46–47; *International Defense Review*, 10/1992, p. 1015; *Jane's Defense Weekly*, February 18, 1995, pp. 29–37.

17. *Inside Defense Electronics*, April 10, 1992, p. 14; IAI Elta Brochure; *Air Force*, November, 1991, p. 50; JINSA, *Security Affairs*, March, 1992, p. 3; *Aviation Week*, June 28, 1993, pp. 46–47; *International Defense Review*, 10/1992, p. 1015; *Jane's Defense Weekly*, February 18, 1995, pp. 29–37.

18. *Jane's Defense Weekly*, October 15, 1988, p. 959.

19. *International Defense Review*, 9/1987, p. 1204.

20. *Defense News*, April 4, 1988, p. 1; *International Defense Review*, 9/1989, pp. 1237–1238.

21. *International Defense Review*, 9/1989, pp. 1237–1238; *Defense News*, July 3, 1995, p. 8.

22. The Harpee and Star-1 may be different systems. *Defense News*, April 4, 1988, p. 1, May 11, 1992, p. 1, July 3, 1995, p. 8.

23. *Defense News*, November 28, 1988, p. 17; Israeli Military Industries (IMI) manufacturer brochures.

24. "The IDF's Security Principles," Office of the IDF Spokesman, April, 1995; Scotty Fisher, "Country Briefing Israel," *Jane's Defense Weekly*, February 18, 1995, pp. 29–38; *Defense News*, February 21, 1993, p. 3, January 10, 1994, p. 6; *International Defense Review*, 10/1994, p. 6; *Wall Street Journal*, January 28, 1994, p. A-3.

25. Dick Pawloski, *Changes in Threat Air Combat Doctrine and Force Structure, 24th Edition*, General Dynamics DWIC-91, Fort Worth Division, February, 1992, pp. I-85 to 1-117.

26. Rostislav Belyakov and Nikolai Buntin, "The MiG 29M Light Multirole Fighter," Military Technology, 8/94, pp. 41–44; Dick Pawloski, *Changes in Threat Air Combat Doctrine and Force Structure, 24th Edition*, General Dynamics DWIC-91, Fort Worth Division, February, 1992, pp. I-85 to 1-117.

27. Dick Pawloski, *Changes in Threat Air Combat Doctrine and Force Structure, 24th Edition*, General Dynamics DWIC-91, Fort Worth Division, February, 1992, pp. I-85 to 1-117.

28. *Aviation Week and Space Technology*, April 10, 1989, pp. 19–20; *New York Times*, April 5, 1989, September 7, 1989; *Washington Times*, January 16, 1989; *FBIS/NES*, April 10, 1989.

29. The Su-24 has a wing area of 575 square feet, an empty weight of 41,845 pounds, carries 3,385 gallons or 22,000 pounds of fuel, has a take-off weight of 871,570 pounds with bombs and two external fuel tanks, carries 2,800 gallons or 18,200 pounds of external fuel, has a combat thrust to weight ratio of 1.02, has a combat wing loading of 96 pounds per square foot, and has a maximum load factor of 7.5G. *Jane's Soviet Intelligence Review*, July, 1990, pp. 298–300; *Jane's Defense Weekly*, June 25, 1985, pp. 1226–1227; and Dick Pawloski, *Changes in Threat Air Combat Doctrine and Force Structure, 24th Edition*, General Dynamics DWIC-91, Fort Worth Division, February, 1992, pp. I-65 and I-110 to 1-117.

30. *Jane's Defense Weekly*, August 20, 1994, p. 6, July 12, 1995, p. 19; *Defense News*, June 26, 1995, p. 12; *Washington Times*, September 28, 1995, p. A-10.

31. *Jane's Defense Weekly*, August 20, 1994, p. 6, July 12, 1995, p. 19; *Defense News*, June 26, 1995, p. 12; *Washington Times*, September 28, 1995, p. A-10.

32. *Jane's Intelligence Review*, October, 1994, p. 456.

33. For a more detailed description of the Israeli AH-64 program, see *Jane's Defense Weekly*, October 10, 1992, p. 7.

34. "The IDF's Security Principles," Office of the IDF Spokesman, April, 1995, and Scotty Fisher, "Country Briefing Israel," *Jane's Defense Weekly*, February 18, 1995, pp. 29–38.

35. *Flight International*, August 24, 1993, p. 12.

36. Based on interviews with British, US, and Israel experts. *Washington Times*, January 16, 1992, p. G-4; *Washington Post*, February 1, 1992, p. A-1, February 2, 1992, pp. A-1 and A-25, February 5, p. A-19; *Financial Times*, February 6, 1992, p. 4; *Christian Science Monitor*, February 6, 1992, p. 19; *Defense News*, February 17, 1992, p. 1.

37. *Jane's Intelligence Review*, October, 1994, p. 456.

38. *Jane's Fighting Ships, 1994–1995*, pp. 322–327; IISS, *Military Balance, 1995–1996*.

39. *Jane's Fighting Ships, 1994–1995*, pp. 322–327; IISS, *Military Balance, 1995–1996*.

40. *Jane's Fighting Ships, 1994–1995*, pp. 322–327; IISS, *Military Balance, 1995–1996*.

41. "The IDF's Security Principles," Office of the IDF Spokesman, April, 1995, and Scotty Fisher, "Country Briefing Israel," *Jane's Defense Weekly*, February 18, 1995, pp. 29–38.

42. *Jane's Fighting Ships, 1994–1995*, pp. 665–666; IISS, *Military Balance, 1995–1996*.

43. *Jane's Fighting Ships, 1994–1995*, pp. 665–666; IISS, *Military Balance, 1995–1996*.

44. *Jane's Fighting Ships, 1994–1995*, pp. 380–383; IISS, *Military Balance, 1995–1996*.

45. *Jane's Fighting Ships, 1994–1995*, pp. 402–403; IISS, *Military Balance, 1995–1996*.

46. *Defense News*, October 23, 1995, pp. 3, 45.

Chapter Four

1. *Jane's Defense Weekly*, May 6, 1995, p. 12.

2. Dick Pawloski, *Changes in Threat Air Combat Doctrine and Force Structure, 24th Edition*, Fort Worth, General Dynamics DWIC-91, February, 1992, pp. II-199 to II-227.

3. The defecting pilot was on maneuver near the Golan, and suddenly turned toward Israel and flew very low and fast low over the Golan and the central Galilee. He landed in a remote civil strip near Megido. This led to a great deal of media comment in Israel, but such incidents are almost unavoidable. Although he flew for seven minutes without being intercepted, he flew at a time when IAF E-2Cs were not in the air and no nearby aircraft were scrambled, when the IAF was in a state of low alert, and flew without using any radar or communications emissions. He also stated later that he did receive warning he was being tracked by Israeli radar. Israel later used the MiG-23ML (G) for training and test and evaluation purposes. *Washington Post*, October 13, 1989, p. A-35, October 14, 1989, p. A-18; *New York Times*, October 12, 1989, p. A-10, October 14, 1989, p. A-2; *Philadelphia Inquirer*, October 12, 1989, p. 18A, October 13, 1989, p. 17A; *Washington Times*, October 12, 1989, p. A-8; *Jane's Defense Weekly*, February 10, 1990, p. 221.

4. Samuel M. Katz, "Israeli Airpower on the Rise," *Air Force*, November, 1991, pp. 44–51.

5. See Emanuel Wald, *The Wald Report: The Decline of Israeli National Security Since 1967*, Boulder, Westview, 1991.

6. *Jane's Defense Weekly*, July 27, 1991, p. 135; Eric Silver, "A Warrior for the Nineties," *The Jerusalem Report*, June 20, 1991, pp. 12–20.

7. Office of IDF spokesman; *Los Angeles Times*, November 1, 1995, p. A-1.

8. *Armed Forces Journal*, October, 1991, p. 30.

9. For an interesting discussion of changes in Israel's manpower system that might affect these vulnerabilities, see Stuart A. Cohen, "Studying the Israel Defense Forces: A Changing Contract with Israeli Society," BESA Center for Strategic Studies No. 20, Ramat Gan, Israel, Bar-Ilan University, 1995.

Chapter Five

1. Herbert J. Tillema, *International Armed Conflict Since 1945*, Boulder, Westview, 1991.

2. Herbert J. Tillema, *International Armed Conflict Since 1945*, Boulder, Westview, 1991.

Chapter Six

1. The original peace agreement authorized 9,000 PLO police officers. IDF reports indicate that 14,000–17,000 have been hired. Prime Minister Rabin also authorized 2,000 more police for Gaza in February, 1995. *Los Angeles Times*, February 10, 1995, p. A-2; *Washington Times*, February 8, 1995, p. A-1; *Christian Science Monitor*, May 17, 1995, p. 7.

2. US Department of State, "Patterns of Global Terrorism, 1994," Washington, GPO, April, 1995, pp. 15–20.

3. For a detailed discussion of this issue, see Elie Rekhess, "The Terrorist Connection— Iran, the Islamic Jihad, and Hamas," *Justice*, Volume 5, May, 1995.

4. US Department of State, "Patterns of Global Terrorism, 1994," Washington, GPO, April, 1995, pp. 15–19; *Washington Post*, November 5, 1995, p. A-33.

5. *Washington Post*, October 17, 1995, p. A-1; Washington Times, September 4, 1995, p. A-9.

6. *New York Times*, October 13, 1995, p. A-5; Executive New Service, October 12, 1995, p. 1330.

7. *Peacewatch*, October 30, 1995, pp. 1–3; *Philadelphia Inquirer*, November 1, 1995, p. A-3; Executive News, October 11, 1995, 0611.

8. Executive News Service, November 6, 1996, 1643.

9. For a detailed discussion of this issue, see Elie Rekhess, "The Terrorist Connection— Iran, the Islamic Jihad, and Hamas," *Justice*, Volume 5, May, 1995.

10. Elie Rekhess, "The Terrorist Connection—Iran, the Islamic Jihad, and Hamas," *Justice*, Volume 5, May, 1995.

11. *Al-Hayat*, December 12, 1994; *Al-Wassat*, December 12, 1994.

12. Radio Nur, December 11, 1994; Iranian TV, November 23, 1994; Associated Press, November 11, 1994.

13. US Department of State, "Patterns of Global Terrorism, 1994," Washington, GPO, April, 1995, pp. 15, 18–19.

14. US Department of State, "Patterns of Global Terrorism, 1994," Washington, GPO, April, 1995, pp. 15, 18–19.

15. US Department of State, "Patterns of Global Terrorism, 1994," Washington, GPO, April, 1995, pp. 17–21 and 20–69; *Washington Post*, November 5, 1995, p. A-33.

16. *Washington Post*, September 26, 1995, p. A-1; *Washington Post*, November 5, 1995, p. A-33; US Department of State, "Patterns of Global Terrorism, 1994," Washington, GPO, April, 1995, pp. 17–21 and 20–69.

17. This analysis is based on US State Department reporting on the Palestinian Authority's compliance with the peace accords in dealing with terrorism.

18. US Department of State, "Patterns of Global Terrorism, 1994," Washington, GPO, April, 1995, pp. 15–19; Executive News, July 13, 1995, 1544.

19. Executive News Service, October 2, 1995, 1147.

20. *Washington Post*, October 17, 1995, p. A-1; *Washington Times*, September 4, 1995, p. A-9.

21. US Department of State 95/06/01 PLO Commitments Compliance Report Bureau of Near Eastern Affairs. PLO Commitments Compliance Report Pursuant to Title VIII of Public Law 101–246, Foreign Relations Authorization Act for Fiscal Year 1990–91, As Amended. This report covers the period from the date of submission of the last PLOCCA report on December 1, 1994, to May 31, 1995. In addition to providing information required by the PLOCCA, this report covers matters that would have been required of a written policy justification under Section 583(b)(1) of the Middle East Peace Facilitation Act, Part E of Title V of Public Law 103–236 (MEPFA). Should the MEPFA be renewed in its current form beyond July 1, 1995, this report will also serve as a written policy justification for using that authority.

22. For a summary of criticism and charges by major Israeli officials, see *Near East Report*, April 24, 1995, p. 54. These criticisms do, however, predate many of the measures taken to strengthen the Palestinian Authority security forces after April, 1995.

23. CIA, *Atlas of the Middle East*, Washington, GPO, January, 1993, pp. 52–53, 62–63.

24. Many of these comments in this section are based on interviews in Gaza, Israel, and Cairo in 1994 and 1995; on detailed security maps of Gaza; and IDF Spokesman, "Gaza-Jericho Agreement: Security Aspects," Tel Aviv, IDF, May, 1994.

25. Based on data released by the International Labor Organization on December 3, 1995, and the data in the CIA, *World Factbook, 1995*, "Gaza." Other sources report an Israeli per capita income of $14,000 and a Gazan per capita income of $1.400 (*New York Times*, November 8, 1995, p. A-19).

26. *New York Times*, February 8, 1995, p. A-19; *Wall Street Journal*, September 26, 1995, p. A-18.

27. Based on data released by the International Labor Organization on December 3, 1995, and the data in the CIA, *World Factbook, 1995*, "Gaza." Other sources report an Israeli per capita income of $14,000 and a Gazan per capita income of $1,400 (*New York Times*, November 8, 1995, p. A-19).

28. Based on the data in the CIA, *World Factbook, 1995*, "Gaza." Other sources report an Israeli per capita income of $14,000 and a Gazan per capita income of $1,400 (*New York Times*, November 8, 1995, p. A-19).

29. Based on the data in the CIA, *World Factbook, 1995*, "Gaza," and *Wall Street Journal*, September 26, 1995, p. A-18. Other sources report an Israeli per capita income of $14,000 and Gazan per capita incomes ranging from $600 to $1,400 (*New York Times*, November 8, 1995, p. A-19; *Washington Times*, July 12, 1995, p. A-18).

30. *Jane's Intelligence Review*, May, 1994, pp. 215–216.

31. Discussions with US and Israeli experts; *Philadelphia Inquirer*, July 28, 1995, p. A-23.

32. Summary text of peace accords, US State Department; Israeli government Internet database, accessed October, 1995; information sheets provided by the Palestinian Authority; *Washington Post*, September 27, 1995, p. A-27; *Jane's Intelligence Review*, February, 1994, pp. 69–70; *Washington Times*, September 28, 1995, p. A-13.

33. Israel has already improved the security of roads inside Gaza and West Bank, and according to one source, it has imported 14,000 low cost Thai workers to replace Palestinian workers. *Middle East Economic Digest*, January 13, 1995, p. 19; *New York Times*, February 8, 1995, p. A-19; *Executive News Service*, December 4, 1995, 1217.

34. *Ha'aretz*, August 23, 1995, and September 13, 1995; *Yediot Ahronont*, August 25, 1995.

35. For detailed complaints about arms smuggling in Gaza and other security problems, see "Peace Watch Report: Weapons Control and the Palestinian Authority," Tel Aviv, Jaffee Center for Strategic Studies, June, 1995.

36. CIA, *Atlas of the Middle East*, Washington, GPO, January, 1993, pp. 52–53, 62–63.

37. Gold, Dore, "Fundamental Factors in a Stabilized Middle East: Security, Territory, and Peace," Washington, JINSA, 1993.

38. Based on the data in the CIA, *World Factbook, 1995*, p. 458. Israel also estimates that 19% of Israel's population, not 17%, is Palestinian.

39. CIA, *World Factbook, 1995*; Clyde Mark, "Palestinians and the Middle East Peace: Issues for the United States," Congressional Research Service, IB92052, December 5, 1994.

40. CIA, *World Factbook, 1995*; Clyde Mark, "Palestinians and the Middle East Peace: Issues for the United States," Congressional Research Service, IB92052, December 5, 1994; *Wall Street Journal*, September 25, 1995, p. A-18; *Washington Times*, August 7, 1995, p. A-11.

41. Executive News, July 17, 1995, 0705; *Christian Science Monitor*, August 3, 1995, p. 6; *Baltimore Sun*, August 25, 1995, p. 6A; *Washington Post*, July 24, 1995, p. A-14, September 10, 1995, p. C-2; *Washington Times*, August 8, 1995, p. A-12. For a discussion of the water issue from a Palestinian perspective, see Center for Policy Analysis on Palestine, *The Water Issue and the Palestinian-Israeli Conflict*, Information Paper No. 2, Washington, Center for Policy Analysis on Palestine, September, 1993.

42. Statistics based on UNRWA data obtained by telephone. For a discussion of the compensation issue, see Center for Policy Analysis on Palestine, *Palestinian Refugee Compensation*, Information Paper No. 3, Washington, Center for Policy Analysis on Palestine, April, 1995. Also see Center for Policy Analysis on Palestine, *Palestinian Refugees: Their Problem and Future*, Information Paper No. 3, Washington, Center for Policy Analysis on Palestine, October, 1994.

43. Gazit, Shlomo, *The Palestinian Refugee Problem, Final Status Issues: Israel-Palestinians*, Study No. 2, Tel Aviv, Jaffee Center for Strategic Studies, 1995, p. 36.

44. Gazit, Shlomo, *The Palestinian Refugee Problem, Final Status Issues: Israel-Palestinians*, Study No. 2, Tel Aviv, Jaffee Center for Strategic Studies, 1995, p. 36.

45. See World Bank, *Integrated Development of the Jordan Rift Valley*, Washington, World Bank, October, 1994; World Bank, *Emergency Assistance Program for the Occupied Territories*, Washington, World Bank, October, 1994; World Bank, *Developing the Occupied Territories: An Investment for Peace*, Washington, World Bank, October, 1994; World Bank, *Peace and the Jordanian Economy*, Washington, World Bank, October, 1994.

46. Statistics based on UNRWA data obtained by telephone. For a discussion of the options from an Israeli perspective, see Shlomo Gazit, *The Palestinian Refugee Problem, Final*

Status Issues: Israel-Palestinians, Study No. 2, Tel Aviv, Jaffee Center for Strategic Studies, 1995.

47. Executive News Service, October 18, 1995, 1430; *Report on Israeli Settlements in the Occupied Territories,* Volume 5, Number 6, November, 1995, p. 3. There are a number of Israeli studies of "adjustments" to the 1967 borders, but they rarely are supported by exact borders and significant demographic details. Discussions with Israeli officials indicate that negotiations are not likely to be based on the assumptions in most such studies, particularly the Allon Plan, and that most such studies will need to be revised as a result of the September, 1995 peace accords. For an excellent Israeli study of the options involved, see Joseph Alpher, *Settlements and Borders,* Tel Aviv, Jaffee Center for Strategic Studies, 1994. There are also a number of good Palestinian studies, including Hisham Sharabi, "Settlements and Peace: The Problem of Jewish Colonization in Palestine," Washington, Center for Policy Analysis on Palestine, July, 1995. Even the most recent of these studies, however, are now dated because of the September, 1995 peace accords.

48. *Washington Times,* October 26, 1995, p. A-17; *Washington Post,* October 25, 1995, p. A-22; New York Times, July 6, 1995, p. A-3; Executive News Service, December 3, 1995, 1433.

49. CIA, *Atlas of the Middle East,* Washington, GPO, January, 1993, pp. 52–53, 62–63.

50. Dore Gold, *Jerusalem,* Tel Aviv, Jaffee Center for Strategic Studies, 1995, p. 7.

51. There are many demographic and historical studies of Jerusalem and a number of studies of options for peace which are referenced in the bibliography. A number of good recent Palestinian studies have been done on this issue, including draft work by Walid Khalidi, a report by Hisham Sharabi, ed. "Settlements and Peace: The Problem of Jewish Colonization in Palestine," Washington, Center for Policy Analysis on Palestine, July, 1995, and Center for Policy Analysis on Palestine, *Jerusalem,* Center for Policy Analysis on Palestine, Washington, February, 1994. There are a number of excellent Israeli studies as well. Two of the best recent studies are Dore Gold, *Jerusalem,* Tel Aviv, Jaffee Center for Strategic Studies, 1995, and Moshe Hirsch, Deborah Housen-Couriel, and Ruth Lapidoth, *Whither Jerusalem?,* London, Martinus Nijhoff, 1995.

52. Prime Minister Rabin made these points several times before his assassination. They were repeated afterward by Shimon Peres and his new foreign minister Ehud Barak, and Yossi Belin, a normally "dovish" minister in Peres's office. See Executive News Service, November 28, 1995, 0419.

53. Summary text of peace accords, US State Department; Israeli government Internet database, accessed October, 1995; information sheets provided by the Palestinian Authority; *Washington Post,* September 27, 1995, p. A-27.

54. Summary text of peace accords, US State Department; Israeli government Internet database, accessed October, 1995; information sheets provided by the Palestinian Authority; *Washington Post,* September 27, 1995, p. A-27; *Christian Science Monitor,* January 18, 1995, p. 19.

55. Summary text of peace accords, US State Department; Israeli government Internet database, accessed October, 1995; information sheets provided by the Palestinian Authority; *Washington Post,* September 27, 1995, p. A-27.

56. Executive News Service, December 4, 1995, 0755.

57. Summary text of peace accords, US State Department; Israeli government Internet database, accessed October, 1995; information sheets provided by the Palestinian Author-

ity; *Washington Post*, September 27, 1995, p. A-27. Also see *The Estimate*, October 13–26, 1995, pp. 5–8.

58. *Washington Post*, April 28, 1995.

59. *Washington Post*, October 17, 1995, p. A-1, October 26, 1995, p. A-20.

60. Executive News Service, October 19, 1995, 1507, November 11, 1995, 1632.

61. Heath Minister Ephraiam Sneh admitted Israel's role in killing a leader of Islamic Jihad in an interview on November 2, 1995, but retracted his remarks. Executive News Service, October 29, 1995, 1431, November 2, 1995, 0704.

62. US State Department, *Country Reports on Human Rights, 1995*, Internet version, accessed October 31, 1995.

63. For Palestinian criticism of Israeli security operations, see Center for Policy Analysis on Palestine, *Targeting to Kill: Israel's Undercover Units*, Center for Policy Analysis on Palestine, Washington, May, 1992, and Center for Policy Analysis on Palestine, *Palestinian Human Rights Under Israeli Rule*, Center for Policy Analysis on Palestine, Washington, May, 1993.

64. Executive News Service, June 28, 1995, 1240; *Philadelphia Inquirer*, June 28, 1995, 1240; September 13, 1995, p. A-1; *Baltimore Sun*, September 9, 1995, p. 4A; *Washington Post*, September 9, 1995, p. A-19.

65. Many of these comments in this section are based on interviews in the West Bank and Jericho, Israel, and Cairo in 1994 and 1995.

66. *Ha'aretz*, August 23, 1995, and September 12, 1995.

67. *Yedit Ahronot*, August 25, 1995.

68. Estimates vary from 68% to 73%. *Christian Science Monitor*, October 17, 1995, p. A-20; *Peacewatch*, October 5, 1995, p. 1.

69. *Christian Science Monitor*, September 20, 1995, p. 6.

70. For detailed descriptions of the IDF's past adaptations in dealing with similar challenges during the Intifada, see Anthony H. Cordesman, *After the Storm*, Boulder, Westview, 1993, and Stuart A. Cohen, "How Did the Intifada Affect the IDF?" *Conflict Quarterly*, Vol. 14. No. 3 (Summer 1994).

71. *Washington Times*, May 16, 1995, p. A-11; *Wall Street Journal*, April 25, 1995, p. A-16.

Chapter Seven

1. Based on data in the relevant country section of the IISS, *Military Balance, 1995–1996*. Estimates in other sources differ.

2. UPI, November 5, 1992, BC cycle.

3. *Jane's Defense Weekly*, July 1, 1995, p. 13; Syrian *Official Gazette*, June 6, 1995.

4. *New York Times*, April 29, 1994, p. A-7; *Middle East Economic Digest MEED)*, December 9, 1994, NEXIS edition; *Defense News*, July 4, 1994, p. 15.

5. "The IDF's Security Principles," Office of the IDF Spokesman, April, 1995, and Scotty Fisher, "Country Briefing Israel," *Jane's Defense Weekly*, February 18, 1995, pp. 29–38.

6. "The IDF's Security Principles," Office of the IDF Spokesman, April, 1995, and Scotty Fisher, "Country Briefing Israel," *Jane's Defense Weekly*, February 18, 1995, pp. 29–38.

7. Based on data in the relevant country section of the IISS, *Military Balance, 1995–1996*. Estimates in other sources differ.

8. *Defense News*, January 11, 1993; Agence France Presse, June 1, 1993; *International Defense Review*, March, 1994, pp. 27–28.

9. *Middle East Economic Digest MEED)*, December 9, 1994, NEXIS edition; *Jane's Defense Weekly*, October 10, 1992, p. 7; *Defense Electronics and Computing*, 10/1992, p. 1035; *International Defense Review*, 10/1994, p. 6.

10. For more detail on this contingency, see the author's *After the Storm*, Boulder, Westview, 1993, and Edward B. Atkeson, "The Syrian-Israeli Military Balance: A Pot That Bears Watching," Arlington, Institute of Land Warfare, Paper No. 10, January, 1992.

11. CIA, *Atlas of the Middle East*, Washington, GPO, January, 1993, pp. 52–53, 62–63.

12. Based on the data in the CIA, *World Factbook, 1995*, "Syria." For a good summary analysis of the location and population of Israeli settlements and related security issues, see "Report on Israeli Settlements in the Occupied Territories: A Golan Heights Primer," Washington, Foundation for Middle East Peace, February, 1995. Extensive additional data are available from the Israeli government and Golani web servers on the Internet.

13. Washington Institute, *Supporting Peace*, Washington, Washington Institute, 1994, pp. 9–12, 79–82; Aryeh Shalev, *Israel and Syria, Peace and Security on the Golan*, Boulder, Westview, 1994.

14. *Jane's Defense Weekly*, April 22, 1995, p. 24; W. Seth Carus and Hirsh Goodman, *The Future Battlefield and the Arab-Israeli Conflict*, London, Transaction Press, 1990, pp. 64–176.

15. Washington Institute, *Supporting Peace*, Washington, Washington Institute, 1994, p. 83.

16. UPI, August 3, 1993.

17. Kenneth S. Brower, "The Middle East Military Balance: Israel Versus the Rest," *International Defense Review*, 7/1986, pp. 910–911.

18. For more detail on this contingency, see the author's *After the Storm*, Boulder, Westview, 1993, and Edward B. Atkeson, "The Syrian-Israeli Military Balance: A Pot That Bears Watching," Arlington, Institute of Land Warfare, Paper No. 10, January, 1992.

19. Some systems can fire rounds longer range, but not accurately. Syria's S-23 guns are its only long range weapons with effective ranges beyond 28 kilometers and they have been in storage for several years.

20. Interviews, *Boston Globe*, June 23, 1995, p. 14; *Los Angeles Times*, May 2, 1994, p. A-4; *Washington Post*, May 3, 1995, p. A-15, May 16, 1995, p. A-7, May 25, 1995, p. A-23; *New York Times*, May 16, 1995, p. A-6, May 25, 1995, p. A-1, May 26, 1995, p. A-2.

21. The Washington Institute, *Policywatch*, No. 117, October 27, 1995; *Christian Science Monitor*, September 28, 1995, p. 6; *Executive News*, October 11, 1995, 0604, October 15, 1995, 0629; *Armed Forces Journal*, October, 1995, p. 15.

22. Executive News Service, November 28, 1995, 0859, 1614.

23. *New York Times*, May 16, 1995, p. A-6, May 25, 1995, p. A-1; *Washington Post*, May 25, 1995, p. A-23.

24. A comprehensive discussion of the technical issues involved require a detailed knowledge of Israeli intelligence sources and methods that is not available to the author. For another view, see Aryeh Shalev, *Israel and Syria, Peace and Security on the Golan*, Boulder, Westview, 1994, pp. 128–139.

25. Israel launched the Ofeq 1 prototype on September 19, 1988. It has a satellite mass of 156 kilograms. It sent up the Ofeq 2 on April 3, 1990, one day after Saddam Hussein threatened to destroy half of Israel with chemical weapons if Israel attacked Baghdad. The Ofeq satellite has a mass of 160 kilograms. *Washington Post*, April 6, 1995, p. 1; *Jane's Intelligence Review*, Volume 7, Number 6, June, 1995, pp. 265–268; *Washington Post*, April 6, 1995, p. 1.

26. For more detail on this contingency, see the author's *After the Storm*, Boulder, Westview, 1993, and Edward B. Atkeson, "The Syrian-Israeli Military Balance: A Pot That Bears Watching," Arlington, Institute of Land Warfare, Paper No. 10, January, 1992.

27. For a discussion of the Syrian military operation that took control of Lebanon, see John Laffin, *The World in Conflict, War Annual 6*, London, Brassey's, 1995, pp. 133–144.

28. *Christian Science Monitor*, September 28, 1995, p. 7; *Middle East Economic Digest*, October 27, 1995, pp. 2–3.

29. *Christian Science Monitor*, October 16, 1995, p. 7; *Baltimore Sun*, October 12, 1995, p. 4; *Middle East Economic Digest*, September 29, 1995, p. 21, October 27, 1995, pp. 2–3; *Washington Post*, October 16, 1995, p. A-1; *New York Times*, October 16, 1995, p. A-1.

30. *Middle East Economic Digest*, September 29, 1995, p. 21.

31. *Washington Post*, December 20, 1994, p. A-30.

32. Washington Institute, *Supporting Peace*, Washington, Washington Institute, 1994, p. 83.

33. The basic salary of Hizbollah fighters seems to have been cut from $300 to $175 per month, and "Islamist" subsidies, like a $100 a month payment to women for wearing the chador, have been largely eliminated. *Washington Post*, December 20, 1994, p. A-30.

34. *Washington Post*, October 16, 1995, p. A-1; *New York Times*, October 16, 1995, p. A-1.

35. For example, an ambush that killed six Israeli soldiers on October 15, 1995. *Washington Times*, October 16, 1995, p. A-1; Executive News Service, October 14, 1995, 0556, October 16, 1995, 1654; *Washington Post*, October 16, 1995, p. A-1; *New York Times*, October 16, 1995, p. A-1.

36. For example, Hizbollah rocket attacks on Qiryat Shemona and other settlements on November 28, 1995, after clashes that killed three members of the Hizbollah. *New York Times*, November 29, 1995, p. A-6; *Washington Post*, November 29, 1995, p. A-1.

37. Interviews, *Boston Globe*, October 27, 1995, p. 2; *New York Times*, October 22, 1995, p. E-14; *Christian Science Monitor*, October 23, 1995, p. 19.

38. For further details, see Clyde R. Mark, "Lebanon," IB89118, Washington, Congressional Research Service, November 14, 1995.

Chapter Eight

1. *Defense News*, December 12, 1994, p. 3; March 8, 1993, p. 1.

2. *Washington Post*, August 16, 1995, p. A-26.

3. Based largely on data in the relevant country section of the IISS, *Military Balance, 1995–1996*. Estimates in other sources differ.

4. Based largely on data in the relevant country section of the IISS, *Military Balance, 1995–1996*. Estimates in other sources differ.

5. Based largely on data in the relevant country section of the IISS, *Military Balance, 1995–1996*. Estimates in other sources differ.

6. *Defense News*, December 12, 1994, p. 3; March 8, 1993, p. 1.

7. *Defense News*, December 12, 1994, p. 3; March 8, 1993, p. 1; November 7, 1994, p. 1, November 29, 1993, p. 1.

8. Press Association Newsfile, July 7, 1993; *The Independent*, June 23, 1993; *Washington Times*, June 17, 1993.

Chapter Ten

1. Based largely on data in the relevant country section of the IISS, *Military Balance, 1995–1996*. Estimates in other sources differ.

2. Based largely on data in the relevant country section of the IISS, *Military Balance, 1995–1996*. Estimates in other sources differ.

3. *Jerusalem Post Magazine*, March 11, 1994, p. 7; *Defense News*, May 9, 1994, May 16, 1994, p. 1, June 20, 1994, p. 54; *Jane's Defense Weekly*, December 17, 1994, p. 6; *Defense Daily*, December 1, 1994, p. 295.

4. Based largely on data in the relevant country section of the IISS, *Military Balance, 1995–1996*. Estimates in other sources differ.

5. Based largely on data in the relevant country section of the IISS, *Military Balance, 1995–1996*. Estimates in other sources differ.

6. Based largely on data in the relevant country section of the IISS, *Military Balance, 1995–1996*. Estimates in other sources differ.

7. This summary is adapted from work by Aryeh Shalev in *Israel and Syria: Peace and Security on the Golan*, JCSS Study No. 24, Tel Aviv, 1994, pp. 173–177.

8. The technical history of the MFO can be traced through the annual reports of the US State Department and through the annual reports to Congress by the General Accounting Office (*Assessment of US Participation in the Multinational Force and Observers*).

9. The author examined both Egyptian and Israeli complaints about such violations in some depth in discussions with Egyptian and Israeli officials. These violations are not normally reported publicly in detail, but they are largely technical in character and have had little—if any—strategic significance.

Chapter Twelve

1. IISS, *Military Balance, 1995–1996*. Some estimates show totals for the Gendarmerie alone. This is incorrect. They have been merged with the national police and some elements of the internal security forces.

2. *New York Times*, May 17, 1995, p. A-3.

3. For a detailed discussion, see Anthony H. Cordesman, *The Threat from the Northern Gulf*, Boulder, Westview, 1994; and Dr. Andrew Rathmell, "Iraq—The Endgame?" *Jane's Intelligence Review*, Volume 7, Number 5, pp. 224–228.

Chapter Thirteen

1. A detailed description of Israel's nuclear and missile effort accompanied by satellite photos is provided in Harold Hough, "Israel's Nuclear Infrastructure," *Jane's Intelligence Weekly*, November, 1994, pp. 505–511. Also see *Chicago Sun-Times*, July 7, 1993, p. 29; *Washington Times*, June 27, 1994, p. A-15; *Sunday Times*, October 5, 1986, pp. 1–3, and October 12, 1986, pp. 1 and 12; Barnaby, *The Invisible Bomb*, London, I. B. Taurus, 1989, pp. 25 and 31; *Science*, March 22, 1974, p. 15; *Washington Times*, October 6, 1986; *Boston Globe*, October 14, 1986; *New York Times*, October 27, 1986; *Washington Post*, October 31, 1986. Recent BBC and ITV reporting efforts seem to give more credibility to the idea that Israel has some form of relatively short range nuclear armed missile. Ranges of anywhere

from 75–930 nautical miles have been reported for the Jericho, with accuracies of anywhere from 0.1 Kilometer to radar correlator guidance packages capable of CEPs of 100 meters.

2. Some US experts like Theodore Taylor speculate that Israel has the technology to build plutonium weapons using only 8.8 pounds (4 kilograms) of material versus the 16–18 pounds normally used to calculate the amount required per weapon. Other work by Frank Barnaby indicates that Israel may have at least 35 weapons with yields boosted up to 100 kilotons or more. Such high yield weapons would largely remove the need for thermonuclear weapons—since Israeli missiles almost certainly have CEPs good enough to hit any regional target close enough to destroy it with such yields, and there are no targets hardened enough to survive such blasts. (Based on work by Leonard Spector; *Sunday Times*, October 5, 1986, pp. 1–3 and October 12, 1986, pp. 1 and 12; *Washington Times*, October 6, 1986; *Boston Globe*, October 14, 1986; *New York Times*, October 27, 1986; and *Washington Post*, October 31, 1986.)

3. *Washington Times*, November 3, 1989, p. A-6.

4. Leonard S. Spector, Mark G. McDonough, and Evan S. Medeiros, *Tracking Nuclear Proliferation*, Washington, Carnegie Endowment, 1995, pp. 135–139. Israel also acquired Meiko Scientific Supercomputers in December, 1992. These supercomputers are sometimes associated with thermonuclear weapons and missile trajectory analysis. While such systems might be an aid to creating such weapons, Israel's existing mini-computers have long been adequate. There is also little incentive to use thermonuclear weapons with accurate IRBMs or in bombs because they consume added material, are more complex, and boosted weapons are adequate to destroy virtually any regional target. *New York Times*, January 9, 1992, p. D-1.

5. Leonard S. Spector, Mark G. McDonough, and Evan S. Medeiros, *Tracking Nuclear Proliferation*, Washington, Carnegie Endowment, 1995, pp. 135–139; *Nucleonics Week*, January 6, 1994, p. 18, February 24, 1994, p. 15.

6. Enhanced radiation or neutron weapons maximize radiation at the expense of blast and do less physical damage, although they still produce large amounts of blast and thermal energy. Enhanced yield weapons boost a nuclear explosion to yields in excess of 100 kilotons and largely eliminate the need for thermonuclear weapons with highly accurate systems. Thermonuclear weapons allow explosions in excess of 25 megatons.

7. Anthony H. Cordesman and Abraham R. Wagner, *The Lessons of Modern War*, Volume 1, Boulder, Westview, 1990, pp. 244–246; *Jane's Defense Weekly*, August 8, 1987, p. 21.

8. For recent reporting on the Israeli nuclear effort, see the *Sunday Times*, October 5, 1986; *Washington Times*, October 6, 1986; *Boston Globe*, October 14, 1986; *New York Times*, October 27, 1986; and *Washington Post*, October 31, 1986.

9. Other reports indicate that the Jericho surface-to-surface missile had a range of up to 300 miles and a 1,000–1,500 pound warhead. Other reports indicate that it could reach a 400 mile range with 226 pound (100 kilogram) nuclear warhead. Data published by Iran after the seizure of the US Embassy in Tehran claimed to have found evidence that Israel was giving Iran missile technology in return for oil and had tested new guidance systems in flights in Iran. *Aerospace Daily*, May 1, 1985, May 7, 1985; Shuey et al., *Missile Proliferation: Survey of Emerging Missile Forces*, p. 56; *International Defense Review*, July, 1987, p. 857; *Defense and Foreign Affairs Daily*, May 9, 1985, pp. 1–2; CIA, "Prospects for Further Proliferation of Nuclear Weapons," DCI NIO 1945/74, September 4, 1974; NBC Nightly News, July 30, 1985; *New York Times*, April 1, 1986; US Arms Control and Disarmament Agency,

World Military Expenditures and Arms Transfers, Washington, GPO, 1989, p. 18; *Jane's Defense Weekly*, November 25, 1989, p. 1143.

10. It is also possible that Israel may have deployed nuclear warheads for its MGM-55C Lance missiles. Israel has 12 Lance transporter-erector-launchers and at least 36 missiles. The Lance is a stored liquid fueled missile with inertial guidance and a range of 5–125 kilometers. It has a warhead weight of 251 kilograms and a CEP of 375 meters. It was deployed in US forces with the W-70 nuclear warhead. *International Defense Review*, 7/1987, p. 857; *Economist*, May 4, 1968, pp. 67–68; *New York Times*, July 22, 1987, p. A-6; *Washington Times*, July 22, 1987, p. D-4; *Defense and Foreign Affairs*, June, 1985, p. 1; *Aerospace Daily*, May 1, 1985, p. 5 and May 17, 1985, p. 100; *Aerospace Daily*, May 1, 1985, May 7, 1985; Shuey et al., *Missile Proliferation: Survey of Emerging Missile Forces*, p. 56; CIA, "Prospects for Further Proliferation of Nuclear Weapons," DCI NIO 1945/74, September 4, 1974; NBC Nightly News, July 30, 1985; *New York Times*, April 1, 1986; US Arms Control and Disarmament Agency, *World Military Expenditures and Arms Transfers*, Washington, GPO, 1989, p. 18; Michael A. Ottenberg, "Israel and the Atom," *American Sentinel*, August 16, 1992, p. 1.

11. *Jane's Defense Weekly*, June 10, 1989, p. 1135.

12. Tass International, 1216 GMT, September 15, 1989; *Washington Post*, September 16, 1989; *Jane's Defense Weekly*, November 19, 1988, September 23, 1989, p. 549; *Washington Times*, July 22, 1987, p. D-4; *International Defense Review*, 7/1987, p. 857; *New York Times*, July 22, 1987, p. A-6, July 29, 1987; *Mideast Markets*, November 23, 1987, p. 11; Harold Hough, "Israel's Nuclear Infrastructure," *Jane's Intelligence Weekly*, November, 1994, pp. 505–511.

13. *Baltimore Sun*, November 23, 1988; *Washington Post*, September 16, 1989.

14. BBC and ITV reporting efforts seem to give more credibility to the idea that Israel has some form of relatively short range nuclear armed missile. Ranges of anywhere from 750–930 nautical miles have been reported, with accuracies of anywhere from 0.1 Kilometer to radar correlator guidance packages capable of CEPs of 100 meters. *Bulletin of Atomic Scientists*, Vol. 46, January/February 1990, p. 48; *Washington Post*, September 16, 1989, p. A-17, November 15, 1989, p. A-14; *Economist*, August 1, 1987, p. 41; Washington Times, July 22, 1987, p. D-4, July 24, 1987, p. A-9, and April 4, 1988, p. 17; *International Defense Review*, 7/1987, p. 857; *New York Times*, July 29, 1987, p. A-10.

15. *Washington Post*, October 26, 1989, p. A-36; *Boston Globe*, October 30, 1989, p. 2; *Newsweek*, November 6, 1989, p. 52.

16. Some experts also feel that Israel deployed large numbers of nuclear artillery rounds after the 1973 war, including rounds for its 175 mm and 203 mm weapons. A few experts feel such rounds include enhanced radiation variants. Such capabilities are very controversial, but they would give Israel the ability to use low yield weapons against Syrian and other Arab armor and artillery formations at ranges of 18–29 kilometers, and could stop massed army formations as long as they remained as much as 12 kilometers from Israeli army formations or civilians. *Jane's Defense Weekly*, July 15, 1989, p. 59 and December 23, 1989, p. 1385; Johannesburg Domestic Service, 1600 GMT, July 5, 1989; *Boston Globe*, October 27, 1989; Fred Francis, NBC Nightly News, October 25 and 26, 1989; *New York Times*, October 27, 1989, p. A-1, November 15, 1989; *Newsweek*, November 6, 1989, p. 52; *Washington Times*, June 20, 1989, p. A-1; *Washington Post*, October 27, 1989, p. A-1, October 29, 1989; Michael A. Ottenberg, "Israel and the Atom," *American Sentinel*, August 16, 1992, p. 1.

17. This information is unconfirmed and based on only one source. Israel does, however, have excellent research facilities; laboratory production of poison gas is essential to

test protection devices, as is the production of biological weapons to test countermeasures and antidotes.

18. *Washington Post*, April 6, 1995, p. 1.

19. *Jane's Defense Weekly*, May 6, 1995, p. 15; *Aviation Week*, June 21, 1993, p. 39.

20. Michael Eisenstadt, "Syria's Strategic Weapons," *Jane's Intelligence Review*, April, 1993, pp. 168–171; Agence French Presse, computer printout, February 10, 1992; *Christian Science Monitor*, March 10, 1992, p. 1; *Washington Post*, December 7, 1991, p. A-26, February 11, 1992, p. A-16; *Daily Telegraph*, November 23, 1991, p. 10; *London Financial Times*, March 27, 1992, p. 4; *Washington Times*, November 24, 1991, p. A-17.

21. J. M. Moreaux, "The Syrian Army," *Defense Update*, No. 69, p. 31.

22. *Baltimore Sun*, October 24, 1995, p. 1A.

23. The analysis in this section is based largely on various interviews. Also see *Jane's Defense Weekly*, July 26, 1986, p. 92, April 2, 1988, p. 613, April 30, 1988, p. 853; *Washington Post*, June 23, 1988, p. 33, September 7, 1988, p. A-25; *Los Angeles Times*, July 14, 1988, p. I-1; *Washington Times*, September 18, 1987, p. 2; *New York Times*, June 22, 1988, p. A-6.

24. *London Sunday Times*, January 10, 1988, p. 1; *Washington Times*, April 8, 1988, p. 9, January 11, 1988, p. 1; *Los Angeles Times*, January 14, 1988, p. 13.

25. Syrian units deploy as close as 10 kilometers from the front line versus 20–25 kilometers for Soviet units.

26. The FROG with a VX chemical warhead carried much less agent. The Soviet version is 540 mm in diameter and weighs about 960 pounds, of which 475 is VX agent. The FROG with a chemical warhead has a maximum range of 40 miles versus 190 miles for the Scud. Michael Eisenstadt, "Syria's Strategic Weapons," *Jane's Intelligence Review*, April, 1993, pp. 168–171; Shuey, Lenhart, Snyder, Donnelly, Mielke, and Moteff, *Missile Proliferation: Survey of Emerging Missile Forces*; Washington, DC, Congressional Research Service, Report 88-642F, February 9, 1989, pp. 34–35; *Jane's Defense Weekly*, February 27, 1988, pp. 370–371; Defense Intelligence Agency, "Soviet Chemical Weapons Threat," DST-1620F-051-85, 1985, p. 8.

27. *New York Times*, June 6, 1986, p. 11; *Washington Post*, June 11, 1986, p. 36; *Defense Week*, April 14, 1986, p. 5; Michael Eisenstadt, "Syria's Strategic Weapons," *Jane's Intelligence Review*, April, 1993, pp. 168–171.

28. *Jane's Defense Weekly*, July 26, 1982, p. 92.

29. Although various other press reports have appeared at different times that Syria has established an SS-23 site, had a brigade of SS-23s, and even had deployed the SS-25, none of these reports are true. See J. M. Moreaux, "The Syrian Army," *Defense Update*, No. 69, p. 31.

30. *The Sunday Correspondent*, October 15, 1989, p. 3; *Al-Ittihad*, July 31, 1989, p. 1; Hong Kong AFP, 0629 GMT, August 7, 1989.

31. *Washington Post*, March 30, 1990, p. 1; *Washington Times*, November 22, 1989; *Defense and Foreign Affairs*, August 14–20, 1989, p. 2.

32. *Jane's Defense Weekly*, December 23, 1989, pp. 1384–1385; *Washington Post*, June 23, 1988, p. A-2, March 29, 1990, pp. A-1 and A-34; *New York Times International*, March 30, 1990, p. A-7; *New York Times*, June 22, 1988, p. 1, January 31, 1992, p. A-1.

33. *Wall Street Journal*, July 10, 1991, p. 12; *Washington Times*, March 10, 1992, p. A-3, March 11, 1992, p. A-3, July 16, 1992, p. A-3; *Time*, March 23, 1992, p. 34; *Washington Post*, February 22, 1992, p. A-15, March 11, 1992, p. A-11, March 13, 1992, p. A-18, July 14, 1992, p. A-1, August 14, 1992, p. A-25; *New York Times*, January 31, 1992, p. A-1, February 21, 1992, p. A-9; *Sunday Times*, December 21, 1991, p. 1.

34. *Defense News*, October 16, 1989, p. 60; *Washington Times*, June 18, 1990, p. A-1; Lora Lumpe, Lisbeth Gronlund, and David C. Wright, "Third World Missiles Fall Short," *The Bulletin of the Atomic Scientists*, March, 1992, pp. 30–36.

35. Michael Eisenstadt, "Syria's Strategic Weapons," *Jane's Intelligence Review*, April, 1993, pp. 168–171.

36. Interviews in Israel, January, 1992 and 1994.

37. The following analysis involves considerable technical speculation by the author. It is based on various Jane's publications and General Dynamics, *The World's Missile Systems*, Pomona, General Dynamics, 8th Edition, 1988.

38. Adapted by the author from various editions of Jane's and Ray Bonds, *Modern Soviet Weapons*, New York, ARCO, 1986, pp. 432–435.

39. *Jane's Defense Weekly*, March 12, 1988, pp. 462–463.

40. *Atlanta Constitution*, October 5, 1988, p. 17A.

41. *London Financial Times*, December 21, 1987, p. 1; June 8, 1988, pp. 20, 38.

42. *Jane's Defense Weekly*, December 16, 1989; *Defense Electronics*, August, 1988, pp. 17, 20; *La Nacion*, July 4, 1988; *Economist*, May 4, 1988, pp. 67–68; *Defense and Foreign Affairs*, June, 1985, p. 1; *Defense and Foreign Affairs Daily*, May 9, 1985, pp. 1–2; *International Defense Review*, July, 1987, p. 857; *New York Times*, July 22, 1987, p. A-6; *Washington Times*, July 22, 1987, p. D-4.

43. For a good summary report, see *Jane's Defense Weekly*, February 17, 1990, p. 295. Also see *Financial Times*, November 21, 1989, p. 1; *Washington Post*, September 20, 1989.

44. *London Financial Times*, December 21, 1987, p. 1; June 8, 1988, pp. 20, 38.

45. The US also detected Egyptian efforts to build additional types of missiles. In 1987 and 1988, Egypt became involved in an attempt to smuggle missile equipment out of the US in a complex operation involving front organizations like the IFAT Corporation of Zug, Switzerland. As a result, the US arrested two Egyptian military officers based at the Egyptian Embassy in Washington on June 23, 1988. They were arrested for conspiring with an Egyptian-born rocket scientist called Abdelkadr Helmy and other Egyptian agents, to export 32 tons of rocket fuel chemicals, 432 pounds of carbon fiber materials for nose cones and rocket motor nozzles, propulsion hardware, telemetry tracking equipment, equipment and materials for making rocket motor casings, and missile assembly plans for the Pershing II missile. These missile plans had been obtained from Messerschmidt in Germany and an Italian firm. The material was carbon-phenolic fabric which is used to make rocket nozzles and rocket heat shields. Helmy received at least $1 million from Egyptian sources to purchase the carbon fabric and other missile components. *Washington Post*, August 20, 1988, p. A-1, April 1, 1989, p. A-15, April 16, 1989, p. A-29; *New York Times*, March 10, 1989, p. A-1, June 11, 1989, p. 6, June 25, 1988, p. 1; *Los Angeles Times*, June 10, 1989, p. 10; *Washington Times*, April 17, 1989, p. A-8, *London Financial Times*, April 18, 1989, p. 5; *Wall Street Journal*, April 4, 1989, p. A-1; *Philadelphia Inquirer*, March 11, 1989, p. 9-A.

46. Abdel Darwish, "China to Update Egypt's Missiles," *The Independent* (UK), June 14, 1990, p. 2.

47. *Al-Ahram*, July 25, 1975; *Al-Akhbar*, July 25, 1975.

48. The results of these orders are uncertain, and there are no confirmed reports of actual production. *Washington Post*, August 20, 1988, p. A-1; *New York Times*, June 25, 1988, p. 1.

49. *Washington Post*, April 1, 1989, p. A-15, April 16, 1989, p. A-29; *Washington Times*, April 17, 1989, p. A-8; *London Financial Times*, April 18, 1989, p. 5; *Wall Street Journal*,

April 4, 1989, p. A-1; *Philadelphia Inquirer*, March 11, 1989, p. 9-A; *New York Times*, March 10, 1989, p. A-1.

50. Leonard S. Spector, Mark G. McDonough, and Evan S. Medeiros, *Tracking Nuclear Proliferation*, Washington, Carnegie Endowment, 1995, pp. 119–123.

51. *Washington Post*, May 17, 1995, p. A-23; *New York Times*, May 19, 1995, p. A-1; Leonard S. Spector, Mark G. McDonough, and Evan S. Medeiros, *Tracking Nuclear Proliferation*, Washington, Carnegie Endowment, 1995, pp. 119–123.

52. Leonard S. Spector, Mark G. McDonough, and Evan S. Medeiros, *Tracking Nuclear Proliferation*, Washington, Carnegie Endowment, 1995, pp. 119–123.

53. *New York Times*, February 23, 1995, May 18, 1995, p. A-11; *Washington Post*, May 8, 1995, p. A-22; *Nucleonics Week*, February 13, 1992, p. 12, October 14, 1993, p. 9, December 16, 1993, p. 11, September 22, 1994, p. 1, October 6, 1994, p. 11; *Washington Post*, February 14, 1992, February 12, 1995; *Nuclear Fuel*, March 14, 1994, p. 9, March 28, 1994, p. 10; *Nuclear Engineering*, April, 1992, p. 67, November, 1994, pp. 4, 10; UPI, November 21, 1994; Reuters, November 20, 1994.

54. According to one report by Zalmay Khalizad in *Survival*, Pakistan was deeply involved in this $10 billion effort, as was China. US experts do not confirm these reports. *Washington Post*, May 17, 1995, p. A-23.

55. *Washington Times*, May 17, 1995, p. A-15.

56. See Anthony H. Cordesman and Abraham R. Wagner, *The Lessons of Modern War*, Volume IV, Boulder, Westview, 1995, Chapter 11; Dr. Andrew Rathmell, "Iraq—The Endgame?" *Jane's Intelligence Review*, Volume 7, Number 5, pp. 224–228; and Leonard S. Spector, Mark G. McDonough, and Evan S. Medeiros, *Tracking Nuclear Proliferation*, Washington, Carnegie Endowment, 1995, pp. 119–123.

Chapter Fourteen

1. The figures cited are based on work published by ACDA and Richard F. Grimmett, updated on the basis of discussion with US government experts.

2. The figures cited are based on work published by ACDA and Richard F. Grimmett, updated on the basis of discussion with US government experts.

3. The figures cited are based on work published by ACDA and Richard F. Grimmett, updated on the basis of discussion with US government experts.

4. The figures cited are based on work published by ACDA and Richard F. Grimmett, updated on the basis of discussion with US government experts.

5. The figures cited are based on work published by ACDA and Richard F. Grimmett, updated on the basis of discussion with US government experts.

6. ACDA, *World Military Expenditures and Arms Transfers, 1993–1994*, Table I.

7. The figures cited are based on work published by ACDA and Richard F. Grimmett, updated on the basis of discussion with US government experts.

Bibliography

Abdelnour, Ziad K., "Lebanon: Israel's True Partner?" *Middle East Quarterly*, Vol. 2, No. 2, June, 1995, pp. 39–44.

Adan, Avrahham (Bren), *On the Banks of the Suez*, San Francisco, Presidio, 1980.

Aerospace Daily, various editions.

Air Force, various editions.

Ajami, Fouad, "The Sorrows of Egypt," *Foreign Affairs*, September-October, 1995, pp. 72–88.

Alpher, Joseph, "Israel: Security After Oslo," *International Affairs*, Vol. 70, No. 2, April, 1994, pp. 229–242.

————, *Settlements and Borders, Final Status—Israel—Palestinians, Study No. 3*, Tel Aviv, JCSS, 1994.

Armed Forces Journal International, various editions.

al-Asad, Hafiz, "Interview with Syrian President Hafiz al-Asad," *Journal of Palestine Studies*, Summer, 1993, 111–121.

Asher, Jerry, and Eric Hammel, *Duel for the Golan*, New York, Morrow, 1987.

Atkeson, Edward B., "The Syrian-Israeli Military Balance: A Pot That Bears Watching," Arlington, Institute of Land Warfare, Paper No. 10, January, 1992.

Aviation Week and Space Technology, various editions.

Badri, Magdoub, and Zohdy, *The Ramadan War, 1973*, New York, Hippocrene, 1974.

Bailey, Clinton, *Jordan's Palestinian Challenge, 1948–1983*, Westview, Boulder, 1984.

Baker, A. D., III ed., *Combat Fleets of the World, Their Ships, Aircraft, and Armament*, Annapolis, Naval Institute Press.

Barker, A. J., *Arab-Israeli Wars*, New York, Hippocrene, 1980.

Barnaby, Frank, *The Invisible Bomb*, London, I. B. Taurus, 1989.

Bass, Gail, and Bonnie Jean Cordes, *Actions Against Non-Nuclear Energy Facilities: September 1981–September 1982*, Santa Monica, Calif., Rand Corporation, April, 1983.

Beit-Hallahmi, Benjamin, *The Israeli Connection: Who Arms Israel and Why*, New York, Pantheon, 1987.

Belyakov, Rostislav, and Nikolai Buntin, "The MiG 29M Light Multirole Fighter," *Military Technology*, 8/94, pp. 41–44.

Ben Horin, Yoav, and Barry Posen, *Israel's Strategic Doctrine*, Santa Monica, Calif., Rand Corporation, September, 1981.

Ben Porat and others, *Kippur, Special Edition*, Tel Aviv, 1973.

Ben-Meir, Alon, "The Israeli-Syrian Battle for Equitable Peace," *Middle East Policy*, Vol. 3, No. 1, 1994, pp. 70–83.

Beres, Louis Rene, *Security or Armageddon*, Lexington, Lexington Books, 1986.

Beres, Rene, "After the Gulf War: Israel, Palestine, and the Risk of Nuclear War in the Middle East," *Strategic Review*, Fall, 1991, pp. 48–55.

Berger, Marshall, "The New Battle for Jerusalem," *Middle East Quarterly*, Vol. 1, No. 4, December, 1994, pp. 23–34.

Bitzinger, Richard, "The Globalization of the Arms Industry," *Foreign Policy*, Summer, 1995, pp. 170–182.

Blechman, Barry M., and Stephan S. Kaplan, *Force Without War*, Washington, D.C., Brookings Institution, 1978.

Bonds, Ray, *Modern Soviet Weapons*, New York, ARCO, 1986, pp. 432–435.

Bowen, David, and Laura Drake, "The Syrian-Israeli Border Conflict, 1949–1967," *The Middle East*, Vol. 1, No. 4, 1992, pp. 17–28.

Bulletin of Atomic Scientists, various editions.

Carus, W. Seth, "The Genie Unleashed: Iraq's Chemical and Biological Weapons Production," *Policy Papers No. 14*, The Washington Institute for Near East Policy, Washington, 1989.

Carver, Michael, *War Since 1945*, London, Weidenfeld and Nicholson, 1980.

Casandra, "The Impending Crisis in Egypt," *Middle East Journal*, Vol. 49, No. 1, Winter, 1995, pp. 9–27.

Center for Policy Analysis on Palestine, *Settlements and Peace: The Problem of Jewish Colonization in Palestine, a Special Report*, Washington, Center for Policy Analysis on Palestine, July, 1995.

———, *Jerusalem*, Washington, Center for Policy Analysis on Palestine, February, 1994.

———, *Palestinian Human Rights Under Israeli Rule*, Center for Policy Analysis on Palestine, Washington, May, 1993.

———, *Palestinian Refugee Compensation*, Information Paper No. 3, Washington, Center for Policy Analysis on Palestine, April, 1995.

———, *Palestinian Refugees: Their Problem and Future*, Information Paper No. 3, Washington, Center for Policy Analysis on Palestine, October, 1994.

———, *Targeting to Kill: Israel's Undercover Units*, Center for Policy Analysis on Palestine, Washington, May, 1992.

———, *The Water Issue and the Palestinian-Israeli Conflict*, Information Paper No. 2, Washington, Center for Policy Analysis on Palestine, September, 1993.

Clarke, Duncan, "Israel's Unauthorized Arms Transfers," *Foreign Policy*, Summer, 1995, pp. 89–111.

Clawson, Patrick, and Howard Rosen, *Economic Consequences of Peace of Israel, the Palestinians, and Jordan*, Washington Institute Policy Papers, No. 25, 1991.

Cohen, Howard A., and Steven Plant, "Quenching the Levant's Thirst," *Middle East Quarterly*, Vol. 2, No. 1, March, 1995, pp. 37–46.

Cohen, Saul, *The Geopolitics of Israel's Border Question*, Tel Aviv, Jaffee Center for Strategic Studies, 1986.

Cohen, Stuart A., "How Did the Intifada Affect the IDF?" *Conflict Quarterly*, Vol. 14, No. 3 (Summer, 1994).

———, "Israel's Changing Military Commitments, 1981–1991," *Journal of Strategic Studies*, Vol. 15, No. 31, September, 1993, pp. 330–351.

———, Studying the Israel Defense Forces: A Changing Contract with Israeli Society," BESA Center for Strategic Studies No. 20, Ramat Gan, Israel, Bar-Ilan University, 1995.

Congressional Budget Office, *Limiting Conventional Arms Transfers to the Middle East,* A CBO Study, Washington, September, 1992.

Cordesman, Anthony H., *After the Storm: The Changing Military Balance in the Middle East,* Boulder, Westview, 1993.

———, *The Arab-Israeli Military Balance and the Art of Operations,* Washington, University Press of America-AEI, 1987.

———, *Jordan and the Middle East Balance,* Washington, Middle East Institute, 1978 and 1985.

———, "The Military Balance in the Mahgreb: The Next Decade," in *Brassey's Military Annual, 1986,* London, Brassey's, pp. 227–254.

———, *The Threat from the Northern Gulf,* Boulder, Westview, 1994.

———, *Weapons of Mass Destruction in the Middle East,* London, Brassey's/RUSI, 1991.

Cordesman, Anthony H., and Abraham R. Wagner, *The Lessons of Modern War: Volume I—The Arab-Israeli Conflicts,* Boulder, Westview, 1990.

———, *The Lessons of Modern War: Volume II—The Iran-Iraq Conflict,* Boulder, Westview, 1990.

———, *The Lessons of Modern War, Volume IV,* Boulder, Westview, 1995.

Darwish, Abdel, "China to Update Egypt's Missiles," *The Independent* (UK), June 14, 1990, p. 2.

Defense and Foreign Affairs Daily, various editions.

Defense News, various editions.

Diab, M. Zuhair, "Have Syria and Israel Opted for Peace?", *Middle East Policy,* Vol. 3, No. 2, 1994, pp. 77–90.

DMS/FI Market Intelligence Reports database.

Dunn, Michael C., "Fundamentalism in Egypt," *Middle East Policy,* Vol. 2, No. 3, 1993, pp. 49–61.

———, "Islamist Parties in Jordan and Yemen," *Middle East Policy,* Vol. 2, No. 2, 1993, pp. 16–28.

Dupuy, Trevor N., *Elusive Victory: The Arab-Israeli Wars, 1947–1974,* New York, Harper & Row, 1978.

Dupuy, Trevor N., and Paul Martell, *Flawed Victory,* Washington, Hero Books, 1985.

Economist, various editions.

Economist Intelligence Unit, various country reports.

Eisenberg, Laur Zittrain, "Passive Belligerence, Israel and the 1991 Gulf War," *Journal of Strategic Studies,* Vol. 15, No. 31, September, 1993, pp. 304–330.

Eisenstadt, Michael, *Like a Phoenix from the Ashes? The Future of Iraqi Military Power,* Washington, The Washington Institute, 1993.

———, "Syria's Strategic Weapons," *Jane's Intelligence Review,* April, 1993, pp. 168–171.

Elazar, Daniel J., *Judea, Samaira, and Gaza: Views on the Present and the Future,* Washington, AEI, 1982.

El-Edroos, Brigadier S. A., *The Hashemite Arab Army, 1908–1979,* Amman, Publishing Committee, 1980.

Elmusa, Sharif, "Dividing the Common Palestinian-Israeli Waters: An International Water Law Approach," *Journal of Palestine Studies,* Spring, 1993, pp. 57–77.

———, "The Jordan-Israel Water Agreement," *Journal of Palestine Studies,* Spring, 1995, pp. 63–73.

El-Shazly, Lt. General Saad, *The Crossing of Suez,* San Franciso, American Mideast Research, 1980.

Eshel, David, *Peace for Galilee*, special edition of the Born in Battle Series, Tel Aviv, Eshel-Dramit, 1982.

———, *War of Desperation*, London, Osprey, 1985.

———, *The Yom Kippur War*, Tel Aviv, Eshel-Dramit, 1978.

Eshel, Tamir, "Israel's Defense Electronics," *Defense Electronics*, October, 1991, pp. 87–90.

Estimate, various editions.

Executive News Service, on-line database.

Fandy, Mamoun, "The Tensions Behind the Violence in Egypt," *Middle East Policy*, Vol. 2, No. 1, 1993, pp. 1–14.

Feiler, Gil, "Palestinian Employment Prospects," *The Middle East Journal*, Vol. 47, No. 4, Autumn, 1993, pp. 633–651.

Feldman, Shai, *Israeli Nuclear Deterrence, a Strategy for the 1980s*, New York, Columbia University Press, 1982.

Feldman, Shai, ed., *Confidence Building and Verification: Prospects in the Middle East*, Tel Aviv, Jaffee Center for Strategic Studies, 1994.

Feldman, Shai, and Ariel Levite, *Arms Control and the New Middle East Security Environment*, Boulder, Westview, 1994.

Fisher, Scotty, "Country Briefing Israel," *Jane's Defense Weekly*, February 18, 1995, pp. 29–38.

Fisher, Stanley, Dani Rodrik, and Elia Turner, *The Economics of a Middle East Peace*, Cambridge, MIT Press, 1993.

Flight International, various editions.

Foreign Intelligence Service of the Russian Federation, *A New Challenge After the Cold War: The Proliferation of Weapons of Mass Destruction, Moscow, 1993*. Available in an FBIS translation of February, 1993 from the Government Operations Committee of the US Senate.

Fromkin, David, *A Peace to End All Peace: The Fall of the Ottoman Empire and the Creation of the Modern Middle East*, New York, Avon Books, 1989.

Gabriel, Richard A., *Fighting Armies: Antagonists in the Middle East, a Combat Assessment*, Westport, Greenwood Press, 1983.

———, *Operation Peace for Galilee*, New York, Hill and Norton, 1983.

Gazit, Shlomo, *The Palestinian Refugee Problem, Final Status Issues: Israel-Palestinians*, Study No. 2, Tel Aviv, Jaffee Center for Strategic Studies, 1995.

General Dynamics, *The World's Missile Systems*, 8th edition, Pomona, General Dynamics, 1988.

Gilbert, Martin, *Jerusalem: Illustrated History Atlas*, London, Martin Gilbert, 1977.

Golan, Galia, "A Palestinian State from an Israeli Point of View," *Middle East Policy*, Vol. 3, No. 1, 1994, pp. 56–70.

———, *The Soviet Union and the Israeli War in Lebanon*, Research Paper 46, Jerusalem, Soviet and East European Research Center, 1982.

Gold, Dore, "Fundamental Factors in a Stabilized Middle East: Security, Territory, and Peace," Washington, JINSA, 1993.

———, *Jerusalem*, Tel Aviv, Jaffe Center for Strategic Studies, 1995.

Goodman, Hirsch, and W. Seth Carus, *The Future Battlefield and the Arab-Israeli Conflict*, Transaction Publishers, New Brunswick, Rutgers, Washington Institute for Middle East Policy, 1989.

Grossman, David, *Yellow Wind*, New York, Farrar, Straus & Giroux, 1988.

Harkabi, Yehoshafat, "Reflections on National Defence Policy," *Jerusalem Quarterly*, No. 18, Winter, 1981, pp. 121–140.

Heikel, Mohammed, *The Road to Ramadan*, New York, Quadrangle, 1975.

Held, Colbert, *Middle East Patterns*, Boulder, Westview, 1989.

Heller, Mark, and Sari Nuseibeh, *No Trumpets, No Drums: A Two-State Settlement of the Israeli-Palestinian Conflict*, New York, Hill and Wang, 1991.

Hersh, Seymour M., *The Samson Option, Israel's Nuclear Arsenal and American Foreign Policy*, New York, Random House, 1991.

Herzog, Chaim, *The Arab-Israeli Wars*, New York, Random House, 1982.

Hirsch, Moshe, Deborah Housen-Couriel, and Ruth Lapidoth, *Whither Jerusalem?*, London, Martinus Nijhoff, 1995.

Hof, Fredericj C. "The Yarmouk and Jordan Rivers in the Israel-Jordan Peace Treaty," *Middle East Policy*, Vol. 3, No. 1, pp. 47–56.

Hough, Harold, "Israel's Nuclear Infrastructure," *Jane's Intelligence Weekly*, November, 1994, pp. 505–511.

Inside Defense Electronics, various editions.

International Defense Review, various editions.

Isby, David C., *Weapons and Tactics of the Soviet Army, Fully Revised Edition*, London, Jane's, 1987.

Israeli government Internet database.

Israeli Military Industries (IMI) manufacturer brochures.

Jaffee Center for Strategic Studies, *Israel's Options for Peace*, Report of a JCSS Study Group, Tel Aviv, Jaffee Center, 1989.

———, *The Middle East Military Balance*, Boulder, Westview, various editions.

Jane's All the World's Aircraft, London, Jane's Publishing, various editions.

Jane's Armor and Artillery, London, Jane's Publishing, various editions.

Jane's Battlefield Surveillance Systems, London, Jane's Publishing, various editions.

Jane's C3I Systems; *Jane's Air-Launched Weapons Systems*, London, Jane's Publishing, various editions.

Jane's Defense Appointments & Procurement Handbook (Middle East Edition), London, Jane's Publishing, various editions.

Jane's Defense Weekly, various editions.

Jane's Fighting Ships, London, Jane's Publishing, various editions.

Jane's Infantry Weapons, London, Jane's Publishing, various editions.

Jane's Intelligence Review, October, 1994, various editions.

Jane's Land-Base Air Defense, London, Jane's Publishing, various editions.

Jane's Military Vehicles and Logistics, London, Jane's Publishing, various editions.

Jane's Naval Weapons Systems, London, Jane's Publishing, various editions.

Jane's Radar and Electronic Warfare Systems, London, Jane's Publishing, various editions.

The Jerusalem Report, various editions.

JINSA, *Security Affairs*, various editions.

Johnson, Major Maxwell Orme, USMC, *The Military as an Instrument of US Policy in Southwest Asia: The Rapid Deployment Joint Task Force, 1979–1982*, Boulder, Westview, 1983. A good description of US military capabilities in the Gulf.

Jones, Rodney W., ed., *Small Nuclear Forces and US Security Policy*, Lexington, Lexington Books, 1984.

Kanovsky, Eliyahu, "Will Arab-Israeli Peace Bring Prosperity?", *Middle East Quarterly*, Vol. 2, No. 2, June, 1994, pp. 3–12.

Kaplan, Stephen S., *Diplomacy of Power*, Washington, Brookings Institution, 1981.

Karam, Simon, "Lebanon, Collapse and Revival," *Middle East Policy*, Vol. 3, No. 1, 1994, pp. 15–24.

Katz, Samuel M., "Israeli Airpower on the Rise," *Air Force*, November, 1991, pp. 44–51.

Keegan, John, *World Armies*, London, Macmillan, 1983.

Kemp, Geoffrey, *The Control of the Middle East Arms Race*, Washington, Carnegie Endowment, 1991.

Khalidi, Rashid, *Under Siege*, New York, Columbia, 1986.

Khalidi Walid, *Conflict and Violence in Lebanon*, Cambridge, Harvard Center for International Affairs, 1984.

Khashan, Hillel, "The Levant: Treaties Without Normalisation," *Middle East Quarterly*, June, 1995, pp. 3–14.

Khazen, Farid el, "Lebanon's First Postwar Parliamentary Election," *Middle East Policy*, Vol. 2, No. 1, 1993, pp. 102–119.

Klieman, Aaron S., *Israel's Global Reach*, London, Pergamon-Brassey's, 1985.

Kollek, Teddy, "Jerusalem," *Policy Papers No. 22,* Washington, The Washington Institute for Near East Policy, 1990.

Kramer, Martin, "Hizbollah's Vision of the West," *Policy Papers No. 16*, Washington, The Washington Institute for Near East Policy, 1989.

Kronsky, Herbert, and Stephen Weissman, *The Islamic Bomb*, New York, Times Books, 1981.

Laffin, John, *The World in Conflict or War Annual*, London, Brassey's, various editions.

Lambeth, Benjamin S., *Moscow's Lessons from the 1982 Lebanon Air War*, Santa Monica, Rand Corporation, 1984.

Levite, Ariel, *Offense and Defense in Israeli Strategy*, Boulder, Westview, 1989.

Lowi, Miriam R., "Bridging the Divide: Transboundary Resource Disputes & the Case of West Bank Water," *International Security*, Summer, 1993, pp. 113–139.

Luttwak, Edward, and Dan Horowitz, *The Israeli Army*, New York, Harper & Row, 1975.

Mark, Clyde R., "Israel: US Foreign Assistance," Congressional Research Service, CRS-IB85066, May 18, 1995.

———, "Middle East and North Africa: US Aid FY1993, 1994, and 1995," CRS 94-274F, *Jane's Defense Weekly*, July 12, 1995, p. 19.

———, "Palestinians and the Middle East Peace: Issues for the United States," Congressional Research Service, IB92052, December 5, 1994.

McLaurin, R. D., "Golan Security in a Middle East Settlement," *Oriente Moderno*, December, 1981, pp. 43–58.

Meir, Alon Ben, "Jerusalem's Final Status," *Middle East Policy*, Vol. 3, No. 3, 1994, pp. 93–110.

Merari, Ariel, and Shlomi Elad, *The International Dimension of Palestinian Terrorism*, Tel Aviv, Jaffee Center, 1986.

Middle East Economic Digest, various editions.

Middle East Policy (formerly *Arab-American Affairs*), various editions.

Military Technology, various editions.

Military Technology, *World Defense Almanac*, Bonn, Monch Publishing Group, various editions.

Moore, James H., "Parting the Waters: Israeli and Palestinian Entitlements to West Bank Aquifers and the Jordan River Basin," *Middle East Policy*, Vol. 3, No. 2, 1994, pp. 91–108.

Moreaux, J. M., "The Syrian Army," *Defense Update*, No. 69, p. 31.

Mushih, Muhammed, "The Golan: Israel, Syria, and Strategic Calculations," *The Middle East Journal*, Vol. 47, No. 4, Autumn, 1993, pp. 611–633.

Nakhleh, Emile A., "Palestinians and Israelis: Options for Coexistence," *Journal of Palestine Studies*, Winter, 1993, pp. 5–16.

Neff, Donald, *Warriors Against Israel*, Battleboro, Amana, 1988.

Norton, Augustus Richard, and Robin Wright, "The Post-Peace Crisis in the Middle East," *Survival*, Winter, 1994–1995, pp. 7–20.

Nuclear Engineering, various editions.

Nuclear Fuel, various editions.

Nucleonics Week, various editions.

O'Ballance, Edgar, *The Electronic War in the Middle East, 1968–1970*, Hamden, Ct., Archon, 1974.

Office of the IDF Spokesman, "The IDF's Security Principles," April, 1995.

Office of Technology Assessment, *Global Arms Trade: Commerce in Advanced Military Technology and Weapons*, Washington, D.C., OTA, Congress of the United States, June, 1991.

Ottenbergy, Michael A., "Israel and the Atom," *American Sentinel*, August 16, 1992, p. 1.

Palestinian Authority, briefing papers.

Pawloski, Dick, *Changes in Threat Air Combat Doctrine and Force Structure, 24th Edition*, Fort Worth, General Dynamics DWIC-91, February, 1992, pp. II-199 to II-227.

Peretz, Don, *Intifada: The Palestinian Uprising*, Boulder, Westview, 1993.

Perlmutter, Amos, "The Israel-PLO Accord is Dead," *Foreign Affairs*, May/June, 1995.

Pipes, Daniel, *Damascus Courts the West: Syrian Politics, 1989–1991*, Washington Institute Policy Papers No. 26, Washington, Washington Institute for Near East Policy, 1992.

Policywatch, various editions.

Pry, Peter, *Israel's Nuclear Arsenal*, Boulder, Westview, 1984.

Quandt, William B., *Camp David, Peacemaking and Politics*, Washington, Brookings, 1986.

———, *The Middle East Ten Years After Camp David*, Washington, Brookings, September, 1988.

———, *Peace Process: American Diplomacy and the Arab-Israeli Conflict*, Berkeley, University of California Press, 1993.

———, *The United States and Egypt*, Washington, Brookings, 1990.

Rabin, Yitzhak, "Deterrence in an Israeli Security Context," in Aharon Klieman and Ariel Levite, eds., *Deterrence in the Middle East: Where Theory and Practice Converge*, Boulder, Westview, 1993, pp. 6–16.

Rabinovich, Itamar, *The War for Lebanon, 1970–1983*, Cornell, Cornell University, 1984.

Rafael briefing sheet; manufacturer offprint of "Rafael: Lessons of Combat" from *Military Technology*, May, 1991.

Randall, Jonathan C., *Going All the Way*, New York, Viking Press, 1983.

Rathnell, Dr. Andrew, "Iraq—The Endgame?" *Jane's Intelligence Review*, Vol. 7, No. 5, pp. 224–228.

Reich, Bernard, and Gershon R. Kieval, *Israeli National Security Policy: Political Actors and Perspectives*, New York, Macmillan, 1985.

Rekhess, Elie, "The Terrorist Connection—Iran, the Islamic Jihad, and Hamas," *Justice*, Vol. 5, May, 1995.

Reuters, on-line access.

Rubenstein, Alvin Z., *Red Star over the Nile*, Princeton University Press, 1977.

Safran, Nadav, *From War to War*, New York, Pegasus, 1969.

Satloff, Robert, The Jordan-Israel Peace Treaty," *Middle East Quarterly*, Vol. 2, No. 1, March, 1995, pp. 47–52.

———, *The Politics of Change in the Middle East*, Boulder, Westview, 1993.

Scarlott, Jennifer, "Nuclear Proliferation After the Gulf War," *World Policy Journal*, Fall, 1991, pp. 687–695.

Schiff, Ze'ev, *Earthquake*, Jerusalem, 1973.

———, *A History of the Israeli Army*, New York, Macmillan, 1985.

———, "Security for Peace: Israel's Minimal Security Requirements in Negotiations with the Palestinians," *Policy Papers No. 15*, Washington, The Washington Institute for Near East Policy, 1989.

Schiff, Ze'ev, and Ehud Ya'ari, *Intifada: The Palestinian Uprising—Israel's Third Front*, New York, Simon and Schuster, 1990.

———, *Israel's War in Lebanon*, New York, Simon and Schuster, 1984.

Schmid, Alex P., *Soviet Military Interventions Since 1945*, New Brunswick, Transaction, Inc., 1985.

SDIO, *Ballistic Missile Proliferation: An Emerging Threat, 1992*, Washington, SDIO, October, 1992.

Seale, Patrick, *Asad, the Struggle for the Middle East*, Berkeley, University of California Press, 1988.

Sella, Amon, *Soviet Political and Military Conduct in the Middle East*, London, Macmillan, 1981.

Shalev, Aryeh, *Israel and Syria: Peace and Security on the Golan*, Tel Aviv, Jaffee Center for Strategic Studies, 1993.

———, *The West Bank: Line of Defense*, New York, Praeger, 1985.

Shimshoni, Jonathan, *Israel and Conventional Deterrence*, Ithaca, Cornell University Press, 1988.

Shuey, Lenhart, Snyder, Donnelly, Mielke, and Moteff, *Missile Proliferation: Survey of Emerging Missile Forces*, Report 88-642F, Washington, Congressional Research Service, February 9, 1989.

Sicherman, Harvey, *Palestinian Self-Government (Autonomy): Its Past and Future*, Washington, Washington Institute, 1991.

Sicker, Martin, *Israel's Quest for Security*, New York, Praeger, 1989.

Sirriyeh, Hussein, *Lebanon: Dimensions of Conflict*, Adelphi Paper 243, IISS, London, 1989.

Skogmo, Bjorn, *UNIFIL: International Peacekeeping in Lebanon, 1978–1988*, Boulder, Lynne Rienner, 1988.

Spector, Leonard S., Mark G. McDonough, and Evan S. Medeiros, *Tracking Nuclear Proliferation*, Washington, Carnegie Endowment, 1995.

Spencer, Claire, *The Maghreb in the 1990s*, Adelphi Paper 274, London, International Institute of Strategic Studies, IISS-Brassey's, February, 1993.

Stockholm International Peace Research Institute, *World Armaments and Disarmament: SIPRI Yearbook*, London, Oxford Press, various editions.

Survival, various editions.

Susser, Asher, *In the Back Door: Jordan's Disengagement and the Middle East Peace Process*, Washington, The Washington Institute, Policy Papers 19, 1990.

Tal, Lawrence, "Dealing with Radical Islam: The Case of Jordan," *Survival*, Autumn, 1995, pp. 139–157.

———, "Is Jordan Doomed," *Foreign Affairs*, Vol. 72, No. 5, November/December, 1993, pp. 110–126.

Talal, Hassan Bin, *Palestinian Self-Determination, a Study of the West Bank and Gaza Strip*, New York, Quartet, 1981.

Tanks of the World (Bernard and Grafe), various editions.

Tillema, Herbert K., *International Conflict Since 1945*, Boulder, Westview, 1991.

UPI, on-line access.

Urban, Mark, "Fire in Galilee," a three-part series in *Armed Forces*, March,

US Arms Control and Disarmament Agency (ACDA), *World Military Expenditures and Arms Transfers*, Washington, GPO, various editions.

US Central Intelligence Agency (CIA), *Handbook of Economic Statistics*, Washington, GPO, various editions.

———, "Prospects for Further Proliferation of Nuclear Weapons," DCI NIO, 1995.

———, *World Factbook*, Washington, CIA, various editions.

US Defense Intelligence Agency (DIA), *Soviet Chemical Weapons Threat*, DST-1620F-051-85, 1985, p. 8.

US Defense Security Assistance Agency (DSAA), "Foreign Military Sales, Foreign Military Construction Sales and Military Assistance Facts as of September 30, 1994," Washington, Department of Defense, 1995.

US Department of Defense, *Conduct of the Persian Gulf War: Final Report to Congress*, Washington, Department of Defense, April, 1992.

US Department of State, *Congressional Presentation for Security Assistance Programs, Fiscal Year 1996*, Washington, Department of State, 1995.

———, *Country Reports on Human Rights, various editions*, Internet version.

———, "Patterns of Global Terrorism," various years, Internet version.

van Creveld, Martin, *Military Lessons of the Yom Kippur War: Historical Perspectives*, Washington Paper no. 24, Beverly Hills, Calif., Sage Publications, 1975.

Vandewalle, Dirk, "The Middle East Peace Process and Economic Integration," *Survival*, Winter, 1994–95, pp. 21–34.

Vatikiotis, J. P., *Politics and the Military in Jordan*, New York, Praeger, 1967.

von Pikva, Otto, *Armies of the Middle East*, New York, Mayflower, 1979.

Wald, Emanuel, *The Wald Report: The Decline of Israeli National Security Since 1967*, Boulder, Westview, 1991.

Warplanes of the World (Bernard and Grafe), various editions.

Weinberger, Naomi, "The Palestinian National Security Debate," *Journal of Palestine Studies*, Winter, 1995, pp. 16–30.

Wendt, James C., and Richard Darilek, *Possible US Roles in Support of a Syrian-Israeli Peace Agreement*, Washington, Rand, 1994.

Weyer's Warships (Bernard and Grafe), various editions.

Whetten, Lawrence L., *The Canal War: Four Power Conflict in the Middle East*, Cambridge, MIT, 1974.

Woolsey, James, "Testimony by Director of Central Intelligence Before the Senate Governmental Affairs Committee," February 24, 1993.

World Bank, *Claiming the Future: Choosing Prosperity in the Middle East and North Africa*, Washington, World Bank, 1995.

———, *Developing the Occupied Territories: An Investment for Peace*, Washington, World Bank, October, 1994.

———, *Emergency Assistance Program for the Occupied Territories*, Washington, World Bank, October, 1994.

———, *Forging a Partnership for Environmental Action*, Washington, World Bank, December, 1994.

———, *Integrated Development of the Jordan Rift Valley*, Washington, World Bank, October, 1994.

———, *Peace and the Jordanian Economy*, Washington, World Bank, October, 1994.

———, *A Population Perspective on Development in the Middle East and North Africa*, Washington, World Bank, August, 1994.

———, *Will Arab Workers Prosper or Be Left Out in the Twenty-First Century*, Washington, World Bank, 1995.

Yaacov, Bar Siman Tov, *The Israeli-Egyptian War of Attrition, 1969–1970*, New York, Columbia, 1980.

Yaniv, Avner, *Deterrence Without the Bomb, the Politics of Israeli Strategy*, Lexington, Lexington Books, 1987.

Zak, Moshe, "The Jordan-Israel Peace Treaty," *Middle East Quarterly*, Vol. 2, No. 1, March, 1995, pp. 53–60.

Zunes, Stephen, "The Israeli-Jordanian Agreement: Peace or Pax Americana," *Middle East Policy*, Vol. 3, No. 3, 1995, pp. 57–68.

———, "Israeli-Syrian Peace, the Long Road Ahead," *Middle East Policy*, Vol. 2, No. 3, 1993, pp. 62–68.

About the Book and Author

Nobody understands the delicate and dangerous balance of power in the Middle East better than Anthony Cordesman. In *Perilous Prospects*, he supplies the first account of the military and security concerns arising out of the Israeli-Palestinian peace process and the recent assassination of Prime Minister Rabin.

Cordesman considers a number of possible futures for the region and their effects on the peace process, ranging from the outbreak of a new *intifada* to war between Israel and Syria over the Golan Heights. He also provides an analysis of the internal security requirements of both Israel and a new Palestinian state, which are the key to any lasting settlement.

Offering hard-headed analysis combined with hope for the future, *Perilous Prospects* is both timely and provocative.

Anthony Cordesman has served in senior positions in the office of the secretary of defense, NATO, and the U.S. Senate. He is currently a senior fellow at the Center for Strategic and International Studies and a special consultant on military affairs for ABC News. He lives in Washington, D.C.